NEW INTERNATIONAL
BIBLICAL COMMENTARY

New Testament Editor,
W. Ward Gasque

1 CORINTHIANS

New Testament Series

NEW INTERNATIONAL BIBLICAL COMMENTARY

1 CORINTHIANS

MARION L. SOARDS

Based on the New International Version

© 1999 by Hendrickson Publishers, Inc.
P. O. Box 3473
Peabody, Massachusetts 01961–3473

First published jointly, 1999, in the United States by Hendrickson Publishers and in the United Kingdom by the Paternoster Press, P. O. Box
300, Carlisle, Cumbria CA3 0QS.

Printed in the United States of America

First printing — August 1999

Library of Congress Cataloging-in-Publication Data

Soards, Marion L., 1952–
    1 Corinthians / Marion L. Soards.
    (New International biblical commentary; 7.   New Testament
series)
    "Based on the New International Version."
    Includes bibliographical references and indexes.
    1. Bible N.T.   Corinthians, 1st Commentaries.   I. Title.   II. Title:
First Corinthians.   III. Series: New International biblical
commentary; 7.
    BS2675.3.S63   1999
    227'.2077—dc21   99–29480
                                                                        CIP

ISBN 0–943575–97–4 (U.S. softcover)
ISBN 1–56563–499–3 (U.S. hardcover)

British Library Cataloguing in Publication Data
A catalogue record for this book is available
from the British Library.

ISBN 0–85364–661–9 (U.K. softcover)

For Whit

Table of Contents

Foreword
New International Biblical Commentary

Although it does not appear on the standard best-seller lists, the Bible continues to outsell all other books. And in spite of growing secularism in the West, there are no signs that interest in its message is abating. Quite to the contrary, more and more men and women are turning to its pages for insight and guidance in the midst of the ever-increasing complexity of modern life.

This renewed interest in Scripture is found both outside and inside the church. It is found among people in Asia and Africa as well as in Europe and North America; indeed, as one moves outside of the traditionally Christian countries, interest in the Bible seems to quicken. Believers associated with the traditional Catholic and Protestant churches manifest the same eagerness for the Word that is found in the newer evangelical churches and fellowships.

We wish to encourage and, indeed, strengthen this world-wide movement of lay Bible study by offering this new commentary series. Although we hope that pastors and teachers will find these volumes helpful in both understanding and communicating the Word of God, we do not write primarily for them. Our aim is to provide for the benefit of every Bible reader reliable guides to the books of the Bible—representing the best of contemporary scholarship presented in a form that does not require formal theological education to understand.

The conviction of editor and authors alike is that the Bible belongs to the people and not merely to the academy. The message of the Bible is too important to be locked up in erudite and esoteric essays and monographs written only for the eyes of theological specialists. Although exact scholarship has its place in the service of Christ, those who share in the teaching office of the church have a responsibility to make the results of their research accessible to the Christian community at large. Thus, the Bible scholars who join in the presentation of this series write with these broader concerns in view.

A wide range of modern translations is available to the contemporary Bible student. Most of them are very good and much to be preferred—for understanding, if not always for beauty—to the older King James Version (the so-called Authorized Version of the Bible). The Revised Standard Version has become the standard English translation in many seminaries and colleges and represents the best of modern Protestant scholarship. It is also available in a slightly altered "common Bible" edition with the Catholic imprimatur, and the New Revised Standard Version appeared in 1989. In addition, the New American Bible is a fresh translation that represents the best of post–Vatican II Roman Catholic biblical scholarship and is in a more contemporary idiom than that of the RSV.

The New Jerusalem Bible, based on the work of French Catholic scholars but vividly rendered into English by a team of British translators, is perhaps the most literary of the recent translations, while the New English Bible is a monument to modern British Protestant research. The Good News Bible is probably the most accessible translation for the person who has little exposure to the Christian tradition or who speaks and reads English as a second language. Each of these is, in its own way, excellent and will be consulted with profit by the serious student of Scripture. Perhaps most will wish to have several versions to read, both for variety and for clarity of understanding—though it should be pointed out that no one of them is by any means flawless or to be received as the last word on any given point. Otherwise, there would be no need for a commentary series like this one!

We have chosen to use the New International Version as the basis for this series, not because it is necessarily the best translation available but because it is becoming increasingly used by lay Bible students and pastors. It is the product of an international team of "evangelical" Bible scholars who have sought to translate the Hebrew and Greek documents of the original into "clear and natural English . . . idiomatic [and] . . . contemporary but not dated," suitable for "young and old, highly educated and less well educated, ministers and laymen [*sic*]." As the translators themselves confess in their preface, this version is not perfect. However, it is as good as any of the others mentioned above and more popular than most of them.

Each volume will contain an introductory chapter detailing the background of the book and its author, important themes, and other helpful information. Then, each section of the book will be expounded as a whole, accompanied by a series of notes on items in the text that need further clarification or more detailed explanation. Appended to the end of each volume will be a bibliographical guide for further study.

Our new series is offered with the prayer that it may be an instrument of authentic renewal and advancement in the world-wide Christian community and a means of commending the faith of the people who lived in biblical times and of those who seek to live by the Bible today.

W. WARD GASQUE

Abbreviations

AB	Anchor Bible
ABD	*Anchor Bible Dictionary*
ABR	*Australian Biblical Review*
BA	*Biblical Archaeologist*
BAR	*Biblical Archaeology Review*
Bib	*Biblica*
BibSac	*Bibliotheca Sacra*
BiTod	*Bible Today*
BT	*The Bible Translator*
BTB	*Biblical Theology Bulletin*
BZ	*Biblische Zeitschrift*
BZNW	Beihefte zur Zeitschrift für die neutestatmentliche Wissenschaft
CBQ	*Catholic Biblical Quarterly*
Chm	*Churchman*
CP	*Classical Philology*
CurTM	*Currents in Theology and Mission*
DSS	Dead Sea Scrolls
EDNT	*Exegetical Dictionary of the New Testament*
1 Esd.	1 Esdras
2 Esd.	2 Esdras
ExpT	*Expository Times*
Gk.	Greek
Greg	*Gregorianum*
HAR	*Hebrew Annual Review*
Hb.	Hebrew
HNTC	Harper's New Testament Commentaries
HTR	*Harvard Theological Review*
IBS	*Irish Biblical Studies*
IDB	*Interpreter's Dictionary of the Bible*
IDBSup	*Interpreter's Dictionary of the Bible: Supplementary Volume*
Int	*Interpretation*
JBR	*Journal of Bible and Religion*

JBL	*Journal of Biblical Literature*
JES	*Journal of Ecumenical Studies*
JETS	*Journal of the Evangelical Theological Society*
JSNT	*Journal for the Study of the New Testament*
JSNTSup	Journal for the Study of the New Testament Supplements
JTS	*Journal of Theological Studies*
Jub.	*Jubilees*
KJV	King James Version
List	*Listening: Journal of Religion and Culture*
lit.	literally
LS	*Louvain Studies*
LSJ	Liddell, Scott, Jones, *A Greek-English Lexicon*
LXX	Septuagint
MSJ	*Master's Seminary Journal*
NA^{27}	*Novum Testamentum Graece*, Nestle-Aland, 27th ed.
NASB	New American Standard Bible
NCB	New Century Bible
Neot	*Neotestamentica*
NICNT	New International Commentary on the New Testament
NIV	New International Version
NovT	*Novum Testamentum*
NovTSup	Novum Testamentum Supplements
NRSV	New Revised Standard Version
NT	New Testament
NTS	*New Testament Studies*
OCD	*Oxford Classical Dictionary*
OT	Old Testament
pl.	plural
RB	*Revue biblique*
REB	Revised English Bible
RefR	*Reformed Review*
ResQ	*Restoration Quarterly*
RevExp	*Review and Expositor*
RSV	Revised Standard Version
SBLDS	Society of Biblical Literature Dissertation Series
SEÅ	*Svensk exegtisk Årsbok*
sing.	singular

SNTSMS	Society for New Testament Studies: Monograph Series
SR	*Studies in Religion*
TD	*Theology Digest*
TDNT	*Theological Dictionary of the New Testament*
ThTo	*Theology Today*
TJ	*Trinity Journal*
TynB	*Tyndale Bulletin*
USQR	*Union Seminary Quarterly Review*
Wis.	Wisdom of Solomon
WTJ	*Westminster Theological Journal*
ZNW	*Zeitschrift für die neutestamentliche Wissenschaft und die Kunde der älteren Kirche*
ZTK	*Zeitschrift für Theologie und Kirche*

Introduction

Paul came to Corinth for the first time around the mid-point of the first century after Christ. Some time later, when he had departed from Corinth, he wrote his fellow Christians a letter that we now know as 1 Corinthians. Preparing to read that letter is a challenging task, since to comprehend what is going on in this truly foreign communication one must understand a variety of background matters. Given the distance (in terms of time, language, culture, geography, and life-experience) between readers of this letter at the turn of the twenty-first century and the original first-century audience to which it was addressed, even information about seemingly small issues—who, what, when, where, why, and how was the letter written—becomes important for a sensible reading of Paul's communication. Thus, before diving into the reading and the study of 1 Corinthians, let us briefly come to terms with some preliminary issues.

Paul and the Corinthians

Precisely locating events in the context of Paul's ministry is a challenge, often a nearly impossible one, because available sources concerning Paul's life and work are both scarce and vague. Paul's involvement with the Corinthians, however, is one of the chapters of the apostle's career about which we can be somewhat certain. According to The Acts of the Apostles, a key secondary source related to Paul's ministry, Paul moved with his colleagues Silas (or Silvanus), Timothy, and others who are unnamed from Asia Minor to Europe, specifically Macedonia and Greece, to preach the gospel. These "evangelists" were active in Philippi, Thessalonica, and Berea before Paul moved alone to Athens and then to Corinth, where he was eventually rejoined by Silas and Timothy (and perhaps others). A sketchy account of an eighteen-month sojourn in Corinth is given in Acts 18:1–18, and although the story is but a brief general summary of the work that Paul and his colleagues did in Corinth, one does garner some important information from the narrative. Paul began his ministry in Corinth by locating the Jewish quarter of the city where he befriended some other Jews: Priscilla (or Prisca) and Aquila. These two were a married couple, and apparently they were already Christians since there is no mention or explanation of the origins of their Christian faith. Priscilla and Aquila had come to Corinth after being banished from Rome under an edict of the Emperor Claudius. In an extrabiblical source by the Roman historian Suetonius (*Claudius* 25) we learn that in or about A.D. 49 Claudius expelled Jews from Rome because of dissension and rioting among the members of the Jewish community. This disturbance was caused by the preaching of "Chrestus" (a garbled reference to "Christ" that most likely indicates the controversial preaching of the gospel in Rome). The couple were, like Paul, tentmakers by trade, and Paul resided with them in Corinth.

Paul engaged in evangelistic missionary activity, at first ministering in the context of the Corinthian synagogue (Acts 18:4). He and his colleagues remained active in this setting until their work aroused sufficient hostility to make it impossible to continue there. The loss of the synagogue as a place for preaching did not end Paul's proclamation of the gospel. Rather, he simply moved with the other members of the now-identifiable Christian community to the house next-door to the synagogue, which belonged to a God-fearing Gentile named Titius Justus (Acts 18:7). Paul's success in the synagogue is reflected in the report in Acts 18:8 that Crispus—who was the president of the synagogue (see also 1 Cor. 1:14)—his household, and many other Corinthians heard, believed, and were baptized. Apparently the proximity of the evangelical ministry and its ongoing success continued to generate controversy, for eventually the members of the synagogue community brought charges against Paul before the Roman proconsul Gallio.

Gallio's involvement with the proceedings against Paul registers an important historical note that aids the effort to locate chronologically the ministry of Paul in Corinth. From various extrabiblical materials, including both a votive inscription at Delphi—the site of the famous oracle and sanctuary of Apollo—and references in several Roman writers, one can be almost certain that Lucius Junius Annaeus Gallio was proconsul of Achaia, the Roman province of which Corinth was capital, during A.D. 52–53. Gallio recognized the religious nature of the dispute and took no interest in the case, actually dismissing it from his court

(Acts 18:14–16). The plaintiffs, however, were not easily dissuaded and gave their new synagogue president Sosthenes ("Sosthenes" is also identified as the co-author of 1 Corinthians; this may or may not be the same person) a beating to show their displeasure with the outcome of the proceedings (Acts 18:17). Gallio was not swayed by the action.

The story in Acts recalls that Paul stayed "many days longer" in Corinth after the incident before Gallio, but then (Acts does not say why) Paul departed from Corinth. Whether or not he was encouraged to leave is impossible to determine from the account in Acts. Nevertheless, having left Corinth, Paul sailed east and came to Ephesus, visiting there before launching out on a tour of the larger region of Asia Minor. Paul brought his travels to a conclusion by returning to Ephesus, where he lived and worked for a period of twenty-seven months. While in residence at Ephesus, Paul exchanged a series of letters with the members of the church in Corinth and even, at one point, paid them a visit. In 1 Corinthians 5:9 Paul refers to a previous correspondence that he had sent to Corinth and to the misinterpretation of his assertions in that letter. Thus, 1 Corinthians is at least the second letter in a larger series of writings that included a previous communication, 2 Corinthians, and seemingly (from references in 2 Corinthians) still other missives. Moreover, from the way that Paul describes his situation in 1 Corinthians 16:5–9, he must have already been in Ephesus for an extended period, for he delineates plans for bringing his stay in Ephesus to a close. He indicates that he was in the final stages of assembling an offering for the poor saints in Jerusalem, which he intended to take to them personally. When he did this he was arrested and incarcerated for some years as one learns from Acts 21–28. Paul may have died at the end of this imprisonment or he may have been released and imprisoned again at a later time. The historical data concerning the end of his life are minimal and unclear. Given this information, 1 Corinthians is most likely a letter from Paul to the church in Corinth written between A.D. 53 and A.D. 55.

The City of Corinth

Corinth was an ancient Greek city, located at a strategic point on the isthmus that connected the Peloponnesian peninsula to the southern mainland section of Greece (which was called Achaia in Paul's day) and to the provinces of Macedonia and Epirus beyond. During the Roman military campaigns of the second-century B.C., in 146 ancient Corinth fell and the Romans demolished the city. A small population lived among the ruins for a century. In 44 B.C. Julius Caesar commissioned the rebuilding and reconstitution of Corinth and secured its success by populating it with an international mix of freedmen. Many of these freedmen were slaves from around the Mediterranean—especially Greece, Syria, Palestine, and Egypt—who were given freedom and a new start in life as a reward for military service. Thus this population was loyal to Rome. From 44 B.C. through the first centuries A.D., Corinth was a prominent Roman colony; various industries, including the prominent bronze and terra-cotta works, were born and grew. This reconstituted or "new" Corinth became a magnet for many persons who were interested in fresh economic opportunities and lively social conditions. The city of Corinth grew and was, despite its reputation for excitement, a peaceful metropolitan area. The Romans named Corinth as capital of Roman Achaia, and the city was the residence of the Roman proconsul from about 29 B.C. With the prosperity of the city reestablished, the Corinthians re-instituted the traditional Isthmian Games, a major panhellenic festival that occurred every two years and focused on athletic, dramatic, musical, and oratorical competitions. In this way they reclaimed the ancient glory of Corinth, perhaps in a form more splendid than originally enjoyed. Trade, travel, and tourism led to the development of a center for banking that added even more prosperity to the cosmopolitan city and its region. Archaeological work done from the late nineteenth century to the present day reveals detailed information about the city, its origins, its reconstitution, its development, and its actual appearance in Paul's day. As a cosmopolitan center of status, Corinth could boast of an abundance of affluent neighborhoods, rental properties, recreational facilities, and establishments for both public and private dining. Politics naturally flourished in this urban climate.

The geographical location of Corinth made it a vital entity. It bordered on two seas: to the west, in the direction of Rome, was the Corinthian Gulf of the Adriatic Sea; to the east, in the direction of Asia Minor, was the Saronic Gulf of the Aegean Sea. Sea trade and travel in antiquity were always risky business, but this was especially true around the turbulent, unpredictable waters south of the Peloponnesus. Therefore, rather than unnecessarily chance lives and precious cargo to the perils of the sea, ship-owners, sailors, and merchants brought their vessels to harbor in one of Corinth's two ports and had the ships brought into dry-dock and unloaded or hauled across the isthmus to be put back in the water at the other gulf harbor. This activity was labor-intensive, so Corinth had a large population of manual workers.

Because the goods of both the East and the West passed through the city, Corinth possessed a truly cosmopolitan atmosphere. Fortunes were made and spent in Corinth. The educated, the elite, the entrepreneur, and the entertainer all flocked to Corinth. People of diverse backgrounds brought to the life of the city a rich mixture of cultures, religions, languages, entertainment, foods, and other amenities. Corinth was vigorous and vivacious; the atmosphere was both pluralistic and syncretistic, with distinctive cultures and worldviews existing independently and mixing together to form novel, often unexamined and illogical combinations. Former slaves found freedom and acquired great wealth that they shared generously, so that at times these freedmen were selected to the highest public offices. Cults thrived and devotees made rounds of the temples to assure favor with all the gods. On one street stood together temples to several gods who often represented parallel or competitive claims to power. Such was the city Paul knew, and those among whom Paul ministered comprised its population.

The Purpose of Paul's Letter

When Paul wrote to the church in Corinth, he did so for concrete reasons related to specific concerns. Indeed, as the reader learns from the letter itself, Paul wrote to the Corinthians after visiting with those who were familiar with the church, talking with some of its members, and receiving a letter of inquiry from the congregation. An exact reconstruction of the situation is impossible, but one may gain sufficient clarity about the circumstances to make the reading of the letter in a later context more sympathetic and precise. First, Paul mentions that he had met with a group that he names as "Chloe's people." Their identity is treated below in the commentary on 1 Corinthians 1:11. From these persons Paul learned of at least some of the problems in Corinth that were causing divisiveness in the life of the congregation. Paul expresses shock, alarm, and apprehension at the quarreling among the Corinthians. Second, Paul received a letter from the church via a letter delegation—specifically Stephanas, Fortunatus, and Achaicus—named in the closing segment of Paul's letter back to the church (see 1 Cor. 16:17). Paul had certainly discussed the Corinthian situation with these letter bearers, and from his reply in writing one can discern those prominent elements of the letter that demanded Paul's attention.

The church had fallen into arguing, forming cliques within the larger congregation, perhaps over one issue or another, or over a combination of issues that even included the varied social status of the members of the church. Paul's particular references to the Corinthians' own letter address such issues as sexual relations, marriage, divorce, the eating of foods associated with pagan gods, the status of spiritual gifts and the practice of those gifts in the assembly of the church, orderly behavior in worship, the resurrection of the dead, and a collection that Paul was assembling for the relief of the poor in Jerusalem.

Seemingly at the root of all these concerns was the desire of certain Corinthian Christians to establish their own spiritual status. The concern with spirituality and the comparison of the spiritual standing of one person or group with that of another took a remarkably diverse set of forms, from parsimonious asceticism to avaricious licentiousness, with many configurations in between. While Paul addresses the specific issues and behaviors, he consistently identifies the will to boast in spiritual arrogance of one's special rank in faith and practice as the fundamental fault of the people and groups in Corinth. Throughout the letter Paul denounces boasting of human or spiritual behaviors and affirms the goodness and achievements of God and God's grace at work in Jesus Christ. Coupled with his criticism of the problems at Corinth is a steady stream of positive teachings concerning the meaning of the experience of God's grace in the life of the individuals and the community.

The Structure of 1 Corinthians

As Paul writes to the Corinthians, one may observe the major and minor lines of his reasoning. The initial elements of the letter are quite clear, forming Paul's versions of a standard salutation (1:1–3) and thanksgiving (1:4–9).

The main segment of 1 Corinthians begins at 1 Corinthians 1:10, but there is vigorous disagreement among interpreters concerning where the body of the letter ends. Since Paul uses the phrase "now about" several times in the letter—often as an obvious reference to matters raised in the previous letter from the Corinthians to the apostle—some suggest that Paul's last use of the phrase "now concerning" at 16:1 is an indication that he is referring to the Corinthians' letter for the last time. Thus they argue that this use signals that Paul is concluding his response to their inquiries and that the body of the letter ends with 16:12. However, it is not certain that 16:1 is citing the Corinthians' letter; Paul may well introduce a new topic there himself. Moreover, from 1:10 through 6:20 there is no clear reference to the letter, although Paul is certainly focusing on the situation in Corinth. For these reasons one can make a strong case that Paul's change of tone and focus in 16:1 signals his transition from the body of the letter to parenesis. The commentary that follows treats 16:1–11 as part of Paul's parenetic materials and views 1:10–15:58 as the body of the letter.

Furthermore, there are various ways in which one may view the divisions of the larger sections of the body of the letter. Some commentators envision 1:10–6:20 as Paul's remarks in reaction to oral reports of the situation in Corinth and 7:1–15:58 (or 7:1–16:12) as his answer to the Corinthians' letter. However, the following commentary treats the letter's body in four large sections because I recognize these portions of the letter to be concerned with different themes. First, 1:10–4:21 is a set of reflections on *the gospel and wisdom;* second, 5:1–11:1 takes up a series of *matters in the everyday life of the Corinthian church;* third, 11:2–14:40 focuses on *the need for orderly worship and the practice of spiritual gifts* in the context of that worship; and fourth, 15:1–58 is a complex but unified meditation on *the truth of the resurrection of the dead.* Other patterns of examining the body of the letter are possible, but considering these materials in terms of unifying themes allows us to appreciate the major concerns Paul addresses when he discusses the many specific matters in this letter.

After the body of the letter one encounters Paul's discussion of several practical matters (16:1–18) and the elements of the formal closing of the letter (16:19–24). In all, the letter is lengthy and complex, and it is helpful to see the flow of the materials in the form of an outline in order to follow the logic and development of Paul's thought.

This outline informs the commentary that follows, assisting the reader of any particular passage to gain a vision of where that segment of the letter belongs in the overall configuration of the letter. At times, however, in the course of offering commentary on particular passages, sections or verses are further subdivided in more discrete units or, by contrast, they are held together in larger coherent pieces to facilitate the interpretation of the text.

Paul's Theological Worldview

To appreciate the worldview from which Paul thought and taught, it is necessary to understand the foundations of Paul's personal background and religious thought. There is an ongoing debate among those seeking to understand Paul over which background best accounts for Paul's own understanding of what he did and said. Prior to the last two or three decades of study, scholars drew hard lines dividing three areas that were commonly accepted as having influenced Paul. Since he was a Pharisee, Palestinian Judaism was thought by some to provide the key to interpreting Paul. Other scholars argued that Hellenism was the most appropriate background for viewing and interpreting Paul, and a third contingent maintained that apocalyptic eschatology was the best framework in which to understand Paul's work. Scholars now recognize that these three backgrounds are not exclusive of one another and that each makes a contribution to a balanced reading of Paul, for Paul was influenced by and drew upon all of them. Nevertheless, the question remains whether one of these is dominant.

Judaism   Paul the Christian had once been Paul the Jew. It is clear from both his own letters and the story of his ministry in Acts that Paul was not only a Jew but also a zealous Pharisee. From time to time Paul boasts of his Jewish past as a way of rebutting other missionaries who caused problems in churches that he had founded (see Phil. 3 and 2 Cor. 11). Acts 22:3 preserves a tradition not attested in Paul's own writings that associates him with Gamaliel I of Jerusalem, one of the most influential figures in first-century Judaism. While Paul does not mention this striking association when rehearsing his Jewish credentials, nonetheless the association of Paul with formal "rabbinic-style" education seems likely, for in his writings Paul manifests signs of "rabbinic" style and logic (although the designation "rabbinic" is anachronistic for Paul's first-century Judaism, since the actual office of "rabbi" is a post–70 development and the rabbinic sources with which comparisons are made come from the third century and later). Paul does midrashic exegesis of the Jewish scriptures;

that is, he provides an imaginative retelling of a Bible story or passage that relates and applies the story or sense of the Scripture to the current concerns of the author and the author's audience. As Paul writes in 1 Corinthians 10 he demonstrates a clear perception of law-observance as the heart of Judaism; and the contrast he draws between Christ and the law shows his disavowal of practicing the law's systemic righteousness that he had once observed with confidence and contentment. These features of Paul's writings locate him within the stream of first-century Pharisaic Judaism. Scholarly discussion of Paul's writings during the past quarter century has focused in a particularly vigorous fashion on Paul's understanding and teaching concerning the law and its pertinence (or lack thereof) for Christianity. That particular issue (Paul and the law) is essentially peripheral to the focused discussion of the contents of 1 Corinthians; yet as will be noted throughout the commentary below, Paul constantly refers to and quotes from the scriptures of Judaism as the authoritative text for comprehending God and the human situation in the context of the Christian church. His use of the so-called Old Testament is complex—it was in some ways typical of Jews of his time, yet it also was quite original in both interpretation and application.

His use of apparently technical language in reference to tradition he had *received* and *delivered* (1 Cor. 15:3) to the churches he founded was taken to indicate his self-understanding and his attitude toward the tradition itself. Moreover, Paul's practice of midrashic exegesis (in which he elaborates on the meaning of a text in a way similar to that done by rabbinic Judaism; see Paul on the exodus in 1 Cor. 10 or on Abraham in Gal. 3) was thought to reveal his approach to the Old Testament, while his concern with the contrast between Christ and the law was determined by his past participation in Pharisaism.

Hellenism   As it is clear that Paul's past was in Pharisaic Judaism, it is also certain that Paul was a Hellenized Jew. Beyond doubt, those among whom Paul worked and ministered and to whom he preached and wrote his letters were residents of a Hellenized world. Whether one elects to name the temporal age of Paul and his contemporaries as "the era of Hellenism" or "the period of post-Hellenism," the world of that time was thoroughly influenced by Greek culture.

According to The Acts of the Apostles, Paul was born outside Palestine in the Greco-Roman trade city of Tarsus. All of

Paul's writings display the hallmarks of Hellenistic education: mastery of the skills of reading, thinking, argumentation, and expression in writing, as well as others. Paul normally quotes the Greek version of the Jewish scriptures, which indicates that he read the Greek version of the Bible at least some of the time, if not exclusively. Paul is thoroughly familiar with the conventions of popular Hellenistic philosophy and methods of literary interpretation. He engaged in a diatribe style of argumentation typical of Stoic and Cynic teaching. Paul did allegorical exegesis, which was a refined Hellenistic interpretive approach to highly regarded writings, when he dealt with the Jewish scriptures (see Paul on Sarah and Hagar in Gal. 4). He refers to himself with the Greek name, *Paul*, not the Jewish name, *Saul;* and the majority of his metaphors are drawn from the Greco-Roman world of households, sports, street life, and the military. Some scholars have held that casting Paul in the context of Hellenism provides interpreters with the prerequisite clues for understanding such basic Pauline notions as the sacraments and Christology. As this argument goes, since Paul was thoroughly Hellenistic in heritage, he would have interpreted baptism and the Lord's Supper in relation to the practices of Hellenistic mystery religions, and he would have understood Christ in terms of a general, Hellenistic myth of a descending and ascending redeemer figure.

For these reasons, among others that will become apparent in the course of studying 1 Corinthians, scholars of the past two decades have focused with steadily increasing energy on the relationship of Paul's letters to the style and devices of Greco-Roman rhetoric. Understanding the rhetorical features of portions of 1 Corinthians will be helpful in attempting to understand and to interpret its significant elements.

Apocalyptic Eschatology   In conjunction with Judaism and Hellenism, a distinctive and crucial element of Paul's religious outlook was his apocalyptic-eschatological outlook. Indeed, this worldview (which may be described as being aware of both the earthly reality and the transcendent divine) is a key for comprehending some of Paul's most difficult teachings. Paul's perspective was consistently theological, with a sharply focused christological cast, and it took into consideration the reality of God and creation, the relationship of God and creation, and the place and role of humanity in relation to both God and the created order. This worldview is truly comprehensive, though it is intimately bound to the language and ideas of the first-century world in which Paul and his contemporaries lived.

It has become increasingly clear through the work of several contemporary scholars (e.g., J. C. Beker, E. Käsemann, and J. L. Martyn) that the apocalyptic-eschatological element provided Paul with a basic framework for his thought and determined his comprehension of the world around him. Paul's language displays his apocalyptic perspective in the way it focuses on wrath, judgment, and the Day of the Lord. His displayed yearning for *the* messianic age is characteristic of all apocalyptic writings. The elements of both Paul's Judaism and Hellenism hang on and relate to this overall apocalyptic structure.

Thus one must ask and answer the question, *What is this apocalyptic-eschatological perspective?* In Greek, *apokalypsis* means "revelation." Paul uses this word to refer to his original encounter with the risen Jesus Christ (Gal. 1:12). That dramatic revelation was the occasion of Paul's call, as well as the time and means of Paul's reception of the gospel that he preached (Gal. 1:11–17). This sort of disruptive intervention of God into someone's life is not unusual in first-century apocalyptic Judaism.

(1) The Jewish elements of Paul's apocalyptic eschatology. In essence, apocalyptic is a special expression of Jewish eschatology that is characterized, as noted, by the dualistic doctrine of two ages. On the one hand there is "the present evil age," and on the other there is "the age to come." The "present evil age" is the world of mundane realities in which human beings live; the "age to come" is the supernatural realm of the power of God. There is no continuity between these ages. Indeed, apocalyptic Jewish thought held that at some future moment "the age to come" would break into the human realm by a supernatural act of God. In this moment of God's intervention, the "present evil age" would pass away and "the age to come" would be established as a new reality, ordained and directed by God. Apocalyptic Judaism held that by this act of God, evil would be annihilated and those who were righteous would be redeemed. Thus "the age to come" was the hope of those who believed in God but found themselves oppressed by the forces of evil in the present world. In Jewish apocalyptic literature the authors usually claim to live in the last days of "the present evil age." Their message to readers is the joint promise and warning that the intervention of God is about to take place.

Throughout his letters Paul's language and patterns of thought reveal elements of this apocalyptic eschatology. For example, Paul frequently uses apocalyptic language: "destined . . . for wrath," "the wrath to come," "the wrath of God," "the day of wrath," "the day of the Lord Jesus Christ," "the day of salvation," "redeemed," "redemption," "this age," "the rulers of this age," "the present evil age," and "the ends of the ages." Moreover, Paul reveals in his letters the conviction that he and his readers are part of the last generation of humanity (1 Thess. 4:13–18, esp. v. 17; 1 Cor. 7:31; 15:51–57).

(2) The Christian elements of Paul's apocalyptic thought. Because Paul does not use the phrase "the age to come," some scholars deny the thoroughly apocalyptic character of his thought. Yet he speaks in distinctively Christian phrases of the same idea when he says, "a new creation" and "the kingdom of God." This difference in phrases indicates a slight but fundamental alteration on the part of Paul. He transforms the pattern of Jewish apocalyptic thought described above into a particularly Christian pattern of apocalyptic thinking that permeates all of his writings. In other words, Paul articulates an apocalyptic perspective that has been modified in light of the Christ-event.

While Jewish apocalyptic eschatology thought in terms of two ages, the present (evil) age and the age to come, these periods were completely distinct, so that one age ended and the other began by an intervening act of God. Thus reality was understood in terms of an absolute temporal (not metaphysical) dualism. As a Christian thinker, Paul has a similar but remarkably distinct view of time. He maintains the temporal dualism characteristic of Jewish apocalyptic, but he modifies the scheme in light of the Christ-event so that there are two distinct ages that are separated and joined by an interim period of time.

For Paul the first temporal epoch is "the present evil age" (Gal. 1:4; 1 Cor. 2:6–8). This age is ruled by the god of this world (2 Cor. 4:4), namely Satan, and by the elemental spirits of the universe (Gal. 4:3; 1 Cor. 2:8). Under the influence of its rulers this age is at odds with God (1 Cor. 15:24–28; Rom. 8:37–39). Nevertheless, this age is passing away (1 Cor. 7:31). The second epoch is the "new creation" (Gal. 6:15; 2 Cor. 5:17). This new age comes as God in Christ defeats the opposing forces (Gal. 6:14; 1 Cor. 7:31; Rom. 5:21), and it is established as the reign of God, an age of glory (1 Thess. 2:10–12; 1 Cor. 15:20–28; 2 Cor. 4:17; Rom. 5:2, 21).

According to Paul, the *present* exists as the juncture or mingling of the two ages (1 Cor. 10:11; 2 Cor. 5:16). Here, 1 Corinthians 10:11 is important. In this verse Paul describes himself and other humans in very striking terms that modern translations often obscure. For example, Paul's words as they were rendered in the RSV read, "upon whom the end of the ages has come." This translation implies that Paul stands at the end of time and looks back at past ages (something like dispensations?)—but, in fact, he does not. The NIV reads "on whom the fulfillment of the ages has come," but Paul's actual phrase literally says, "upon whom the ends of the ages have met"; as the NRSV now translates the words. Paul perceives that he and other humans live at the juncture of the ages. This juncture came about as a result of the cross of Christ (1 Cor. 1:17–18) and it will conclude at the coming of Christ from heaven—which will mark the absolute end of the present evil age (1 Thess. 2:19; 3:13; 4:13–18; 1 Cor. 15:23–28). This interim period is the time in which Paul was called and in which he thought, worked, and preached. Much of Paul's message derives from his understanding of this juncture and of the fact that it came about as a result of the cross of Christ (1 Cor. 1:17–18). In essence Paul thought and taught that sin has been defeated (Gal. 1:4; 1 Cor. 15:3; Rom. 4:25); that death has been condemned (1 Cor. 15:54–57; Rom. 8:31–39); that the law has been exposed for what it is—powerless (Gal. 2:21; 3:24–25; Rom. 7:7–12); that Christ has discharged humanity from the curse of the law (Gal. 3:13–14; Rom. 7:4–6); that although the battle goes on toward God's final victory, creation has been reclaimed by God (1 Cor. 15:20–28; Rom. 8:18–25); that God's sovereignty has been established (Rom. 8:31–39); and that all creation presently awaits the grand judicial inquest (1 Thess. 5:2–11; 1 Cor. 6:2–3; 15:20–28; Rom. 8:18–25); and while the kingdom of God has not yet been fully established in glory, for Christians the present is effectively *already* the messianic age in which, for now, everything is to be viewed from the vantage point of the cross (2 Cor. 5:16). In the commentary that follows, this understanding of Paul's theological vision of reality will constantly underlie and inform the interpretation of Paul's correspondence to the Corinthians.

§1 Salutation (1 Cor. 1:1–3)

Letters in the Greco-Roman world had a fairly standard form. They would begin with a salutation, followed by a conventional thanksgiving (often in the form of a prosaic prayer). Next came the body of the letter, often followed by *parenesis* (concrete directions), and then the closing of the letter. The salutation itself normally contained three parts that first named the sender, then named the recipient, and finally offered a greeting.

A typical non-Christian letter from Paul's day might open as follows: "Gaius, to Quartus, greetings." The salutations in Paul's letters are rarely so concise. Rather, Paul modified the form of the salutation by expanding it and giving it a distinctively Christian cast. Even when Paul's salutation is brief, as it is in 1 Thessalonians, it has a clearly theological tone. The salutation here in 1 Corinthians is quite elaborate.

1:1 / Paul describes himself as one **called to be an apostle of Christ Jesus by the will of God.** This designation emphasizes God's divine initiative in setting Paul about the work that he did in founding and forming churches in the first-century world. While Paul literally writes, "called apostle" (the NIV supplies the words "to be"), he does not merely wish to report a title he received from God. *Apostolos,* from the verb *apostellō* meaning "to send," describes Paul as "one who is sent," so while **apostle** could serve as a title, the word defined what Paul did as a result of God's call. Moreover, Paul informs the Corinthians that he was an apostle *of Christ Jesus.* This phrase concerning Paul's apostleship can only mean that he is one who is sent out in behalf of Christ. He is Christ's own agent; indeed, one might understand that Christ Jesus himself sent Paul. Thus, Paul is one sent under the authority of Christ. Paul reminds the Corinthians of his relationship to Christ Jesus because in the rest of this letter he will deal with them as the agent of Christ, as one authorized by Christ, whose authority is not his own, but Christ Jesus' authority. Furthermore, Paul's being commissioned and going on behalf of Christ Jesus are **through the will of God**. He did not simply decide to be Christ's agent; God willed it and now Paul works under and with the authority of Christ Jesus. The result of God's acting in Paul's life was that Paul became active in the world.

Along with Paul, **Sosthenes** is named as the co-author of this letter. From the letters preserved from the Greco-Roman world, it does not appear that joint authorship was a normal procedure. Why Paul wrote this way is open to speculation, and perhaps the motives differed from one letter to another. In the other instances of co-authorship the persons named with Paul were known to the churches to which they were writing, and from Paul's use of "I" and "we" throughout the letters we see that he did not always understand his co-authors to play equally active roles in the composition of the letters. The inclusion of Sosthenes here is especially striking since this reference is the only mention of Sosthenes in this or any other Pauline letter. Nevertheless, Paul calls him "Sosthenes the brother." In other letters of Paul the designation "brother" identifies one of his fellow workers, and that may be the case here (see Rom. 16:23; 1 Cor. 16:20; 2 Cor. 1:1; 2:13; 8:18, 22; 12:18; Phil. 2:25; 1 Thess. 3:2; Phlm. 1, 7, 20; and Eph. 6:21; Col. 1:1; 4:7, 9). From Acts 18:17 we know that someone named Sosthenes was the ruler of the synagogue community in Corinth at the time when some members of the synagogue brought Paul before the tribunal of Gallio. The charge against Paul was not successful, and the Acts account reports that Sosthenes suffered a beating from his fellow Jews when their case failed. We do not know whether the Sosthenes of Acts and the Sosthenes named here are the same person. If the two references are to one person, we do not know how he became a Christian or how he came to work with Paul away from Corinth, but we would gain insight into Paul's possible motive for naming Sosthenes as the co-author of 1 Corinthians.

1:2 / Paul refers to the Corinthians in an elaborate and deliberate manner. He refers to them as a **church**. The Greek word *ekklēsia* can be translated "church," "congregation," or "assembly" and was used in different contexts. In secular Greco-Roman literature it named a political assembly, especially one brought together for decisive action. Yet the word had religious usage in Judaism that Paul would likely have known. The LXX uses *ekklēsia* to render the Hebrew word *qahal* that both named the Israelites at points in their desert wanderings during the exodus and referred to their later assemblies at the temple for various kinds of worship. There is no reason or way to force a decision between the secular and religious uses of *ekklēsia* in order to understand how Paul and the Corinthians thought about the nature of the company of Christians in Corinth. More crucial for understanding Paul's vision of the church than isolating a particular background for the word *ekklēsia* is to notice that he calls the Corinthians the **church of God.** The church exists because of God's initiatives. Thus, Paul refers to the location of the congregation **in Corinth** only as a secondary identification, for primarily the Corinthian church belongs to God (6:19–20), not merely to a place.

Paul continues to clarify the true theological identity of the Corinthians by referring to them as **those sanctified in Christ Jesus.** "Those sanctified" translates a Greek word that comes from a verb *(hagiazō)* that means "to make holy." In mentioning the sanctified state of the Corinthians in this way, Paul recognizes that God's own past activity, not that of the Corinthians, forged out their new life in Christ. To be sanctified means to be made holy, to be set apart for special service to God. The Corinthians are to reflect God's own holiness in their devotion to God. The form of the word here literally means "having been sanctified" and implies a completed past action that may indicate the conversion of the Corinthians to Christian faith. Clearly they have their identity in Christ Jesus, and perhaps Paul even means to remind them that they are "in Christ" and no longer "of the world" (see 1:27–30).

As Paul was (literally) "called apostle," i.e., called to be one sent by God, so the Corinthians are (literally) "called holy ones," i.e., called to be holy. The word translated **holy** in the NIV is sometimes rendered "saints" in other translations, but today that term has taken on connotations that could be misleading for understanding Paul's remark. The same basic root in Greek lies behind both the word that was translated "those sanctified" and the word that is construed with **holy** in this verse. Paul is not, however, being redundant; rather, he is emphasizing that God's divine calling imparts an identity that gives a new, clear purpose to life. As Paul was called apostle to be sent by God, so the Corinthians were sanctified to be set apart for service to God. Although persons and tasks differ, there is always a missional dimension to Christian identity and existence.

Furthermore, Paul acknowledges that the Corinthians were sanctified and called to be holy **together with all those everywhere who call on the name of our Lord Jesus Christ—their Lord and ours.** By informing the Corinthians of their common bond with all others who affirm the lordship of Jesus Christ, Paul registers an identity that will prove to be a large part of the solution to the problematic situation that existed in Corinth. While Paul has not yet mentioned any of the difficulties that exist among the Corinthians, it becomes clear in the rest of the letter that some in Corinth were manifesting lifestyles that were inconsistent with the manner of life advocated by Paul and embraced by the members of other churches. Later Paul will chide the Corinthians for their inappropriate independence (14:36), and he will repeatedly confront their arrogant tendency to strike a novel path of life (4:6, 17; 5:1–2; 11:16; 14:33b; 15:1–2). Even as he opens this letter, Paul reminds the Corinthians that they are not an unrestrained holy group that is detached from the larger community of Christian faith. Rather, they and all other Christians live in a dependent relationship to the Lord Jesus Christ that establishes a mutuality that transcends the worldly boundaries of human relations. Shared devotion to the Lord Jesus Christ, who through the calling of God has authority over the lives of all believers, focuses existence and draws Christians beyond themselves and their immediate congregation into a universal fellowship of faith.

1:3 / The standard word for hailing the recipient in the salutation of a Greco-Roman letter was "greetings!" The Greek verb *chairō,* meaning literally "to rejoice," was used for this purpose. Paul's letters make a slight modification that gives theological emphasis to the greeting. Rather than *chairō,* Paul writes *charis,* meaning grace; and to that greeting he adds the traditional Jewish greeting, "peace." This combination of **grace and peace** occurs in every letter attributed to Paul in the New Testament (although the triad of "grace, mercy, and peace" forms the greetings in 1 and 2 Timothy). The word "grace" summarizes Paul's understanding of God's full generosity in dealing with humanity; indeed, grace is the way, the means, and even the presence and power of God at work in relation to humans (1:4; 3:10; above all, 15:10). The result of God's gracious dealings with humanity is summarized by "peace," which is far more than the mere absence of strife. Peace means wholeness and well-being; it is the divine result of the divine gift of grace. Paul consistently couples grace and peace, because he understands that grace creates peace and peace comes about through grace.

Moreover, Paul's greeting recognizes the source of both grace and peace to be **God our Father and the Lord Jesus Christ.** All that God does is through Jesus Christ. In turn, as Paul calls God our Father he preserves Jesus' own language for God and he fosters the understanding of and attitude toward God that Jesus taught to his initial disciples. The religious significance of calling God "Father" has nothing to do with the idea that God is male, which idea has fallen under much sharp criticism today. God is not male or female; but the cast of this address inspires one to relate to God in the best terms of the love that is experienced in a healthy family. Moreover, relating to God as loving heavenly parent inspires Christians to relate to one another as sympathetic members of the family of faith. Indeed, because he regards God as Father, Paul regards Sosthenes as his "brother" and still other believers as his "brothers and sisters."

Paul ends this salutation with the name of the Lord Jesus Christ. Thus, we see Paul's overriding christological outlook from the beginning to the end of the opening three verses of this letter. Paul designated himself as an apostle of Christ Jesus. He recognized the church of God in Corinth to be those sanctified in Christ Jesus along with everyone else who called on Jesus Christ as Lord. Finally, Paul understood that the very grace and peace of God came to Christians from both God and the Lord Jesus Christ.

Additional Notes §1

1:1 / Frequently in the seven undisputed epistles (Rom., 1 Cor., 2 Cor., Gal., Phil., 1 Thess., and Phlm.), Paul names a colleague as co-author of the letter; all of these writings except Rom. and Gal. refer to co-authors. Those named as co-authors with Paul include Sosthenes (1 Cor.), Timothy (2 Cor., Phil., 1 Thess., Phlm.), and Silvanus (1 Thess.). In the six epistles that are disputed (Eph., Col., 2 Thess., 1 Tim., 2 Tim., and Titus), Col. and 2 Thess. mention co-authors: Timothy (Col., 2 Thess.) and Silvanus (2 Thess.).

J. Murphy-O'Connor ("Co-Authorship in the Corinthian Correspondence," *RB* 100 [1993], pp. 562–79) studies the role of the co-authors with Paul and recognizes different levels of involvement from one letter to another and even from one section of a letter to another section of the same letter. He argues that Sosthenes made more of a contribution to the composition of 1 Corinthians than past scholarship has suggested.

1:2 / Two grammatical issues mark the phrases **together with all those everywhere who call on the name of our Lord Jesus Christ— their Lord and ours.** First, the statement could belong with either (1) Paul and Sosthenes, or (2) **the church of God in Corinth,** or (3) those **called to be holy.** Thus, the line could mean (1) that Paul and Sosthenes envision the church universal joining them as they write the Corinthians—a thought that makes little sense; or (2) that the church in Corinth is being addressed along with the church universal—a striking image that locates the Corinthians as part of the whole church; or (3) that the Corinthians are called to be God's holy ones along with the rest of the church universal—a sensible idea. Similar statements in 2 Cor. 1:1 and Phil. 1:1 strengthen the case for (2), despite the idea in (3) being easier to comprehend. Nevertheless, the fact that both (2) and (3) associate the Corinthians with all other Christians may mean that it is unnecessary to decide between these options; indeed, Paul and Sosthenes may have shades of both thoughts in mind, so that the ambiguity is deliberate.

The second grammatical issue is that scholars suggest that the phrase "those . . . who call on the name of our Lord" is a confessional statement from the life of the early church and that it is related to a range of texts and images in the OT. When Paul uses the phrase in the opening of 1 Corinthians he seems to be emphasizing the church universal—a church that is unified by the devotion of all its believers to the Lord Jesus Christ. Thus, the phrase implies that factions are to be condemned and that unity is the solution to the situation in Corinth. The significance of common calling on the name of the Lord for Christian unity was explicated by O. Cullmann ("All Who Call on the Name of Our Lord Jesus Christ," *JES* 1 [1964], pp. 1–21).

1:3 / C. K. Barrett (*The First Epistle to the Corinthians* [HNTC; New York: Harper & Row, 1968], p. 34) notes that the combination of "grace and peace" also occurs in 2 *Bar.* 78.2 and 2 Macc. 1:1. Thus, these theological terms are found in close association in these two other writings from Hellenistic Judaism.

§2 *Thanksgiving (1 Cor. 1:4–9)*

The second typical normal element of a Greco-Roman letter—after the salutation—is a statement of thanksgiving or a thanksgiving prayer. Usually the lines mean little more than "I hope all is well with you," although the writer typically makes some reference to "the gods." Paul again follows the basic pattern of the standard letter of his day, but he modifies the form so that it becomes "Christian" and takes on a dynamic function in the letter. Scholars have long recognized that as a formal element of Paul's letters the thanksgiving (or thanksgiving prayer) serves several purposes. First, the thanksgiving terminates the opening portion of the letter. Second, it signals the basic theme or themes of the letter that will follow. Third, the thanksgiving can sometimes even outline the major topics to be treated in the epistle. In 1:4–9, Paul acknowledges God's grace as active among the Corinthians to the end that they are in every way enriched in Christ Jesus, in speech and knowledge of every kind. Among the Corinthians the real gifts of speech and knowledge are at the heart of their problematic thoughts and actions. At once Paul names the genuine strengths and weaknesses of the Corinthian church. The members experience the endowments of grace, but as the remainder of the letter reveals, their concern with and use of these gifts is completely out of hand.

1:4 / Paul reports his giving thanks to God at the outset of this section. He reiterates such thanksgiving later in the letter at 14:18. Paul does not mention prayer per se at this point, but the fact that his thanksgiving is directed to God indicates that he has prayerful activity in mind. The word **always** in this report emphasizes Paul's regularity and constancy in remembering and rejoicing over the Corinthians. Paul's thankfulness, however, is not primarily because of the Corinthians themselves, but rather because of the grace of God that affects the lives of the Corinthians. God as the source of grace and the giver of grace is the object of Paul's thanksgiving. **Grace** itself in this statement is the experience of salvation, but not merely as the moment of initial faith. Rather, the following comments show that for Paul grace is the ongoing experience of God's endowing the Corinthians with spiritual gifts that redefine their lives.

Paul's references to grace make it clear that the Corinthians experience grace as a gift from God. Grace is given by God; there is no foundation for boasting (a major concern of the rest of the letter) in the Corinthians' experience of grace. The grace the Corinthians have, the gifts that are manifested among them, are God's and not their capacities and achievements (cf. 4:7–8). Moreover, Paul locates the experience of God's grace specifically in relation to Christ Jesus. In the context of Christian faith and life the Corinthians are the recipients of God's gift of grace, so that the grace is never purely at their disposal. Grace comes in a context and for a purpose, as Paul makes plain throughout the entire letter. God's endowments are for specific reasons in the context of the Christians' relationship to Christ and his community of faith.

1:5 / Paul explicates his thanksgiving further by specifying the reason for his gratitude: that in Christ Jesus the Corinthians are **enriched in every way.** The enrichment, said to be complete, is still not the property or privilege of the Corinthians; it is theirs specifically in the context of Christ Jesus, that is, in the context of the new life God created by working through him. In particular, Paul says the Corinthians have been enriched in all speaking and all knowledge. In the context of this letter **all your speaking** probably means the more specific phenomenon of spiritual assertions, not merely all the talking that they do. The mention of **all your knowledge** most likely indicates the Corinthians' perception of the truth of divine revelation, not merely a set of facts. Paul thinks here of both speaking and knowledge as phenomena of grace, i.e., as divine gifts. Remarkably, as one sees in the rest of the letter, the Corinthians' practice of making spiritual assertions (6:12–13; 10:23; 12:3; 14:1–40) and their concern with spiritual knowledge or wisdom (1:19–31; 8:1–2, 7–13; 13:2, 8) are serious problems in the life of the church. Thus, interpreters often suggest that here in the thanksgiving Paul is using sarcasm or irony. Yet such an interpretation fails to grasp the range of Paul's thought. Paul is a genuine charismatic who believes in, practices, and celebrates the reality of God's spiritual gifts. He can easily distinguish between the use and the abuse of spiritual gifts. He offers thanks for the gracious gifts that the Corinthians received because they came to them from God. Paul emphasizes speaking and knowledge in his thanksgiving because, as major sections of the letter indicate, these gifts are prominent in the life of the Corinthian church. Later, Paul can take up the misuse of these endowments and express his unquestionable distress over the misappropriation of God's gifts. The gifts themselves, however, are real, and Paul rejoices over them because they are God's gifts—even in the face of their abuse. Paul's confidence lies with God, the giver of gifts; his *concern* lies with the Corinthians.

1:6 / Paul continues his thanksgiving with another word of explanation, although the rendering of the Greek word *kathōs* as **because** in the NIV (compare the translation in the NRSV, "just as") gives the mistaken impression that Paul is adding a causal remark to what he has said. Rather, here he forms a comparison between the reality of God's endowing the Corinthians with spiritual gifts and God's initial act of grace in bring the Corinthians to faith in Christ. Thus, Paul refers literally to "the testimony of Christ" (NIV: **our testimony about Christ**) that he says was **confirmed in** the Corinthians. Paul rarely uses the word "testimony" in his letters, so the meaning of this word is not immediately apparent. He says the testimony of Christ was confirmed without stating explicitly who brought about the confirmation; the verb is in a passive construction that assumes God as the subject of the action. That God confirmed Christ's testimony most sensibly refers to God's establishment of faith in Christ in Corinth, so "the testimony of Christ" is another way of referring to *the gospel.* Paul's point here, then, is that God gives grace and enriches the Corinthians in the same way that God established faith in the gospel in the lives of the Corinthians.

1:7 / Paul continues the sentence he began in verse 4 with still another elaboration that serves to round out the idea of his thanksgiving. The phrase here begins with the Greek word *hōste,* which means "so that" or **therefore** and indicates that Paul means to explain the results of what he has been saying. Thus he says the Corinthians **do not lack any spiritual gift,** for as he has said, God enriched them "in every way" (1:5). Paul underscores the reality of the spiritual gifts in Corinth in recognition of the magnitude of God's grace. He continues, however, in a way that qualifies God's complete enrichment of the Corinthians by saying that they experience these gifts (lit.) "as [they] eagerly await the revelation of our Lord Jesus Christ." This crucial circumscription gives a clear eschatological cast to the spiritual gifts in Corinth. *Already* the Corinthians have faith in Christ, but *not yet* are their hopes in Christ realized. *Already* the Corinthians are enriched by God's grace, but *not yet* has the full reality of divine grace been made real. Rather, Paul says the Corinthians **eagerly wait for** [the] **Lord Jesus Christ to be revealed.** Thus, Paul affirms the reality of the Corinthians' experience of grace and the reality of God's gifts to them, but he emphasizes that their involvement with grace is not as principal actors—they experience the reality of God's grace, they do not initiate it. Moreover, even as they are enriched by God, they live in expectation, for they enthusiastically look forward to the "revelation" of Christ. Paul certainly means to refer to the return of Christ, but his use here of "revelation" (Gk. *apokalypsis*) rather than his more usual term "coming" (Gk. *parousia*) gives further emphasis to God's priority in Christian life (cf. Gal. 1:15–17). Thus Paul says the Corinthians live their enriched lives looking forward to what God will do in and through the Lord Jesus Christ. God's purposes and God's future are greater than the present experience of God's grace in Corinth, so Paul implies that the Corinthians should not be overly self-satisfied with the richness of God's gifts to them. The Corinthians live in relation to a promise of the final revelation of the Lord Jesus Christ, so the full experience of God's grace lies beyond the present in God's future action, and the sole basis of the eager expectation of the Corinthians in God's future, as Paul will declare, is that "God is faithful" (1:9).

1:8 / The final clause of Paul's complex Greek sentence functions as a confessional statement. The grammar is ambiguous, however, and interpreters debate whether the remark in this clause is about the "Lord Jesus Christ," who was named at the end of verse 7, or about God, who has been the unstated subject of a number of passive verbs throughout the preceding lines. The clause begins with a word that may be translated **he** or "who" (Gk. *hos*). The NIV translates the verb that follows this subject as "keep strong," although it is the same verb that was translated "confirm" in verse 6. The passive form of the verb in verse 6 assumed God for a subject, thus God was the one who did the confirming, but Paul could have shifted his point of view so that now in verse 8 he has "the Lord Jesus Christ" in mind as the one who sustains the Corinthians. Even if this is the case, he would still understand that God was the one who was acting in and through Christ in relation to the Corinthians. While the easiest way to read verse 8 would be to translate the subject as "who," in reference to the immediately preceding Greek words "our Lord Jesus Christ," the declaration that follows in verse 9, "God is faithful," may be an indication of Paul's intended subject in verse 8. The creation of a separate sentence that begins with "He" in the NIV and the NRSV accurately reflects the ambiguity of the Greek (the RSV reads "who" in reference to Christ and does not begin a new sentence at v. 8). Whether Paul means to speak here of God or of the Lord Jesus Christ, the Corinthians should gather that the basis of their security is not with themselves or their endowments, but with the divine action (of God or Christ) on their behalf.

Paul continues the eschatological emphasis that was registered in verse 7 as he speaks of the Corinthians' being kept strong **to the end.** Here Paul has in mind the endpoint of time as we know it in our earthy existence. Paul thought and taught that he and the Corinthians (and all others) lived at the juncture of two ages (see the Introduction, p. 15, and 10:11)—"the present evil age" (Gal. 1:4) that had started to pass away with the cross of Christ (see 1 Cor. 7:31b) and the new age, the "new creation" (2 Cor. 5:17) or "kingdom" (see 1 Cor. 15:24), that had begun but that would not be fully present until the coming of Christ (Phil. 3:20; 1 Thess. 4:13–18; 5:1–11; see 1 Cor. 15:23–24).

The outcome of the Corinthians' being kept strong is that they would be **blameless on the day of** [the] **Lord Jesus Christ.** The language here is part of a legal metaphor that depicts being without guilt in relation to the law. The implication of this image is that the Day of the Lord would bring judgment at the end. The reference to the Day of the Lord Jesus Christ takes up language and thinking from the OT (Ezek. 30:3; Joel 2:31; Amos 5:18, 20; Zeph. 1:14–16), although in the OT texts the one who executes judgment on the Day of the Lord is *the Lord God,* whereas here Paul plainly understands that one to be *the Lord Jesus Christ.* Paul preserves the theological vision of the OT and gives it christological focus that makes the promise of the Day of the Lord all the more specific and real.

Finally, Paul's unswerving confidence in the Corinthians' future is remarkable, for from the remainder of the letter one sees that he faced grave problems in the life of the Corinthian congregation. Yet Paul's remarks in this thanksgiving show that whatever confidence he had for the outcome of the problems in Corinth was based in God and God's working among the Corinthians through the Lord Jesus Christ, not in the Corinthians themselves. Indeed, Paul's declaration of confidence in God concerning the Corinthians should have directed the attention of the Corinthians toward God and away from themselves.

1:9 / All Paul's elaborate thinking and thanksgiving are epitomized in this crisp—but loaded—statement. Paul declares, above all, that **God . . . is faithful.** This truth is the foundation of Paul's confidence concerning the Corinthians. God's faithfulness is a major theme of the OT, where God is remembered and praised as a faithful God. Yet as we see in Paul's declaration here, he has in mind God's faithfulness as he and the Corinthians know it specifically through Jesus Christ. God had begun and was continuing a work among the Corinthians that had an assured outcome because of God's own character. The declaration of God's faithfulness will be repeated at 10:13, where Paul recognizes the reality of the temptation that the Corinthians must face and tells them that God's own faithfulness assures that they will not be tempted beyond what they can bear—indeed, God's faithfulness guarantees that "he will provide a way so that [they] can stand up under [temptation]." Already in 1 Thessalonians 5:24 Paul had written of God's faithfulness, coupling the idea with the memory of God's calling the Thessalonians to faith in a manner quite similar to his statement here. In 2 Corinthians 1:18 Paul again speaks of God's faithfulness—here in such a way as to reveal that Paul considered God's faithfulness beyond question.

God's faithfulness undergirds his calling the Corinthians, and as Paul explains, God's initiative in calling the Corinthians was related to a specific goal. Through God's call they were brought **into fellowship with . . . Jesus Christ.** Moreover, the Christocentric character of Christian fellowship creates a dynamic relationship between God and humanity, for on the one hand, Jesus Christ is God's Son, and on the other hand, he is the Lord of those God calls into fellowship with him. With this sketch of relations, Paul directs the attention of the Corinthians away from themselves toward their fellowship with Jesus Christ and through him to God. What God does for humanity, he does through Jesus Christ; and, at the same time, humanity relates to God in and through the divinely created fellowship with Jesus Christ.

Additional Notes §2

1:4 / The NIV reads, **I always thank God,** although the Gk. text of NA[27] reads, *eucharistō tō theō mou pantote,* literally "I give thanks to my God always." The pronoun "my" is missing in two of the oldest and most reliable manuscripts (א* and B), but it is present in a wide variety of other texts, including some that are ancient and typically accurate. The easiest explanation for this discrepancy is that the pronoun was accidentally omitted in א* and B, for the variety of texts that do include this otherwise innocuous pronoun are striking.

The Greek phrase for giving thanks to God is a feature of several Pauline letters: Rom. 1:8; 14:6; 1 Cor. 1:4; 14:18; Phil. 1:3; 1 Thess. 1:2; 2:13; Phlm. 4; and Col. 1:3; 3:17; 2 Thess. 2:13. On the significance of the thanksgivings in Paul's letters, see P. Schubert, *Form and Function of the Pauline Thanksgivings* (BZNW 20; Berlin: Töpelmann, 1939); P. T. O'Brien, "Thanksgiving and the Gospel in Paul," *NTS* 21 (1974), pp. 144–55 and idem, *Introductory Thanksgivings in the Letters of Paul* (NovTSup 49; Leiden: Brill, 1977). These studies make clear the thorough and profoundly Christian character of this part of Paul's writings.

1:5 / The NIV translation **in all your speaking** is far too broad to reflect Paul's thought here. A reader can be easily and unfortunately misled by this rendering of Paul's statement. Rather than having all speaking in Corinth in mind, Paul is concerned with God's grace that manifests itself in inspired speech or spiritual utterance. In agreement see G. D. Fee, *The First Epistle to the Corinthians* (NICNT; Grand Rapids: Eerdmans, 1987), p. 39.

K. Grayston ("Not With a Rod," *ExpT* 88 [1976], pp. 13–16) over-reads Paul's phrases *en panti logō kai pasē gnōsei* when he asserts that they refer to divisions in the church between those advocating *logos* and those involved with *gnōsis.* Rather, in Paul's discussion of the situation in Corinth (12:8; 14:6–25) the concerns with speaking and **knowledge** seem intimately connected.

1:7 / The subject of "spiritual gifts" that Paul raises already in the thanksgiving is a major topic of discussion in ch. 12 of the letter; and Paul mentions this matter in the course of his comments at both Rom. 12:6 and 1 Cor. 7:7. These gifts are clearly not thought to be birthright capacities; rather, they are divine endowments that come for the work of the Christian mission.

1:8 / While the NIV includes the phrase **our Lord Jesus Christ,** there is a division in the manuscript tradition between texts reading "our Lord Jesus" and "our Lord Jesus Christ." Two ancient and authoritative witnesses, P[46] and B, omit "Christ"; while others (א A C D F G and many others, including ancient versions and Ambrosiaster) include "Christ." Fee (*Epistle,* p. 35 n. 4) suggests that the absence of the title was a very early accidental omission that resulted from the juxtaposition of abbreviations for the genitive forms of Jesus and Christ ($\overline{IY}$ and $\overline{XY}$).

1:9 / Paul says here (lit.), "God is faithful, through whom you were called into fellowship with his son Jesus Christ our Lord." The NIV obscures both Paul's pattern of speech and the essence of his thought. The loss of precision in language is unfortunate, for Paul's statement contains the unusual idea that God is the agent *through* whom the Corinthians were called. In every other instance that Paul uses the phrase "through whom" (Gk. *di' hou*), he is referring to the Lord Jesus Christ as the one through whom God acts in relation to humanity—cf. Rom. 1:5; 5:2, 11; 1 Cor. 8:6; Gal. 6:14 (this last reference is ambiguous and may mean "through which" in reference to the cross of the Lord Jesus Christ).

§3 Factions in the Congregation (1 Cor. 1:10–17)

This first major segment of the body of Paul's letter forms a coherent reflection on the specific situation in Corinth in relation to and in the light of basic matters of Christian belief. Paul examines and explains the character of the gospel itself, so that the Corinthians are directed to evaluate their situation in the light of the gospel of God's saving work in Jesus Christ and the implication of God's work for their lives. Paul argues against understanding the gospel as a kind of mysterious wisdom teaching, especially as a teaching that would elevate those who have certain information above others who do not. He reminds the Corinthians of their calling, of the message they heard and believed, of the way that God reveals truth to humanity, of God's certain judgment of their life in Christ, of the inappropriateness of spiritual boasting, and of the necessity of their taking stock of and then changing their behavior.

1:10 / Paul begins by making an appeal to the Corinthians. In Paul's direct address to the Corinthians the NRSV's translation, "brothers and sisters" is preferable to the NIV's **brothers.** The Greek word *adelphoi* is one of Paul's most familiar forms of address for Christians. He uses the word twenty times in 1 Corinthians alone as a way of speaking directly to the Corinthians. In Greek the male plural form of address was the standard form for addressing mixed assemblies of men and women (the same is true of Latin and other languages, including English in a former time). Paul repeatedly uses *adelphoi* as the form of address for the Corinthian congregation, even in instances in which he is clearly concerned to address the Corinthian women (esp. chs. 7, 11, 14). Thus *adelphoi*, despite its literal male cast, should be translated as the NRSV and other recent versions render it: "brothers and sisters."

When Paul says **I appeal to you,** the verb "to appeal" (Gk. *parakaleō*) could indicate either a formal petition as in a court of

law or a simple request that has no special urgency. The seriousness of the situation in Corinth and the way that Paul words the
rest of this sentence show that he speaks urgently and in an offi-
cial fashion. Paul specifies that he appeals to the Corinthians (lit.)
"through the name of our Lord Jesus Christ." Translations that
read "by the name . . ." are closer to the sense of Paul's statement
than the NIV's **in the name . . .** , for Paul is continuing the
christological emphasis that he registered in the salutation and
thanksgiving and is now making it the basis and means of his appeal to the Corinthians. The substance of his appeal is given in
the remainder of verse 10 in a series of three phrases that, by the
form of Paul's Greek, state not only *what* he appeals for, but even
the *purpose* of his appeal. The phrases of the appeal are positive,
then negative, and positive again. He urges that they all say the
same thing (positive), and that there not be divisions among
them (negative), but that they be perfectly united in the same
mind and in the same conviction (positive).

The word **mind,** which Paul uses in the last phrase, usually
has the sense of disposition or mentality; the word translated
here as **thought** may be rendered "judgment," "opinion," "advice," and "consent" (see 7:25, 40; 2 Cor. 8:10; Phlm. 14). In this
christologically focused appeal for unity, Paul is making a plea
similar to the well-known one he issued in Philippians 2:5. This
call for unity aims at eliminating divisions that encumber the
church and hinder its mission. Paul is not interested in imposing
uniformity on the congregation, he is concerned that the community of Christian faith not suffer a tear in the fabric of its life
that would weaken its faith and life in Christ. By choosing to
make this statement his starting point in the body of the letter,
Paul provides valuable insight into his primary purpose for writing to the Corinthians.

1:11 / Paul tells the Corinthians how he became aware
of the problem he addresses: his information came as a report on
the Corinthians from **Chloe's household** or (lit.) "the ones of
Chloe," who apparently had witnessed the strained relations in
Corinth. The statement here raises a series of issues that are impossible to answer with certainty. (1) We cannot tell whether
Chloe herself is a Christian. (2) We cannot tell whether she
and her household are from Corinth or Asia (perhaps Ephesus).
(3) We cannot tell whether these people are member of Chloe's
family, her slaves, or freedmen in her employ. Since they know

the situation in the Corinthian church and bring the news to Paul in Ephesus, they are apparently themselves Christians. They are not to be confused with the Corinthians who came to Ephesus with a letter from the Corinthians to Paul (Stephanas, Fortunatas, and Achaicus—see 16:17). Identifying Chloe's people precisely is not, fortunately, crucial for understanding Paul's remarks to the Corinthians.

1:12 / Paul elaborates his concern by reporting that he has heard that some of the Corinthians are saying, "I am of . . ." and then naming either Paul, Apollos, Cephas, or Christ. The way Paul words his remarks is telling, for he says that "each" (NIV = **one**) of the Corinthians is making such declarations, so they are acting as individuals, not as groups; for each of them is speaking as "I," not "we." This shows us that, despite the suggestion of many scholars, there are not formal parties or fixed divisions in the church. Paul's report does not create the image of clusters or clear factions that are set over against one another. Rather, we see a congregation in which its members are in general turmoil.

Moreover, the way Paul constructs this report also indicates that, incongruous as it is, Christ has been cast into the mix as one of a number of people with whom the individual Corinthians are claiming to identify (along with Paul, Apollos, and Cephas). Identifying oneself as being "of Christ" would normally have Paul's approval, but the way he refers to the Corinthian situation indicates that perhaps in this case the claim to belong to Christ is not necessarily laudable. Exactly what the Corinthians think they are achieving by declaring such identities is not clear from Paul's discussion at this point, but they apparently think such identities give them some kind of status. Yet what they are attempting to accomplish is uncertain. Their actions raise questions that cannot be answered conclusively: (1) How did this problem begin? (2) How did some in Corinth come to identify themselves with Cephas (Simon Peter)? Had he been to Corinth, or had they known him elsewhere and then moved to Corinth themselves? (3) How could Christ come to be one among several with whom the Corinthians identify? Would his name not naturally be more impressive than those of Paul, Apollos, and Cephas?

1:13 / The activity of the Corinthians in declaring these diverse identities causes Paul to compose a series of rhetorical questions in this verse that aim at exposing the absurdity, the inappropriateness, and the danger of what they are doing. The grammatical construction of the questions signals that Paul expects the answers all to be "no." Yet because of ambiguity in the vocabulary that Paul uses, interpreters debate exactly how the questions should be answered. The difficulty relates to the sense of the first question, **Is Christ divided?** If "Christ" in this question is a surrogate for "church," then some argue the three questions in this verse are to be answered "yes—although to divide the church is erroneous and inappropriate," "no—certainly Paul was not crucified for us," and "no—of course we were not baptized into the name of Paul." This would, however, be an unusual use of Christ by Paul—one that uses a very different meaning of Christ than that of verse 12. But then, what does Paul mean by asking "Is Christ divided?" In fact, the verb translated here as "divided" more normally means "to apportion out," so Paul may be asking, "Is Christ apportioned out [as one option among several viable options]?" If this is the sense of Paul's first question, then the answers to the three questions are "no," "no," "no." In either case, in the sequence of these questions, the first identifies the problem and the following two questions make it obvious that the situation in Corinth is senseless. The third question, concerning baptism, will become Paul's point of departure in the ensuing verses as he first argues that who baptizes whom is unimportant and second explains the central concern of his ministry—preaching the gospel in a way that does not draw attention to Paul's ministry, but that ensures that the power of the cross is preserved and made effective.

1:14–16 / In an initial reading, Paul's remarks in these verses appear to exhibit a surprisingly, even shockingly supercilious view of baptism. Paul is not, however, attempting to explain his theological understanding of baptism; rather, he is combating the Corinthians' own obviously erroneous understanding of baptism as some kind of magical ritual (see 15:29 and the commentary on that part of the letter). Paul is grateful here that he baptized only a few persons in Corinth, for this means that not many will be apt to say they were baptized **into the name of Paul** (1:13) and then declare that they "follow Paul" (1:12).

As he registers this disclaimer, Paul recalls that he did baptize Crispus and Gaius. Crispus is surely the former president of the synagogue in Corinth who is mentioned in Acts 18:8, and the

Gaius referred to here may be the same Gaius mentioned in Romans 16:23 who, Paul says, hosted him and the whole church in Corinth. (Paul wrote to the Romans as he was in Corinth and about to go to Jerusalem with the collection he had assembled for the church there.) Thus, Paul's immediate memory is that he baptized only two prominent persons in Corinth—although he remembers (or someone like Sosthenes or Stephanas reminds him) that he also baptized the household of Stephanas. Later, at 16:15 Paul relates that Stephanas and his household were among the first converts in Achaia. The subsequent reference to Stephanas in 16:17 as one of the letter delegation may name the same person, although that is not certain since the name was not uncommon. There is certainly sarcasm in these lines as Paul attempts to jolt the Corinthians out of their boastful comparisons concerning their status in the church.

1:17 / As one sees from Paul's statement in here (1:17), he is able to relativize the importance of baptism (which the Corinthians apparently think gives them special identities and status) because he understands his call as a call to preach. The sentence begins with **for** and looks back to the last phrase of verse 16, "I don't remember if I baptized anyone else." Baptism is a part of the larger picture of Christian faith and practice, but Paul's principal interest is in the proclamation of the gospel. Given the particular problem in Corinth with the Corinthians' concern with baptism and spiritual boasting, Paul claims that he is thankful that baptism per se was not his primary ministry. Paul understands his primary ministry to be **to preach the gospel,** that is, **the cross of Christ**.

As Paul continues he creates a remarkable contrast between **wisdom** and the cross—literally, "the wisdom of word" and the cross of Christ. He articulates disdain for sheer eloquence, for in Paul's evaluation, loquacious rhetoric that wins allegiance merely through its beauty is inadequate, since it draws attention to itself or to the one who utters such lovely lines. The good news of God's saving work in the cross of Christ, however, is not a message that is to be sold through elegant presentation. The cross is not a pretty sight, and sheer manipulative eloquence is not a medium that can bear the weight of the message of Christ's cross. Above all, the shocking claim that God saves humanity in the cross of Jesus Christ demonstrates that God works in defiance of this world's norms. Paul's unstated point here is that the substance of the gospel—the message of the cross of Christ—determines the appropriate style of the proclamation of that message. Human wisdom is smooth and easy to hear, but the gospel confronts humanity with power that is real and urgent, even offensive. Paul's statements here are an aggressive apology for the form of his work and preaching but also for the gospel itself, which is his ultimate concern. Only as the Corinthians hear and heed the gospel will they exist as the church in the way God intends.

Additional Notes §3

1:10 / Paul uses the title or address **brothers** (Gk. *adelphoi*) regularly in his letters. The word occurs eighty-one times in the undisputed Pauline letters and fourteen times in those that are disputed; the word occurs twenty-seven times in 1 Corinthians. Of these ninety-five uses, sixty-nine occurrences are the vocative form of direct address (which indicates the persons being addressed), sixty-two times in the undisputed letters and seven times in the disputed; the vocative form occurs twenty times in this letter.

The appeal through "the name of our Lord Jesus Christ" is unique in the Pauline letters. Similar phrases are found in his writings, however. He uses the phrases "in the name of the Lord Jesus" (5:4) and "in the name of the Lord Jesus Christ" (6:11) in this letter. In Phil. 2:10 Paul employs the phrase "at/by the name of Jesus." In these cases Paul invokes the authority, the person, and even the presence of Christ.

1:11 / The identity of Chloe's household is a riddle without a solution, but Fee (*Epistle*, pp. 54–55) makes a strong, persuasive case for these people's not being from Corinth. He reasons, in part, that were they Corinthians, they would have been regarded by others as "Paul's people." Thus, Paul's use of a report from them as trustworthy, authoritative witnesses would not have assisted him in the attempt to critique and correct the situation in Corinth. This suggestion is sensible, but it does not settle the matter, as Fee recognizes.

The word translated **quarrels** in the NIV (Gk. *eris*) is referred to as a vice in Paul's other uses of the term. Cf. Rom. 1:29; 13:13; 1 Cor. 3:3; 2 Cor. 12:20; Gal. 5:20; Phil. 1:15; 1 Tim. 6:4; Titus 3:9.

1:12 / The references to **Cephas** here and in Gal. 1:18 and 2:11 regularly motivate scholarly discussion of whether in fact Cephas is to be identified with Simon Peter. From time to time suggestions are made that the two are distinct, but such interpretations have not found support among the vast majority of scholars.

P. Lampe ("Theological Wisdom and the 'Word About the Cross.' The Rhetorical Scheme in I Corinthians 1–4," *Int* 44 [1990], pp. 117–31) argues that this reference to **Apollos** and Cephas is a key to all of Paul's remarks in 1:18–2:16, wherein Paul makes a covert speech *(schēma)* that critiques the faction among the Corinthians without directly focusing on Apollos and Cephas in a way that could be offensive to them. Earlier, B. Fiore (" 'Covert Allusion' in 1 Corinthians 1–4," *CBQ* 47 [1985], pp. 85–102) suggested that the rhetoric that forms 1 Corinthians 1–4 is a recognizable covert technical device *(logos eschēmatismenos)* that Paul abandons only at 4:6 in order to call the Corinthians overtly to focus on the crucified Christ as the locus of the salvation offered to them by God.

Attempts to identify the distinct theological perspectives of those who would claim affiliation with one or the other of those named by Paul here are not persuasive and are necessarily speculative—e.g., W. O. Fitch, "Paul, Apollos, Christ: [1 Cor 1:12]," *Theology* 74 (1971), pp. 18–24.

1:13 / Paul's vigorous introduction of the matter of baptism in the context of discussing the controversy in Corinth suggests that the Corinthians themselves make much of baptism. Paul's reference to the exceptional baptismal practice in 15:29 suggests that the Corinthians regard baptism as being more than sacramental; perhaps they view it as magical. Although Paul takes no such view, he does not critique this attitude toward the practices; rather, here he attacks the Corinthians' attempt to derive status from the ones who baptized them.

1:14 / The textual evidence is divided for this verse. The matter is not serious, but the NIV does not have "to God" after **I am thankful,** whereas NA²⁷ has the words *tō theō* (to God) in the text in brackets. The NRSV reads, "I thank God" and offers a footnote explaining the problem. Some ancient witnesses read simply, "I am thankful" (including ℵ and B), whereas others (including ℵ², C, D) include "to God" in the statement.

1:17 / When Paul says, **Christ did not send me to baptize,** he constructs a negative formula using the verb "to send" (Gk. *apostellō*) that is related to his normal assertion that he is "an apostle [a sent one] of Christ" (1:1). Paul was one who was sent by Christ (to preach), but Christ did not send him primarily to baptize or to preach an ostensibly erudite message. On this issue of the congruence of the messenger with the message, see N. M. Watson, " 'The Philosopher Should Bathe and Brush His Teeth': Congruence between Word and Deed in Graeco-Roman Philosophy and Paul's Letter to the Corinthian," *ABR* 42 (1994), pp. 1–16.

The reference here to **wisdom** (Gk. *sophia*) is rendered **human wisdom** in the NIV to indicate the nuance of Paul's remark. M. D. Goulder ("*Sophia* in 1 Corinthians," *NTS* 37 [1991], pp. 516–34) has argued that *sophia* in Paul's discussion in chs. 1–3 actually refers to the law and law-observance, but there is nothing in Paul's rhetoric and vocabulary to suggest that he is thinking of the law. R. A. Horsley's suggestion ("Wisdom of Word and Words of Wisdom in Corinth," *CBQ* 39

[1977], pp. 224–39) that relates Paul's comments about wisdom to the Hellenistic-Jewish appreciation as found in Philo and Wisdom of Solomon is much nearer the mark, although the concern for wisdom in Corinth could be non-Jewish in its origin and could reflect a form of religiosity parallel to that of pagan mystery religions—see H. Conzelmann, *1 Corinthians* (Hermeneia; Philadelphia: Fortress, 1975), esp. pp. 14–16, 38–39. As Barrett points out, Paul can use "wisdom" in a variety of ways to indicate both good and bad phenomena. The particular remark and its context determine the understanding the reader should attribute to Paul's use of the word. Negatively, regardless of the "background" from which "wisdom" originated in Corinth, Paul denounces an understanding of "wisdom" as either "a manner of preaching, involving the use of logical and rhetorical devices which were designed to convince the hearer" or "the stuff of salvation itself" (Barrett, *Epistle,* p. 18).

§4 God's Peculiar, Powerful Way (1 Cor. 1:18–25)

This paragraph is crucial, both in the context of this partic-ular letter and for the overall understanding of Paul's theology. Here he delivers the heart and essence of the gospel he believed and proclaimed. Paul's lines reveal that God works in a most pe-culiar way—first, God works in defiance of the standards of this world as they are understood or construed by humanity, and second, God's work is powerful so that it incapacitates, reverses, even turns upside down the values of this world as they are ob-jectively established and understood by humans. Paul declares this way of God's working as a fact—it is God's saving activity that amounts to the soteriological reality of the cross of Jesus Christ.

1:18 / Paul sets up a rhetorical contrast scheme that captures the heart of the gospel as he understands it. He begins the sentence with the word **For,** showing that it is an extension of his statement in verse 17. Now Paul explains that declaration more precisely in relation to the theme of "the word of the cross," or **the message of the cross.** In speaking of the proclamation of the saving death of Jesus Christ, Paul refers to humanity in two groups. The division he envisions is eschatological, for it super-sedes older divisions that were real, but humanly constructed—e.g., Jew and Gentile, Greco-Roman and barbarian, slave and free, male and female—and this eschatological division occurs as an act of God. Thus, on the one hand, there are those who regard the word of the cross as **foolishness;** Paul says they **are perish-ing.** The word typically translated foolishness (Gk. *mōria*) refers to something stronger or more problematic than that which is merely silliness or simplistic. The English word "moron" comes from the Greek root of this word, so perhaps it should be trans-lated "moronity" to ensure that we see the degree of disdain that those who are perishing have for the message of the cross. On the other hand, there are those **who are being saved.** Paul includes himself and most likely those to whom he is writing in this group. The passive voice of the verb "being saved" acknowledges that God is the actor, the one who is saving. Moreover, in the scheme of this contrast, perishing versus being saved, one finds foolishness contrasted with **the power of God.** The natural opposite of foolishness in this context would be "wisdom," so if the Corinthians are paying careful attention they will be surprised at this.

Paul's rhetoric trips the logic of his readers. Remarkably, Paul says that it is what God does, not what humans know, that saves. God acted in the cross of Christ, and that action produces a division among humanity that itself reveals God's unexpected power. Paul is not decrying the value of sensible reflection; rather, he is insisting that humans cannot discern the reality of God through their reason based only upon their own experience. God's self-revelation in the cross is the key to comprehending God, it is the necessary starting point for valid comprehension of the divine, and without the cross we are bound to misunderstand God. The apostle himself employs reason, but always in reflection on the significance of God's revelation in and through the cross. Paul's point was not popular among many in the first-century church—witness the attraction to law-observance in Galatia and the fascination with power in 2 Corinthians. Often today people still do not like this message.

1:19 / To underscore the authenticity and authority of his argument, Paul quotes Isaiah 29:14—which is a declaration that records God's judgment of human wisdom. In the original context in Isaiah the saying is a warning for Israel because of its indifference and arrogance toward God. The saying fits Paul's argument well, although he changes the original verb "shall be hidden" to read **will frustrate,** so as to fit the citation more precisely to the situation in Corinth. This reference by Paul to Scripture as the evidence or precedent for the way God works through the cross of Christ is not a simple prooftext; it is an eschatological interpretation of the way God is working in the message of the cross. The divine overthrow of human wisdom that God promised is now real through the cross of Jesus Christ. Paul is pointing out that the Corinthians are witnessing—perhaps even experiencing—God's baffling work.

1:20 / In turn, Paul calls for three groups of persons, **Where is the wise man? . . . the scholar? . . . the philosopher of**

this age? In doing this he may be using synonyms to refer to a collective class of persons, or he may be drawing together different sets that mutually experience the God-created frustration of the message of the cross. Perhaps, given the references to Jews and Greeks in the following verses, one should choose the latter option and understand "the wise [one]" to refer to Greco-Roman philosophers, the "scribe" (NIV = scholar) to designate Jewish experts in the law, and the "debater of this age" (NIV = philosopher of this age) to refer collectively to all those who live and evaluate life by the wisdom of the world.

Paul's purpose in asking after these people is not self-evident. Perhaps he is summoning them to a challenge, but from the flow of his argument it seems more likely that Paul is indicating that God's destruction and frustration of the wisdom of the world has dismissed their standards and made their logic irrelevant: **Has not God made foolish the wisdom of the world?** God has acted in such a way that worldly wisdom becomes moronic, or completely incapable of properly evaluating the significance of God's work through the cross. Paul's argument here locates where the wisdom of the merely human wise [one], scholar, and philosopher originate—namely in this age, and therefore not with God.

1:21 / As Paul explains here, God's **wisdom** exposes the shallowness and inaccuracy of mere human wisdom: even the loftiest theology is **foolishness** if it is disengaged from the primary revelation of God in Jesus Christ. Humans simply cannot reason their way to God. If salvation depended on human reason, then the gospel would depend upon human intelligence and perception, and the message would be for an elite. But God saves humanity (and the world) by the cross of Christ and the message of God's work done there, which is, by this world's standards, foolishness. Christ, preached as crucified, brings a crisis of separation. Those who deny the saving significance of the cross are in bondage to **the world,** whereas **those who believe** (1:21) are called by God (1:2), grasped by the power of God—a demonstration that Christ is God's wisdom. At this juncture in the letter Paul is declaring the significance of the cross and the preaching of Christ crucified, but he constructs rhetorical schemes that proclaim as well as explain. In other words, Paul gives a kerygmatic explanation. In chapter 2 Paul will attempt to explicate God's work and humanity's experience of God's revelation.

1:22–24 / These lines create an evolving rhetorical scheme that contrasts the concerns and experiences of those who judge the message of the cross to be foolishness and do not believe, with the concerns and experiences of those who are called by God and do believe the message of the cross. The first group Paul names comprises both **Jews** and **Greeks.** While the description of these two subgroups draws distinctions between them, they are alike in that the priorities of both cause them to seek evidence of God and authentication of his work in something other than the revelation of God delivered in the message of the cross. Paul says the Jews demand **miraculous signs** on the order of those done by Moses and the prophets. The OT records such works, and the gospels recall that Jesus' Jewish contemporaries insisted that he give them a sign (Matt. 12:38–39; 16:1–4; Mark 8:11–13; Luke 11:15–20; John 6:26–29, 30–34). The Greeks look for **wisdom.** This is a characteristic in Corinth, but the concern with wisdom has been a characteristic of Greek culture and life throughout the self-conscious memory of Greece. Already in Herodotus (ca. 484–420 BC) there are reports of Greek concern with wisdom (1.30, 60, 68), learning (4.77), and foolishness (1.146). Similarly, in Acts one reads, "Now all the Athenians and the foreigners living there would spend their time in nothing but telling or hearing something new" (17:21). Thus, Paul implies that *power* and *reason* are the worldly standards that precluded certain Jews and Greeks from hearing and believing the message of the cross.

The second group named, **we** who **preach Christ crucified,** includes Paul and other early Christians. To the demand for power, they present a message of weakness that is offensive, for it tells of a crucified Messiah—an unthinkable paradox for the Jewish mind. To the longing for reason, they present an outright absurdity. In this way, God has defied humanly established criteria for discerning the divine. For Paul, in this rejection of human norms, God truly shows himself to be God precisely because he refuses to let humans dictate terms; and so he acts in sheer defiance of their expectations so that God's own way of working is presented as a saving reality that humans can experience only on God's terms. Humans are forced to shelve their standards and to swallow their pride; they either accept or reject God for who he shows himself to be. But, Paul declares, Jews and Gentiles who hear God's call, who believe in God's saving work in the cross of Christ, receive a revelation of God's true power and wisdom.

1:25 / Finally, Paul summarizes his argument in this whole section by making a theological pronouncement in this verse. He declares that God's wisdom or power expressed in the cross of Christ renders worldly wisdom into foolishness as a demonstration of the reality of the power of God. God shows himself to be both wiser and stronger than humans, who cannot predict or control God!

Additional Notes §4

1:18 / J. Louis Martyn first brought the rhetorical scheme of this verse with its inherent defiance of logic to my attention in a graduate seminar at Union Theological Seminary in New York nearly twenty years ago. His observations on grammar led to incisive remarks about the crux of Paul's theology and provided a springboard for many other insights into Paul's thinking and teaching.

Fee (*Epistle*, p. 68 n. 6) recognizes the infrequent use of the Gk. *sōzomenois* ("the ones being saved") but argues correctly that "this is probably the most comprehensive word in Paul's vocabulary for God's redemptive event."

J. M. Reese ("Paul Proclaims the Wisdom of the Cross: Scandal and Foolishness," *BTB* 9 [1979], pp. 147–53) concluded that Paul presented the crucifixion of Jesus, specifically his death on the cross, as an apocalyptic act in which God created a new form of discernment, an eschatological wisdom that allowed Christians to live in conformity with the cross. For Paul the word of the cross is clearly an unprecedented message that both saves and enlightens the believer as an intervening act of God.

L. Lucy's attempt ("Talbott on Paul as a Universalist," *Christian Scholar's Review* 21 [1992], pp. 395–407) to read 1:18 as Paul's declaration of the reality of eternal destruction that indicates a denial of universalism reads more into the text than out of it. Paul's rhetorical contrast is designed to register that it is what God does, not what humans know, that achieves salvation. Paul is concerned neither to advocate nor to deny universalism in this verse; more relevant to this topic are Rom. 9–11, 1 Cor. 15, and Phil. 2:5–11, although even in these passages Paul is not directly concerned with the theme of universalism.

1:19 / The phrase **for it is written** (Gk. *gegraptai gar*) always signals the citation of the OT in Paul; he cites no other writings in order to argue that God's purposes and promises have been brought to fulfillment. Cf. Rom. 12:19; 14:11; 1 Cor. 3:19; Gal. 3:10; 4:22, 27.

The final verb in the lines from the LXX is "[I] will hide" (Gk. *krypsō*), whereas Paul writes [I] **will frustrate** (*athetēsō*); so there can be no question of his deliberateness here.

1:21 / The verb "to please" (Gk. *eudokeō*) implies both great pleasure and intense discrimination in Paul's usage. Cf. Rom. 15:26, 27; 1 Cor. 10:5; 2 Cor. 5:8; 12:10; Gal. 1:15; 1 Thess. 2:8; 3:1; Col. 1:19; 2 Thess. 2:12. A. J. M. Wedderburn ("*en tē sophia tou theou*—1 Kor 1:21," *ZNW* 64 [1973], pp. 132–34) relates the earlier phrase "in the wisdom of God" to the phrase "God was pleased" to suggest that *en* should be understood to have an adverbial function indicating attendant circumstances, thus "in the wisdom of God" names a divine context to which Paul's ensuing remarks relate.

Paul says that God's great pleasure was expressed "through . . . preaching," and the NIV explicates the sense of Paul's remark with the translation **through . . . what was preached,** that is, the message of the cross.

1:23 / On the topic of crucifixion in the ancient world, see M. Hengel, *Crucifixion* (Philadelphia: Fortress, 1977). Hengel's careful survey of ancient literature is helpful, for twentieth-century persons have seen the cross so often as a religious symbol that we forget the brutal reality of this practice and often fail to comprehend how scandalous was the early Christian message of God's saving humanity through the crucifixion of Jesus.

1:24 / Paul's alternation in this paragraph between Greeks and Gentiles may be not simply the use of synonyms for good form. In v. 22 he spoke of the Greeks in relation to wisdom, a genuinely Greek concern. Then, in v. 23 he mentioned the Gentiles in relation to the message of Christ crucified, and Gentiles other than Greeks would have found such a message to be moronity. Finally, he refers to the Greeks again in this verse as he returns to the idea of wisdom. Paul frequently refers to Gentiles: forty-seven times in all the letters, thirty-eight in the undisputed epistles—but only three times in 1 Corinthians (1:23; 5:1; 12:2); he speaks of Greeks much less often: thirteen times in all the epistles, twelve times in the undisputed letter—but four times in 1 Corinthians (1:22, 24; 10:32; 12:13).

H.-J. Klauck (" 'Christus, Gottes Kraft und Gottes Weisheit' [1 Kor 1,24]. Jüdische Weisheitsüberlieferungen im Neuen Testament," *Wissenschaft und Weisheit* 55 [1992], pp. 3–22) moves toward reading Paul's remarks in this verse as articulating a wisdom Christology; but as A. van Roon ("The Relation between Christ and the Wisdom of God according to Paul," *NovT* 16 [1974], pp. 207–39) recognizes, Paul's letters do not present a wisdom christology that would work from an identification of Christ with Wisdom as Wisdom is presented in Hellenistic-Jewish Wisdom literature. Indeed, as R. A. Horsley ("Wisdom," pp. 224–39) correctly recognizes, "Paul rejects *sophia* as the means of salvation (1:21–24) by replacing it with the crucified Christ as the true 'power' and 'wisdom' of God" (p. 237).

§5 Before and After God's Call (1 Cor. 1:26–31)

The verses of this paragraph are packed with theological substance and significance. Paul directs the Corinthians to remember and reflect upon themselves both when they were called (*at* or *before* the time of their call) and *in* or *after* their calling. Before God chose them most of the Corinthians were nobodies. After being called by God, however, the Corinthians are instruments of God's own power with Christ Jesus as the source of their lives. To make this argument Paul engages in a careful, deliberate play on the LXX version of Jeremiah 9:23–24. His citation of Scripture is clear in verse 31, where he quotes Jeremiah 9:24 LXX; but already in verses 26–27 mentions of the wise, the influential, and the strong echo the language of Jeremiah. Paul creates this contrast scheme to humble the Corinthians in order to check their boasting and heighten their appreciation for the saving work of God in Jesus Christ. Paul tells the Corinthians that in light of what God has done in Jesus Christ the only legitimate boasting that Christians can do is to boast about what God has done.

1:26 / Paul begins this section of the letter with the word "for" (untranslated in the NIV), because he is explaining what he had said in verses 18–25 through personal illustration and application to the Corinthians. His remarks to the Corinthians are clear and straightforward: "brothers and sisters" (in the NIV, **brothers;** see the discussion of this form of salutation in the commentary on 1:10–17). Paul tells the Corinthians to **think** about their calling—this admonition may be either a command (imperative) or an observation (indicative), since the same form of the word serves both purposes in Greek; yet the tone seems directive. The remark continues the theme of calling that Paul registered at 1:1, 2, 9, 24. His concern at this point, however, is specifically related to who the Corinthians were at the time of their calling. Paul wants the Corinthians to recognize that God did not choose them according to the standards of the world ("according to the flesh"; Gk. *kata sarka;* NIV = **by human standards**). Thus, God's way of relating to the Corinthians actually judges their standards, revealing their inadequacy and the inappropriateness of the way some of them have been evaluating others (including Paul). Paul explicitly denies that many of the Corinthians were **wise, . . . influential, . . . of noble birth.** The language at this point reflects Jeremiah 9:23 LXX with some changes:

> Paul: "wise ones" *(sophoi)*
> Jeremiah: "wise one" *(sophos)*
>
> Paul: "influential ones" *(dynatoi)*
> Jeremiah: "mighty one" *(ischyros)*
>
> Paul: "well-born" *(eugeneis;* NIV has "of noble birth")
> Jeremiah: "wealthy one" *(plousios)*

In the first case, the difference between Paul and Jeremiah is simply that Paul has used a plural rather than a singular. In the second case, the difference is the slight one between *influence* as social strength and *might* as raw physical power. In the third case, the difference is between heritage and accumulated assets. Jeremiah's remark was inclusive and meant to name those who would be self-satisfied with their physical goods. Paul's reference to being well-born could relate to wealth, but the connection is not necessary.

The language may reflect the Corinthians' own boasts. Indeed, in the verses that follow, Paul's remarks will locate his rhetorical audience—although the identities of those to whom Paul speaks are not to be pressed excessively. Verse 26 has been simplistically interpreted in a literal fashion in the past: commentators have suggested that the members of the early church were from the low, even lowest, classes of society. But the text merely recognizes that only some of the Corinthian Christians were from the upper classes of social order. The church was likely made up predominantly of middle-class craftspersons and merchants, and persons who were well-to-do, as well as slaves, some of whom could have been people of means and education (cf. 7:21–24). The most remarkable sociological feature of the early church was that it was genuinely transsocial, including members from all classes of society. But Paul is not here primarily concerned with sociology; rather, his point is theological—God is no respecter of persons! God freely chooses whomever God pleases at will, and not in a manner beholden to human standards. God's grace does not necessarily correlate to social order or human patterns of evaluation.

1:27–28 / Paul extends the basic rhetoric of verse 26 in these two verses, and the lines reflect the language of Jeremiah even more closely than before. The initial word "but" calls attention to the juxtaposition of these lines to the preceding remarks and prepares for the ensuing contrast scheme in these verses. Again, Paul offers three sets of comparisons:

IN OPPOSITION TO:	GOD CHOSE:
the wise	the foolish things of the world
the strong	the weak things of the world
the things that are	the lowly things of [the] world, the despised things—and the things that are not.

God's choices defy and demolish the logic, power, and recognized standards of the world. God's freedom and sovereignty are demonstrated in God's inexplicable actions that reveal God's grace.

Paul's rhetoric explicitly states the purposes of God's seemingly odd choices. First, God's actions **shame** the wise and the strong. In both the LXX and the NT the word for shame (Gk. *kataischynō*) means "to be disgraced," particularly as a result of divine judgment. Thus, the verb implicitly registers eschatological divine action. Second, Paul says God chose **the lowly, the despised,** and **the things that are not** in order **to nullify the things that are.** In other words, God chose nobodies or low-bodies to undo the somebodies of this world. To nullify (Gk. *katargeō*) indicates divine eschatological elimination, as one sees from the consistent use of this verb in Romans and 1 and 2 Corinthians. Paul uses this rhetorical flourish to confront the Corinthians with the fact that God's calling of them, like God's saving action through the cross of Christ, defies the world's standards and even judges those standards to be inadequate and inaccurate. In doing this God reveals a graciousness and authority that is independent of the world's norms and judgments.

1:29 / Paul continues to explain the purpose of God's choices by completing the sentence that began with verse 26. This final clause states what God's ultimate purpose is in making choices that themselves have the aims of shaming and nullifying those who are recognized by the world. Paul says God disgraced and disqualified those who are honored in the world **so that** no human could **boast before** God. The cross of Christ and the calling of the most lowly Corinthians occurred so as to eliminate the possibility that humans would feel self-satisfied and would arrogantly elevate themselves before God. Paul makes frequent use of the verb **to boast** (in the NT outside the thirteen Pauline letters only James employs this verb [twice]). For Paul "to boast" is to do far more than merely to brag or to self-promote. For a human "to boast" is for the person to glorify the self in a way that either refuses to recognize God or presumes that God is bound to recognize the human's status. Paul can use this verb positively with the connotation that humans recognize the glory of God's actions and "boast" of what God has done (see Rom. 2:17; 5:2, 11; 1 Cor. 1:29, 31; 2 Cor. 10:17; Phil. 3:3). In the present verse Paul has human self-satisfied and self-praising boasting in mind.

1:30 / Here, Paul again addresses the Corinthians directly. This new sentence informs them of what they should already know, but apparently have forgotten—that it is by God's own work that they have been established in Christ Jesus. The Corinthians have whatever life they now live only as a result of God's work in and through Christ, not by means of their own efforts. Thus, by God's own actions Christ Jesus has become **wisdom**—unlike that of the world—to and for the Corinthians. Jesus Christ informs the Corinthians of who God is and how God relates to humanity. Paul explains Christ as wisdom **from God** in an explanatory phrase (the NIV casts his argument well), **that is,** [Christ Jesus is] **our righteousness, holiness, and redemption.** Thus, Paul's focus is on God's saving work in Christ; he is not elaborating abstract christology here. As God unsettles the world's wisdom in Christ and eliminates the possibility of humans laying claims on God's grace, God demonstrates a peculiar power that sets people (by God's choice) right with God (righteousness), sets people apart for God's purposes and service (holiness—as in *sanctification,* not a status but an identity in terms of devotion to God's intentions), and delivers people from estrangement from God for devotion to and a relationship with God. The description of salvation that Paul offers here is not strictly sequential; rather, he refers to facets of the gem of grace. At most, Paul's observations may mean that humans are redeemed as God's work in Christ Jesus sets them right and sets them apart.

1:31 / Paul returns to the theme of boasting, although now he has a positive image in mind. He explains the reasonable results of God's justifying, sanctifying, and redeeming work. His point is self-evident: God is the source of legitimate Christian glory. Paul modifies a quotation from Jeremiah so that it fits the Corinthian situation more precisely. Jeremiah says, "Let the one who boasts boast about this"—this line introduces the legitimate reasons for boasting (" 'that [the person] understands and knows me, that I am the Lord, who exercises kindness, justice and righteousness on earth, for in these I delight,' declares the Lord"). Paul does not give the full quotation, rather he replaces "about this" with **in the Lord** and thus truncates the statement so that it defines for the Corinthians appropriate boasting. In Paul's declaration, the Lord is Christ Jesus who has been identified in the saving activity that Paul delineated in verse 30. Recognition of the lordship of Christ Jesus is the key to correcting the situation in Corinth.

Additional Notes §5

On the profound theological content and implications of the verses of this section, see L. E. Keck, "God the Other Who Acts Otherwise: An Exegetical Essay on 1 Cor. 1:26–31," *Word & World* 16 (1996), pp. 437–43.

1:26 / **By human standards:** literally this is "according to the flesh" (Gk. *kata sarka*). The phrase occurs nineteen times in the Pauline letters, twice in 1 Cor. (1:26; 10:18). The dynamic equivalence translation of the NIV catches the sense of Paul's statement, but the phrase "according to the flesh" is important for Paul. He uses this phrase to name the world with its human standards over against the new creation of God that is presently struggling toward full realization through the cross of Jesus Christ. The incisive work of J. Louis Martyn ("Epistemology at the Turn of the Ages: 2 Corinthians 5:16," in *Christian History and Interpretation: Studies Presented to John Knox* [ed. W. R. Farmer, C. F. D. Moule, and R. R. Niebuhr; Cambridge: Cambridge University Press, 1967], pp. 269–87) on this phrase, esp. its occurrence in 2 Cor. 5:16, demonstrates that for Paul there are two ways of knowing: either *kata sarka* or *kata stauron*—which is either according to the old age or according to the "painful and gracious juncture" of the ages brought about through Christ's cross ("Epistemology," p. 285 n. 1).

In the past, scholars have assumed, based on v. 26, that the Corinthian Christians were of the lowest social classes—e.g., G. A. Deissmann, *Light from the Ancient East: The New Testament Illustrated by Recently Discovered Texts of the Graeco-Roman World* (trans. L. R. M. Strachan; 1927; repr., Peabody, Mass.: Hendrickson, 1995) and *Paul: A Study in Social and Religious History* (2d ed.; trans. W. E. Wilson; 1926; repr., New York: Harper, 1957). Recent interpreters employing sophisticated sociological methods of interpretation have come to see the church as comprised of a mixture of social classes, most likely dominated by the members of the urban middle class. See E. A. Judge, *The Social Pattern of Christian Groups in the First Century* (London: Tyndale, 1960), esp. pp. 49–61; R. MacMullen, *Roman Social Relations* (New Haven/London: Yale University Press, 1974); G. Theissen, *The Social Setting of Pauline Christianity: Essays on Corinth* (Philadelphia: Fortress, 1982), esp. pp. 69–119, and *Social Reality and the Early Christians: Theology, Ethics, and the World of the New Testament* (Minneapolis: Fortress, 1992), esp. pp. 159–227; A. J. Malherbe, *Social Aspects of Early Christianity* (Baton Rouge/London: Louisiana State University Press, 1977); W. A. Meeks, *The First Urban Christians: The Social World of the Apostle Paul* (New Haven/London: Yale University Press, 1983); and J. E. Stambaugh and D. L. Balch, *The New Testament in Its Social Environment* (Library of Early Christianity 2; Philadelphia: Westminster, 1986), esp. pp. 107–67.

1:27–28 / The presence of the contrasting phrases **the things that are not** (Gk. *ta mē onta*) and **the things that are** (Gk. *ta onta*) sometimes provokes philosophical discussions of creation, but as Fee (*Epistle*, p. 83) correctly recognizes, Paul's employment of the verb **to nullify** (cf. 2:6; 6:13; 13:8 [2x], 10; 15:24, 26) "makes certain that this is rhetorical, eschatological language, not philosophical." Outside of 1 Cor. "to nullify" (*katargeō*) occurs in the Pauline letters in Rom. 3:3, 31; 4:14; 6:6; 7:2, 6; 2 Cor. 3:7, 11, 13–14; Gal. 3:17; 5:4, 11; Eph. 2:15; 2 Thess. 2:8; 2 Tim. 1:10.

1:29 / **So that** translates the Gk. word *hopōs*, which is coupled here with the negative particle *mē* and a subjunctive form of the verb "to boast" (Gk. *kauchaomai*), a construction that clearly and strongly indicates a statement of purpose.

1:30 / The theological vocabulary of this verse is complex and rich with significance. **Righteousness** (Gk. *dikaiosynē*) is a central term in Paul's reflections on soteriology—"For Paul *dikaiosynē* stands in close relation to the central salvific event, which has its historical place in the death and resurrection of Jesus" (*EDNT* 1:326). Righteousness is granted to the human as grace, but it demands a complete service of righteousness in a transformed life of obedience to God. **Holiness** (Gk. *hagiasmos*) denotes *consecration*, so that "through God's calling and Christ's work of redemption those who believe are saints," i.e., *holy people* who are set apart through divine action—"they have not created their own salvation" (*EDNT* 1:19). **Redemption** (Gk. *apolytrōsis*) in Paul's usages refers to the central content of the gospel.

> It denotes the "redemption" which God offers in the death of God's Son; its location, therefore, is "in Christ Jesus" . . . Redemption is God's gracious turning to humanity in its need for redemption, and this grace is experienced as remission of sins—in faith in Jesus Christ. [The word can designate] Jesus Christ as the redeemer himself. (*EDNT* 1:138)

1:31 / Paul's citation of Jer. 9:24 LXX is remarkable. Jeremiah reads, *all' ē en toutō kauchasthō ho kauchōmenos;* but Paul cites, *ho kauchōmenos en kyriō kauchasthō.* He rearranges the words and even alters the phrase to make it a call to boasting in Christ Jesus rather than in oneself. This seemingly minor change reflects and reveals Paul's concerns, strategy, and goal in 1 Cor. Paul is concerned with the Corinthians' inappropriate boasting that results from sheer confidence in themselves and that indicates a lack of recognition of God's gracious work in Christ. He employs rhetoric and the force of tradition to call the Corinthians to a proper way of thinking and living, and he aims at firmly fixing the focus of the congregation's life on God as revealed through Christ Jesus.

G. R. O'Day's helpful study of 1 Cor. 1:26–31 ("Jeremiah 9:22–23 and 1 Corinthians 1:26–31: A Study in Intertextuality," *JBL* 109 [1990], pp. 259–67) examines verbal, structural, and theological parallels between Paul and Jeremiah to conclude, "Jeremiah's critique of wisdom, power, and wealth as false sources of identity that violate the covenant are re-imaged by Paul as a critique of wisdom, power, and wealth that impede God's saving acts in Jesus Christ" (p. 267).

§6 Paul's Apostolic Ministry and Message (1 Cor. 2:1–5)

Paul focuses in this section of the letter on the character and rationale of his *apostolic* message and ministry. His comments come in two complex sentences: First, verses 1–2 elucidate the continuity between the form and content or the shape and substance of the apostle's preaching. Second, verses 3–5 demonstrate the continuity of the message and the demeanor of the preacher. Paul's statements are intensely personal. His remarks make clear that the style of his ministry was deliberate. The sentences are, however, ambiguous and subject to misreading and misunderstanding. Paul is not saying, "I preached the cross only instead of the cross and something more"; rather, he insists that he put aside any devices for persuasion and proclaimed the cross without extra rhetorical frills. Paul presents himself as ministering in **weakness** and explains this kind of behavior by using the traditional Jewish image of **fear and trembling**—which is a reference to his worshipful recognition of the actuality of God! Paul tells the Corinthians that his message was one that allowed the Spirit and God's power to show themselves as they worked through his preaching and ministry. Paul reminds the Corinthians that they came to believe, not as a result of showy human effort, but through the working of God's own power. Paul's remarks reveal that although humans are God's agents, God alone is the one who saves humanity.

2:1 / Paul recalls his original work among the Corinthians in or about AD 50, approximately five years before his writing of this letter. In referring back to his earlier ministry, Paul continues to explain the basic teaching he had articulated in 1:18–25: God's work defies and even reverses the standards of this world. He had already provided one kind of explanation in 1:26–31, but now he focuses on himself, especially his style of ministry and his message, as illustrations of the truth of the gospel of Christ-crucified. The initial statement is awkward in Greek, but it echoes and amplifies the previous remark in 1:17 that led to Paul's theological exposition of the cross in 1:18–25. Paul writes, "And when I came to you, I came not according to the excellence of word or of wisdom . . ."; so that the NIV translation misrepresents the sense of the statement by placing **superior** (= "excellence") in relation to **wisdom** alone. Rather, Paul names two forms of excellence, that of word and that of wisdom, both of which he refused to practice in preaching the gospel. **Eloquence** in the NIV intends to name the first form of excellence that Paul rejected, but he may have meant to imply the content as well as the form of the word he refused to preach. This point is certainly clear from the second excellence he names: wisdom. Paul's **testimony** to God's work in the cross of Christ was not put in a slick package or toned down to a humanly reasonable level.

2:2 / Paul continues to explain why **(for)** he ministered as he did. Paul's resolve **to know nothing** other than **Jesus Christ and him crucified** was the result of his understanding of the centrality and significance of the cross. The crucial reality of the cross as God's work for salvation relativized all other knowledge, so that by comparison all other knowledge was unimportant. The qualifying phrase "and him crucified" identifies Jesus Christ in terms of his cross, because Paul understood Christ's death on the cross to be the revealed reality of God's extraordinary saving power. Paul points to the power of God effecting salvation in the cross and in the cross alone. The remarks in this verse logically precede the ensuing discussion that will follow in 2:6–16, but before making those statements Paul will offer still further explanation.

2:3 / This next sentence begins exactly as did the last (2:1–2), literally, "And I"; so that the Greek text signals the connection of this sentence, which runs to the end of 2:5, with the foregoing comments. The NIV renders the Greek verb **came,** although the word may mean either "came" or "was with." Following 2:1–2, the latter sense of the verb ("was with") seems preferable, so that Paul is explaining the conditions of his stay and ministry, not merely the style of his arrival. Paul refers to his **weakness, fear,** and **trembling.** By referring to weakness, Paul reiterates the language of 1:25, now applying the notion of weakness to himself. Paul is fond of this image of his person and work; he uses "weakness" in key texts such as Romans 8:26;

1 Corinthians 15:43; 2 Corinthians 11:30; 12:9; 13:4. Especially from Paul's discussions of weakness in 2 Corinthians, one learns that he valued weakness not for its own sake (as if he were a masochist), but because in, through, and despite Paul's weakness God's power was at work in his ministry. The contrast of Paul's weakness and God's powerful, sustaining grace reveals that the power and the results of that power are property and achievements of God alone (see 2 Cor. 4:1–12).

Paul's uses of fear and trembling conjure up obvious, crucial biblical categories of profound piety that recognize the difference between human frailty and divine strength. The NIV rendering "in weakness and fear, and with much trembling" is peculiar in that it couples weakness and fear and separates trembling from the other two terms. This translation slightly distorts Paul's statement which (lit.) reads, "And I in weakness and in fear and in much trembling was with you." While Paul's statement is enigmatic (since today one cannot know exactly what his words described), still his point is clear: Paul's manner of ministry was far removed from a polished and persuasive performance; his behavior allowed the reality of God's power alone to bring the Corinthians into the experience of salvation.

2:4–5 / The NIV breaks Paul's complex sentence (2:3–5) into two parts so that his fluid reasoning is easier to follow in English. Paul refers directly to his **message** (lit. "word") and his **preaching,** declaring that they **were not with wise and persuasive words,** but (lit.) "in demonstration of the Spirit and of power." This statement is ambiguous in Greek and may mean either that his proclamation told of the Spirit and power or that his proclamation allowed the Spirit and power to be shown in working through his (weakly formed) message. In context the latter understanding is preferable. Obviously Paul's preaching produced results, but he insists that it was not his rhetoric but **the Spirit's power** that persuaded people. The NIV wisely renders Paul's phrase (lit.) "of the Spirit and of power" with the words "the Spirit's power," recognizing that in Paul's thought "the Spirit" and "the power" are practically synonymous ways of referring to God's presence and efficacy.

Moreover, it is the Spirit's power that brings about the combination of Paul's "word" and "proclamation" (NIV = "my message and my preaching"). Whereas the Corinthians were concerned with "word" and "wisdom," which they believed ennobled those "in the know," the Spirit's power at work through Paul brought message into preaching that transformed lives. The power of the Spirit used Paul, it moved him toward others, energizing and directing him beyond his weak self. Paul's ministry was missional: it was for the well-being of others who were in need of the transforming power of God's salvation.

Finally it is instructive to notice that these verses introduce the Spirit into Paul's correspondence with the Corinthians. Earlier Paul denied that humans are saved by what they know; what they know does not make them who they are. Then, he pointed to his own weakness and to his style of ministry that selflessly conformed to the cross of Christ. Only after registering these crucial lessons did Paul refer to the Spirit. He didn't want the Corinthians to view the Spirit as a powerful possession that would grant them a special guarantee of salvation. In reality, the Spirit is the foundation of **faith** that moves those who are saved beyond themselves and into the vulnerability of life lived for God and for others. Thus, Paul explained the inappropriateness and uselessness of wise and persuasive words in his message and preaching. His proclamation served as a vehicle for the revelation of the Spirit's power that formed faith on the foundation of God's power, so that devoid of crafty rhetoric and content, the gospel (viewed from the perspectives of human values) gave the impression of foolishness (1:21).

Additional Notes §6

2:1 / Translations vary regarding this verse because some ancient manuscripts include the words **the testimony about God,** whereas others read "the mystery of God." In Gk. the difference is not great, for the word for "testimony" is *martyrion* and the word for "mystery" is *mystērion,* a matter of three letters. Moreover, the sense of Paul's statement is not dramatically altered from one reading to the other. Nevertheless, the NIV does not follow the text of the latest critical editions of the Gk. text that prefer "mystery" over "testimony." The word "mystery" definitely occurs in 2:7, and ancient scribes may have made the more difficult word "testimony" of 2:1 conform to the less problematic "mystery" of 2:7. For a defense of *mystērion* as the original reading see B. M. Metzger, *A Textual Commentary on the Greek New Testament* (Stuttgart: United Bible Societies, 1971), p. 545; R. E. Brown, "The

Semitic Background of the New Testament *Mysterion* (I)," *Bib* 39 (1958), pp. 426–48.

On the matter of the chronology of Paul's ministry, including his first stay in Corinth and his writing of 1 Corinthians, see M. L. Soards, "Paul," in *Mercer Dictionary of the Bible* (ed. W. E. Mills; Macon, Ga.: Mercer University Press, 1990), pp. 657–62.

2:3 / L. Hartman ("Some remarks on 1 Cor. 2:1–5," *SEÅ* 39 [1974], pp. 109–20) suggests that an intertextual echo occurs in this verse as Paul ponders his weakness as a fulfillment of Jer. 9:23–24, which Paul cited in part at 1 Cor. 1:31.

On **fear** and **trembling,** see Exod. 15:15; Ps. 2:11; 55:5; Jdt. 15:2; 2 Esd. 15:33; 4 Macc. 4:10; cf. 2 Cor. 7:15; Eph. 6:5; Phil. 2:12.

Fee (*Epistle,* pp. 92–93) argues for translating *egenomēn* as "was with" by pointing to the occurrence of the same verb in 16:10 (there, NIV = "is with") as a clear reference to Timothy's stay with the Corinthians.

2:4–5 / The textual evidence regarding the phrase **with wise and persuasive words** is problematic. The NIV reflects the current critical Gk. texts, which themselves include words in brackets to suggest that they were probably not originally a part of Paul's letter. Some ancient manuscripts offer the reading translated by the NIV, but others offer still different combinations. Fee (*Epistle,* p. 88 n. 2) argues reluctantly but convincingly that the original text may have read, "My message and my preaching were not with the persuasion of wisdom, but with the Spirit's power."

T. H. Lim (" 'Not in Persuasive Words of Wisdom, but in the Demonstration of the Spirit and Power' [I Cor. 2:4]," *NovT* 29 [1987], pp. 137–49) recognizes that Paul was not rejecting effective communications in general; rather he was refusing to conform Christian preaching to the craft of persuasion that Greco-Roman orators and rhetoricians valued and practiced.

Finally, one should note that the section ends in 2:5 with a purpose clause in Gk. that states the reason that all Paul said in 2:3–4 (or, perhaps, 2:1–4 or even 1:18–2:4) was true. Again, Paul contrasts human wisdom with divine power (and divine wisdom) as revealed in the cross of Christ.

§7 Insights on the Operation of Revelation (1 Cor. 2:6–16)

These verses form something of an excursus on the wisdom of God and the spiritual discernment of Christians, although the discussion is symmetrically similar to 1:18–25. In these verses, however, Paul seems to be describing reality from God's point of view. To avoid misunderstanding Paul's thought in these lines one must recall that he designated his message "the word of the cross." Paul would tell about the cross, and he would explicate its meaning. Clearly, Paul interprets the saving significance of the cross throughout his letters by applying the meaning of the cross to the lives of his readers. The cross was not merely something that once happened to Jesus; it was an event that continues to give new shape and meaning to those who hear and believe the gospel. Paul declares that by the mysterious grace of God the cross transforms the lives of Christians. Thus, it is not that Paul had a special teaching for some, but that he could explain more of the significance of Christ's cross to the more spiritually mature than to the less spiritually mature. That there are different levels of comprehension on the part of believers was the basis for Paul's distinction between the **mature** and the **spiritual** person on the one hand and the one **without the Spirit** or the "unspiritual" person on the other.

Paul taught that God's wisdom is not simply available to inquiring minds. The depths of God's will and work are apparent to humanity only as God chooses to reveal such things through the working of the Spirit. One sees here that Paul explained the necessity of divine revelation through an argument on the principle of "like by like"—saying that a person is the only one who knows the inner secrets of him- or herself. It is likewise with God. Paul states that an unspiritual human is unable to receive the things of the Spirit of God because these things are discernible only by the Spirit. Yet by contrast Paul boldly declares that Christians have **the Spirit who is from God** and **the mind of Christ,** so that they experienced the gift of God's wisdom as the Spirit imparted it to them.

2:6 / Paul's language both ties the verses of this section to what had preceded and signals a turn in his direction. This development is indicated by the word **however** (this word *de* is often translated as "but"). Having denied that he came to the Corinthians with an eloquent and polished message, he now states that he did preach **a message of wisdom among the mature.** Some interpreters accuse Paul of inconsistency and elitism, suggesting that he had a special message for a privileged group among the larger body of believers. However, that interpretation badly distorts what Paul wrote here. Paul's message was his proclamation of "Christ and him crucified" (2:2), "the message of the cross" (1:18); and the wisdom he taught was "the wisdom of God" (1:21), "Christ the power of God and the wisdom of God" (1:24). As Paul states in a negative form, this message of wisdom was **not . . . of this age.** Those whose lives still manifest elements of this age, even if they are Christians, are "mere infants in Christ" (3:1), not the mature whose lives are "enriched" by God (1:5) and among whom Paul can proclaim "the deep things of God" (2:10) "destined for [the Christians'] glory before time began" (2:7). Paul writes that among Christians of developed religious sensibilities he was able to explicate in fuller detail the significance of the saving power of the cross of Christ.

In referring to this age, Paul sounds an eschatological note concerning God's transformation of the ages (see 10:11) through the cross of Christ. The effect of God's work is that **the rulers of this age** are now **coming to nothing.** Paul is thinking of God's eschatological judgment, but it is not immediately clear who the rulers of this age are. Three interpretations are most often given: Either (1) the rulers of this age are super-human demonic forces that are set in opposition to God, or (2) they are the human political and religious authorities who are working in this world under the influence of the demonic powers, or (3) they are simply human political and religious leaders. Paul's cosmology is complex, and he often personifies evil (Rom. 16:20; 1 Cor. 5:5; 2 Cor. 11:14; 12:7) and sin (Rom. 5:12; 7:8–9, 11); but in this context the rulers of this age, who are coming to nothing, are those who "crucified the Lord of glory" (2:8). Linguistically and conceptually there is no reason to understand these rulers to be anyone other than human political and religious authorities.

2:7 / In this verse Paul describes positively the nature of his "message of wisdom" that he preached "among the mature." The **No** of the NIV translates Paul's word *alla,* so that he is again drawing a contrast to the immediately preceding remarks. He explains that his message of **wisdom** is **God's,** that it is **secret,** that it had **been hidden,** that **God destined** this wisdom for the Christians' **glory,** and that God did this **before time began.** Thus, Paul explains that the message of salvation through the cross of Jesus Christ was God's eternal purpose, predestined for humanity, and available to humans not through nature or reason but only as disclosed by God in the reality of the cross of Christ. Implicit in this description are the crucial theological notions of the providence and sovereignty of God.

2:8 / Paul has already stated that the message of God's wisdom was not openly available to humanity prior to the manifestation of that wisdom as reality in the cross of Christ. God's wisdom, not of this age, effectively brought **the rulers of this age** to nothing. Because they did not possess God's wisdom, the rulers acted without understanding, even to the point that they **crucified the Lord of glory.** Indeed, the wisdom of this age, with which the Corinthians were unduly and ill-advisedly concerned, proved itself not only inadequate but even evil in what it produced: the crucifixion of Christ. Paul's comment registers negatively the power of God's work in Christ, and it expresses a deep irony. Acting in ignorance, the rulers crucified Christ, who as the crucified Christ was the powerful wisdom of God. Opposition in ignorance produced results that ultimately brought the undoing of evil and the salvation of humanity.

2:9–10a / The word **however** (again *alla*) connects and creates a contrast to the previous remarks. The sense of the beginning of this verse is, "Nevertheless, as it is written . . ." Then Paul cites Scripture as the precedent for his teaching, although it is impossible to identify with precision the passage he has in mind. This "quotation" seems, in the main, to be from the LXX of Isaiah 64:4 and 65:16; although it may also be a pastiche of lines from Psalm 31:20; Isaiah 52:15; Jeremiah 3:16; Sirach 1:10. One encounters the same statement in the same form in *Ascension of Isaiah* 11.34, so that it is likely that Paul is not freely paraphrasing,

but that he is drawing the lines from the same otherwise unknown source used by the author of *Ascension of Isaiah.*

The NIV translation ignores elements of the Greek and rearranges the sense and the logic of Paul's quotation. More literally the citation says,

> Things which   an eye did not see
>   and an ear did not hear
>   and on a human heart did not come up—
> things which   God prepared for the ones loving him.

Viewed in this more literal form and wording, the sense of Paul's
statement is more intelligible. By mentioning the **eye, ear,** and
heart Paul registers that humans (in "this age") did not and could
not perceive God's will and work. All of these are things that
God has prepared for those who love him. Thus, the human
senses could not apprehend what God has prepared. What God
prepared for those who love him was Christ-crucified, the power
of God for salvation (2:6–8).

Verse 10a completes and articulates the central point toward which Paul has been pressing in this section: **God has revealed it to us by his Spirit.** The meaning of his statement in
2:10a is self-evident: God has revealed God's previously unper-
ceived wisdom to the Christians by his Spirit. God's people know
God's wisdom only because God's Spirit reveals it to them, so the
Spirit alone perceives and reveals. Once stated explicitly, this
idea becomes the theme for the remainder of chapter 2.

2:10b–11 / Paul adds two further explanatory remarks
in these lines. The NIV fails to signal the explanatory nature of the
second sentence in 2:10 by omitting the word "for" from the
translation of the Greek, which literally reads, "For **the Spirit
searches all things, even the deep things of God.**" The omission
of "for" is unfortunate, since in Greek the presence of this and
the subsequent "for" in 2:11 signals that Paul seeks to argue the
validity of his position. His rhetorical strategy is a "like by like"
argument that was a well-known philosophical principle of the
Greco-Roman world. Like things are able to be known by like
things. The human knows the human, and God alone knows
God, so the Spirit is a necessary link between God and humanity,
for otherwise humanity would not be able to know God. Humans are unable to perceive the reality of the divine, for God's
greatness and holy-otherness (the deep things of God) are beyond the comprehension and grasp of the finite human mind.

Thus, **the Spirit of God** who **knows the thoughts of God** has been given by God to "those who love him," so that the Spirit can reveal to such humans the otherwise imperceptible wisdom of God (Christ crucified, the saving power of God).

2:12–13 / The two verses form one complex sentence in Greek. Paul reiterates his central point that humans cannot themselves comprehend God and that the Spirit is an absolute necessity, given by God and received by humanity, in order that humans may understand God's will and work. Having reiterated this crucial contention, Paul returns to the theme of this preaching, commenting on its contents and character. Once again Paul insists that **the spirit of the world,** an age out of congruity with God, does not understand God. This contention is part of Paul's apocalyptically formed worldview: There are two ages, one in bondage to the forces of evil and the other formed and revealed by the intervening power of God. For Paul, the character of this world requires that whatever truth humans know about God must come to them from God as a powerful, gracious gift. In a backhanded fashion Paul strikes another blow against human claims of knowledge about God and human efforts to fathom the divine. God's goodness and grace are seen in the gift of **the Spirit who is from God** so that the Christians **may understand what God has freely given** in the cross of Jesus Christ.

As the gift of the Spirit enabled understanding, so also the presence and the power of the Spirit taught Paul the spiritual truths that he expressed in spiritual words. In other words, the Spirit enabled Paul's preaching, determining both its content and constitution. Here, 2:13 echoes the lines of 2:1–5. Having been taught by the Spirit about God's will and work, by the power of the Spirit Paul explained these things to others. Implicit in Paul's remarks is an understanding of the missional character of the presence and the power of the Spirit. The Spirit and the truths about God are not grasped and possessed by humans, rather, they themselves grasp humanity and direct persons toward others as the agents of God's saving work.

2:14 / With the words of this verse Paul returns to an argument he initiated in 1:18. The thrust of the argument is negative and echoes similar elements already encountered in 2:6, 8–9, 12–13. Along with presenting the positive case that God's wisdom revealed by the Spirit is nothing other than Christ crucified, Paul vigorously denounces human wisdom as an inadequate avenue to understanding God. Mere reason does not bring humanity into a true relationship with God and the transforming power of God's work. Indeed, **without the Spirit** humanity resists or rejects as **foolishness** the revelations of the Spirit **(the things that come from the Spirit of God).** The Spirit alone provides perception that enlightens and transforms humanity by bringing the human into a divinely initiated relationship with God. And, finally, it is important to notice that, while Paul's language in this verse refers to the individual, the context of his comments in this section clearly indicates that he is thinking of the common human experiences of belief and disbelief. His concern is with a corporate, not a private, spiritual awakening.

2:15–16 / Paul closes this portion of the letter with a statement of the benefits of the reception of the Spirit, which he substantiates with a quotation of Scripture. The shape or logic of the lines is remarkable. First, in 2:15a Paul makes a positive statement—**the spiritual man makes** [is able to make] **judgments about all things**—that reverses the image of the unspiritual person's lack of spiritual discernment (2:14). The remainder of 2:15, then, makes a statement in contrast to the first part of the verse: **but he himself is not subject to any man's judgment.** The power of spiritual discernment means freedom from human scrutiny. The first part of 2:16 offers a reworked version of the LXX's Isaiah 40:13, and it seems to corroborate that the one who receives the Spirit is free from human judgment. The quotation both instructs the Corinthians about true freedom and shields Paul from any criticism the Corinthians might make of him. Finally, Paul boldly answers the rhetorical question of the line from Isaiah by declaring, **But we have the mind of Christ.** Those who experience the illuminating and transforming power of the Spirit are granted Christ's own capacity of spiritual discernment and the freedom that comes with it.

Additional Notes §7

Recent scholarship has made a series of striking observations about 2:6–16: (1) The content of these verses has resulted in scholarly debate on whether gnosticism was an issue in Corinth. On 2:6–16, see J. L. Kovacs ("The Archons, the Spirit, and the Death of Christ: Do we

Need the Hypothesis of Gnostic Opponents to Explain 1 Corinthians 2:6–16?" in *Apocalyptic and the New Testament. Essays in Honor of J. Louis Martyn* [ed. J. Marcus and M. L. Soards; Sheffield: JSOT Press, 1989], pp. 217–36), who argues that positing the existence of gnostics in Corinth hinders the understanding of this passage. (2) Working from a "psychological" perspective, G. Theissen (*Psychological Aspects of Pauline Theology* [Philadelphia: Fortress, 1987], pp. 343–93) understands that "wisdom" for the "perfect" in Corinthians, especially as seen in 1 Cor. 2:6–16, is equivalent to the psycho-dynamic category of "higher consciousness." That is, the "perfect" are able to maintain a more complete and accurate knowledge of and communion with God. (3) R. A. Horsley ("Pneumatikos vs. Psychikos: Distinctions of Spiritual Status among the Corinthians," *HTR* 69 [1976], pp. 269–88) identifies the anthropological distinction between *immortal spirit (pneuma)* and *mortal soul (psychē)* as labels for different levels of spiritual status achieved through different relations between the human and "wisdom," so that the Corinthians are comparing themselves in terms of their relationship to "Sophia/ Wisdom." (4) In turn, W. Willis ("The 'Mind of Christ' in 1 Corinthians 2,16," *Bib* 70 [1989], pp. 110–22) insists that ethical problems in the life of the church, not linguistic distinctions and terms, are the key to understanding Paul's polemic in this passage. These lines are a storm-center for contemporary interpretation.

2:6 / Paul's reference to "the perfect ones" or **the mature** (Gk. *teleioi*) should be seen to anticipate his naming a second group in Corinth in 3:1, "mere infants" (Gk. *nēpioi*), so while the Corinthians may call themselves "perfect" or "mature," Paul's use of the Gk. word *teleioi* (mature) could at times be sarcastic.

2:8 / O. Cullmann's work (*Christ and Time: The Primitive Christian Conception of Time and History* [Philadelphia: Westminster, 1950; rev. ed., 1962) suggested that in the mind of Paul angelic or demonic powers lay behind the activity of earthly rulers. That interpretation was taken up by numerous other scholars whose works have been extremely influential. Thus, today one often encounters this interpretation as if it were a self-evident truth. Nevertheless, a brief essay by T. Ling ("A Note on 1 Corinthians ii.8," *ExpT* 68 [1956], p. 26) works with OT and NT texts to argue that "the rulers of this world" is a more probable rendering of the Gk. word *archon* in this passage than "spirit powers." Later, in a perceptive critique (unfortunately often ignored) of Cullmann's position, W. Carr ("The Rulers of This Age: I Corinthians II.6–8," *NTS* [1976], pp. 20–35) tends to minimize the significance of cosmology for Paul, but correctly faults Cullmann on lexical and contextual grounds for unnecessarily introducing the idea of angels or demons into the reading of 1 Cor. 1–3. Carr later published his insightful work as a monograph: *Angels and Principalities: The Background, Meaning and Development of the Pauline Phrase* haiarchai kai exousiai (SNTSMS 42; Cambridge: Cambridge University Press, 1981).

2:9 / Fee (*Epistle*, pp. 107–9) interprets the two main sections of the citation (marked off by "which things") as a dramatic contrast between (1) human ignorance and (2) God's saving power.

A. Feuillet goes against the tendency to understand the citation as coming from a combination before Paul's time that drew on portions of Isa., or the other texts listed above ("The enigma of 1 Cor 2:9," *TD* 14 [1966], pp. 143–48). He suggests that Paul himself introduced elements into the text by drawing on Job 28 or Bar. 3 (which depends on Job 28).

2:10a / While the NIV begins this verse with the word "but" (Gk. *de*), there is a textual variant that reads "for" (Gk. *gar*). The current critical editions of the Gk. text offer "but" as the probable original reading, although several scholars argue vigorously for the originality of "for." If the reading is "but," then Paul is taking exception to the first part of the citation in 2:9 ("Things which . . . eye . . . ear . . . heart . . . did not come up with"), whereas if the reading is "for," then Paul is completing what he began to say through the last part of the citation ("things that God prepared for the ones loving him").

2:11 / B. E. Gärtner ("The Pauline and Johannine Idea of 'to know God' against the Hellenistic Background: The Greek Philosophical Principle 'Like by Like' in Paul and John," *NTS* 14 [1968], pp. 209–31) compares portions of Paul and John to suggest that these two NT authors demonstrate the particularly Christian use and development of the Gk. philosophical principle "like by like." These authors struggled independently, but similarly, with the question of how humans know God. Gärtner identifies that problem as the fundamental issue underlying Paul's statements in 1 Cor. 2:6–16.

2:14 / The NIV translation, **the man without the Spirit**, interprets but somewhat obscures the linguistic contrast that Paul is making in this verse and in this section of the letter. Paul uses the Gk. words *psychikos* in 2:14 (lit. "natural person") and *pneumatikos* in 2:15 (lit. "spiritual person") to contrast two radically different kinds of persons. The "natural person" belongs to "this age" and so cannot understand God; whereas the "spiritual person" is freed by the Spirit from the encumbrances of human existence through the endowment of the mind of Christ. Thus, Paul's basic concern is epistemological; he is thinking about what can and cannot be known.

2:15 / While Paul does not explicitly say that he is quoting Scripture here, it is certain that he freely reworked lines from Isa. 40:13 into his argument. Nevertheless, Paul omits some words from the original statement. The LXX of Isa. 40:13 literally reads, "Who knows the mind of the Lord, and who is his counselor, that he may instruct him." Paul alters the form of the verb "to instruct" in a minor manner, but he completely drops the phrase that asks who might be the Lord's counselor, apparently because it is superfluous to his concern at this point.

Regarding the OT citations in this verse and in the rest of 1 Cor., R. L. Omanson ("Acknowledging Paul's Quotations," *BT* 43 [1992], pp. 201–13) assesses the possibility of determining an objective criterion for recognizing Paul's full use of the OT. Among the verses treated are 2:15–16; 4:6; 6:12–13, 18; 7:1, 26, 34; 8:1, 4, 8–10; 10:23, 29–30; 11:2; 14:21–22, 33–35; 15:12. This effort is laudable, even if one differs with particular portions of the exegesis of the texts.

§8 Working toward Unity and Edification (1 Cor. 3:1–17)

Paul's teaching in this part of the letter is vivid and relatively straightforward. He begins by tying together what he has been saying since 1:17. The cardinal idea in these remarks is that the Corinthians are immature. Nevertheless, Paul does at least regard the Corinthians as "infants"; he does not deny they are persons of faith. The statements are insulting, as Paul repeatedly says the Corinthians are worldly (lit. "fleshly"). The Corinthians value wisdom and declare their status as mature believers or "spiritual ones," but Paul contradicts their assertions.

Having brusquely denied the claims of the Corinthians, Paul takes up a series of metaphors in order to instruct the church. His aim is to correct the Corinthians' misunderstandings and to move them in the direction of unity and mutual edification. Thus, in 3:5–9 Paul teaches the Corinthians by offering himself and Apollos as examples of proper attitude and behavior. Paul casts himself and Apollos in the role of field servants who serve the higher authority of their Lord. In this picture of divine farming God grows the crop while the field hands, whose assignments are different, simply do God's will. As God's servants Paul and Apollos are equal, and they are paid according to their labor. God's servants do not form competitive groups, for they are united in their efforts under the sole authority of God. Paul recognizes God's authority over the apostles and over the church in Corinth, which he calls "God's field."

At the end of 3:9 Paul shifts metaphors. The Corinthians are "God's field," but they are also "God's building." Using this new image Paul speaks in the role of a sophisticated master builder and refers to the foundation he laid, which was none other than Jesus Christ. That foundation cannot be changed, although others may erect an edifice on the foundation. Going further with his explanation, Paul informs the Corinthians that when persons build on the foundation of Jesus Christ, not all buildings are equal. To illustrate this point, 1 Corinthians 3:12 catalogues a variety of building materials, and the following discussion promises a testing of the materials. This testing is an eschatological judgment on the future, promised "Day" (of the Lord). Thus, those who build on the foundation of Jesus Christ are to anticipate reward or loss in accordance with the quality and durability of the material they used. Paul's lesson admonishes the Corinthians to a careful selection of materials, to a way of life as a church that is fitting for the foundation of Jesus Christ. In Paul's portrayal, Christian works do not bring salvation—God accomplished that in the cross of Christ—but what Christians do with their lives makes a difference in God's eyes. Paul applies the metaphor of "God's building" in order to inform the Corinthians of their identity as God's temple as they experience the indwelling of the Holy Spirit among them. Finally, Paul plainly counsels that God will give a fitting reward to any who destroy God's temple. Indeed, 3:17 bluntly states that behavior that destroys the church will ultimately be destroyed by God.

3:1 / Paul opens this section of the letter in a fashion similar to that which he employed at 2:1. First, he makes a direct personal reference, "And I myself," which the NIV leaves untranslated; second, he address the Corinthians directly as a group, brothers. While the form of "brothers" is a masculine plural, in antiquity that manner of address functioned inclusively, so that the Corinthians would have understood that Paul was speaking to all the brothers and sisters in the congregation.

Paul's rhetoric is deliberate in its form and word selection. Most interpreters understand that Paul is using the Corinthians' own language against them in his argumentation. He says he was unable to address them as **spiritual** people (perhaps their self-designation), not because they did not have the Spirit—from 2:10 it is clear that they did, and for Paul there was no Christian life without the Spirit—but because the Corinthians think and behave in such a way as to deny the true experience of the Spirit. Thus, Paul calls them **worldly**, identifying them as still part of this world. The NIV does not preserve the nuances of Paul's language at this point. He refers to the Corinthians with the Greek word *sarkinoi*, which means "made of flesh," implying that they give the appearance of belonging to this age rather than to the Spirit. In 3:3 Paul alters his language slightly (though the NIV re-

peats **worldly**) as he labels the Corinthians with the Greek word
sarkikoi, which means "having the character of flesh," a term with
ethical implications. Paul's language here highlights that the Corinthians were of the world rather than of the Spirit, whereas in
3:3 he indicates that they behave in a worldly fashion that does
not conform to the activity of the Spirit. One should note in both
instances that Paul has not denied the presence of the Spirit entirely as he had earlier in 2:14, when he wrote of "the man without the Spirit" by using the Greek word *psychikos*.

Paul describes the situation in Corinth for what he perceived it to be. Having been given the gospel, the Corinthians
have not grown up in the gospel. They are **mere infants** (Gk.
nēpioi). He does not merely say they were children (Gk. *tekna*);
they were immature—stuck in infancy, because they have sought
human or worldly wisdom rather than focusing on the crucified
Christ and the meaning of the message of the cross for their lives.
They were **in Christ,** but they had made no progress in Christian
life and thought because they had the wrong focus. They had
been given and had received the gospel, but by longing for
human wisdom rather than God's powerful wisdom in Christ,
they had stunted their growth in Christ.

3:2a / It is crucial to avoid misreading this statement. In
the context of 1 Corinthians and the corpus of Paul's letters, one
sees that Paul did not preach a two-tier message. Rather, different audiences had differing abilities to grasp the significance of
the gospel of Christ crucified. Thus, after labeling the Corinthians "worldly" rather than "spiritual," Paul plays on that contrast
with the metaphor of **milk** versus **solid food.** Paul's discussion
should be understood in relation to the different comprehen-
sions of his preaching by different hearers of the gospel. Having
drunk the milk of the gospel, the Corinthians could not feed on
the solid food of the cross of Christ. They could not digest the
solid food of the message of the cross because they were looking
for a wisdom different from God's revealed wisdom. Their improper concerns left them immature, unable to be nourished by
the bountiful banquet inherent in the gospel; as Paul explains,
they **were not yet ready for it.**

3:2b–3 / Paul strengthens his accusations against the
inappropriate thought and life among the Corinthians with the
words **Indeed, you are still not ready.** In all the lines of this section the pronoun "you" is in the plural form, so one should

understand that Paul intends to address the entire congregation. It may be that some had perceived the depth of the significance of the gospel, but Paul calls the whole congregation, not simply a faction, to accountability. They, not he, are responsible for their shallow appreciation of the significance of the gospel.

Having confronted them with their immaturity, Paul continues: **you are still worldly** (see the comment on "worldly" at 3:1). The NIV leaves untranslated the explanatory word "for" (Gk. *gar*) with which Paul launches his explanation. Paul had already used this word in 3:2a ("for you were not ready for it"), and he will use it again to introduce lines of explanation in 3:3 and in 3:4, so his rhetoric becomes judicial as he explains and calls for the Corinthians to form a proper judgment concerning their situation.

The Corinthian situation is "worldly" (Gk. *sarkikoi* implies "unethical"), as is clear from the **jealousy** and **quarreling** among them. Here Paul reintroduces the language of 1 Corinthians 1:11, which he used in reference to the divisions or factions that existed in the church. Paul's choice of words suggests that the Corinthian predicament was one of destructive, inappropriate party strife. Thus Paul again accuses them of being **worldly** (*sarkikoi*), adding that they were **acting like mere men** rather than like people whose lives were being shaped and directed by the presence and the power of the Spirit. They live as though they were citizens of the old age prior to the revelation of the powerful wisdom of God in the cross of Christ. The Corinthians had the Spirit, but they acted like those outside the church who had not experienced God's gracious gift.

3:4 / Paul's final explanatory line comes in this verse **(For)**. Having moved back to the language of 1:11 in 3:3, Paul now returns explicitly to the problem he began to address in 1:10–12—the competitive appeal to various leaders whereby the Corinthians distinguish one group from another. Paul repeats their slogans, **I follow Paul** and **I follow Apollos**, which prove their inappropriate and unethical behavior that demonstrates that they are living like **mere men**. This mention of the appeals in Corinth to Paul and Apollos rounds out Paul's case against the inappropriate, Spirit-denying behavior in the life of the church, and it sets up the subsequent segments of Paul's discussion in 3:1–17 and 3:18–23.

3:5 / This verse follows immediately on the rhetorical question posed in 3:4. From their slogans (quoted in 3:4—"I follow . . . ," lit. "I am of . . .") one sees that the Corinthians misunderstood the nature of Christian leadership, the church, and the character of Christian ministry. The Corinthians seem to assume that the ones who ministered among them had some status and that by being identified with this or that person they gained some status-giving identity. Thus, ministry was taken to be about self and status, not about service.

To counter and correct such thinking Paul engages in sharp rhetoric and sarcasm. **What,** he asks, **after all, is Apollos? And what is Paul?** His questions denigrate both Apollos and himself from the level of obvious status to that of questionable significance. Having called Apollos's and his standing into question, Paul provides a two-part answer that aims to educate the Corinthians. First, Apollos and Paul are **servants,** people who perform a service for the sake of others. Paul specifies that the service was bringing the Corinthians to faith **(through whom you came to believe).** The significance of Apollos and Paul was that they acted for the well-being of others. The service Apollos and Paul performed had two distinct but related dimensions: They served **the Lord;** and they acted for the sake of the Corinthians who came to believe in the Lord. It was not Paul and Apollos with whom the Corinthians were to identify. Second, they were God's servants who worked according to God's will **(the Lord has assigned to each his task).** Implicit in Paul's remarks is the recognition that the faithful execution of God's will meant that he and Apollos performed different but complementary tasks in ministry. They were different in the kind of ministry they did, but they were the same in that they were both servants doing what their Lord assigned them to do: work for the Lord for the sake of others. Paul transfers the focus of the Corinthians' devotion away from Apollos and himself to the Lord.

3:6 / In order to make his points clear, Paul offers an analogy wherein he casts himself and Apollos as laborers on a farm where God is the owner. The image was a common one in antiquity, for the world was essentially an agrarian economy in which even city dwellers were closely connected with farming. Indeed, in the first-century Mediterranean world, the majority of persons were slaves or servants on large, plantation-style enterprises. The lowest-ranking slave was the field hand who was directly involved with planting, watering, tending, and harvesting the crops. For Paul to apply this image to himself and Apollos is remarkable, for the picture is far from flattering. Lest the Corinthians think that those called to preach and teach the gospel were persons of superior status with whom they could be associated and from whom they could acquire standing, Paul conjures up an image that precludes such misunderstanding. Paul founded the church **(I planted)** and Apollos ministered to the congregation **(Apollos watered)**, but God was the Lord of the church **(God made it grow)** and the Corinthians belonged to him, not to his servants. Whatever standing the Corinthians had came from their belonging to God, not from their association with any one of God's servants.

3:7 / Paul seeks to explain this seemingly clear image. Neither he nor Apollos is important. Only God matters. The Corinthians are so worldly that they cannot see beyond the human ministers, God's servants, who labor among them in distinct but complementary and equally necessary ways. If there are differences between God's servants, those differences exist because God has assigned different tasks to his workers. The tasks are important, but there is no reason to esteem one of God's servants more than another. Rather, God is the one with whom the Corinthians are to be concerned and the one to whom the Corinthians are to give their devotion **(only God . . . makes things grow)**.

3:8 / This verse reiterates and nuances the point that Paul made and explained in the previous verse. Now, however, Paul emphasizes that the different servants of God share **one purpose**. Alike, they do their Lord's will to bring in the Lord's crop, and, given the metaphor, the bigger the crop the better. Paul writes (lit.), "The one planting and the one watering are one." Then he adds a cryptic line that the NIV translates correctly, **and each will be rewarded according to his own labor**. Again, Paul makes the point that the different servants of God have independent responsibilities, although now he registers the additional point that they will be rewarded individually for the quality of their work. Nevertheless, the overriding concern of these lines is to emphasize that the ministers of the gospel—and by implication all Christians—share a common concern with working God's will. Paul will return to this matter later in this section.

3:9 / Paul's interest in explaining his concerns is evident as once again he begins with the word **For**. The NIV translation of this verse is unfortunate, however. That **we** [Paul, Apollos, the Corinthians?] **are God's fellow workers** may be the farthest idea from Paul's mind. Literally this verse says, "For God's we are, fellow workers; God's field, God's building you are." There is a shift in or mixture of metaphors, but Paul's thinking is clear. He recognizes that he and Apollos are fellow workers, and he recognizes that as fellow workers they both belong to God. They do not labor with God; they are God's servants, and they labor with each other. Paul's syntax emphasizes God and God's priority in the tasks and the doing of ministry. The church is **God's field, God's building,** so that to claim allegiance to or status from one or another of God's servants is nonsense. With the alteration of images—from field to building—Paul sets up the lines that follow.

3:10 / The verse has two parts: first, Paul expands the metaphor about building that he began in 3:9; second, he issues a confident warning to anyone who engages in the development of the church. While the language in this verses and those that follow is metaphorical and cryptic because of the presence of several indefinite pronouns, Paul's logic is cyclical and progressive. He is concerned that those who are leading the church act in ways that will be consistent with and enhance the basic gospel of Jesus Christ crucified.

Paul's remarks are aimed at the entire congregation, although those in positions of leadership would have heard themselves addressed in particular. As Paul writes, he assumes his role as the founder of the Corinthian congregation (although from the preceding lines it is clear that Paul knows God to be the owner of the building he "founded"). Paul formed the congregation in Corinth because of the will and work of God in his own life **(By the grace God has given me).** Paul's particular gift was the founding of churches (Rom. 15:18–21), and in exercising this endowment he had laid a foundation that required the erection of an edifice consistent with its nature. Moreover, Paul did this work with exceptional ability—he was **an expert builder.** His words are ironic, for he literally says he was a "wise" (Gk. *sophos*) "architect." Thus, as he laid the foundation of Jesus Christ he exercised true wisdom, not the human wisdom that was causing problems in Corinth; and his actions anticipated and even determined how others would work after him **(someone else is building on it).**

When Paul finally issues his warning, **But each one should be careful how he builds,** he is focusing on the situation in Corinth, not on Apollos and Cephas, who were named as special characters in 1:12. Paul's complaint is aimed at the current situation in Corinth, not at his fellow workers to whom the Corinthians made their appeals. This interpretation is confirmed by all that follows in chapter 3.

3:11 / Paul makes a curt negative statement that denies the validity of developments inconsistent with the original work he had done in Corinth. Paul names the foundation **already laid, which is Jesus Christ,** to remind the Corinthians of the groundwork of their faith. The negative form of the statement results from Paul's perception that the foundation he laid in Corinth was being eroded by an inappropriate concern with "wisdom."

When Paul declares Jesus Christ to be the foundation of the church in Corinth, he is not attempting to assert all the christological concerns of later periods. But he does establish that Christian faith and practice are intricately bound to the person and work of Jesus Christ, especially Jesus' crucifixion. Paul located salvation at the cross, and to lose sight of that reality was to pervert the truth of the gospel. The church cannot be refounded on a foundation other than Jesus Christ. Such a renovation is corruption or destruction, not expert building.

3:12–13 / Paul's concern is that the developments in Corinth be consistent with the foundation of the church—Christ and him crucified. This verse is not an allegory, although it has frequently been interpreted in that way. Paul is not primarily concerned with the building or the materials with which it is built but with the builders themselves and their methods and motives. They must work in a manner and with aims that are consistent with the nature of the church's one foundation, Jesus Christ. He registers the heart of his concern, mentioning six different materials that may be used in building. Paul's primary concern regarding building materials is that those who build the church in Corinth use quality materials (3:13).

The first three materials mentioned are valuable and would endure fire, but the next three materials named would be consumed by fire. In the context of Paul's discussion and concerns in 1 Corinthians, **gold, silver,** and **costly stones** are materials fit for construction on the **foundation** of the gospel of Christ crucified, because they are worthy of that foundation and fit to endure

fire; wood, hay, and **straw** are materials unfit for construction on the foundation Paul laid and are unable to survive the fire. These materials are the perishable stuff of human wisdom that finds the gospel foolish. The builders had to evaluate their materials.

The testing **fire** in these lines is an eschatological image of judgment, as one sees from the mention of **the Day** (the OT "Day of the Lord," a day of final judgment by God). Paul uses this terminology elsewhere in his letters (e.g., Rom. 2:5, 16; 1 Cor. 1:8; 5:5; 2 Cor. 1:14; Phil. 1:6, 10; 2:16; 1 Thess. 5:2), and one also encounters such language in prophetic literature (e.g., Amos 5:18–20; Zeph. 1:7–18; 2:2–3; 3:8). The eschatological fire will reveal the quality of the building materials. There is no thought here of the purifying function of fire. It will "show," "bring to light," "reveal," and test the quality of each person's work. While the language of these verses seems threatening, one should see that there is an eschatological promise in the idea that each person's **work will be shown for what it is.** Early Christians heard this promise of judgment and understood the message to be good news of God's concern with and authority over what people did in the life of the church. The promise of retribution too often overshadows the equal or more important promise of God's ultimate vindication of the life of the faithful. Paul will elaborate on both dimensions of God's eschatological judgment in 3:14–15.

The language of the NIV is artificially and inaccurately restrictive with respect to whose work will be tested. Paul refers to "anyone" building on the foundation of Christ, to that person's work being exposed and tested. At times it is crucial to notice that Paul is addressing either men or women, not both; but when the original language assumes that the remarks are pertinent to all believers, male and female, the translation and interpretation should not introduce gender-specific or gender-exclusive designations. Paul has been accused of addressing the males in a congregation and rendering the females passive observers. That criticism is unfounded, but unfortunately some translations reinforce that misperception.

3:14–15 / Paul makes a pair of statements in contrast to each other in these verses, both of which begin (lit.), "If what the work" (Gk. *ei tinos to ergon*). Verse 14 is positive; verse 15 is initially negative, then positive in a qualified way. These verses have produced much debate among interpreters, for they seem to say that God's saving grace comes with differing scales of pay that are determined by human efforts. At one level this is the plain sense of the text, so that one should recognize that Paul inherited and affirmed Judaism's contention that God would **reward** the righteous. At the same time, one should notice that while both appear to be saved, neither the one receiving the reward (3:14) nor the one suffering the **loss** of efforts (3:15) was saved by works. What both persons did with their lives obviously made a difference in God's eyes. Only the one whose work built on the foundation of Christ and survived the test of eschatological fire on the day of judgment received a reward. Grace brings salvation for both persons who built on the foundation of Christ, but divine judgment did not find all efforts and accomplishments to be of equal value. As Paul stated in 3:10, "Each one should be careful how he builds"; for in the end, God distinguishes between the quality of human efforts.

Paul's words are a metaphor, which means that one cannot press the images. In the case of neither reward nor loss does Paul specify how and what is the difference. Rather, his discussion focuses on why there is a difference. The foundation of Jesus Christ sets a standard that determines the appropriateness and worth of all our efforts as Christians. One may derive materials for building on Christ from a variety of resources—philosophy, sociology, science, psychology, business, arts, anthropology, and other areas (some seemingly good, some seemingly bad)—but no matter what the worldly value of such systems, their consistency with Christ and the truth of his gospel ultimately determines their value in relation to the building of the Christian community.

3:16 / Paul extends or expands the metaphor of the Corinthians' being God's building. He begins this verse with a rhetorical jab, **Don't you know . . . ?** Thus, he implies that they do not know the important matter that he is about to take up with them. Paul refers to the Corinthian congregation as **God's temple** and explains **that God's Spirit lives in** them. By selecting the particular word for "temple" that he uses here (Gk. *naos*) and by introducing the issue of the Spirit's indwelling the Christian community, Paul raises the crucial topic of the nature of the church. Paul's word "temple" is the word for the inner sanctuary of God's temple, not merely for the general site of the temple. Inherent in this word are the themes of God's presence and holiness, as becomes clear through the reference to the **Spirit,** even to those who might not perceive Paul's nuance in the Greek.

At issue is the reality of God's Spirit among them that means that as a church they are the special locus of God's presence and power at work in Corinth. The character of their community and its presence in the world are to embody God's will and work. Instead of focusing on themselves and forming destructive factions, they are to live out God's holiness, which in Christ has been revealed to be a saving presence and power. As they live as God's people, God's presence is made a physical reality in Corinth, and God's will and work come to expression in that city. This verse explicitly reminds the Corinthians of their identity as the corporate people of God, among whom the Spirit lived. At the same time, the statement implies the missional identity of the church as the real presence, power, will, and work of the Spirit.

3:17 / The final line of this section of chapter 3 is a stunning statement that has troubled interpreters as it must have troubled the Corinthians who first heard or read it. Paul has said that those experiencing God's grace and doing God's will would be saved and receive their reward, but those who experience grace and build inappropriately on Christ will suffer loss while being saved. Now, however, he writes, **If anyone destroys God's temple, God will destroy him.** Is Paul inconsistent, or does he mean now to add that some person(s) mangling and distorting the church will suffer the greater loss of full destruction by God?

This verse is the subject of elaborate theological discussions about the eternal quality of salvation and the security of believers. But, since Paul knows nothing of those concerns in this letter, one should not press this statement to form a resolution to those debates. Indeed, one cannot tell whether Paul's word "if" refers to a reality he knows or to a development he fears and intends to thwart. While the exact nature of Paul's remark is not self-evident, his reason for issuing the warning comes in the clear clause of 3:17: **God's temple is sacred, and** [the members of the Corinthian congregation] **are that temple.** The security of God's people is found not so much in their individuality ("if *anyone* destroys") as in their membership in the corporate people of God ("you *are* that temple"). God formed and God guards God's temple from destruction. Paul tells the Corinthians who they are, calls them to appropriate patterns of life in relationship to God and to one another, and promises that God cares for and guards God's people. God's freedom in forming the temple, in caring for it, and in guarding it inform and inspire Paul's bold word in this declaration.

Additional Notes §8

3:1 / According to Paul there is no Christian life without the Spirit (see Rom. 8:9; 1 Cor. 3:16; 2 Cor. 6:16; Gal. 3:2–5; 4:6; 5:5, 16, 22, 25), although reception of the Spirit is no guarantee of problem-free existence for Christians.

As J. Francis (" 'As babes in Christ'—Some proposals regarding 1 Corinthians 3.1–3," *JSNT* 7 [1980], pp. 41–60) observes, Paul's use of *nēpioi* does not refer to a stage of development or growth in Christian faith that is to be outgrown as one moves on to deeper matters; rather *nēpios* names immaturity that is incapable of spiritual understanding. Thus, the problem is lack of understanding, not lack of growth.

3:2a / G. D. Fee (*Epistle,* p. 126) sums up Paul's argument in this sentence: "The problem, he insists, is not on his side, but on theirs. 'I could not' (explain the cross as God's wisdom in mystery) 'because you could not' (so understand it, given your 'advancement' in the wrong direction)." And, similarly, M. D. Hooker ("Hard Sayings: I Corinthians 3:2," *Theology* 69 [1966], pp. 19–22) observes that Paul's meat and milk differed little, but the capacity of the Corinthians to digest determined what they ate. What they took for meat, Paul rejected as inappropriate fare.

3:2b–3 / Paul's apocalyptically structured worldview lies behind the distinctions he makes in these lines. Although the Corinthians had received the Spirit, they were still attached to this age rather than to God's Spirit-created new creation.

Paul literally says that the Corinthians "walk" in a human way (Gk. *kata anthrōpon peripateite*); contrast this accusation with Paul's admonition in Gal. 5:16 to "live by the Spirit" (Gk. *pneumati peripateite*). The language of walking is nearly always ethical in focus for Paul; see J. O. Holloway, *PERIPATEŌ as a Thematic Marker in Pauline Ethics* (San Francisco: Mellen Research University Press, 1992).

3:5 / Paul is not blaming Apollos, and there is no reason to speculate that there was strife between the two. A helpful study by A. Dittberner (" 'Who Is Apollos and Who Is Paul?'—I Cor. 3:5," *BiTod* 71 [1974], pp. 1549–52) makes this point nicely. Nevertheless, the translation "who" rather than **what** (*tis* rather than *ti* in Gk.) follows a textual tradition that should be laid to rest. The oldest and best texts read "what," not "who," so that one should understand that Paul is questioning the significance, not the persons, of God's servants.

3:6 / Conzelmann (*1 Corinthians*, p. 73) notes and lists parallels to this agricultural metaphor in classical literature, the DSS, and extrabiblical Jewish literature. He also notices that the verbs for **planted** and **watered**—alluding to Paul's and Apollos's human actions—are aorists, indicating an action completed in the past, whereas the verb **made grow**—in reference to God's activity—is imperfect, which indicates a more enduring past action; this simple contrast distinguishes the limited nature of human action from the vital and enduring activity of God.

3:9 / The NIV is theologically problematic at this point. Whereas the NIV and other translations read "we are God's fellow workers," an idea that makes little sense in the context of the previous lines, the NRSV more accurately renders the ambiguous Gk. as "we are God's servants, working together." Paul's concern is with the sovereignty and priority of God, not with identifying himself and Apollos simultaneously with God. See D. W. Kuck, *Judgment and Community Conflict: Paul's Use of Apocalyptic Judgment Language in 1 Corinthians 3:5–4:5* (NovTSup 66; Leiden: Brill, 1992). Above all on this point, see V. P. Furnish, " 'Fellow Workers in God's Service,' " *JBL* 80 (1961), pp. 364–70.

3:10 / This and the following verses of this section are concerned with appropriate edification, a theological term that has fallen out of vogue. As Paul's discussion reveals, however, the issue of edification is far from a concern only with personal piety. The discussion focuses on the life of the community. Paul's striking statements address issues of service to the community of faith, but they seem simultaneously concerned with the mission of the community of faith to the larger community in which it existed.

3:11 / Interpreters observe that this verse interrupts the flow of the metaphor, begun in 3:10 and continued in 3:12–13. Conzelmann (*1 Corinthians*, p. 75 n. 69) records a comment by J. Weiss, "Paul is no longer thinking metaphorically, but has in mind the thing itself." One may reasonably suspect that Paul was never thinking metaphorically, at least in a pure and detached way, but that he had the situation in Corinth in mind and wrapped a dramatic, didactic metaphor around it to bring the Corinthians to their senses.

3:12–13 / H. W. Hollander ("The Testing by Fire of the Builders' Works: 1 Corinthians 3.10–15," *NTS* 40 [1994], pp. 89–104) makes the point that the fire in this eschatological judgment is no more the fire of wrath than the fire of purification; rather, the image of fire signifies the testing of the quality of the works. The good endures, and the inadequate does not survive.

A possible connection between these verses and the *Testament of Abraham* 13 is often recognized, but C. W. Fishburne ("I Corinthians III.10–15 and the Testament of Abraham," *NTS* 17 [1970], pp. 109–15) is practically alone in arguing that Paul depended on the *Testament*. If the majority of scholars is correct, then comparison of the two texts is instructive to see how Paul's letter was read and used by a near contemporary.

While interpreters (particularly Roman Catholics) of another era attempted occasionally to relate these verses to purgatory, almost no scholar working today would make that connection, regardless of confessional persuasion or background.

3:14–15 / Both verses are conditional sentences in Gk., as the NIV reflects. The degree of reality assumed by the stated condition is essentially impossible to determine, although the grammatical form may be named with precision. Indeed, the inadvisability of pressing Paul's language for a high degree of precision may be seen in that his metaphor shifts to the level of a cliché at the end of 3:15: **only as one escaping through the flames.** See Conzelmann (*1 Corinthians*, p. 77 n. 85) for a list of parallels in both biblical and classical literature.

Conzelmann (*1 Corinthians*, p. 77) summarized the significance of these two verses: "This is the reverse side of the fact that works do not bring about salvation. But we remain responsible for our works before God (2 Cor 5:11); for the life of believers is service."

3:16 / As Fee (*Epistle*, p. 147) has pointed out, if Paul is still thinking eschatologically in this verse, as he clearly was in the preceding verses, he may have in mind the realization of God's promise to dwell among the people at the end of time.

3:17 / As is usually the case in this letter, Paul's focus is on the community. This verse is often contorted and applied merely to matters of personal piety, but the concern is much larger than with the fate of an individual or some individuals. This "warning" has implications for the life of the individual believer, but never outside the context of the community of faith.

§9 Evaluating by God's Standards
(1 Cor. 3:18–23)

Paul returns to the original concerns he identified and discussed at 1:18–25: the contrast between God's mysterious saving activity in the cross of Christ and the arrogant activity of the Corinthians that resulted from their erroneous preoccupation with wisdom. Paul calls the behavior of the Corinthians what he perceives it to be, sheer self-deception. Focusing on their own knowledge as a key to their spiritual standing, they avoided involvement with the amazing power of God. Paul calls for the Corinthians to take a proper attitude toward wisdom: in comparison with the saving power of God it is of little value. In order to intensify his argument Paul cites two passages from the LXX as prooftexts. Neither citation is precise, though Paul's particular renderings of the texts make them fit the situation in Corinth in a more intelligible way: God's wisdom, not worldly wisdom, is supreme.

Paul continues with a surprising statement. He informs the Corinthians that they do not claim enough. By dividing themselves into cliques or factions they fail to embrace the saving reality that God called into being through the cross of Christ. All that belongs to God is available to the Corinthians as they are faithful followers of Christ. In and through Christ God unifies a redeemed creation, and the Corinthians are called to a new life in that new cosmic unity.

3:18 / The verse opens with an exhortation. The NIV translation, **Do not deceive yourselves,** is inaccurate in rendering the line with a plural form ("yourselves"). Paul's remark is singular ("yourself"); it applies to each and perhaps every person, but not to all as a group.

The words that follow make evident the specific issues of self-deception that Paul has in mind in issuing this stern warning, **If any one of you thinks he is wise by the standards of this**

age. The matter over which the Corinthians might have been in danger of self-deception or delusion was worldly wisdom. Some of the Corinthians were persuaded that they were sophisticated in terms of wisdom, so that one should not miss the deep irony of Paul's remark. Paul has had to labor assiduously to bring the Corinthians to their proper Christian senses precisely because some of them have gone off the foundation of the gospel through their misguided concern with wisdom and the spiritual status that came from possessing special wisdom.

Paul offers an ironic, conditional piece of advice: If someone in Corinth thinks he or she is wise, then that person **should become a "fool" so that he** [or she] **may become wise.** Paul continues the strong tone of his advice, using the imperative form of the verb to say (lit.), "let him (or her) become foolish, in order that he (or she) may become wise." The statement stands on its head the value system that Paul opposed in Corinth. Thinking themselves wise, some Corinthians were fools, for their wisdom caused them to scoff at or ignore the wisdom of God that was revealed in the cross of Christ. By embracing the seemingly foolish wisdom of God, they would become fools to the world but wise in the sight of God. Paul has made this point repeatedly in chapters 1–3, but he reiterates it here in rhetorically deliberate summary fashion to call anyone who confided in anything other than the saving power of God and who derived essential self-esteem from anything other than God's care (seen in the cross) back to an absolute trust in God.

3:19–20 / The initial word, **For,** indicates that Paul is offering an explanation for the command and advice he gave in verse 18. Although the NIV leaves the word untranslated, "for" reoccurs in 3:19b in the introduction to the first scriptural citation. **As it is written** literally reads, "For it is written." Thus, the line **For the wisdom of this world is foolishness in God's sight** is a modified inversion of what Paul said in 1:18a, "For the message of the cross is foolishness to those who are perishing." By inverting the dynamics of the controversy, Paul gives a theological explanation for his insistence that any Corinthian wishing to be wise must first become a **fool,** and he describes the wisdom of this world from God's point of view: it is foolishness. Paul's explanation itself requires supporting arguments (in 3:19b–20) and further explanation (in 3:21–23).

Paul offers a combination of explication, precedent, and proof by citing two passages of Scripture in support of his argument, Job 5:13 and then Psalm 94:11 (93:11 LXX). The citation from Job seems very loosely related to the original text, for the LXX refers to God literally as "the one who takes the wise ones in [their] prudence," whereas Paul names God as "the one who **catches the wise** ones **in their craftiness.**" Paul comes closer to the psalm text in 3:20, simply altering the word "humans" in the psalm to read **wise.** These passages present vivid images. The verb "catch" in Job comes from the language of hunting, so that Paul's employment of this particular verse presents a divine irony. As people craftily try to avoid God's will and work through their involvement with "wisdom," God uses their very craftiness to capture them; for as they posture themselves before God and humanity as the wise, such persons turn out to be real fools. Given the existence of this kind of foolishness in Corinth, Paul cites the psalm to verify and give weight to what is obvious in his argument, **The Lord knows that the thoughts of the wise are futile.** The introductory formula to this citation is simply stated, **and again,** showing that Paul's thoughts are connected to the initial "for," so that in this citation he is still offering words of explanation.

3:21a / Paul signals that he shifts from explanation to drawing conclusions with the emphatic introductory phrase, **So then.** His words are cast as a command, saying literally, "Let no one boast in humans!" The NIV captures the basic sense of Paul's declaration: **no more boasting about men!** Although the minor shift away from the more literal sense of Paul's words casts his admonition in an even more impersonal form than he stated the directive, nevertheless one should see that this remark harks back to Paul's comments in 1:10–12 (echoed in 3:4–5), and it anticipates the explicit denial of the validity of certain Corinthians who claim allegiance to either Paul, Apollos, or Cephas in 3:22. Paul's criticism is aimed at the formation of factions, but his real critique here is of the tendency in Corinth to engage in boasting. The confidence of the Christian is to be in God alone, in God's work in the cross of Christ, not in the mere human agents of God or in any form of human wisdom that focuses on something other than Christ crucified.

3:21b–22 / Paul gives the theological rationale for what he said in the lines immediately preceding these verses and in all that he had written previously. That Paul is offering an explanation is clear in the Greek. The statement begins with the word "for," which the NIV leaves untranslated, although what Paul says in these lines is founded on the grand statement that follows in 3:23.

In one sense Paul's words are self-evident; he begins, **All things are yours.** The importance of this declaration is clear from Paul's literal repetition of the words at the end of 3:22 (without the word "for" in Gk.). The Corinthians have said, "I am of" Paul, or Apollos, or Cephas; but Paul obliterates the reductionistic tendency of such thinking by informing them that **all things** are theirs. The Corinthians viewed themselves as individuals ("I am of . . ."), but Paul looks at them in terms of their corporate identity (**yours,** Gk. plural form). By isolating themselves from one another and thinking about their personal status, the Corinthians have missed the glorious truth of the gospel that Paul makes plain in these verses. The Corinthians had reduced the reality of God's saving work in Christ to a new personal status, whereas the cosmic salvation God achieved in the cross of Christ carved out a new reality that set the Corinthians into a new pattern of relations wherein they were not isolated, competitive, status-seeking individuals or cliques.

Included in the list of all things that Paul names are **Paul, Apollos, Cephas, the world, life, death, the present,** and **the future.** The three persons are those whose names came to Paul's attention from the controversy in Corinth (1:10–12); but these figures represent any or all humans to whom the Corinthian Christians might be tempted to look for identity and status. These three are but human; they are not God (or Christ). In turn, Paul's list of the following five items—the world, life, death, the present, and the future—summarizes all things. Paul forms this remarkable list and insists, All things are yours.

3:23 / The bold claim Paul made in the preceding lines is explained from a purely theological vantage point: **and you are of Christ, and Christ is of God.** Paul did not mean to say that the Corinthians were the lords over everything imaginable; rather, because they belong to Christ and because Christ belongs to God, "all things" belong to them, since all things ultimately belong to God. Only as they are **of Christ** are they related to "all things" in such a way that they are free from the need to attach themselves to someone or something so that they can find identity and status. The one God of the cosmos acted in the cross of Christ to assert sovereign power over all creation. Paul insists that apart from this action, no knowledge or affiliation grants the saving experience of the power of God. Yet because they belong to Christ and Christ belongs to God, the Corinthians already have the status they foolishly sought through wisdom and special affiliations with other seemingly prominent humans.

At times interpreters have struggled with this verse because it seems to present a subordinationist christology that denies the equality of God and Christ as members of the Trinity. Paul, however, knew nothing about such doctrinal considerations, nor was he trying to make a doctrinal statement that would clarify the relationship of God and Christ. Rather, Paul was speaking in a functional fashion, so that whatever christology one encounters here is best taken soteriologically, not ontologically. God acted through Christ. Christ served God's will in doing God's work for the salvation of humanity. So Paul thought and so he spoke. Christ is cast as a mediating figure in Paul's thought, for the Christians belong to Christ who belongs to God, so that in belonging to Christ the Christians belong to God through Christ.

Additional Notes §9

3:18 / With the first three words of the Gk. text (*mēdeis heauton exapatatō:* "no one himself [herself] let deceive"), Paul mandates change by using the imperative form of the Gk. word "deceive" *(exapataō)*. Moreover, Paul is fond of the rhetorical form employed in the words that follow, **If any one of you thinks** (Gk. *ei tis dokei*). It occurs here and at 1 Cor. 8:2; 11:16; 14:37; Gal. 6:3; and Phil. 3:4. As Fee (*Epistle,* p. 151 n. 5) observes, it consistently introduces the position of those whom he opposes, and in an ironic fashion Paul seeks to persuade them by presenting his counterargument. Overall, this verse is a shrewdly crafted bit of simple but effective rhetoric.

In addition, one should not overlook the highly eschatological character of Paul's language here and in the following verse when he forms contrasts between **the standards of this age** and **God's sight** (3:19).

3:19–20 / Comparison of the texts from Job and Paul is instructive:

Job (LXX):   the one who takes the wise ones in [their] prudence
ho katalambanōn sophous en tē phronēsei

Paul: the one who catches the wise ones in their craftiness
ho drassomenos tous sophous en tēi panourgia autōn

Because of the striking differences, one is tempted to argue that Paul is freely translating from his memory of the Hb. text into Gk. But that is certainly not the way he works throughout the rest of this and his other letters. Moreover, a form of the striking word **craftiness** (Gk. *panourgia*) in Paul's citation of Job 5:13 occurs in the LXX of Job 5:12—"frustrating the plans of the crafty" *(diallassonta boulas panourgōn)*—so that Paul may be conflating lines as he cites them from memory of the LXX. Whatever the origin(s) of these citations, they represent the simplest ways in which Paul uses Scripture in his letters, as forthright explanation or evidence of his position.

3:21a / Contrast this negative directive to the positive formulation in 1:31, "Therefore, as it is written: 'Let him who boasts boast in the Lord.' " Conzelmann (*1 Corinthians*, p. 80) states Paul's point positively, "The act, seemingly negative of refraining from 'human' boasting is, positively speaking, freedom."

3:21b–22 / Interpreters (e.g., Barrett, *Epistle*, p. 96; Conzelmann, *1 Corinthians*, p. 80 nn. 16–17; Fee, *Epistle*, pp. 154–55) often observe parallels between Stoic and to a lesser degree Cynic thought and Paul's contention that **all things are yours**, although—as is often recognized—the point of such claims in the philosophers was to establish the self-sufficiency or self-reliance of humans. The value of such comparisons is that one discovers that Paul's point is the opposite: only as persons belong entirely to God do they experience an equality and freedom in relation to all things.

3:23 / One way to avoid engaging in anachronistic debates about subordinationist christology is to think of texts such as this one in terms of divine agency. Thus, G. B. Caird and L. D. Hurst (*New Testament Theology* [Oxford: Clarendon Press, 1994], p. 303) write, "The concept of agency is an essential and undeniable element of New Testament theology. . . . There can be no 'higher' Christology than one which transfers to Jesus the role of Old Testament divine intermediaries who in one way or another represent God to His creatures: prophet, priest, Son of David, Messiah, Son of God, Servant of God, *logos*, wisdom, and Lord."

§10 God as the Only Real Judge (1 Cor. 4:1–5)

The thought and logic of this passage are clear, although in Greek much of Paul's language is awkward. Any translation struggles to render Paul's statements in a sensible and reliable way.

These verses begin by informing the Corinthians how they are to regard Paul, Apollos, Cephas, and all other early Christian workers. They are merely servants and stewards who are called to serve Christ as agents of the proclamation of the mysteries of God's grace. A single quality must characterize stewards: trustworthiness. Or, more literally, they must prove faithful. God requires that Paul and the others be faithful executors of the trust that has been placed in them. In turn, Paul informs the Corinthians that what they think of him as God's steward is of little or no importance. In fact, he says that his opinion of himself is irrelevant, because the Lord is the only one who judges. In a sense Paul is freed by the Lord's being his sole judge, for he needs neither to worry about what others think nor to be obsessed with evaluating his own performance. Paul is free to strive to be faithful, for in the end Christ will judge him and all others. Then God will give whatever praise is appropriate.

4:1 / Paul looks back to the image of the apostles as servants (3:5–9), although he now shifts the metaphor slightly by focusing on their servanthood as that of stewardship **(those entrusted)** rather than in terms of their work as field hands (3:5–9). The plural forms of the words indicate that Paul has not only his own service but also that of others in mind. This point of view characterizes 4:1–2, but one should note that in 4:3–5 Paul shifts to the singular form and seems to be discussing only his own ministry.

The word "servant" in Greek refers to an assistant, indicating one responsible to manage the concerns of another. The Greek word behind "those entrusted" more literally means "stewards," a now anachronistic designation that named the domestic servants who oversaw the operations of a household or an estate. In antiquity, both **servants** and stewards were most often slaves, although in many cases such slaves had enormous power despite their low social standing. Nevertheless, they worked under the authority and judgment of their masters. Thus, one issue for Paul in the use of these images is accountability, as is evident in the words those entrusted **with the secret things of God.** This concern comes through in the idea of judgment in the following verses. Moreover, as those verses will indicate, Paul employs the images of servants and stewards because implicit in such service was the matter of delegated authority, the secondary concern of Paul's remarks in chapter 4.

4:2 / This verse follows closely on the preceding sentence, as is evident in the unusual, complex, awkward beginning in Greek, which literally says, "Here, moreover" or "In this connection, in addition" *(hōde loipon)*. The phrase is an odd rhetorical indication that Paul intends to elaborate on the metaphor he established in 4:1, and so he does, literally: "One looks among stewards in order that someone be found faithful." One looks for one thing in stewards, faithfulness. In the context of this discussion, Paul can only mean that stewards are to be **faithful** to the gospel, to the message of the cross, to the proclamation of Christ crucified.

By registering this solitary desideratum Paul denies that "eloquence" and "wisdom" (see 2:1) were necessary, perhaps even desirable, traits for God's stewards. In saying that faithfulness to the trust is what God requires of his servants, Paul once again indirectly emphasizes God's authority over the apostles and that the character of the gospel determines the shape and substance of the ministry to which the apostles are commissioned.

4:3 / Having established faithfulness as the standard for the evaluation of a steward, Paul reflects on the judgment of himself as the Lord's steward. The shift of focus in 4:3–5 from God's stewards to Paul alone leads interpreters to conclude that Paul is responding to criticisms of himself and his style of ministry. This concern in the situation Paul was facing in Corinth has already surfaced in Paul's discussion (1:17; 2:1–5, 15; 3:1–4, 10), and the motif of judgment was prominent in 2:15 and 3:12–15.

As he takes up this matter Paul begins bluntly by stating, literally, "But it is of the least importance to me that I may be judged by you or by any human day." The language is eschatological, contrasting judgment by humans on a "human day" with divine judgment by the Lord on "the Day" (3:13). The NIV agrees with most other translations in rendering the Greek word "day" as **court**, recognizing that "day" indicated a fixed time such as a court date for passing judgment. Nevertheless, one should not allow this shift in terminology to reduce the critical eschatological quality of these lines.

The motivation for Paul's energetic disavowal is not immediately apparent, for in a sense he has inverted the logical progression of this thought in this section of the letter. Encountering this abrupt statement, one could conclude that Paul is indifferent to what others think of him, that he is arrogant or unconcerned; but that is not the case. Rather, when in 4:4b Paul says, "It is the Lord who judges me," he reveals the reason for his disinterest in human opinions. Paul is the Lord's steward, and the Lord judges Paul; therefore, all other opinions are of little or no consequence for accurate evaluation of Paul's faithfulness. Paul thinks eschatologically, so that the Lord and the Lord's future determine the value of his present activity. No human, including Paul **(indeed, I do not even judge myself)**, is in a position to evaluate his faithfulness. Paul labored with others and among others, and he ministered to others; but he was the servant of the Lord and worked for the Lord alone.

4:4 / The initial portion of this verse explicates Paul's eschatological freedom from concern with judgment. The NIV again fails to signal that Paul connects this statement to the preceding lines as a word of explanation by leaving the word "for" untranslated. Paul literally starts out, "For I am conscious of nothing against myself." The statement registers a profound eschatological conviction, namely, that human consciousness (or "conscience") is neither a valid nor an ultimate arbiter of divine truth. Even one who was attuned to the eschatological work of God in Christ was not in a position to allow **conscience** to pronounce a final verdict. Only **the Lord** can make the final judgment concerning the faithfulness of the steward.

As the NIV translates, a clean conscience **does not make me innocent.** While that rendering is accurate, it stops short of the full sense of Paul's statement. The verb translated "make . . .

innocent" is often rendered "to justify," "to make righteous," or "to put in a right relationship [with God]" (Gk. *dikaioō*). Paul at least means to say that having a clean conscience does not guarantee that he is right with God. Human opinion can never guarantee such a relationship. Only divine action achieves and ensures that humanity and God are in a right relationship. This theological conviction has stimulated Paul's engagement with the Corinthians from the beginning of this letter, as he denied the value of their quest for human wisdom over against an absolute confidence in the work of God in the cross of Jesus Christ. Perhaps the best way to render this important verse is as follows: "For I am conscious of nothing against myself, but in this I am not made right with God—the one judging me is the Lord."

Paul informs the Corinthians that he was accountable to the Lord for his faithfulness to the gospel. His point is clear, although as interpreters recognize, the identity of the Lord is not immediately apparent. Paul mentioned God in 4:1 and refers to God explicitly in 4:5, so that some commentators argue that the Lord is God. That conclusion seems ill-advised, however, for it is Paul's normal pattern to use "the Lord" (without an identity specified) in reference to Jesus Christ. Moreover, in the following verse Paul writes of the coming of the Lord, a clear indication that one should understand "the Lord" in this section to refer to Christ. Thus, in 4:4 Paul informs the Corinthians that because Christ is his judge, he does not judge himself, for although he is not aware of failure in his faithfulness, his own opinion does not justify him in God's sight.

4:5 / Paul draws to a close the metaphor that he began at 4:1. The emphatic character of his statement is evident from the beginning of the verse, **Therefore.** The words that follow are a single complex construction in Greek, as one sees in the three correlated sentences into which the NIV breaks the verse. These lines reiterate the thought of 3:10–15, where Paul used the metaphors of building and fire to call for "faithful" and appropriate construction on the foundation of Christ crucified.

Paul now applies the logic of the preceding lines to the Corinthians. Paul exhorts them, saying, Therefore **judge nothing before the appointed time.** An overreading of the decree takes the statement to mean that they are to refrain from all evaluation, but Paul's ensuing discussions in chapters 5–6 make that interpretation impossible. Moreover, in context Paul is discussing the Corinthians' tendency to criticize and compare various stewards of God for the purposes of their own boasting. His command here should not be taken out of that context. Thus, "before the appointed time" refers to the predilection of the Corinthians to judge from a human perspective, a mistaken tendency not to think eschatologically in terms of God's ultimate values. The Corinthians are disqualified from judging in the present matters over which **the Lord** alone has a final say; they are to **wait till** the Lord **comes.** Then judgment will take place.

The promise of judgment comes in striking form, in the language of apocalyptic eschatology. Paul expects the coming of Christ in the end, saying that his coming will create a separation of **light** and **darkness,** apocalyptic language for good and evil. Christ's final judgment will be universal, disclosing and exposing all things, **what is hidden in** darkness, even **the motives of** [the] **heart.** Nothing can be or will be concealed from the Lord at the appointed time. In the end, the focus turns to **God,** who enacts the results of the judgment that Christ effected by giving **each** whatever **praise** is due. One should not miss this essentially positive conclusion to a discussion that was less than purely positive in tone. Despite present difficulties, Paul expects the Lord's judgment to result in good things from God!

Additional Notes §10

4:1 / Fee (*Epistle,* p. 158 n. 3) criticizes the NIV rendering of the Gk. word *houtōs* as **So then.** His criticism depends on an artificially rigid sense of Paul's grammar. The metaphor of servant in these verses and the issues of "judgment" and "receiving praise" are clearly related to elements of ch. 3. Paul's argument moves forward and does not merely reiterate past points. Nevertheless, Paul's logic spirals at this point, looking back and looking forward at once. Paul did not write with a Gk. grammar in hand, worrying about the rules. Fee presses Paul's language too hard here.

The phrase **the secret things of God** lit. says, "God's mysteries" (Gk. *mystērion theou*). Exactly what Paul means by these words is debatable, although since he already used this phrase in 2:7, he most likely means "the gospel," as he did in using the phrase in the context of 2:1–10. Thus, **the secret things of God** are God's eternal will and work for the salvation of humanity, things that were incomprehensible apart from their revelation in Christ and him crucified.

4:2 / Compare Paul's argument here with his previous statements in 1:17; 2:1–5, regarding his commissioned ministry. In addition, there is a small but meaningful textual problem with this verse that is not indicated in the NIV. Some ancient texts read "one looks" (Gk. *zēteitai*), as in "one looks for faithfulness in stewards"; whereas several significant manuscripts read "you [plural] look" (Gk. *zēteite*), as in "you [the Corinthians] look for faithfulness in stewards." The differences completely alter the sense of the statement. Which did Paul mean? Indeed, the reading with "you look" could even be taken to be an imperative, so that Paul is ordering them, "You, look for faithfulness . . . " Textual critics have preferred the reading "one looks," but the quality of the manuscripts with the alternative reading is also impressive. If "you look" is original, then in context it makes sense only if Paul is issuing a command for the Corinthians to look for faithfulness, not wisdom and eloquence.

4:3 / As A. T. Robertson observed concerning Paul's dramatic disavowal of concern with "human" judgment: " 'by human day,' in contrast to the Lord's Day . . . in 3:13. '*That* is the tribunal which the Apostle recognizes; a *human* tribunal he does not care to satisfy' " (*Word Pictures in the New Testament* [Nashville: Broadman, 1931], p. 103).

In a scholarly insight with significance for pastoral work, B. Fiore (" 'Covert Allusion,' " pp. 85–102) identifies 4:3–6, with its singular focus on Paul, as a key element in the development of Paul's model of a paternal relationship with the Corinthian community. He understands Paul's rhetoric to come from his sense of responsibility to mediate Christ to his Corinthian children in both belief and practice.

4:4 / Conzelmann (*1 Corinthians*, p. 83 n. 18) notes that Paul's reference to his consciousness (Gk. verb: *synioda* = "I am conscious") is related to the "conscience" as the seat of judgment (Gk. noun: *syneidēsis*), so that the NIV translation makes a valid transition by rendering Paul's words in practical paraphrase, **My conscience is clear.**

4:5 / The image of God searching hearts is frequent in the OT. Paul uses this metaphor for God's judgment here and at Rom. 8:27; 1 Cor. 14:25; 1 Thess. 2:4. Similarly, he writes of God's knowing the secrets of humanity at Rom. 2:16; 2 Cor. 4:2–4.

G. Theissen (*Psychological Aspects*, pp. 59–66) offers a basic exegetical probe of 4:1–5 that is often both precise and insightful. He argues that Paul had a notion of an unconscious dimension within the human being where there lay repressed deeds and unconscious plans and motives. While the conscious and unconscious dimensions of human life were not necessarily at odds, the unconscious dimension was inscrutable to the conscious, and only divine judgment could shed light on that psychological dimension of human existence.

§11 Exposing Inappropriate Boasting
(1 Cor. 4:6–13)

Paul illustrates matters with reference to himself and Apollos, but what he says is intended to apply to the Corinthians for their benefit (4:6). Paul's argument in the ensuing verses comes in two strokes. Verse 7 lays the foundation for an assault on the Corinthians' practice of judging, comparing, and boasting. Then in a series of steps (4:8–13) Paul marshals the attack. At the outset Paul is quite sarcastic. He mocks the Corinthians for their pride, false pride as Paul would see it. As he confronts the Corinthians' arrogance Paul counters with the example of the apostles themselves. He contends that God uses the real oppression of the apostles to a positive end. He then contrasts the state of the apostles with the exalted status that the Corinthians claim to possess in order to show that something is wrong in their lives. His rhetoric is patterned, so that the wording draws the Corinthians' attention away from themselves and focuses on the sufferings of the apostles. Thus, he portrays the nature of a genuine apostolic style of ministry characterized by "weakness" (4:10; see 2:3). The image offered in these lines presents Christian life and ministry as selfless, sacrificial, suffering service for the sake of others rather than life lived for the benefit of self.

4:6 / Paul looks back to the foregoing sections of the letter (**these things**) in summarizing and applying his argument to the Corinthians (**for your benefit**). Paul states clearly that he wants the Corinthians to take a lesson from his discussion of himself and Apollos, but his precise concern is difficult to comprehend. The Greek has two purpose clauses (**so that . . . Then;** lit. "in order that . . . in order that"), indicating that Paul wants the Corinthians to learn for two reasons: so that they will understand and apply the saying "Nothing **beyond what is written**"; and so that then they will refrain from forming clashing, competitive factions because of arrogant prejudices. At a surface level these purposes are plain, but exactly what lesson Paul would have the Corinthians gain from his earlier metaphors about farming and building is not immediately apparent. As Paul elaborates his argument, the meaning of the quoted saying itself is not clear. By "what is written" Paul may mean to indicate the Scripture he quoted in the sections prior to the metaphorical arguments in 4:1–5. If so, then Paul is reiterating or reflecting on his point from 3:18–23, again emphasizing that by forming factions the Corinthians defy the unity that God in Christ is creating and to which they themselves are called.

The second purpose clause is clearer, although the NIV translation is unduly restrictive: Then **you will not take pride in one man over against another.** Paul literally says, "Lest you are puffed up one in behalf of one against the other." The statement suggests that he has in mind the Corinthians' claiming one or another of the apostles as their own special leader. His concern, however, is caused by the controversy that results from their identifying with one or another apostle as they compare the apostles and boast about one over against the other(s).

While Paul's point about not boasting in "one against the other" is clear, one wonders whether Paul has in mind a specific competitive comparison of Apollos and himself or the more general problem of setting any one of the apostles over against the other(s). Paul's specific reference to Apollos and himself may indicate that the problem is specific, although all such friction among factions would be inappropriate in the Christian community.

4:7 / With the initial word **for,** Paul signals that he is about to provide reasons for his case against those who are puffed up. To make his point, he uses a series of rhetorical questions to attack the position of the Corinthians. The form of these inquiries is similar to that of the diatribe, a philosophical form of reasoning that uses imaginative irony in a dialog to undermine the position that is being criticized. Paul asks, sarcastically, "What makes you think you're so special?"

Explicitly, the Corinthians think that their association with one or another of the apostles gives them superior status. But implicit in Paul's questions is the true answer to the question of what makes them special—the grace of God! The assumption of this implicit truth underlies the rhetorical questions that follow. Because grace made the Corinthians whatever they now are,

Paul confronts the Corinthians with the reality of their experience of salvation. They were not saved by anything they had or because of anything they did. Rather, they received grace freely—from God, not merely from one of the apostles—and because of the free nature of the gift and their reception of it, they are in no position to boast. In fact, Paul implies that their boasting in humans denies the reality of the nature of grace, for when they boast they act as if grace was not given to them freely by God. The dilemma Paul confronts has two dimensions. On the one hand, the Corinthians are arrogant, acting as if they are above one another; on the other hand, they are unappreciative, acting as if they were not indebted to God for what they had received. Spiritual arrogance and boasting are in contradiction to the true character of God's dealings with humanity. Such behavior is a perverse development that Paul can only oppose.

4:8 / Paul's irony becomes more caustic. The lines of this verse may be translated as either statements or questions. The NIV renders the comments as declarations, and given the force of the remarks, Paul's words are more likely bold assertions than further biting questions. In any case, these lines are the initial portion of a series of sarcastic contrasts that will continue through 4:10 before Paul launches a final acrimonious harangue in 4:11–13. The only goal such rhetoric can serve is to startle the Corinthians into moving away from their improper practices.

Paul's thoroughly eschatological outlook becomes clear in this verse. He repeats himself, **Already . . . already,** thereby registering the nature of the problem he confronted in Corinth. To some degree the Corinthians acted as if the reality of the promised end were already upon them, claiming for themselves in the present world the privileges and the promises that Christian faith taught them to look forward to and to expect at the time of God's completed work of cosmic reconciliation. Instead of looking forward to the glory of the eschaton, they claimed already to be enjoying its arrival. Thus, Paul uses three phrases to label their inappropriate attitude and behavior. First, he says already [they] **have all** [they] **want.** The verb normally refers to being satiated with food, so that one was full and not in need of further nourishment. Second, he says already [they] **have become rich,** a further metaphor indicating their claim to possess an abundance of spiritual, and perhaps physical, assets. Third, from these two metaphors Paul moves to an image of reigning over a kingdom.

The NIV translates, **You have become kings,** but more exactly Paul's words refer to taking up or entering into kingly power. It its not so much their identity as their activity that Paul critiques; he focuses not on who they claim to be but on what they claim to be doing. They claim for themselves the privilege of the promised gift of God, that the saints would share in God's (the one true King's) reign in the age of eschatological fulfillment.

Paul sketches the problem with the opening words of his phrases, Already . . . already . . . **without us . . .** In a selfish manner that ignores the selfless service of the apostles, the Corinthians claimed to possess eschatological privileges without regard for the servants of God who brought and taught them the truth of God's saving grace. The Corinthians claim to reign, but their behavior suggests that the apostles have been left out of God's eschatological kingdom. Thus, Paul adds a sad and sarcastic comment, **How I wish that you really had** [entered your reign] **so that we might** [reign] **with you.** For Paul, God was already establishing the kingdom over which one day God would reign with the saints. But God had not yet granted the privilege of reigning to Christians, who were still living with the all-too-real lingering power of evil around them. Paul's sarcasm seeks to remind the Corinthians that they have gotten ahead of themselves, the apostles, and God; that they should be embarrassed by their behavior (despite what he says in 4:14); and that they should take up a more appropriate pattern of life (see 4:17b).

4:9 / Paul explains his sarcasm concerning his conviction that the Corinthians had not entered into a kingly reign, as the initial word **for** indicates. He offers a stark contrast between the apostles' plight and the arrogant, boastful claims of the Corinthians. By naming the apostles together, Paul disallows any exception that would make one or another of the apostles (here, perhaps, Paul, Apollos, Cephas, or others) superior to the others. In fact, Paul casts the apostles together as a unified group over against the Corinthians with their divisions.

The NIV reads, For **it seems to me that God has put us apostles on display at the end of the procession, like men condemned to die in the arena.** This translation is rich with images, but the language of the verse is less specific than the translation suggests. Paul literally writes, "For I suppose God set us apostles forth last, as those doomed to death." Interpreters debate whether Paul employs a single or a compounded metaphor. Does he intend to cast the apostles in the role of those brought forth last to die in the arena, or does he mean more dramatically to present the apostles led along as "booty" at the end of a victory parade and then to picture them brought forth for execution in the arena? The NIV elects to employ the richer imagery of the parade and the arena. The distinction is not crucial for understanding, and in any case Paul pictures the apostles as being humiliated, condemned, and suffering, not as reigning in kingly power. Paul insists that apostolic ministry conforms to the shape of the cross of Christ. Christian life in the present world is consistent with the reality of Christ crucified, as Paul well knows from the experience of the apostles; and their experience demonstrates the invalidity and inappropriateness of the claims and the behavior of the Corinthians.

In the final lines of this verse, Paul writes, **We have been made a spectacle to the whole universe, to angels as well as to** [humans]. The phrases are set in apposition, registering the same thought in complementary ways that explain each other as they coalesce to provide a basic point. Both phrases, speaking of the whole universe and angels, employ cosmic imagery that registers the eschatological nature of the apostles' divinely appointed experience. Indeed, Paul's eschatologically shaped understanding of God's will and work is the perspective from which he can contrast the life of the apostles with the life the Corinthians claim—"already" Christians are being saved (1:18), but "not yet" have they entered with God into an eschatological reign.

4:10 / In three parallel statements Paul contrasts the stark experience of the apostles with the glib claims of the Corinthians. His rhetoric is sarcastic, and again he seems to aim at shaming the Corinthians for their presumptuousness. The language reflects the contours of major sections of previous portions of the letter, especially 1:26–31; and in each of the three contrasts, Paul's comments both critique and correct the matters they address.

First, Paul contrasts the apostles, who are **fools for Christ,** with the Corinthians, who claim to be **wise in Christ** (the Gk. text does not have **so,** which the NIV introduces as a heightening element in the contrast). The apostles are fools in the eyes of the world, and yet the "foolishness" in which they participate (1:21) exposes the wisdom of the world to be true, godless foolishness. Oddly, the Corinthians are more concerned to be wise in the eyes of the world than to be faithful to the truth of the gospel. In Christ they are beneficiaries of the saving wisdom and power of God that was manifested in the cross of Christ. But when they claim to be wise they set themselves on the side of this world and in opposition to the reality of God's saving work (1:18). As God's fools, the apostles are truly wise; but the Corinthians, who are wise in this age, are fools before God.

Second, Paul declares the apostles to be **weak,** in contrast to the Corinthians, who claim to be **strong.** Already Paul has referred to his "weakness" at 2:3, indicating that this characteristic of his own ministry manifested the reality of the power of the Spirit (2:4). In weakness Paul ministered in a manner that was consistent with the cross of Christ, although that style of ministry was apparently judged to be unimpressive by those Corinthians who were looking for power, wisdom, and eloquence on the part of the apostles. Paul understood "the weakness of God" to be stronger than any human or worldly strength (1:25). Thus, the apostles' ministry in weakness put them on God's side against the illusory strength of the world, which God's weakness had confounded in the cross of Christ. By aligning themselves with worldly forces of strength, the Corinthians were in fact made weak because they distanced themselves from God's powerful weakness.

Third, Paul says the Corinthians **are honored,** while the apostles **are dishonored.** Again, the sarcasm and double meaning of the words aim to sting the smug Corinthians. As those in Christ the Corinthians are honored by God, although if they lived their lives in conformity to the cross of Christ they would be thought to be weak, foolish, and embarrassments by the world. By claiming honor in worldly terms, they side with the forces that dishonor God and judge the power and wisdom of God in the cross of Christ to be weakness and foolishness. The apostles, by contrast, are dishonored in the eyes of the world, while in God's eyes they are truly honored. The world that dishonored Christ also dishonors the apostles because of their style of ministry, but God, who honored Christ by raising him from the dead and by making his cross the central event of salvation, also honors the apostles because of the way their ministry conforms to the reality of the cross. Wisdom and foolishness, strength and weakness, honor and dishonor, are all turned upside down by God in the cross and in the lifestyle of obedient believers.

4:11–13 / In these three verses Paul moves from sarcasm and irony to straightforward language and exposition. He focuses on the apostles, their life and work, leaving behind the explicit contrasts with the claims of the Corinthians. The logic of Paul's presentation is self-evident. First, the apostles have been having a rough time as they ministered in a way that was consistent with the cross of Christ. Paul lists six forms of tribulation to illustrate this dimension of their service. His point is that they have not enjoyed privilege, prestige, position, or pleasure. In this world they have suffered, and all the while they have carried their own weight before the eyes of a world that disdained them (4:11–12a). Second, despite their difficult circumstances and the manner in which they are treated by the world, the apostles never return evil for evil; rather, they always return good for evil, thus manifesting the gracious reality of God's saving grace. Three sets of opposites illustrate this point (4:12b–13a). Third, to the world the apostles are objects of contempt—fools, weak, dishonored; but they are God's faithful servants who are committed to doing God's will no matter what the circumstances.

Paul's language is vivid as he catalogues the hardships and activities of the apostles. He frames the comments in this section with two synonymous phrases at the beginning and end of the verses: **To this very hour** (4:11) . . . **up to this moment** (4:13). Thus, he highlights the cross-centered character of apostolic life in the present and implicitly critiques the Corinthians' claims to privilege in the present world. Whereas the Corinthians are declaring themselves to be satiated, rich, and reigning (4:8), the apostles are **hungry, thirsty, in rags, brutally treated, homeless,** and working **hard with** their **own hands.** As Paul continues, he records how the apostles are "brutally treated" and how they respond to such abuses: **when . . . cursed, we bless; when . . . persecuted, we endure it; when . . . slandered, we answer kindly.** Earlier, Paul said he ministered in weakness in order to demonstrate the power of the Spirit (2:1–5), and in a poignant passage in 2 Corinthians, he lists apostolic hardships and reactions to make this point explicitly (2 Cor. 4:1, 7–12). He likely means to illustrate how the power of the Spirit allows him and the other apostles to minister in the face of abuse so that the reality of God's grace is manifested. In being abused and then responding with grace, the apostles exhibit the reality of God's saving will and work in a manner consistent with the cross and resurrection of Christ.

Paul's argument to this point raises a question: What is the purpose of the suffering that the apostles endure? The last two clauses of 4:13 speak to this question, but they are notoriously difficult to understand. The NIV reads **Up to this moment we have become the scum of the earth, the refuse of the world.** Similarly, the NRSV translates the verse, "We have become like the rubbish of the world, the dregs of all things, to this very day." Thus, both these translations present Paul's statement as an indication that the apostles have become scum ("rubbish") and refuse ("dregs") in their sufferings. In describing the plight of the apostles, both translations understand that Paul offers two negative descriptions in apposition. The Anchor Bible, however, translates 4:13b, "we have become, as it were, until now the dirt scoured from the world, that which cleanses all"; the dirt was poured upon Paul and the other apostles, who, by taking the dirt upon themselves, cleanse the world. Thus, the dirt is read as a negative image that is superseded by the positive one of cleansing.

Remarkably, when the Greek word *perikatharma*—which does not occur anywhere else in the NT and is translated here as scum, "rubbish," or "dirt scoured"—occurs in Proverbs 21:18 (LXX) it means "expiation" or "ransom." The Greek word *peripsēma*—which is also a hapaxlegomenon, and which is translated as refuse, "dregs," or "that which cleanses"—occurs in Tobit 5:18, where it means "ransom" or "scapegoat." Thus, it is possible that rather than ending with two negative images in apposition (scum or "rubbish," refuse or "dregs") or in a negative image that is superseded by a contrasting positive one ("dirt scoured," "that which cleanses"), Paul may ultimately define the positive meaning of the genuine suffering he and the others apostles endure. He may mean to offer two positive images of ransom in apposition. Moreover, there may be a deep ironic double entendre in what Paul writes. If the suffering of the cross of Christ, which ultimately brought about the salvation of humanity, is indeed the paradigm of the labors of the apostles—as Paul's argument has repeatedly indicated that it was (1:17; 2:1–5; 3:18–23)—then it makes good sense to understand that by labeling the apostles "the scum of the earth, the refuse of the world," Paul also names them as God's agents in salvation: "an expiation for the world, a ransom for all." Perhaps, then, one should translate 4:13 in this way, "Being slandered, we call out, having become like scum—an expiation for the world, refuse—a ransom for all until now." If this rendering is correct, then Paul is not merely saying that Christian suffering is a bad fate that can be endured; rather, Christian suffering plays a vital role in God's work of reconciliation.

Additional Notes §11

4:6 / The meaning of the phrase **not . . . beyond what is written** troubles interpreters. To what does this refer? Some have suggested dropping the words from the translation, arguing they are either incomprehensible or a gloss or both. Others suggest that the words refer generally to Paul's citations of Scripture(s) in his epistle. Still others take the phrase to designate the OT or Scripture in general. Some interpreters understand the words to be a popular maxim that referred to established norms of behavior rather than to any particular writing or set of writings. Others argue that Paul is referring to what he wrote in the metaphors about planting and building in ch. 3. The interpretive suggestion made above is the least radical of the options, viz., that Paul is referring in context to the Scripture(s) he had cited in the foregoing lines of this letter, so that no "unknown" factor needs to be identified to make sense of Paul's remark.

4:7 / Fee draws a helpful comparison between Paul's digging rhetorical questions in this verse and "equally devastating questions in the OT in which one is brought face to face with the truth about oneself before God: e.g., Isa. 40:14 . . . Job 38" (*Epistle*, p. 171 n. 32).

In response to the three questions in this verse, Conzelmann suggests the answer to the first two is "nothing," whereas the third question seeks to cut off the possibility of giving an answer to the questions. However, the correct answer to the first question is "grace," which means that the answer to the second question is "nothing" and to the third is "we shouldn't."

4:8 / Interpreters speculate whether Paul's wish at the end of this verse is genuine or ironic. Perhaps it is both, but whatever the sense, the line **How I wish . . . with you!** brings Paul's argument to a point that naturally leads to his reflection on the apostles' paradoxical style of suffering ministry in the verses that follow. With this wish Paul will momentarily shift his focus off the fantasy of the Corinthians and onto the reality of the ministry of the apostles.

4:9 / Commentators frequently conclude that Paul is responding to criticisms of his style of ministry in this verse and in this larger section of the letter. Thus, they argue that Paul was aware that some of the Corinthians found him unimpressive because of a perceived lack of wisdom and eloquence. This reading means that Paul's remarks are as much concerned with apologetics as with correcting and directing the Corinthians in their life together. While there is much to commend this interpretation of the letter, one may still read the comments here as primarily if not exclusively didactic. Indeed, in the context of the church today, one is hard pressed to relate the apparent apologetic dimensions of the text to a reaction to Paul as "unimpressive." Paul's problem with readers today is that they fault him for having too much authority and for being something of an arrogant autocrat—a reaction that has little or no foundation in history.

4:10 / Paul's reference to the **wise** employs the Gk. word *phronimos,* not *sophos.* This is likely a mere rhetorical variation (Conzelmann, *1 Corinthians,* p. 89; Fee, *Epistle,* p. 176 n. 60); but translations might better render the word as "sensible" or "prudent" in order to distinguish the nuances of Paul's statements concerning wisdom in this letter.

4:11–13 / For a similar but more extensive catalogue of hardships that Paul reports to have endured in 4:11–12a, see 2 Cor. 11:23–29. There too the apostle lists his tribulations in an attempt to confront the Corinthians for their behavior in relation to him. Lists of tribulation are found in Greco-Roman writings and function there in a variety of ways. For a careful study of Paul's remarks in the larger context of Greco-Roman literature, see J. T. Fitzgerald, *Cracks in an Earthen Vessel: An Examination of the Catalogues of Hardships in the Corinthian Correspondence* (SBLDS 99; Atlanta: Scholars Press, 1988).

The matter of Paul's working with his hands appears here and in 2 Cor. (chs. 11–12), 1 Thess. (2:6, 9; 4:11–12), and 2 Thess. (3:7–10). In Greco-Roman antiquity manual labor was not dishonorable, but it brought no honor to those who did such work. Those who were persons of honor or high social status did not engage in manual labor; they lived by other, "more honorable" means. Jewish rabbis undertook manual labor in order to leave their minds free for reflection on Torah, but Gentiles had no such positive use for menial work. Paul's comments on working with his hands reflect nothing of the positive rabbinic disposition toward manual labor. Rather, Paul interpreted his labor as apostolic hardship in conformity to the cross of Christ. He didn't live on the contributions of his congregations; he took on the burden of labor as a symbol of suffering service so that he created no hardship for others but "suffered" for their sakes to spare them the responsibility for his support.

In their discussions of 4:13, Fee (*Epistle,* p. 180) and Conzelmann (*1 Corinthians,* p. 90 n. 49) fail to recognize the possibility of double entendre and dismiss any positive sense to Paul's image. Also arguing for a negative sense to Paul's declaration, A. Hanson ("1 Corinthians 4:13b and Lamentations 3:45," *ExpT* 93 [1982], pp. 214–15) relates Paul's terms *perikatharma* and *peripsēma* to the Hb. text of Lam. 3:45, which he also connects with Christ's passion and death.

§12 A Paternal Appeal and Admonition (1 Cor. 4:14–21)

Paul introduces a new metaphor, and his tone changes as he explains his motives for writing and then issues an appeal to the Corinthians. He portrays himself as a father and the congregation as his children. He refers to the special relationship he has with the Corinthians, and he explains this intimate association as the natural result of his having founded the church through the preaching of the gospel of Jesus Christ. Paul develops the metaphor of a father in a way that the Corinthians would easily comprehend. They are urged to follow Paul's example. Moreover, in order to direct the Corinthians, Paul informs them that he is sending Timothy, who in the pattern of relations named here would be a sibling to the Corinthians. Paul appeals to the Corinthians to take up or return to the standards of life that informed all the congregations that Paul founded.

Thus, again Paul calls the Corinthians away from idiosyncratic, haughty behavior as he reminds them that they are part of the larger church that God in Christ is calling into being. Finally, with his basic point having been made, Paul expands the family metaphor by writing as a father to rowdy children and issuing an unambiguous parental threat.

4:14 / Paul's denial that he was attempting to shame the Corinthians seems hard to believe, unless, as seems likely, he means to indicate that shaming them was not in itself his primary purpose. The word Paul uses (Gk. *entrepō*) carries the sense of "turning in [on oneself]"; and while it does not mean "to devastate" or "to disgrace," it could imply "to demoralize." In the context of this letter, Paul's criticisms of the Corinthians cannot be understood as an attempt to render the congregation passive. Perhaps one should understand that Paul designed his sharp rhetoric to induce a sense of embarrassment in order to accomplish another goal. As his remarks continue one can see Paul's more positive purposes.

Paul states his real goal: **to warn** [the Corinthians], **as** [his] **dear children.** The word translated as "to warn" by the NIV may be better rendered "to instruct" or "to teach," since it most often functions in Greek in reference to admonishing that puts one in mind of a lesson in a didactic fashion. "Warning" in English connotes a more negative sense than Paul may mean to suggest. Indeed, the positive tone of his purpose comes through in his reference to the Corinthians as "my dear [lit. 'beloved'] children," so that one perceives that Paul is more a mentor to his children than a referee or a police officer.

4:15 / Paul explains the reason he was concerned for the Corinthians, but the NIV leaves untranslated the explanatory word "for" that introduces this sentence in Greek. In fact, this verse adds one explanation to another to make Paul's point clear (he writes lit. "For" . . . **for;** NIV omits the first of these but translates the second).

The language is heavily metaphorical, but Paul's logic is straightforward. There are many other leaders who will have important, influential relationships with the Corinthians **(ten thousand guardians),** but all others than Paul are only guardians (Gk. *paidagōgos*), a term that designated a slave charged by the father of a child to escort the child to school in order to guarantee the child's safety and attendance. Such persons played a vital role in the upbringing of children, but they in no way were as crucially related to the children as was the father. Thus, while admitting the presence, significance, and authority of others, Paul claims for himself a special connection, responsibility, and authority in relation to the Corinthians.

In a second word of explanation, Paul adds, **for in Christ Jesus I became your father through the gospel**—which more literally reads, "For in Christ Jesus through the gospel I myself begot you." The statement explains or elaborates Paul's point that the Corinthians **do not have many fathers.** One should notice, however, that in Greek Paul places the phrases **in Christ Jesus** and **through the gospel** at the beginning of his statement to emphasize the particular identity in which and the particular means by which he founded the congregation in Corinth. His relationship to the Corinthians has special meaning because he gave them birth in Christ and because they came into their father-child relationship through the gospel. Paul values the relationship because it came into being as a result of God's saving power at work in the world in the cross of Christ, not merely because human relationships are inherently wonderful.

4:16 / Paul focuses and strengthens his appeal. **Therefore** indicates that he means to make a specific point from his remarks. He then "urges" the Corinthians, using a word (Gk. *parakaleō*) that often functioned in courts of law to make an appeal to a judge or a jury to draw a particular conclusion or to reach a particular verdict. The rhetoric is strong, and in that vein Paul says, **imitate me.** As their one father "in Christ Jesus" Paul teaches his children the way in which they are to live by offering himself to them as an example. This call to imitation may seem arrogant, egotistical, or self-righteous, but in 11:1 it becomes clear that in this call to imitation Paul is urging the Corinthians to Christlike living, for there he plainly says (lit.), "Be imitators of me, even as I am of Christ" (11:1). Moreover, one should keep in mind the pattern of life that Paul had described in the verses immediately prior to this section (see 4:11–13). The concept of imitation had a rich history both in the Greco-Roman world and in Judaism. Children imitated parents and disciples imitated masters. In no case was the imitative behavior understood to be simple mimicry. Children and disciples internalized the values, thoughts, and behaviors of their role models so that they became very much like them.

As Paul calls the Corinthians to imitate his behavior, which he understood to be an imitation of Christ, he calls the church to its mission. They are not merely to behave in a decent and upright manner; they are called to active service, as Paul himself was. Their life in Christ is to be lived lovingly for the sake of others, never selfishly. In mission they should live as Paul did, sacrificially offering their very selves to God for the execution of God's will and work in the world. As the Corinthians become Paul-like, they will be Christlike; and in turn they will live in a godly fashion as the real people of God present and at work in Corinth.

4:17 / Paul writes of sending Timothy to the Corinthians in order to help them live according to his example. Paul's statement may mean either that he had already sent Timothy or that he is about to do so. The NIV translates this in a way that suggests the latter, but the matter is ambiguous and not crucial.

More important is the description of Timothy: **my son, whom I love, who is faithful in the Lord.** As Paul's son (Gk., lit. "child") Timothy is in a position not only to tell the Corinthians about Paul's ways but also to show them the manner of life to which they are called. Timothy is already known to the Corinthians, since according to the account of Paul's original ministry in Corinth (Acts 18:1–18) Timothy had joined him in the city (18:5) and perhaps remained after his departure (18:18). Yet, the subsequent remarks in 1 Corinthians 16:10–11 suggest that Paul was uncertain or anxious about the welcome that Timothy might receive from the Corinthians. The uncertainty extends from the role that Timothy was to play in Corinth; he goes as Paul's representative. If Paul is under fire in Corinth, his agent would experience the same kind of scrutiny and criticism, since his task is to remind them of Paul's **way of life in Christ Jesus.** Paul's declaration of personal affection ("whom I love") and his praise of Timothy's Christian conscientiousness ("who is faithful in the Lord") are strong words of recommendation.

Paul qualifies the lifestyle and teaching that Timothy would represent to the Corinthians with the phrase **which agrees with what I teach everywhere in every church.** Thus, what Timothy brings them from Paul is not novel. It is the universal way of Christian thought and life that Paul promulgated among all the congregations he founded. Any deviation or innovation in Corinth would need to be evaluated against the generally recognized way of life in Christ Jesus that had been laid as the foundation of the Corinthians' faith (3:10–15).

4:18–20 / These verses form one long, complex sentence in Greek, but the NIV sensibly follows the versification of the text and renders Paul's lines in three related sentences. First, he names the problem in a specific way. Up to this point he has addressed the congregation as a whole, but now he narrows his focus to isolate **some** in the congregation who apparently are the primary troublemakers. Now, clearly one sees that the situation is not only that the Corinthians are forming factions; in addition, there are some who are causing problems because they are critical of Paul. Thus, he writes, **Some of you have become arrogant, as if I were not coming to you.** The grammar is unclear, although it is plain that they have taken a position that Paul judges "to be puffed up" (Gk. *physioō*). This is the same word Paul used in 4:6 to describe the formation of the factions, so the factions and the criticisms of Paul are related phenomena, perhaps facets of the central problem of "boasting" that Paul condemned at 1:29; 3:21; 4:7.

Second, lest those who were puffed up and critical of Paul take advantage of his words, Paul immediately declares his intention to **come very soon** (lit. "quickly") to the Corinthians. His tone is sharp in verses 19–20, not at all conciliatory as it was in 4:14–17. He holds the discussion of his specific travel plans until near the end of the letter (16:5–9), registering here that he intends to come as soon as possible. At this point he informs the Corinthians that they can be sure he will come, but he does not say when. Moreover, he adds, **if the Lord is willing.** These words are easily misunderstood today as a pious euphemism for "maybe." Paul is not, however, hedging on his plans; he is an eschatological thinker who knows that the future belongs to God and that nothing will transpire in his life that does not serve God's purposes.

Third, the force of Paul's thought and the purpose of his future visit become clear in the final clause of 4:19, **and then I will find out not only how these arrogant people are talking, but what power they have.** This translation captures the sense of Paul's more wooden statement, "and I shall know not the word of the ones who have been puffed up but the power." Paul probably means to be ironic at this point, for the contrast he draws pits "word" (*logos*) against "power" (*dynamis*), thus picking up the language of the earlier portions of the letter, where Paul indicated that his critics in Corinth found his "word" to be unimpressive (1:17; 2:1–5) when judged from the "powerful" perspective they claimed for themselves (1:21; 2:1; 3:2). Now, Paul confronts them as having a "word" that is devoid of power, because true power is found only in the gospel (1:17), the cross of Christ (1:17–18, 23–24), and the Spirit (2:4; 2:10, 12, 14)—all of which Paul's critics repudiate through their involvement with worldly wisdom.

Paul has already made clear that he stakes his life on the "power" of the "weakness of God" (1:25) and that he ministers in a manner consistent with God's weakness (1:18–25; 2:1–5; 4:9–13). Here he takes that same position as he sets God's peculiar power over against the word and the power that "some" in Corinth claim to possess. Verse 20 makes Paul's position explicit. Opening with the explanatory word **for,** Paul writes, For **the kingdom of God is not a matter of talk** [lit. "word"] **but of power.**

The eloquent worldly wisdom valued by some Corinthians, which leads some to criticize Paul's ministry, has nothing to do with God's true power, mysteriously demonstrated in the cross of Christ and made effective through preaching the gospel and the work of the Spirit. Paul's declaration applies the logic of 1:18 ("For the message of the cross is foolishness to those who are perishing, but to us who are being saved it is the power of God") to the situation in Corinth to make even clearer the error of the path that some of the Corinthians had taken.

4:21 / Paul continues the father-child metaphor with a rhetorical form that functions as a multiple-choice question. The use of the imagery ties together 4:14–21 as a unit and brings the argument to a conclusion, rounding off all of Paul's reflection from 1:10 to 4:21. The question is plain and seemingly innocent: **What do you prefer?** But the options he offers the Corinthians show that Paul speaks now from an assumed position of authority and responsibility. Apologetics are absent. As a stern parent facing rebellious, unreasonable children, Paul threatens parental discipline: **Shall I come with a [rod], or in love and with a gentle spirit?** The questions are posed to the entire community, not merely to the troublemakers—in part because the community tolerates and participates in the problems, but also because the community itself has lost the capacity to exercise discipline (see chs. 5–6).

The NIV reference to a **whip** is peculiar and inappropriate, following inferior or misguided lexical studies. Paul's word (Gk. *hrabdos*) plainly means "rod." This mention of a "rod" employs the language and the imagery of the OT "rod of correction" to name one option for Paul's coming to the Corinthians. The passage has come under fire because of this image. But, contemporary critics who fault Paul for speaking and thinking in a way that promotes child abuse miss his point in this verse. Paul uses traditional language to speak metaphorically about discipline. He is not suggesting a literal rod. And he is neither condoning nor promoting harsh treatment of children. Rather, he suggests an undesirable manner of relating to the Corinthians (with a "rod") in order to heighten the desirability of the other option that he offers: his coming in love and with a gentle spirit. Love, as chapter 13 will make clear, is the necessary standard of all Christian interaction and relations. And love most naturally produces a gentle spirit, although at times love must take a firm hand in relationships that are troubled, as Paul recognizes. The larger letter reveals, however, that Paul would insist that even in administering strict discipline in the context of the Christian community, love must be the guiding force in all Christian actions. With these words Paul draws the first major section of the letter to a close.

Additional Notes §12

4:14 / Conzelmann (*1 Corinthians*, p. 91 n. 56) refers to Wis. 11:10 and a passage from Josephus's *Jewish Wars* (1.481), where the verb *nouthetein* means "to admonish" children, as it does here in Paul's remarks. Looking forward from this verse to the remarks in 4:15, Conzelmann argues that Paul's rhetoric casts "admonition" as the activity of the "father," whereas "to shame" is the work of the "pedagogue" or "guardian."

4:15 / On the distinctions between the roles of **guardians** (*paidagōgos*), "teachers" (*didaskalos*), and **fathers** (*patēr*), consult *EDNT* and *TDNT*: G. Schneider, *"paidagōgos," EDNT* 3:2–3; G. Bertram, *"paideuō/paidagōgos," TDNT* 5:596–625, esp. 624–25; K. H. Rengstorf, *"didaskō/didaskalos," TDNT* 2:135–65, esp. 148–51, 157–59; O. Michel, *"patēr," EDNT* 3:53–57, esp. 56–57; G. Schrenk, *"patēr," TDNT* 5:945–1022, esp. 1005.

Regarding 1 Cor. 4:15, Schneider (*EDNT* 3:3) writes,

> In 1 Cor 4:15 παιδαγωγοί are mentioned as persons who along with πατέρες are deserving of respect.... After Paul has emphasized that he is admonishing the Corinthians as his "beloved children" (v. 14), he underscores his unique relationship with the Corinthian congregation. He is the "father" of the Corinthians, since he "begat" them: "Although you may have ten thousand *disciplinarians* in Christ, you will not have many fathers; for I (ἐγώ) begat you in Jesus Christ through the gospel" (v. 15). The difference between fatherly admonition (v. 14b: νουθετέω) and the berating of a παιδαγωγός (v. 14a: ἐντρέπω) is found in the fact that the father summons the children to imitation of himself (v. 16).

In turn, with regard to *patēr*, Schrenk (*TDNT* 5:1005) observes, "What is denoted by *patēr* is the fact of mediation of life"; and Michel (*EDNT* 3:56–57) argues, "The rabbi becomes a 'father' of believers as a teacher, the mystagogue through initiation in the mysteries, and Paul by proclaiming the gospel. In his mission he seeks people that they might be begotten and born...."

4:16 / Concerning this verse, Conzelmann (*1 Corinthians*, p. 92) comments incisively, "The summons cannot be separated from Paul's missionary work." Moreover, E. A. Castelli (*Imitating Paul: A Discourse of Power* [Literary Currents in Biblical Interpretation; Louisville, Ky.:

Westminster John Knox, 1991]) illuminates the full force and significance of Paul's strategy in this call to imitation by surveying the idea of
mimēsis in ancient literature.

A few inferior and late manuscripts add the words "just as even
I [imitate] Christ" to the end of this verse. The addition is clearly not
original, but it shows that scribes connected this statement with Paul's
words in 1 Cor. 11:1, as did the interpretation above.

4:17 / Beyond the mention of Timothy in this verse, from the
range of references to him in Paul's letters a remarkable image of Timothy emerges. He was one of Paul's fellow workers (1 Thess. 1:1; 1 Cor.
16:10–11; 2 Cor. 1:1; Rom. 16:21; Phil. 1:1; Phlm. 1) who served as Paul's
agent on various occasions (1 Thess. 3:2; Phil. 2:19) and co-authored
several of the letters with Paul (1 Thess. 1:1; 2 Cor. 1:1; Phil. 1:1; Col. 1:1;
Phlm. 1). Both 1 and 2 Timothy are addressed to him.

Contemporary translations of 4:17 are fairly uniform in rendering the third clause of this verse as "who [he] will remind you of my
ways [way of life] in Christ Jesus," but there is a significant textual
variant concerning the name "Christ Jesus." Some manuscripts read
"Christ," others read "Lord Jesus," and still others read "Christ Jesus."
The critical edition of the Gk. NT places *Christ* in brackets to signify that
it is an old, important reading but not likely part of the original text. The
reading "Lord Jesus" has little support and is almost certainly secondary, but the other readings are equally impressive and equally logical. A
final decision is impossible, so that given the uncertainty of the text no
theological hay should be made of the name "Jesus" here.

4:18–20 / When Paul writes, **Some of you have become arrogant, as if I were not coming to you,** he speaks ambiguously. His remark may mean either that their arrogance was in defiance of his
possible coming to them or that their arrogance came about because he
had not come to them in recent memory. Thus, the exact cause of the arrogance of some of the Corinthians is unclear; however, Paul's opinion
of them is not: they are "puffed up" *(physioō)*.

From 2 Corinthians one finds that after writing this letter Paul
did pay a visit to the Corinthians, which proved to be unpleasant and
difficult. Still later, he faced severe criticism and became embroiled in a
controversy because he apparently altered further travel plans that he
had communicated to the Corinthians. For the original travel plans see
1 Cor. 16:5–9 and for the report of the visit see 2 Cor. 1:15–2:4; 12:19–21;
for a final word on Paul's visits to the Corinthians see 2 Cor. 13:1–4.

4:21 / Concerning the "rod of correction," Fee (*Epistle,* p. 193
n. 49) lists Exod. 21:20; 2 Sam. 7:14; Prov. 10:13; 22:15; Isa. 10:24; Lam.
3:1 as possible OT passages that influenced Paul's language.

§13 Shocking Sexual Immorality (1 Cor. 5:1–13)

The move from chapter 4 with its discussion of the ministry of the apostles to chapter 5 with the focused discussion of immorality may seem to be an illogical leap on the part of Paul. Quick shifts in focus such as this one have led a few interpreters to suggest that the document called 1 Corinthians is not a unified composition; but that reading of the text is an overreaction to the diversity of Paul's remarks. Indeed, in 4:18 Paul confronted some of the Corinthians because they were **arrogant** (*ephysiōthēsan*, from *physioō*), and after seeming to shift the focus in 5:1 with the reference to immorality Paul repeats the confrontative accusation that the Corinthians are arrogant (*pephysiōmenoi*, from *physioō*) in 5:2. Unfortunately this connection is lost in the NIV's translation of the first declaration as "arrogant" (4:18) and the second as "proud" (5:2). Nevertheless, Paul's choice and use of words indicate continuity of concern. From the mention of Corinthian arrogance in reaction to the apostles' style of ministry in chapter 4, Paul specifies an instance of that arrogance by taking up the topic of immorality; thus Paul concretizes his criticism and illustrates the validity of his accusation. Moreover, behind the censure of arrogance in both chapters is Paul's overarching concern to recall and to redirect the Corinthians into a manner of life that embodies and fulfills God's commission of the Christian community to mission. As one sees through a careful, close reading of the text, Paul is upset because of the immorality in Corinth, but he treats that flamboyant phenomenon as a symptom of the true, deeper problem that he faces among the Corinthians, namely, their spiritual arrogance, which produces elitism or indifference that renders the congregation inactive and ineffective in living out God's will for their lives in this world.

Three distinct, interrelated sets of verses bring the new issues into play in Paul's communication to the Corinthians. First, in 5:1–5 Paul identifies an incident of sexual immorality in the Corinthian congregation, wherein "someone has his father's wife." He declares his shock and announces that he has already passed judgment; then he instructs the church about what to do and why. Paul's reference to the problem raises questions, but most likely the situation is that a man is living with his former stepmother. In turn, the language related to Paul's judgment, his instructions to the Corinthians, and his explanation of the prescribed action are difficult and produce at least two challenges for interpretation. The language of Paul's directions concerning the action the Corinthians are to take is ambiguous. Moreover, Paul's purpose is unclear when he tells the Corinthians, literally, "Give this one to Satan unto destruction of the flesh, in order that the spirit may be saved in the day of the Lord." What does "unto destruction of the flesh" mean? Whose "spirit" is it that "may be saved"? There are no easy answers.

Second, in 5:6–8 Paul turns to the community and their problem of boasting. The lines pick up the mention of arrogance in 5:2, and Paul criticizes the Corinthians' boasting by using the image of leaven. His point is that a little undesirable boasting goes a long way. Paul continues by declaring that the motivation for Christian purity and discipline is Christ himself, whom Paul acclaims and interprets as the paschal lamb. This traditional image registers the reality of the saving significance of Jesus' death and reminds the Corinthians that what God has done in Christ calls forth an altered manner of living for those who hear and believe the message of Christ.

Third, a new but still related line of thought comes in 5:9–13. Paul refers to a former letter that he says the Corinthians badly misunderstood. He means for the Corinthians to dissociate themselves from immoral persons in the church, not from those outside. He tells them plainly that God attends to those outside the church. In all of this, Paul's point is that the church, as those called by God in Christ, cannot tolerate within it the kind of immorality that existed in the Corinthian church. Paul urges the Corinthians to be the church that God called them to be and to live responsibly in relation to God's will for their life. Above all, he beckons the congregation away from its errors and toward its mission to the world.

5:1 / Remarkably, as Paul takes up this matter of sexual impropriety, he never directly addresses the principal parties participating in the scandal. The behavior in view here contrasts sharply with the "imitation" that the apostle advised in the prior section, and as he registers his judgment concerning the issue Paul reveals the fallacy of those who are "arrogant, as if [he] were not coming to [them]" (4:18).

Paul identifies the situation in Corinth as one of **sexual immorality**, using the Greek word *porneia*, a term commonly used for prostitution. This reference is comprehensive and was used to cover, always in a negative way, almost all forms of sexual activity outside of marriage. Jewish ethical writings reveal a particular disdain for such activity (Wis. 14; *Jub.* 25; and Acts 15:20; Rom. 1–3); and while Greco-Roman culture was generally more tolerant of casual sex than was Judaism, Paul's words **(of a kind that does not occur even among pagans)** show that Hellenism was not entirely promiscuous.

Paul's manner of describing the situation **(a man has his father's wife)** is enlightening. First, the verb **has** indicates a somewhat permanent relationship. Second, both Jewish and Roman law forbade incest, and the descriptive phrase **his father's wife** (see Lev. 18:7–8; 20:11) most likely refers to a stepmother with no indication that adultery was in mind. Specifically, Roman law forbade marriage both between adoptive parents and children and between steprelatives; thus, the man's father could be dead or divorced from this woman, and an unacceptable liaison would be formed if the "son" and the "wife" became involved sexually.

5:2 / Paul names an even greater problem: the pride, boastfulness, or arrogance of the Corinthians **(you are proud)** regarding the sexual situation identified in the previous verse. The failure of the congregation to act appropriately in relation to such a situation is the heart of Paul's concern. Not only has the Corinthian congregation condoned this culturally unacceptable behavior; Paul declares that they also are puffed up over the circumstances, and their conceit causes the apostle theological distress.

In chapter 4 Paul referred to the pride or boasting of the Corinthians, and here one finds an illustration of their assumed spiritual superiority. Paul's sarcasm indicates that the Corinthian Christians thought they were above being rankled by behavior that was deemed unacceptable by their society. The claim of spiritual superiority made them morally complacent according to Paul; thus, not only were they guilty of benign tolerance of the unacceptable, but also they were remiss in taking no action to address and to correct the situation. Being proud they showed no **grief** and took no action. So Paul faults the congregation's behavior and tells them that they should have **put out of** their midst the one **who did this** deed. This observation often seems harsh, but as the following verses show, Paul is not so much advising about discipline as he is articulating a remarkable theological truth from his apocalyptic-eschatological point of view.

5:3 / The NIV works to make clear a grammatical jumble in Greek that has often vexed translators and produced some awkward and unfortunate readings of verses 3–5. Simply put, Paul is absent "in body" but present **in spirit.** Whether he means to indicate that he is spiritually present or present in the power of the Holy Spirit is impossible to determine, but given that **judgment** is being discussed and that Paul understands his apostolic call, commission, and mission to come from God (1:1) and to be empowered by the Spirit (2:4), one should not understand him to be acting independently or autonomously. Rather, his judgment of this affair is Spirit-empowered and in the Spirit, even if Paul is referring to his being spiritually present with the Corinthians. Yet, the likelihood that Paul is emphasizing the universal presence of the Spirit over his own spiritual presence is increased by his saying that he had **already passed** judgment **on the one who did this, just as if I were present.** While the Spirit had already enlightened Paul's thinking, Paul was not yet spiritually present in the assembly of the church, which had still to meet according to his instructions.

5:4 / In the Greek, this verse begins with **in the name of** [the] **Lord Jesus.** Some translations attach this phrase to the end of verse 3 ("judgment in the name of the Lord Jesus"), but the NIV understands these words to introduce Paul's next comment concerning the congregation's gathering together for worship and fellowship (**when you are assembled** in the name of [the] Lord Jesus . . .). Both translations are defensible, although the first option is the more natural reading of the phrase.

Nevertheless, Paul assumes the Corinthians will assemble. In this context, he declares that his **spirit** will be present with **the power of** [the] **Lord Jesus.** The sentence is difficult, and the NIV seeks to clarify Paul's words by breaking the line into two complementary parts (**I am with you in** spirit, **and** the power of our Lord Jesus **is present**), although the results do not literally reflect the plain sense of the text. The difficulty for late twentieth-century readers comes in part because we do not appreciate Paul's vivid sense of the reality of the Holy Spirit as God's universal power and presence and his conviction of the real presence of the Lord Jesus. Paul assumes that the Spirit is real, that the Lord Jesus is present and powerful, and that since as a Christian he is in the Spirit, then he is truly spiritually present among the Corinthian assembly in the power of the presence of the Holy Spirit.

5:5 / Paul offers concrete instructions, but the plain sense of his words is not immediately apparent, so the NIV moves closer to paraphrase than literal translation. Quite literally Paul says, "Hand over this one to Satan unto destruction of the flesh, in order that the spirit may be saved in the day of the Lord." What does he mean?

The mention of **the day of the Lord** qualifies Paul's instructions from the perspective of future, final, apocalyptic eschatology. Thus, to grasp the sense of Paul's directions we must think in terms of a future day of final divine judgment that relativizes all current earthly existence. For Paul, the day of the Lord would bring the end to all the forces of evil (see 1 Cor. 15; 1 Thess. 4–5), but until that day evil is real and active in the world. Only God has the power to combat evil, and as God works through Jesus Christ to save humanity from the reality of sin and evil **(Satan)**, God delivers those saved from "the present evil age" (Gal. 1:4) and brings them into the realm of the Spirit. The church itself is God's newly gained "kingdom" (1 Cor. 4:20) in an otherwise fading world (1:18; 7:29–31).

For the church in Corinth to tolerate the immoral behavior of this particular man is a tragedy, for in the context of the church he is assumed to be freed from the power of evil and set at liberty in the power of the Spirit (cf. 6:12–20). If the church fails to judge this behavior, if such activity is tolerated and considered evidence of spiritual freedom, the condition of the man is hopeless. The church is charged with the responsibility of judging and disciplining those whom God has brought into the life of the church (see 5:9–13; 6:1–11), but if the members fail to live responsibly in relation to one another, the condition is dangerous. In the church God trusts the assembly, empowered by the Spirit, to judge and to correct one another. In relation to those outside the church, the battle against sin is God's work.

Because the church has failed miserably to live up to God's commission, Paul demands that the man engaging in particularly deplorable activity be thrown out of the church. This action accomplishes three important results. First, the church has to confront its own failure to do God's work. Second, the church has to live up to its responsibilities. Third, the man who was **hand**[ed] **over to Satan** is put back in the context of the world, where the church can no longer fail him and where his only real hope is the saving power of God at work in Jesus Christ. As cruel as Paul's advice may seem, he probably views this action as a final effort to save both the man and the church from hopeless corruption. Fee summarizes the issues succinctly with these observations, "What the grammar suggests, then, is that the 'destruction of his flesh' is the anticipated result of the man's being put back out into Satan's domain, while the express purpose of the action is his redemption" (*Epistle*, p. 209).

5:6 / Paul summarizes his point of view and advances his argument in this and the following verses. First, he bluntly states the point he has made repeatedly: **Your boasting is not good.** Having driven that conviction home, Paul introduces the metaphor of leaven in a rhetorical question. In antiquity **yeast** was a common image for a small matter that had the potential to affect a much larger or more significant situation. The implication of Paul's sarcastic question is that the Corinthians ought to, but apparently do not, know better than to tolerate "a little" immorality.

5:7 / Having introduced the metaphor of leaven or **yeast,** Paul proceeds to develop that image to bolster his previous insistence that the man engaging in immoral sexual activity be put out of the congregation. To make this point Paul relates the image of yeast to the celebration of unleavened bread that made up part of the Passover ritual. At Passover the custom in Judaism was to cleanse the home of all yeast so as to ensure that the bread for the festival would be unleavened. This cleansing ritual itself symbolized for Paul and all Jews the elimination of all forms of wickedness from the life of the devout Jew. The original image of bread that was made so quickly that it had no time to rise was superseded by the image of cleansing, and Paul builds on that idea. He advises the Corinthians to eliminate the **old** yeast in order to guarantee that they would themselves be **a new batch**

[of dough] **without yeast,** that their new life as Christians would
be free from immorality or corruption.

Paul registers this thought in two bold statements. First, he
declares that the members of the Corinthian congregation **really
are** new, unleavened dough. They are what they are by God's
grace, and now they have only to live up to who God has called
them and empowered them by the Spirit to be. Second, in a
further development of the Passover theme, Paul declares the
power of God that makes all this new life real, saying, **For Christ,
our Passover lamb, has been sacrificed.** Here Paul refers to the
saving significance of Jesus' death in a simple metaphor that is
often misunderstood. This image is one of divine provision in
dealing with the perils faced by humanity. The Passover lamb
was not technically a sacrifice, but it was a means through which
God marked out the chosen people in order to save them from
wrathful destruction. While the image of sacrifice is not brought
into play in this statement, one should not miss Paul's clear
point: because of what God has done and is doing in Jesus Christ,
humans are set free to eliminate corruption from their lives
and to become the persons that God's Spirit is empowering
them to be.

5:8 / Once more Paul extends the imagery of the Passover metaphor in order to call the Corinthians to a manner of living consistent with God's will for their lives. He admonishes
them and apparently all other Christians, **Therefore let us keep
the Festival.** If Christ is the lamb and **yeast** is immorality, those
celebrating Christ are to free themselves by the power of God of
malice and wickedness and to devote themselves to **sincerity
and truth.** This admonition is not a mere exercise in moral cheer-
leading; rather, Paul is calling the Corinthians to live freed from
sin and freed for godliness because God has already acted in
Christ to make provision for the reality of their new living.

5:9–10 / Having raised the issue of eliminating evil from
life, Paul revisits a misunderstanding of a previous letter he had
sent to Corinth. From Paul's comments in these verses one gath-
ers the degree of misunderstanding was nearly complete, and
while it is impossible to determine whether the Corinthians deliberately ignored or misinterpreted Paul, the earlier reference to
arrogant disregard of the apostle (4:18) may indicate active resis-
tance to Paul's directions. In either case, Paul clarifies his position to preclude further misunderstanding.

Paul had advised the Corinthian Christians **not to associate with sexually immoral people.** Apparently that advice was misconstrued. The church had blithely tolerated the behavior of the man who had taken up with his father's wife; yet some people tried to shun the sexually immoral outside the church. Paul clarifies his remarks: the Corinthians are not to condone sexual immorality in the church, nor are they to treat those outside the church with disdain; neither activity is part of the life to which they are called.

Put differently, Paul's concerns seem to be with Christian witness and mission. The failure to deal with sexual immorality within the congregation exposes the church to criticism by those outside the church who themselves know better than to approve of such behavior. Moreover, an aloof attitude toward those outside the church who have not yet experienced God's saving power hinders involvement with non-Christians, so that the members of the church can neither evangelize nor conduct mission. Rather than prescribing a spiritual isolationism, Paul anticipates ongoing involvement of the members of the congregation with all of those who are outside the church, whether moral or immoral.

5:11 / Paul reiterates and expands his basic point: the members of the Corinthian congregation are neither to tolerate nor to associate with anyone in the church who manifests wickedness. Paul's tone and context make it clear that he is not calling for Christian condescension or arrogance; nor is he encouraging a judgmental spirit, although his advice has been badly misinterpreted in that direction. Rather, Paul tells the Corinthians not to have dealings with those who would attempt both to be part of the church and to continue to live in a manner unworthy of the truth of the gospel. Paul mentions so-called Christians who are **sexually immoral, greedy, an idolater, a slanderer, a drunkard, or a swindler.** This list is illustrative, not exhaustive. Paul is calling for the Corinthians to exercise discretion; he is not attempting to catalogue activities that are unacceptable for Christians. In turn, Paul directs the Corinthians not even to eat with such a so-called Christian. This remark is general, prohibiting meal fellowship in all forms and not merely restricting association at community meals or at the celebration of the Lord's Supper, although those specific settings were to be avoided.

5:12–13 / Four short statements—two rhetorical questions, a declaration, and a quote from the LXX—summarize and epitomize Paul's directions to the Corinthians concerning judgment. First, he queries, **What business is it of mine to judge those outside the church?** This question assumes that judging those outside the church is not a task given to Christians, and it implies that the judgment of the world is God's responsibility. Second, Paul asks, **Are you not to judge those inside?** The question is put to the congregation as a whole, not to each individual; and although there is a negative cast to this question, the Greek grammar assumes the answer, "Yes, we ourselves are to judge those in the church."

Following these questions Paul makes a brief declaration that clarifies the anticipated answer to both questions, **God will judge those outside.** This comment gives the basis for the two previous points. Because God judges those outside the church, Christians should not judge them. Because God judges those outside the church, Christians have the responsibility to judge those who are part of the church. Paul's declaration looks back to these two points, but in context it anticipates and clarifies the point he makes in the citation of Deuteronomy 17:7, "**Expel the wicked man from among you.**" The church failed to render responsible judgment, so Paul quotes Scripture to certify his point that the man must be returned to the world, where God alone executes judgment. The sad situation is that the church failed God, itself, and the man who was in error. The only hope in this hopeless situation is the drastic action of returning the man to the context of the world, where God alone is his hope—not the church and not the man's own sensibilities. The church's failure to correct the man, not merely the man's wickedness or Paul's vindictiveness, necessitated this seemingly harsh course of action.

Additional Notes §13

Points of continuity between chs. 4 and 5 were noted in my introduction to ch. 5. Nevertheless, not all interpreters see the points of connection. M. C. De Boer ("The Composition of 1 Corinthians," *NTS* 40 [1994], pp. 229–45) makes a careful study of the relationship of chs. 1–4 to chs. 5–16 and concludes that there were two phases to the composition of the letter, so that effectively 1 Corinthians is a combination of two practically independent letters. Most important, De Boer argues that there was a double occasion for the writing of the single, compound writing: conversation with Chloe's people (chs. 1–4) and the visit by Stephanas, Fortunatus, and Achaicus, who bore a letter to Paul from Corinth (chs. 5–16). Thus, De Boer sees Paul launching out here in a new direction.

5:1 / The word translated as "pagans" is the Gk. word *ethnos,* which is frequently rendered as "Gentile" or "nation." Late twentieth-century connotations of "pagan" may mislead the reader to conclude that Paul is offering a moral judgment on Gentile culture at large. But one should recall that Paul uses the designation *ethnos* at Gal. 1:16 and Rom. 1:5 in reference to his work among the "Gentiles." Already in 1 Cor. the NIV translated *ethnos* using "Gentile" at 1:23. Paul's usage suggests he means to designate non-Jews with this term.

One sees elements of Greco-Roman law concerning such incestuous relations in the frequently cited passages in Gaius's *Institutiones* 1.63 and Cicero's *Pro Cluentio* 6(15). For further information on ancient Greek and Roman laws of marriage see A. Berger and B. Nicholas, "Marriage, Law of," *OCD,* pp. 649–50.

5:2 / The word for **proud** in this sentence literally means "to be puffed up"; it is the same word that Paul used in discussing the pride or arrogance of the Corinthians concerning spirituality (ch. 4). The graphic quality of Paul's language continues with his choice of words concerning the Corinthians' being **filled with grief,** which is the language of mourning (Gk. *pentheō*) associated with death or insurmountable loss. From the clue provided by the reference to mourning, B. S. Rosner (" *'ouchi mallon epenthēsate':* Corporate Responsibility in 1 Corinthians 5," *NTS* 38 [1992], pp. 470–73) makes connections with the LXX in arguing that Paul viewed expulsion as necessary for the protection of the church in relationship to God. Whether that is the only dynamic at work is debatable, but Paul is concerned throughout this letter with the edification of the church; corruption would hinder edification or perhaps make it impossible.

5:3 / Paul introduces the language of judgment in this verse, a theme related to the issue of church discipline (see G. Harris, "The Beginnings of Church Discipline: 1 Corinthians 5," *NTS* 37 [1991], pp. 1–21; S. J. Kistemaker, " 'Deliver This Man to Satan' [1 Cor 5:5]: A Case Study in Church Discipline," *MSJ* 3 [1992], pp. 33–46). The theme colors the remaining discussion, but the language of judgment (Gk. *krinō*) abates until v. 12, when Paul employs the verb "to judge" three times with great rhetorical force.

5:4 / The Gk. manuscript evidence is divided as to whether Paul wrote **in the name of our Lord Jesus,** "in the name of the Lord," "in the name of the Lord Jesus," "in the name of our Lord Jesus Christ," or "in the name of the Lord Jesus Christ." While a final determination is impossible, the NIV seems prudent in its choice of texts, since the pronoun "our" is appropriate to the situation and compatible with the other usages in this section. But the title "Christ" was more likely added than omitted from so solemn a pronouncement as Paul makes here. Had he written "Christ" originally, it would not likely have been omitted.

5:5 / The mention of **Satan** in this verse is one of ten references to this figure in the Pauline corpus: Rom. 16:20; 1 Cor. 5:5; 7:5; 2 Cor. 2:11; 11:14; 12:7; 1 Thess. 2:18; 2 Thess. 2:9; 1 Tim. 1:20; 5:15. The general pattern of Paul's mentioning Satan shows that he understood Satan to be an adversary who opposed or hindered God's will and work among God's people.

The day of the Lord was an eschatological day of judgment that Paul expected and to which he taught other early Christians to look forward despite the association of wrath with that day, for it was God's day of salvation in and through the Lord Jesus Christ. See 1 Cor. 1:8; 5:5; 2 Cor. 1:14; 1 Thess. 5:2; 2 Thess. 2:2; also Rom. 2:5, 16; 2 Cor. 6:2; 2 Thess. 1:10; 2 Tim. 1:18; 4:8; and cf. Eph. 6:13. Paul's use of the phrase in the current context of controversy, difficulty, and judgment still focuses on the salvific nature of that time, which occurs ultimately for the good of the Christian community. See T. Worden, "The Remission of Sins—I," *Scripture* 9 (1957), pp. 65–79.

The NIV employs the phrase **his spirit saved,** implying that Paul's directions aim at saving "the spirit" of the man who is to be ejected from the church. The Gk. text does not have the possessive pronoun "his"; rather, it literally reads "the spirit may be saved," so that from the original text one is uncertain whose or what "spirit" Paul had in mind, the man's, the church's, or the Spirit per se and the Spirit's efforts.

5:6 / The further mention of **boasting** in this verse echoes the major theme of chs. 1–3 and resounds the note struck at 4:7. This theme is never far out of sight, no matter what Paul's focus in the various sections of 1 Cor.

5:7–8 / The OT directives concerning **yeast** at the time of the Passover **Festival** are at Exod. 12:14–20; 13:6–10; Deut. 16:3–8.

On 5:1–8, see the helpful study by J. T. South ("A Critique of the 'Curse/Death' Interpretation of 1 Corinthians 5:1–8," *NTS* 39 [1993], pp. 539–61), who effectively shows that Paul's final objective in dealing with the man in question was his expulsion, not more. For a reading of this chapter that takes seriously Paul's concerns for the church, not simply its dealings with the man, see L. Vander Broek, "Discipline and Community: Another Look at 1 Corinthians 5," *Ref R* 48 (1994), pp. 5–13; furthermore, in attempting to recognize and comprehend the ethical dimension of this ecclesiological discussion, see R. B. Hays ("Ecclesiology and Ethics in 1 Corinthians," *Ex Auditu* 10 [1994], pp. 31–43), who makes the important point that for Paul ethical concerns are always related to ecclesiology.

5:9 / The verb translated "associate with" in Gk. is *synanamignysthai,* a vivid piece of vocabulary that indicates "mingling" or "mixing" with someone or something. Paul is referring not to casual associations or chance encounters but to regular and prolonged contact or interaction. Given the vivacious character of Paul's words, perhaps modern translations would do well to paraphrase the verb partially as "to hang around with."

5:10–11 / The references in these verses anticipate the more extensive listing that follows shortly in 1 Cor. 6:9–10. Paul deems certain behaviors and characteristics unacceptable and intolerable in the life of the Christian community. The descriptive categories used here to name persons and behaviors that are unacceptable are similar to other catalogues of vices and virtues commonly found in NT writings and other literature from the Greco-Roman period. Nevertheless, P. S. Zaas ("Catalogues and Context: 1 Corinthians 5 and 6," *NTS* 34 [1988], pp. 622–29) argues persuasively that the items named here by Paul are chosen as pertinent and appropriate illustrations of the real situation of which he was aware in Corinth.

5:13 / This citation comes mainly from Deut. 17:7 LXX, but it also reflects the language and thought of Deut. 19:19; 21:21; 22:21, 24; 24:7.

§14 Going to Judgment before Non-Christians (1 Cor. 6:1–11)

Having raised the issue of the relations of Christians both to other Christians and to those outside the church, Paul's mind seems to move to the matter of how Christians relate to one another outside the life of the church. His discussion focuses on the issue of Christians suing each other in pagan courts of law. One cannot determine how Paul knows about this problem; nevertheless, he discusses the matter in some detail. Although interpreters regularly refer to these verses as an excursus, the discussion is not simply a digression from the main lines of thought.

6:1 / Paul views Christians taking one another into pagan courts as an example of the degree of the Corinthians' lack of understanding—or better, love—as will become clear later in the letter (ch. 13). He launches his critique of the Corinthians' misbehavior with a rhetorical question that is cast in a conditional form: "If X, then Y?" If someone **has a dispute with another,** then does that one **dare** to go to **the ungodly for judgment?** There is biting irony in the question, for Paul's query implies two things: that the Corinthian Christians are suing Christians before non-Christians; and that it is absurd, unthinkable, and inappropriate for a Christian to take another Christian before non-Christians for judgment. Paul calls the non-Christians **the ungodly,** more literally "the unjust" (Gk. *tōn adikōn*), which is not so much a description of the moral state of the non-Christian as it is Paul's description of their current relationship to God's justifying work in Jesus Christ. This Corinthian behavior is an explicit failure of the members of the church to live up to their God-given responsibilities. Paul elaborates the inappropriateness of the Corinthians' behavior and by implication corrects their misunderstanding and misbehavior.

6:2–3 / Paul fires off three more sharp rhetorical questions that point out that what the Corinthians should know they either do not know or ignore. The image of the **saints** judging **the world** adapts a motif of Jewish apocalyptic eschatology that depicts the day of final reckoning as including judgment (Dan. 7:22; *1 Enoch* 1.9; Wis. 3:8). One must ask, however, whether this statement contradicts what Paul had already said about the church's capacity to judge in 5:9–13—that the members of the church are not given the responsibility to judge those outside the church. How can Christians not judge non-Christians and **judge** the world at the same time? Obviously, Paul is thinking about two distinct times. The instructions in 5:9–13 are for the Corinthians' present time; the judgment being discussed in 6:2–3 is a particular instance of future judgment. Employing a rhetorical device, Paul is formulating an argument from greater to lesser—from future to present, from **angels** to **the things of this life** (in the context of the Christian community). Paul argues that if Christians will judge the world in a great apocalyptic future judgment, then they should be capable of exercising judgment over the lesser concern of their own internal affairs here and now. Paul's admonition is for the Corinthians to take life in Christ's community seriously, acting with a sense of responsibility toward one another now that befits their responsibility in the future.

6:4 / The NIV seems to miss the point with the translation of this sentence. The critical Greek text of NA[27] and the English translation of the majority of other versions punctuates this line as a question, not as a declaration. Paul continues with sarcasm, as is evident in the reference to those outside the church as those **of little account in the church,** and the more likely sense of his words is that he poses yet another rhetorical question. The NRSV renders the Greek accurately and in the seemingly preferable form of a question, "If you have ordinary cases, then, do you appoint as judges those who have no standing in the church?" This question assumes the answer would be, "Of course not!" Yet, by taking the matters between Christians to legal settings where non-Christians have the final say, the Corinthians were effectively appointing as judges those who had no standing in the church.

6:5 / Paul's intentional rhetoric of sarcasm becomes explicit in this verse as he explains that he intended to shame the Corinthians. Late twentieth-century culture is generally suspi-

cious and even disdainful of **shame,** but without trying to re-
habilitate that ploy or encourage that emotion, one should
remember that honor and shame were two of the most powerful
cultural currents in antiquity. From such a point of view, if persons acted in ways that were not honorable—and the Corinthians were not acting honorably in Paul's theological estimation—
then they were acting shamefully. Paul's effort to shame the
Corinthians is a sincere effort to register the inappropriateness of
the Corinthians' behavior in a stark and persuasive fashion.
Today, one might paraphrase, "I say this to show you that you
are a failure!" This statement is still not a pleasant confrontation,
but it is not necessarily a psychologically devious method. With
such clear purpose, Paul adds yet another rhetorical question implying the absurdity of the Corinthians' behavior: **Is it possible
that there is nobody among you wise enough to judge a dispute
between believers?**

6:6 / The wording and grammar of this brief verse allow one to understand the sentence as either a statement or a
question. The NIV renders the words in the form of a declaration,
but as H. Conzelmann observes, "Standing as it does between
verses 5 and 7 this should be taken as a question" (*1 Corinthians,*
p. 105). Understood in this way, the NRSV translation seems preferable, "but a believer goes to court against a believer—and before unbelievers at that?" Paul's rhetorical question registers the
degree of his incredulity at the Corinthians' practices.

6:7–8 / In these lines Paul advances his argument by declaring bluntly that the will to assert one's own rights at the expense of others and at the expense of the general image of the
community is defeat. The rhetoric of sarcasm and shame are
gone at this point as he directly confronts the Corinthians with
the factual meaning of their actions. Yet the urgency of his appeal comes through again in two further rhetorical questions
(Why not rather be wronged? Why not rather be cheated?). Paul
implies that it would be better to be wronged and cheated than to
act as they have been conducting themselves, taking their problems out of the context of the church and into the world, where
they are appearing before nonbelievers for judgment. The implication of Paul's comments is that by doing what they have done,
the Corinthians have failed to live up to their God-given responsibilities for maintaining the life of the community; moreover, by
parading their problems before non-Christians the Corinthians

both have presented a shameful image and have failed to bear the witness to those outside the church that is their privilege and responsibility to communicate.

6:9–10 / Once again a rhetorical question opens this new segment of the discussion. The wording is deliberate: **Do you not know that the wicked will not inherit the kingdom of God?** Paul implies that the Corinthians should know this theological truth, even though their behavior suggests that they do not. Paul is not saying that the wicked will not inherit the kingdom of God because they are not good enough; the Corinthians were once just as wicked. Rather, he is reminding the Corinthians that God's triumph over evil eliminates unrighteousness. Wickedness has no future with God, and so those who are devoting themselves to ungodly behaviors are forming lifestyles that are contrary to God's will and work and that will not be given a place in God's kingdom. Don't delude yourselves, says Paul; some things do not belong in God's kingdom. The list begun in verse 9 and continued in verse 10 is, as was the listing in 5:9–11, a catalogue to illustrate certain characteristics and conditions that will not gain entry into the kingdom of God.

These lines become a brief meditation on "unrighteousness" (Gk. *adikos*). The NIV translates the Greek word **wicked,** while the NRSV renders it with "wrongdoers," which catches Paul's focus on actions. Nevertheless, either English rendering runs the danger of minimizing Paul's point throughout this discussion that improper behavior results from a faulty theology that fails to recognize the reality of divine transformation in the human experience of salvation. In this instance Paul's true concern is not to catalogue persons who are guilty of scandalous actions, **the sexually immoral, idolaters, adulterers, male prostitutes, homosexual offenders, slanderers, swindlers,** and so forth. Paul's true concern is to remind the Corinthians of their pre-Christian pasts, as becomes clear in the following lines.

6:11 / This verse is the most important statement in this section. From a frank recognition of the character of **some** of the Corinthians before their conversion, Paul elaborates why they now are, and in turn ought to be, different. They are **washed, sanctified,** and **justified.** These terms do not aim at delineating various states of grace or various stages of Christian existence. They are a set of metaphors attempting to describe the indescribably multifaceted experience of God's transforming grace. With this rich description Paul locates the Corinthians theologically, identifying them in relation to Christ, and recognizes the priority of God in their salvation and in their current conduct. In hearing these words the Corinthians would surely think of their baptism, the gift of the Holy Spirit, and their new, right relationship with God—recalling them as a magnificent and incomprehensible movement of God's gracious **Spirit** through **the name of the Lord Jesus Christ.** Above all, in the entire dramatic declaration, Paul makes it clear that all this transformation that the Corinthians experienced comes, as the series of passive verbs that Paul employs show, through the work of God's Spirit in Jesus Christ.

Additional Notes §14

On the relationship between chs. 5 and 6, see W. Deming ("The Unity of 1 Corinthians 5–6," *JBL* 115 [1996], pp. 289–312), who creatively suggests that there are not two but one background against which the materials in both these chapters should be read; that is, there has been a single case of sexual misconduct that has resulted in the Corinthians' engaging in legal actions in secular courts.

6:1 / For a concise overview of the legal system and its operation that Paul would have had in mind at this point, see A. Berger and B. Nicholas, "Law and Procedure, Roman," *OCD*, pp. 583–90.

6:2 / Paul's rhetorical phrase, **Do you not know . . . ,** occurs again in vv. 3, 9, 15–16, 19. The question may imply that Paul had earlier offered the Corinthians teaching on this subject, but he may be assuming that the points he is making are self-evident to anyone who thinks about the issues.

The image of judging at the final judgment is part of and typical of Jewish apocalyptic thought. While the idea of God's elect taking part in the acts of final judgment may be developed throughout the apocalyptic tradition from Dan. 7:22, the notion of God's people enacting Christian judgment is found in and consistent with the eschatological teachings of Jesus: Matt. 19:28–29; Luke 22:30; Rev. 3:21—cf. *Psalms of Solomon* 17:26, 29.

6:7 / Paul consistently employs plural forms of both Gk. pronouns and verb endings in this discussion, so he has the entire community in view in his remarks. Nevertheless, as N. Watson (*The First Epistle to the Corinthians* [Epworth Commentaries; London: Epworth, 1992], p. 55) astutely observes, Paul's point of view shifts in his address to the community. Initially he seems to be speaking to the initiators of the lawsuits who have suffered some kind of wrong; then he turns toward the perpetrators of the wrongdoing, although still addressing them in the context of the full congregation. He does what he tells them to do: handle the situation in the context of the church.

6:9–10 / This verse contains Paul's first of three references to "God's kingdom" (*theou basileia* or *basileia theou*) in this letter—see 6:9–10; 15:50. The same phrase occurs in a similar context at Gal. 5:21, although Paul knows and uses a synonymous phrase, "the kingdom of God" (*basileia tou theou*) in other settings: Rom. 14:17; 1 Cor. 4:20; Col. 4:11; 2 Thess. 1:5. In both cases Paul is using a traditional phrase from apocalyptic-eschatological Jewish thought, and he seems to indicate by these phrases the time, place, and experience of God's supreme, exclusive rule.

Certain elements of Paul's list of **wicked** persons and behaviors have caught the attention of much of the church in late twentieth-century discussions of church life. The pertinent materials merit careful attention. As we have seen, in 1 Cor. 6:9–11 Paul chides the Corinthians for their spiritual arrogance that led to their failure to address immorality and interchurch disputes in a responsible fashion. In exhorting the Corinthians to faithful action Paul contrasts the Corinthians' present quality of life in Christ with their past unrighteousness or wickedness. To make his point Paul catalogues in a stereotypical fashion the previous unrighteous characteristics of the now-justified Corinthians. He describes those who belong to this world, not God's kingdom, in this way: "Do not be deceived: Neither the sexually immoral nor idolaters nor adulterers nor male prostitutes nor homosexual offenders nor thieves nor the greedy nor drunkards nor slanderers nor swindlers will inherit the kingdom of God. And that is what some of you were."

The word translated in the NIV as "male prostitutes" is *malakoi* in Gk. and literally means "soft ones," probably referring to the so-called passive partner in homosexual activity. The word translated as "homosexual offenders" is *arsenokoitai* in Gk. and literally means "male bedders," perhaps referring to the other partner in the homosexual arrangement. These words have sorely vexed interpreters and translators, as consulting several translations reveals. Sometimes, because of the influential work of John Boswell (*Christianity, Social Tolerance, and Homosexuality: Gay People in Western Europe from the Beginning of the Christian Era to the Fourteenth Century* [Chicago: University of Chicago, 1980]) one reads or hears that *malakoi* indicated "unrestrained," "wanton," or "dissolute" and *arsenokoitai* indicated "male prostitutes," so that there is no denunciation in 1 Cor. 6 of homosexual activity. Today, however, because of the incisive work of Robin Scroggs (*The New Testament and Homosexuality: Contextual Background for Contemporary Debate* [Philadelphia: Fortress, 1983]) interpreters almost universally understand the word *arsenokoitai* in 1 Cor. 6:9 to be an idiom derived from the LXX of Lev. 18:22, which in part reads *kai meta arsenos ou koimēthēsē koitēn gynaikeian* ("and you shall not sleep in bed with a man as with a woman") and Lev. 20:13, which contains the words *kai hos an koimēthē meta arsenos koitēn gynaikos* ("and whoever may lie in bed with a man as with a woman"), so that Paul's declaration presupposes the condemnation of homosexual acts by the Holiness Code of Lev. 18:22 and 20:13.

Nevertheless, Watson (*First Epistle,* p. 56) makes the insightful observation that if there is a prevalent point between the items Paul has chosen to include in this listing, it is the common characteristic of "ruthless self-gratification, reckless of other people's rights." Such an attitude, which produces deplorable behaviors, is the ungodliness Paul is concerned to criticize; he is not aiming at ranking or rating sins.

6:11 / The threefold listing **(washed, sanctified, justified)** is most likely a forceful rhetorical reminder, not a description of spiritual operations and mysteries. Paul adamantly argues that Christian life must be consistent with the truth of the gospel, and he reminds the Corinthians that the experience of God's grace means the reality of the believers' obedience to God's will.

§15 The Character of Christian Freedom (1 Cor. 6:12–20)

These nine verses form a complex segment of the letter. One finds here quotations from the Corinthians and a citation of the LXX. The verses are largely cast in the diatribe style of popular Hellenistic philosophy. One also encounters traditional elements of early Christian doctrine. All of this material is woven together in service to Paul's deliberate line of argumentation.

Paul builds and argues a case in verses 12–17 in response to the thinking and declarations of the Corinthians. As the NIV and other translations recognize by placing the statement **"Everything is permissible for me"** in quotations, Paul employs a pattern of rhetoric wherein he quotes the position of those with whom he is in imaginary dialogue in order to respond to their thinking. The hypothetical conversation goes back and forth. In verses 18–20 Paul's rhetoric takes the form of a clear frontal attack. He directs the Corinthians to **flee from sexual immorality.** Then, he informs the Corinthians that their **body** is **a temple of the Holy Spirit within** [them]. He speaks to the entire congregation, bluntly telling them, **You are not your own.** Paul reminds them that they were bought with a price. The language is a metaphorical reference to redemption as ransom, and it alludes in an undeveloped way to the death of Jesus. That the Corinthians belong to God is the ultimate qualification of their freedom.

One should see that throughout this section Paul jabs his readers with the rhetorical refrain, **Do you not know . . . ?** The implication is that the Corinthians do not know what they ought to know. Paul writes to factor into the Corinthians' thinking new information that should correct their ignorance.

6:12–13 / At a glance Paul seems to launch into a new topic or in a new direction, but as careful examination reveals, he is merely developing his current lines of thought and discussion at new levels as he takes up still further, specific elements of the situation he faced among the Corinthians. Initially, the level of reflection is general, referring to **everything**. Today we would describe this discussion as being concerned with the lifestyle of believers. At issue in this deliberation is what the Corinthian Christians are free to do as a result of having been "saved" in Christ and freed from "perishing" (see 1:18). Perhaps the best way to follow Paul's imaginary conversation with the Corinthians in these diatribe-style verses is to set out the lines of verses 12–13a in the form of a drama:

Corinthians:	**"Everything is permissible for me";**
Paul:	**but not everything is beneficial.**
Corinthians:	**"Everything is permissible for me";**
Paul:	**but I will not be mastered by anything.**
Corinthians:	**"Food for the stomach and the stomach for food";**
Paul:	**but God will destroy them both.**

The Corinthians' slogan literally says, "All things to me permissible." This is a remarkable claim, and they may have learned this statement from Paul himself, for he never denies its validity; rather, he qualifies the idea with his arguments. Beyond the generic notion of everything, Paul initially mentions **food,** which will become the subject of detailed discussion in later chapters of the letter. For now, one should know that in antiquity many meals were served in pagan temples, and often the food itself was from the sacrifice(s) offered to a pagan god or goddess. In this connection, some Corinthians must have maintained that it made no difference what or where they ate.

The Corinthians' claim was controversial, and Paul recognizes the problematic nature of this assertion briefly before moving to the issue of sexual relations (sexual promiscuity or **sexual immorality,** as Paul terms it). In this regard, it may also be pertinent that at times sacred prostitution was practiced as part of pagan worship, especially in fertility cults, although nonreligious prostitution was often commonplace in the ancient world. Regardless of the specific circumstances in Corinth, Paul focuses the discussion in terms of eating/food and sexual relations. The earlier observations in chapter 5 introduced the matter of sexual behavior, which now is treated in conjunction with comestibles—a remarkable coupling that shows the deeper issues are not copulation and consumption but the nature of Christian freedom and the theological significance of believers' behavior. In this way, Paul's critique moves forward to call the Corinthians into a responsible relationship to **the Lord.** By articulating the paradox that **the body is ... meant ... for** the Lord, **and the Lord for the body,** Paul tells the Corinthians that freedom is for the Lord, not merely for personal pleasure.

In developing the argument in this manner Paul thinks corporately about the "body" of the Corinthian believers who are the church, as is clear in the plural "you" forms of the subsequent verses. This form contrasts sharply with the Corinthians' individualism, "all things for me permissible." Paul's concern is with more than personal or individual morality, although his words to the church have clear and unmistakable implications for each and every believer. Few statements in Scripture articulate the profoundly relational nature of Christian existence and identity as well as the words "the body ... for the Lord, and the Lord for the body." Moreover, in this insight one finds the basis of the missional nature of Christian life—believers live in all aspects of life for the Lord who himself lives for, in, and through the words and deeds of his people.

6:14 / The seemingly abrupt introduction of the subject of the resurrection is an early anticipation of the extensive discussion of this topic, which was apparently a source of controversy among the Corinthians, that will eventually follow in chapter 15. While Paul here introduces that crucial topic, his main concern is to register the awe-inspiring truth of the power of God. God's power, demonstrated in its ultimate form in the resurrection of Jesus Christ, is a power that lays claim on the life of the believers, both in the future through resurrection per se and already as the believers live in this world. God's claim means that the body of the believer—or better, the body of the believers—and the bodies of the believers—do not belong to the believer(s). They belong to the power of God, which raises them from the dead and which already works to transform them in the present. God has a clear claim on the believers; they do not merely have the freedom to make claims because of God. Indeed, God's own mission manifests itself powerfully in resurrection and transformation of human life.

The Corinthians contended that what they knew or thought they knew had given them an abstract principle, freedom, that could and had produced less than desirable results. But Paul does not deal in abstractions. Freedom, according to Paul, is characterized by pursuing what it best; freedom does not lead to a new form of slavery. The Corinthians mistakenly claim an inner freedom that places them above the mundane realities of the world, and they are eager to demonstrate their liberation. Yet Paul reminds them that God's power is over their lives now through the resurrection of the Lord and in the future in their own anticipated resurrection.

6:15 / If Paul's remarks about the Corinthians' attitude toward food and sexual activity is accurate, the will to display freedom had gotten out of hand, although one should not forget that Paul creates deliberate distortions in his arguments in order to score his points. The Corinthians seem to assume that freedom means they are at liberty to gratify their every appetite. Paul expresses mild shock that some Corinthians, aware of their freedom, work from the notion that all foods are fit for consumption to conclude that engaging in casual sex with a prostitute is a celebration of their freedom.

Paul challenges and corrects such thinking with the rhetorical question, **Do you not know that your bodies are members of Christ himself?** Again, he anticipates the major discussion of the body of Christ that will follow in chapter 12, although for now he is content to make the point that belonging to Christ or being a part of Christ's body should mean that the believers give priority to Christ and his concerns rather than to their own questionable desires. Paul's rhetoric is both ironic and sarcastic as he continues his query, **Shall I then take the members of Christ and unite them with a prostitute? Never!** The form of this question and answer would register immediately with the Corinthians as a diatribe, setting up an assumed false position and then knocking it down. The tone is strong and colloquial, and the readers in Corinth would recognize Paul's intention to expose the shamefully absurd character of their behavior.

6:16 / Again Paul queries the Corinthians in rhetorical fashion to show their error and ignorance, **Do you not know ...?** His description becomes graphic: **he who unites himself with a prostitute is one with her in body.** The reference to body emphasizes the relational nature of life and hints in the context of this religious discussion at much more than a mere physical union. To make his point with all possible force, Paul quotes Genesis 2:24 in the second portion of this verse. On the one hand, he uses Scripture to denounce involvement with prostitutes; on the other hand, the citation sets up the following verse (6:17), a crucial statement of the nature of the spiritual union of Christians with the Lord.

6:17 / This statement shows clearly that Paul is thinking of the relational nature of interpersonal involvements as he writes concerning the unacceptable behavior of some in Corinth. Yet note that Paul does not say that when the believer **unites with the Lord,** they are one body. Rather, when the believer unites with the Lord, the two become **one in spirit.** Paul labors to say that the relationship between believers and the risen Lord is as real as that which exists between two persons in a sexual union, although the different character of the union of the Christian and the Lord is registered in Paul's reference to the spirit. Such a relationship precludes the believer from asserting his or her own will independently of the will of the Lord, for as they are united the believer comes into a relationship to the Lord who is himself the Lord of the one spirit that unites them.

6:18 / Paul's command to the Corinthians is both brief and clear, **"Flee** fornication!" The sense of the words that follow are not, however, so easily discernible: **All other sins a man commits are outside his body, but he who sins sexually sins against his own body.** Part of the problem for understanding this statement is that in Greek the word "other" does not occur in the sentence. Quite literally Paul writes, "Every sinful act that a person does is outside the body, but the one fornicating sins in/into one's very own body." While few translations suggest such an understanding, perhaps Paul is trying to say that fornicating is like all sin and is something more, not merely that fornicating is different from other sins. Since Paul clearly disapproves of fornication, he would understand fornicating to be joining into an inappropriate relationship. How exactly Paul understands this particular illegitimate alliance to be different from other unacceptable unions is not clear from his comments. His sweeping rhetoric is not detailed, but there can be no doubt about the apostle's basic point—fornicating or sexual involvement with a prostitute is not appropriate conduct for the believer, who is united with Christ in spirit and so defiles the body (perhaps the body of Christ) with such sinful behavior. In chapter 7, Paul insists that marriage is the only relationship in which sexual union is appropriate and permissible.

6:19 / Paul turns more directly to religious imagery in the following lines. In this verse he reiterates the point he made earlier in 3:16, **your body is a temple of the Holy Spirit.** Paul's pronouns are plural, addressing the entire body of believers in Corinth. He does not single out only those who have been fornicating, for while those particular persons have acted inappropriately, they have acted in a manner that ultimately touches and shapes the life of the Christian community. Thus, the community is in need of instruction, for in different but complementary ways all have been involved in the degradation of the body of believers.

Moreover, Paul qualifies his reference to the Holy Spirit by adding the phrases **who is in you, whom you have received from God.** All the pronouns are plural, indicating that Paul directs his remarks to all the believers at once. With these brief lines Paul registers at least four crucial theological truths. First, the Spirit is present and active among the Corinthians, empowering them to live the life to which they have been called. Second, the Spirit comes to them from God, whose will is to be manifest in the life of the Spirit-filled community of the Corinthian believers. God's authority, will, presence, and power form and should inform the shape of the temple of believers in Corinth. Third, the Holy Spirit was received by the Corinthians. They did not earn or produce the Spirit's presence among them; God acted graciously in bestowing the Spirit on the Christian community in Corinth. Fourth, the Spirit dwells in the temple so that the Corinthians are bound into an intimate relationship to God through the presence of God's Spirit. They are not independently blessed, but they live in relation to the life that God lives among them.

Paul's final words in this verse, **you are not your own,** may form the final part of the question that began at the outset of the verse: **Do you not know that . . .** you are not your own? The sense is self-evident: the Corinthians are neither autonomous individuals nor an autonomous community of human beings. God founded, forms, and holds a claim on the lives of these and all other believers. No greater truth can be brought home to the church and its members in every generation. How often do discussions of personal and community affairs (freedoms? rights? responsibilities?) take their start and find their course from the reality that every aspect of the life of believers belongs to God? Nothing we have is ours to have and to do with as we please. All of life belongs to God, and it is ultimately God's will and work that is to be accomplished in our lives and in our life together. The believer and the believers find identity, purpose, direction, and meaning from the foundational nature of the relationship that God has established in creating us and in reclaiming us in Jesus Christ and the power of the Holy Spirit.

6:20 / In concluding his deliberation as it extends through chapter 6, Paul expounds the foundation of the relationship that forms each element of life in relationship to God. Stated bluntly, believers have been bought by God! In 7:23 Paul will reiterate this same idea, **you were bought at a price,** which he makes here as the crescendo of his argument. In 6:11 Paul used the metaphors of washing, sanctification, and justification to elaborate the meaning of Christian existence. Now, he reaches back to and through those images of the ongoing nature of Christian life to give a glimpse of the creation and nature of Christian existence. God did something, humans did not. God paid a price, humans did not. God bought, and so God owns or has a claim on the lives of the believers.

The language Paul uses is vivid and would have been familiar to the Corinthians, who were accustomed to the purchasing of slaves in the marketplaces. Today we are unfamiliar with this practice, but the idea is simple. Slaves were bought and sold, and in the purchase they came under the absolute authority of the one who paid the price for them. Paul's statement can be literally rendered, "You were bought for cash!" He does not state, and he may not care, to whom the purchase price was paid; his concern is to underscore the initiative and the rightful authority of God in the relationship between the believers and God.

Therefore, Paul utters his final words of instruction, **Therefore honor God with your body.** The address is a command in the plural form, saying more literally, "Therefore you all glorify God in your body." The NIV attempts to make sense of Paul's command by translating "honor" rather than "glorify" and by using "with" instead of "in," but the result is questionable. Paul may intend to say more than "Act honorably," which is the simplest understanding of the NIV. "Your body" includes all the individual bodies of the Corinthians, but it literally names the corporate body of all the believers, so that the life manifested by the Christian community in both moral and mission-related dimensions of existence brings praise and honor to God's work in the world.

Additional Notes §15

6:12 / The qualifications to the argument that Paul offers are standards that were recognized by popular philosophy during Paul's time: **Beneficial** or "best" (Stoics); **be mastered** or "freedom" (Cynics). Thus Paul uses what would be considered reasonable arguments at the outset of his deliberations. For an argument against reading this and the complementary verses as a slogan from the Corinthians, see B. J. Dodd, "Paul's Paradigmatic 'I' and 1 Corinthians 6.12," *JSNT* 59 (1995), pp. 39–58. Dodd looks at the first-person cast of the discussion in terms of rhetoric.

6:13 / Conzelmann (*1 Corinthians*, pp. 108–10) makes the important point that *porneia* was far more than a remnant of the community's past life in paganism. Indeed, the problematic members of the church were behaving in these unacceptable ways because they were seeking to demonstrate their newfound freedom in Christ.

The activity of the Corinthians and their slogans show that they were assuming a basic dualism as the starting point for their religious life. On the one hand, soul/spirit were set free; so that on the other hand, body/flesh became the avenue for demonstrating freedom. The soul/spirit was unaffected by the activities of the body/flesh, and the Corinthians were proving it in noticeable ways.

6:15 / The Gk. formula *mē genoito*, translated **Never!** was a common convention of diatribe argumentation that could either end the argument or provide a transition (see A. J. Malherbe, "*MĒ GENOITO* in the Diatribe and Paul," *HTR* 73 [1980], pp. 231–40). The form of the verb *ginomai* is telling: it is a rare NT optative, probably preserving a traditional formula rather than registering a distinct nuance to the verb; moreover, it is impersonal and translated "may it be," although in the religious context of this discussion, God is the assumed actor, so that the true force of the statement is "God forbid!"

6:16 / The quotation of Gen. 2:24 occurs in the teaching of Jesus concerning marriage/divorce in Mark 10:8 pars. Paul's use of this citation, which includes the Gk. word *sarx*, is striking since he uses the Gk. word *sōma* in the first part of the verse in reference to the physical union between the client and the prostitute. Paul's use of "body" indicates his concern with relationship, although his employment of "flesh" indicates his concrete concern with the physical nature of human relations. Paul is capable of using both *sarx* and *sōma* in technical and nontechnical ways. One must assess the context of the usage to determine its immediate sense. Here it is the combination of terms that is most telling.

6:18 / Some commentators read portions of this verse as Paul's quotation of another of the Corinthians' slogans; thus Paul quotes them as saying, "All sin is outside the body." There is merit to this suggestion, although the majority of interpreters simply add the word "other" to the line (NIV: **all other sins**) while understanding Paul himself to be coining this phrase (see J. Murphy-O'Connor, "Corinthian Slogans in 1 Cor 6:12–20," *CBQ* 40 [1978], pp. 391–96). I argued above that the words were Paul's, although I am not certain that Paul meant to refer to **all other sins** in contrast to fornication.

On the possible background of Paul's remarks in the Judaism of his time, see B. N. Fisk (*"PORNEUEIN* as Body Violation: The Unique Nature of Sexual Sin in 1 Corinthians 6.18," *NTS* 42 [1996], pp. 540–58), who relates the statement(s) here to notions of body union in sexual relations.

6:19 / One commentator after another (e.g., Conzelmann, *1 Corinthians,* p. 112; Fee, *Epistle,* p. 264) states that Paul uses body/temple in reference to the individual. This contention is hard to comprehend and perhaps seriously misleading, given that there are six explicit plural forms in v. 19 alone, followed by three plural forms in v. 20. There are no singular forms.

§16 General Remarks on Marriage (1 Cor. 7:1–7)

The seventh chapter of Paul's letter to Corinth is a complex and challenging series of related observations and directions that have often lost or puzzled later readers of the epistle. Paul's statements in these verses are more often misunderstood than grasped and appreciated for what they say. The commentary that follows will focus on smaller segments of the writing in an effort to elucidate and explicate Paul's thinking and teachings.

Verse 1 states the Corinthians' position.
Verse 2 states Paul's objection or reservations.
Verse 3 *declares Paul's own position.*
Verses 4–7 explicates Paul's point.

At the outset, one must recognize that Paul is taking up the letter sent to him from Corinth with its variety of inquiries. In replying to the Corinthians' questions, the apostle employs common rhetorical features that his readers would have followed easily, although many generations of translators and commentators, as well as everyday readers of the Bible, have not succeeded in tracking Paul's line of reasoning.

7:1 / Paul explicitly refers to a letter from Corinth. We already know that Paul has met with Chloe's people (mentioned in 1:11), and later in the epistle we will encounter the names of three persons from Corinth (see 16:17) who "supplied what was lacking from [the Corinthians]." In the present verse we encounter the first of several overt references to and citations from the letter that came to Paul from Corinth (cf. 8:1; 12:1; 16:1). The NIV attempts to recognize that Paul has and refers to the letter from Corinth by placing a colon after the words **Now for the matters you wrote about** and then by beginning the next line with capitalization **It is good for a man not to marry.** Similarly, in the NRSV one finds an introductory phrase followed by a colon, "Now concerning the matters about which you wrote:"; but then one finds quotation marks around the words "It is well for a man not to touch a woman." This punctuation correctly indicates that Paul refers to and quotes a line from the Corinthians' letter. In sum, the position of some of the Corinthians is that "it is well for a man not to touch a woman." Obviously the point was debated, for the Corinthians wrote to get Paul's thinking on this point. The NIV leaves Paul's rhetorical ploy somewhat unclear and runs the danger of perpetuating the misunderstanding that Paul himself thought men ought not to have physical dealings with women, but nothing could be further from Paul's own thinking and teaching.

The rendering of the second part of verse 1 in the NIV is questionable, **It is good for a man not to marry.** Literally the Greek reads, "It is good for a man not to touch a woman." The NIV's translation mistakenly focuses on the issue of marriage, whereas the Greek words speak of sexual relations between a man and a woman, obviously in the context of marriage. In the lines that follow, it becomes apparent that Paul is particularly concerned, as were the Corinthians, about whether or not there were to be sexual relations in the context of marriage.

7:2 / Paul's thinking comes clear in this verse. In Greek Paul uses an imperative, so that he declares, "Because of instances of sexual immorality, let each man have his own wife and let each woman have her own husband." This statement is often described as a concession; that is, Paul doesn't want people to marry, but he gives in on this point. However, the imperative force of the declaration calls that description into question. Paul's assumption is that marriage is a normal, natural necessity. He recognizes the potential problem of immorality in order to explain and to verify his basic understanding that marriage is the rule, not the exception.

7:3 / Having laid the foundation for his teachings by first referring to the Corinthians' assertion and then stating his own understanding, Paul works with the assumption that people are already married. He instructs the husbands to give their wives their due and, likewise, the wives to give their husbands their due. At issue are so-called conjugal rights, which Paul assumes do exist. He refers to the mutual responsibility of husbands and wives with the Greek word *hē opheilē*, a term that refers to a debt or something owed to someone, frequently connoting a profit or an advantage. In other words, Paul understands sexual relations to be a basic element in the economy of marriage. Paul's statement is straightforward, although the NIV translation seems to squirm about with a euphemistic reference to **marital duty.** While there is nothing bawdy or lewd in Paul's language, there is nothing oblique. Paul assumes that sexual relations are a standard, natural, even necessary part of marriage; and one should recall that he works from the assumption that marriage per se is necessary and normal. Some persons in the church in Corinth may contend that partners in marriage are above or freed from sexual relations, but Paul does not agree, and his teaching makes that clear. Mutual fulfillment in sexual relations is Paul's plain understanding of the essential, normal condition of marriage.

7:4 / Paul juxtaposes a pair of balanced statements in this verse that give the social or anthropological assumptions behind his directions, although recalling 6:16 we should not understand that Paul has abandoned theological perspectives and concerns. Remarkably, at this point Paul assumes a genuine mutuality in marital relations. The authority over each spouse's body is attributed to the other marital partner. There is little to no historical or cultural precedent for what Paul says. While male-dominant society was the predominant culture of antiquity, Paul understands the dynamics of marital relations in a strikingly egalitarian way—at least at this point in his discussion of sexual rights and responsibilities. In marriage, Paul teaches that one's "other," be that husband or wife, holds the authority over the mate's **body.** The verb translated **belong to** in the NIV more literally means "to have authority over," so Paul is not concerned with ownership or property rights but with relationship and relatedness.

7:5 / In verses 1–4 Paul initially encourages sexual union in the context of marriage, but in this verse he allows for abstinence for special times of devotion to prayer. This practice, as he outlines it, is Paul's true concession. Paul speaks to both partners in the marriage and recognizes that they must be in true agreement on this matter. From Paul's manner of reasoning one sees that some of the Corinthians assume that ascetic restraint in sexual relations in marriage is an element or encouragement of spirituality. But Paul does not follow their line. Rather, he recognizes that refraining from sexual union in a marriage is not a necessary path to spirituality, although he does allow for limited abstinence in special circumstances. Nevertheless, the sharp apocalyptic or cosmic note struck in mentioning **Satan** and temptation recognizes that even sincere humanly designed practices (here, abstinence for prayer) may open persons to the forces of evil.

Paul recognizes the reality and the insidiously subtle nature of evil. Humans are not superhuman, and efforts to practice or display spirituality may backfire despite the best intentions. **Self-control** as a human commodity, even in its most sincere form, has limited potential for accomplishing good. Indeed, the power of evil can even use good, noble, honest intentions against those who seek to do what is good. Paul's warning should be a sobering reminder to the Corinthians that they live out the reality of God's salvation, not by their own decisions and efforts, but through the presence and the power of God's Spirit at work in their lives.

7:6 / When in the following verse Paul says, **I say this as a concession, not as a command,** he is merely qualifying his statement in verse 5 that allowed for sexual continence for prayer. In other words, Paul himself does not think that married persons need necessarily refrain from sexual activity "by mutual consent and for a time" in order to devote themselves to prayer. Asceticism is a possibility in very qualified circumstances, not a norm or mode of Christian life.

7:7 / Paul's further remark, **I wish that all** [persons] **were as I am,** is often misunderstood or misinterpreted. The heart of Paul's thinking and teaching about marriage and sex in marriage comes through clearly at this point, but one must listen carefully. The ensuing line is crucial, **But each** [person] **has** [a personal] **gift from God; one has this gift, another has that.** Paul's language is inclusive, as he addresses both the men and the women, the husbands and the wives, in the Corinthian congregation. Paul's point is that chastity, the capacity not to marry, freedom from a desire for sex in the context of a marriage, is a spiritual gift from God. Such a gift from God brings freedom and opportunity for extensive service to God. One must see, however, that for Paul not marrying is preferable only if the capacity to remain single is given by God; but the gift of chastity is not universal, and it is not necessary. Either one has it, or one does not. Paul's prejudices come out clearly in his comments, since he understands the gift of remaining unmarried to be an opportunity for freedom from marital responsibilities. The teaching is clear, not cryptic, though brief. Later in this chapter Paul develops additional aspects of his thoughts along this line (see 7:32–35). For now, one should note that Paul sees each believer as gifted in some particular way by God; and so each person is responsible and privileged to use whatever gift God has given her or him for God's own purposes. Mission, not manipulation, is God's will for the life of the believer.

Additional Notes §16

7:1 / The rhetorical phrase introducing a reference to the Corinthians' letter and questions begins "concerning" or "now concerning" (Gk. *peri*) and occurs at 7:1, 25; 8:1; 12:1; 16:1, 12, although commentators debate whether every instance of this phrase cites a statement in the Corinthians' letter. On this rhetorical form see W. E. Phipps ("Is Paul's Attitude toward Sexual Relations Contained in 1 Cor 7.1?" *NTS* 28 [1982], pp. 125–31) whose otherwise idiosyncratic analysis pursues additional interests. When Paul begins v. 1 by writing *Peri de hōn egrapsate* (lit. "But about those things of which you wrote"), he employs a rhetorical device that an educated reader would have understood to be introducing a quotation from the source to which Paul refers. Thus, he refers to the Corinthians' letter and then quotes their own statement that Paul read in their letter to him, *kalon anthrōpō gynaikos mē haptesthai* (lit. "good for the man a woman not to touch").

For a thorough critique of the inadequacy of the NIV translation of this verse, see G. D. Fee, "1 Corinthians 7:1 in the NIV," *JETS* 23 (1980), pp. 307–14; for a thorough critique of the use and misuse of archaeological data in assessing these verses and sections of chs. 8, 11, 12, see R. E. Oster, "Use, Misuse and Neglect of Archaeological Evidence in Some Modern Works on 1 Corinthians (1 Cor 7,1–5; 8,10; 11,2–16; 12,14–26," *ZNW* 83 (1992), pp. 52–73.

7:2 / This particular teaching about sexual relations in marriage focuses on the rights of each partner in the marriage—they have equal rights—although, as the remainder of the letter and even this discussion show, that concept was not an abstract principle that Paul invoked or applied in relation to all situations. Rather, the criteria for the application of this principle were determined for Paul by the theological category or reality of spiritual gifts, which are not always—but here are between the marital partners—distributed equally.

Commentators regularly recognize that Paul attempts no positive theological statement on marriage here—understandably, since he is reacting to the Corinthians' assertion. Paul's purpose is to explain the problem with asceticism and the necessity of marriage in the eschatological context in which he understood Christian congregates to live. (See D. E. Garland, "The Christian's Posture Toward Marriage and Celibacy: 1 Corinthians 7," *RevExp* 80 [1983], pp. 351–62; V. L. Wimbush, "The Ascetic Impulse in Ancient Christianity," *ThTo* 50 [1993], pp. 417–28; J. M. Gundry-Volf, "Celibate Pneumatics and Social Power: On the Motivations for Sexual Asceticism in Corinth," *USQR* 48 [1994], pp. 105–26.) Paul came closer to a positive theology of marriage in 6:16 when he cited Gen. 2:24 in his denouncement of prostitution. Further analysis of Paul's thoughts on marriage in conjunction with the present discussion are mere speculation.

7:4 / Fee (*Epistle*, p. 280) summarizes the dynamics of Paul's reasoning incisively, "Paul's emphasis, it must be noted, is not on 'You owe me,' but on 'I owe you.' " The emphasis falls on giving, not receiving; and on the other, not on the self, rights, and personal autonomy. Paul refrains from detaching the person from the relational reality of human existence.

7:5 / The statement **Do not deprive** is noteworthy, as Paul uses the verb *apostereō*, a word carrying a negative connotation of cheating or defrauding another. In turn, the NIV introduces Paul's concession with **except**, more literally "unless perhaps" (Gk. *ei mēti an*)—a conditional phrase in Gk. designating a hypothetical proposition.

7:6 / Paul's concession has often been turned into a rigid command, against the plain sense and the plain intention of his remark. Fee notes, "Here is a passage that has suffered much in the church" (*Epistle*, p. 285).

7:7 / Paul's wording, **I wish** (Gk. *thelō*), states a personal preference, informed by theological reasoning but not intended as a principle. Moreover, exactly what Paul wished is debated, although in grammar and context one should understand that Paul wished all to have the gift of celibacy, not merely that they refrain from marriage. See Fee, *Epistle*, p. 284.

§17 Directions to the Unmarried (1 Cor. 7:8–9)

With the general subject of marriage having been raised through the foregoing discussion of the appropriateness, benefit, and necessity of sexual relations in marriage, Paul extends his field of concern to include a series of particular groups other than those who are married. In this brief segment of the letter, Paul addresses some of those who are not currently married, but as we shall see, exactly with whom he intended to reason is not certain.

7:8 / With the words "**Now to the unmarried and the widows,**" the NIV translates Paul's remarks to address two different groups. These groups would have in common that they were not married at present, but reflection on this rendering of the text reveals that one possible group is conspicuously absent from the appeal, namely, the widowers. Careful study by G. D. Fee (*Epistle*, pp. 287–88) suggests that the word normally rendered "unmarried" by the NIV and other translations may be intended as an address to widowers. The specific course of Paul's previous comments on the necessity of marriage (7:2) and his later remarks on "virgins" (7:25–26) do not fit well with the understanding of Paul's remarks here being directed to both the unmarried and widows. More sensibly, verses 8–9 reflect on the remarriage of those who have lost a spouse through death, so that Paul is writing to men and women, widowers and widows, at this point.

In any case, however, having discussed marriage, the advisability of sexual union in marriage, and the spiritual gift of remaining single, Paul turns directly to this distinct group of members of the Corinthian congregation. He declares that he himself considers it better to remain unmarried than to marry (or, in the case of those previously married but now single, to remarry), and his manner of expression shows that he is offering his own thinking on this subject. Paul suggests that **it is good for them to stay unmarried, as I am.** Later in this chapter he explains that he holds this position because of the eschatological character of the time in which he believes he and the Corinthians live. Paul's comments seem to recognize that before Christ, in the old world, there was no value to single life from the human point of view. But now, as part of the gospel, there is a new sense or value to single life—lived in complete devotion to Christ—in the context of the new Christian life. For now, however, he suggests that should they be as he was—gifted with celibacy—they are in a good position. One does not force celibacy; one accepts it as a gift if it is given by God.

7:9 / Nevertheless, Paul continues and tells this particular group that they **should marry** in certain circumstances. Paul reasons from the charismatically formed assumption that the capacity to remain unmarried is a spiritual gift. The translation of this line in the NIV and other similar translations, **But if they cannot control themselves, they** should marry, is easily misunderstood. Paul is not saying, "If you are not practicing self-control, get married." In Paul's well-known list of the fruit of the Spirit at Galatians 5:23 one finds the noun "self-control," so although Paul uses the verbal form of "self-control" (translated as "control themselves," meaning "to practice self-control"), he is referring to a Spirit-empowered directing of one's self. If an unmarried person in Corinth does not have the Spirit-given ability to be chaste, then Paul says that person should marry. Paul is not so much saying "Fight the urge" as he is advising "Recognize the gift or its absence." Such honesty according to Paul **is better** than trying to accomplish something (refraining from marriage and sexual relations in that context) that God has not given one the gift to do.

Additional Notes §17

7:8 / Paul's first designation of a group in the Corinthian congregation uses the Gk. word *agamos,* most often translated literally as **unmarried**. The problem of this understanding in the context of this discussion was noted above. Moreover, later Paul refers to such unmarried persons with the Gk. word *parthenos,* lit. "virgin" (see 7:25). W. F. Orr and J. A. Walther (*I Corinthians.* [AB 32; Garden City, N.Y.: Doubleday, 1976], p. 210) argue that while *"agamois* means etymologically 'unmarried,' the word may indicate either one who has not been married or one who has been but is no longer married." Fee (*Epistle,* pp. 287–88) recognizes that in the NT period there are no preserved usages of *chēros,* the Gk. word for "widower," but that *agamos* seems to have taken the place of the older, more specific word for widower.

Note the initial element of contrast in this verse as Paul discusses what is "well" or **good** (Gk. *kalon*) before he discusses what is **better** (Gk. *kreitton*) in v. 9. Paul is not discussing right and wrong or good and bad, but **good** and **better** from a point of view he expounds later in this chapter.

7:9 / Paul's reference to "self-control" (Gk. *egkrateia*) uses the form of a verb (Gk. *egkrateuomai,* "to practice self-control"), **control themselves.** Outside the NT in general, "self-control" was considered a virtue in Greco-Roman culture, although Paul's usage in Gal. 5:23 and here shows that he understood this "virtue" to be an endowment of God's Spirit, not a humanly generated personal discipline. Cf. 2 Pet. 1:6; Acts 24:25; *1 Clement* 38.2; 1 Cor. 9:25.

Paul's use of *pyrousthai* (infinitive passive of *pyroō,* "to be burned/ inflamed"), creates discussion among interpreters. Could Paul mean that those who do not marry, despite their desires, will be subjected to the fires of final judgment—so M. Barré, "To Marry or to Burn: *pyrousthai* in 1 Cor 7:9," *CBQ* 36 (1974), pp. 193–202? Or does Paul mean, as the majority of scholars agree, that those aflame with passion should marry to avoid such a condition? Paul's apocalyptic-eschatological point of view is undeniable, but nothing in the present discussion suggests that Paul is issuing a threat or a promise of judgment.

§18 Directions to the Married (1 Cor. 7:10–11)

Once again Paul writes to the married, although now he is interested in the potential of divorce, not in the matter of sexual relations in marriage. As he begins his remarks Paul makes plain that he is not giving his own opinion; instead, he is delivering a word from the Lord to the Corinthians. Accordingly, Paul's words are measured and weighty, coming in the forms of established pronouncements.

7:10 / The tradition to which Paul refers or which he cites may lie behind the materials in passages such as Mark 10:2–9 and Luke 16:18 or Matthew 5:32. This dominical word is a firm denial of the validity of divorce. The **command** from **the Lord,** however, is restricted to verse 10 and does not include or extend to verse 11. Commentators discuss and speculate about Paul's source for this authoritative saying, suggesting either that he learned it from earlier followers of Jesus or that he had this teaching as a revelation from the risen Lord. In the current context, such a discussion is fruitless and distracts from the sense of gravity that Paul attaches to these words. Wherever and however Paul possessed this statement from the Lord, he took it with utter seriousness and offered it in its briefest, unqualified form: **a wife must not separate from her husband.**

7:11 / The series of phrases in this verse is remarkable. Because of its printed form, the NIV can be misread as if this line were continuing the command of the Lord from the previous verse. Nothing could be more wrong. A better presentation is that of the NRSV, which correctly places verse 11 in parentheses. In this verse, Paul states a real possibility—that despite the command of the Lord a believer may enact a divorce. The statement is not an exception clause from Paul, however; rather, it provides directions in the event that persons practice divorce despite the word from the Lord.

The specific way that Paul casts this discussion, focusing on the wife, commenting and reasoning on the divorce in relation to her role in the action, implies that he may be treating a specific situation that the Corinthians would recognize but about which later readers are uninformed. Normally in Greco-Roman cultures such discussions focus on the husband. Only after dealing with the wife and divorce does Paul eventually tag on the line **And a husband must not divorce his wife.**

Whatever we are to make of the situation that lay behind Paul's comments, we should notice the remarkable way in which Paul deals with this situation and subject. Having clearly and plainly reiterated the command of the Lord, Paul does not turn the Lord's word into a new law. Moreover, facing the reality of a divorce that is obviously contrary to the advice from the Lord, Paul does not denounce the divorced person. He has other advice, seemingly his own opinion, that the wife **must remain unmarried or else be reconciled to her husband.** Paul does not imagine or comment on the possibility that such a reconciliation is impossible. Although one may only speculate, perhaps given the reality of God's reconciliation of the world through the mystery of the cross of Jesus Christ, Paul could not imagine that reconciliation was impossible in the context of the Christian community. Paul's comments raise issues for twentieth-century readers that his remarks do not address or resolve.

Paul's logic takes another direction in this verse. Indeed, his comments once more assume that in marriage both wives and husbands have rights and responsibilities and can take initiatives. Paul's directions raise many issues, deal clearly with some, and do not give attention to others. Above all, however, we should notice that Paul takes the words of the Lord seriously, but he never lapses into a new legalism in Jesus' name. Unfortunately, this remarkable combination of faithfulness and flexibility is often difficult to comprehend and emulate.

Additional Notes §18

7:10 / Scholars sometimes suggest that extremists in Corinth were advocating the absolution of marriage or the practice of so-called spiritual marriage that was without sexual relations. The earlier portion of ch. 7 does relate to some such practices among the Corinthians, but it is not clear that the present discussion relates to that same problem.

Commentators also attempt to explain Paul's focusing predominately on a/the **wife** in these lines by relating his remarks to a group of so-called eschatological women in Corinth who are thought to have been seeking divorce as a demonstration of their eschatological freedom from earthly existence. This possibility is not a certainty.

The most important angle for viewing the verse(s) is Paul's parenthetical explanation **(not I, but the Lord)**—cf. v. 12, ("I, not the Lord")—which demonstrates Paul's knowledge of, respect for, and use of the teachings of the Lord. Reiterating the words of the Lord, Paul says, **I give this command;** whereas offering his own apostolic opinion, he writes, "I say this. . . ."

Finally, the use of "to **separate**" rather than "to divorce" is incidental, since in antiquity divorce most often happened through real separation rather than through legal documentation. Paul uses these two verbs interchangeably in the following lines (vv. 13, 15). For information on Greek and Roman divorce practices see A. Berger and B. Nicholas, "Marriage, Law of," *OCD*, pp. 649–50.

7:11 / Commenting on these verses, Watson (*First Epistle*, p. 69) makes a difficult but critical observation: "No doubt, some Christians pass over their own failure to live by the teaching of Paul (and Jesus) on this subject [of divorce] by talking too readily of the failure of their marriage rather than of their own failure as married people."

§19 Regarding "Mixed" Marriages (1 Cor. 7:12–16)

Having directed remarks to unmarried Christians and to Christians married to each other, Paul writes to **the rest**, or those Christians who are married to unbelieving partners. Paul works from the assumption that divorce is contrary to the teaching of the Lord (7:10–11); yet as he reflects on the situation in Corinth, he recognizes and reasons that the involvement of an unbelieving partner in a marriage creates a different set of circumstances. Paul's advice to the Christian partners is that they remain in their marriages if their non-Christian spouses agree. Paul's reasoning supports or maintains Christian freedom—freedom to remain in an agreeable marriage or freedom to divorce in situations where the non-Christian partner will not accept the faith of the Christian—although the ideas of reconciliation and peace (God's work) are at the foundations of his thought. Peace, not the conflict of a divorce, is the characteristic of Christian life. Moreover, as Paul elaborates his thinking, he ponders not only the role of the believer and the presence of the unbeliever in such marriages but also the circumstances or state of the children of these unions.

7:12–13 / The form of Paul's remarks is notable, because he plainly states that he is offering his own advice, not a further word or command from the Lord. Yet his advice is not simply reasonable thinking, for, as he will reveal later in 7:40, Paul understands his reasoning in relation to such circumstances to be inspired or informed by God's Spirit at work in him. Paul's thinking is formed not by a principle, no matter how ethical, but by the reality of God. Moreover, Paul shifts the viewpoint from "a/the wife," in the preceding verses, to **any brother,** although he will reverse the angle of vision before ending his observations, writing to **a woman** whose **husband** is **not a believer.** Although the church has attempted to work from these lines in formulating policies about so-called mixed marriages, the present verses do not deal with the majority of interfaith marriages as we know them in the late twentieth century. Paul is writing to first-century, first-generation converts, many of whom had religious backgrounds in paganism and many of whom might have spouses who were not believers. Today only a small number of Christians in mixed marriages become Christians through conversion while their spouses remain in another religion. The closest Paul comes to offering advice on mixed marriages as we encounter them is in 7:39, where he instructs Christian women to marry Christian men.

In relation to the Corinthian situation, these verses are simple and clear. Believers are to remain in their marriages if their nonbelieving partners agree. Paul's teaching excludes the possibility of the Christian member of a marriage initiating a divorce from a nonbeliever, especially because the spouse is an unbeliever.

7:14 / Portions of verse 14 are enigmatic and difficult to comprehend, although other elements are straightforward. Because of the situation that Paul has described in verses 12–13, one should probably understand that Paul assumes that non-Christian spouses are involved in pagan religions. Thus he makes this exceptional series of statements to recognize that no pagan deity plays a part in the Christians' dealings with pagan spouses. His reference to the children of mixed marriages illustrates the ultimate power of the Lord. In brief, he assures the Corinthians that Christians are not defiled by pagan spouses; rather, the Christian's presence in the family and the Spirit's presence in the life of the believer sanctify the relationship. Paul does not attempt to explain the mechanics of such an operation of sanctification. He observes that **the unbelieving husband has been sanctified through his wife, and the unbelieving wife has been sanctified through her . . . husband,** and that the **children . . . are holy.** God graciously works to bring about the sanctification of the non-Christian spouse and the children through the believer in the family.

The Greek verb *hagiazō*, translated "has been sanctified," is a perfect (past completed action) passive (the subject is acted on rather than acts). Thus, this mention of sanctification refers to a present reality accomplished in the past without specifying when and how the action took place. The implication of the passive is that God did the work. In attempting to understand what Paul thinks about sanctification that would have led him to refer to the unbelieving marital partner as having been sanctified, Conzelmann (p. 122) writes:

> The world is desacralized. By this means freedom is brought to light. Through the believing partner, the marriage between a pagan and a Christian is withdrawn from the control of the powers of the world. In living together with the world, the "saints" are the stronger party. The decisive idea lies not in an ontological definition of the state of the non-Christian members of the family, but in the assertion that no alien power plays any part in the Christian's dealing with them.

7:15 / Three related statements form this striking verse. First, Paul says that should the non-Christian spouse act to end the marriage, the Christian should let it be. Second, in these situations, Christian husbands or wives are not **bound,** or literally enslaved; they are not reduced to being victims of circumstances. They are free, apparently, from the marital vows that were broken by the nonbeliever's actions. Third, Paul explains that **God** calls Christians to **peace.** Neither fighting against a divorce nor suffering the stigma, circumstances, and aftermath of a divorce are God's will for the Christian who is married to an unbelieving spouse. God's peace is relational, and it does not exist in or promote the presence of destructive strife. Paul's words here recognize the freedom of the believers despite the difficulties of divorce that may affect their lives. God's peace is to be the end result of both marriage and divorce.

7:16 / In turn, verse 16 summarizes the intention and motive of Paul's teaching that, if possible, Christians should remain married to non-Christian spouses. Critical editions of the Greek text suggest the two sentences are questions, to be rendered as in the NIV, although other translations make statements out of these lines. Yet the energy of the argument at this point favors the form of a set of rhetorical questions that are designed to drive home Paul's point. Nevertheless, the basic sense of the sentences is clear, and either way, what Paul says may seem peculiar at a glance: Do Christian husbands and wives have the power to **save** their spouses? Certainly not. One sees from Paul's total writings that he does not think humans ever save themselves or one another; God does the saving through Christ. These lines are best and only understood to say that God may work through a

Christian spouse (as is explicit in v. 14) to save an unbelieving partner. A sensible paraphrase of Paul's rhetorical appeal might read, "How will you ever know, if you don't give it a chance, whether God will work through you to save your spouse?"

Additional Notes §19

7:12–13 / These verses form a pair of balanced sentences in Gk. that once again, as in earlier portions of this chapter, treat male and female marital partners who are Christians in the same manner.

7:14 / Some manuscripts add qualifications to the references to unbelieving and believing spouses to explicate Paul's concise statement. At the end of this verse the NIV accepts and translates one of these variants with the words **through her believing husband.** The oldest and best manuscripts, however, contain neither the qualifier "believing" nor the word **husband,** but rather read "brother" (Gk. *adelphos*). The line is best translated "through the brother," meaning a brother who was a believing husband, as the scribal alterations clarified.

On this difficult and fascinating passage, see E. Best ("1 Corinthians 7:14 and Children in the Church," *IBS* 12 [1990], pp. 158–66), who examines ancient currents of thought to explicate the theological and ethical dimensions of this verse.

7:15 / The Gk. text of a portion of this line literally reads, "The brother or the sister is not bound," so the NIV alters Paul's wording with the paraphrase **a believing man or woman is not bound.**

7:16 / The grammar of this rhetorical question is conditional, and the verb translated **you will save** is future tense in reference to a potential act that is not yet and may or may not be realized. See S. Kubo ("I Corinthians vii.16: Optimistic or Pessimistic?" *NTS* 24 [1978], pp. 539–44), who examines similar parallel statements in ancient literature to argue that Paul's tone is one of uncertainty, neither clearly optimistic nor certainly pessimistic.

§20 God's Gifts and the Corinthians' Calling (1 Cor. 7:17–24)

This section is still addressed to "the rest" (v. 12), which may indicate that having addressed the various groups he named regarding the questions of how men and women are to relate in terms of marriage, sex, and divorce, Paul thinks he has covered those related fields of concern. Therefore, he shifts the focus in this next segment of the letter, although he is still concerned with the general issue of the Christians' need or desire to alter their present social status, perhaps as a demonstration of Christian freedom. In brief, Paul tells the Corinthians that they are to live in the state that they were allotted by the Lord. In turn, Paul illustrates this idea by referring to circumcision and to slavery. Then the concluding lines of this section reiterate the basic idea that the Corinthians are to remain before God in the state in which God called them. How is the reader of today to comprehend and apply this notion? Is there relevance?

Some preliminary observations may aid comprehension. Above all, Paul's thought is relative to his thoroughgoing apocalyptic eschatology, as is clear from what follows in 7:31b, "For this world in its present form is passing away." Paul maintains that God saves the believers regardless of their worldly social status; remaining in the social state in which one was called demonstrates that what humans do does not effect salvation; worldly social change is not equivalent to salvation. Ultimately, the calling of Christians by God creates real freedom. All who are called are freed, in spite of social circumstances, to obey God. Paul argues vigorously that the saving work of God eliminates the boundaries of sacred and profane, for God's saving work knows no sociological limitations.

Nevertheless, Paul's first-century, apocalyptic-eschatologically formed convictions produce statements that rankle the social and ethical sensibilities of some later readers. Paul's point of view is not ours, however, so grasping the simple sense of his words and viewing them in relation to Paul's own day and age and eschatological convictions should mitigate inappropriate criticism of his teachings.

7:17 / Paul refocuses the deliberations in this verse. Quite literally he writes, "At any rate, to each as the Lord allotted, each as God has called; thus let one walk—and thus in all the churches I direct." Paul's grammar is simple, but his choice of words is subtle, even enigmatic; so translations supply words and phrases to clarify Paul's elusive statements. The NIV's introduction of the verb **should retain**, the phrase **to which**, and the explanatory paraphrasing **This is the rule I lay down** together add a tone of moral oughtness, depersonalize the focus of Paul's thought, and lapse into heavy, static moralizing. This rendering misses the personal concern of Paul's statement, its dynamic confidence in God, and its gentle tone of encouragement and direction.

Far from being heavy-handed, Paul is concerned that the Corinthians alter their social status in celebration and display of their Christian freedom, and he assures them that God attends to their lives as they are. Whatever place in life was granted to the believer by the God-given gift of life, that is the capacity in which God came to the Corinthians and called them. Thus, the Corinthian Christians are able to live with the assurance of God's concern and in the dignity of knowing that God had brought them to a new life in faith and in the church in their present earthly statuses. Moreover, Paul assures the Corinthians that they are not alone in this endeavor, for all the churches are called and directed in this same manner, even as Paul himself lives this way. The subtlety of Paul's statement suggests that one should imagine his gently checking, nudging, and encouraging the believers in Corinth. Reading and hearing from this point of view, one perceives a different Paul and even a different God from the one suggested by the severe and clumsy rendering of the NIV and most other translations. One may easily misread the NIV to reveal a cold-hearted Paul and a capricious and indifferent God, but that understanding does not fit in the context of this epistle.

7:18 / Moving from the general idea that social change is unnecessary, perhaps even undesirable, Paul takes up the issue of being circumcised. He applies or illustrates the idea of the Christians' remaining in the state in which God called them by telling the Corinthian men neither to get uncircumcised nor to be circumcised. Such change was ill-advised, and Paul offers no exception to his declarations.

At the heart of this matter is the question of the necessity for Christians to take on the sign of God's covenant of circumcision with Abraham and the Jews. In antiquity, unlike today, this issue was crucial. Baths were public places, and in Greco-Roman settings Jews often suffered ridicule from non-Jews who viewed their religious practice as barbarian. Indeed, some Jews underwent the tedious and painful process of eliminating the physical impression of circumcision in order to avoid stigmatization. In regard to such a controversial matter, Paul says, Don't bother. Jews could be scandalized even as some Gentiles might be comforted by the advice.

7:19 / To emphasize his contention, Paul bluntly states the irrelevance of the matter in two simple, balanced rhetorical phrases, literally, **Circumcision is nothing and uncircumcision is nothing.** Then, he offers clarification in rhetorical juxtaposition, literally, "but observance of God's commandments." Yet for the Jew, being circumcised was God's commandment, and if a Gentile were to become one of God's people, circumcision seemed a necessary sign of obedience. Paul disagrees, which is remarkable for someone who was trained as a Pharisee.

Behind Paul's bold declaration is the recognition that symbolic, even physical acts are not the heart of the matter of keeping God's commands. Rather, as Paul has said, "The body is . . . meant . . . for the Lord, and the Lord for the body" (6:13). The essence of Christian life is relational; the believers are brought by God into a new relationship through Jesus Christ and in that relationship they are empowered by God to live faithfully and freely, not merely to do things to demonstrate their freedom (see 1:8). For Paul, obedience to God is the natural outcome of living in a faithful relationship to God through the gift of grace.

7:20 / This verse briefly states the point that Paul has made and remade throughout this segment of the letter. The statement functions here to reiterate what was said about circumcision and to prepare the way for what is to follow concerning slavery and freedom.

7:21 / Circumcision may no longer pose the problem it did for the Corinthians, but these remarks about slavery seem vital in a world that has known and still knows the inhumane practice of one human's being so arrogant as to own another. Moreover, the implications of this specific issue are taken as analogous to the dynamics of other patterns of human relatedness, such as management/labor, business owner/employee, privileged/deprived, and powerful/vulnerable. Thus, from our perspective Paul may seem callous or cold. Again, however, one must remember that given Paul's apocalyptic-eschatologically formed perspective—"the form of this world is passing away" (7:31b)—current social status is ultimately unimportant. Rather, in one's life on this earth, one is to be concerned with developing one's new relationship to God in the context of the church and the world and living a life in continuity with God's grace. Freedom per se is a secondary concern for Paul. As one interpreter summarized Paul's attitude, "Why hustle to join a lame-duck administration?"

7:22 / Paul works through rhetorical phrases to elaborate and explain his advice. He offers an off-balance contrast in verse 22:

> a Christian slave is the Lord's free person in the Lord;
> likewise, a free person is the Lord's slave.

The emphasis of Paul's wording indicates that the idea of being "in the Lord" dominates simple social conventions. The category "in the Lord" supersedes all else, and in that context all other qualifiers are made relatively unimportant. The call of God releases the slave to the new freedom of an ultimate relationship with God, as the call of God enslaves the free person to that same ultimate relatedness. Essentially Paul portrays all humans as being on a level playing field from a theological point of view. From Paul's short-sighted apocalyptic perspective, social status is unimportant and not worth one's ultimate concern. From a later Christian vantage point, since we know from Paul that social standing means nothing to God, we are free to judge and alter social patterns, always remembering that such changes are not of ultimate importance (that's why they may be made!), that social status is not salvation, and that the status quo of human social order does not have God's imprimatur for eternity.

7:23 / Having grouped slaves and free together "in the Lord," Paul now makes a statement that is beautifully ambiguous: **You were bought at a price.** The forms of "you" here and throughout the verse are plural, so that Paul is addressing all previously named parties—slave and free—with this declaration. Thus, slaves would hear the words to mean that they were ransomed, into either freedom or a new lordship or both; the free would hear that they had been purchased into bondage to the one who had paid the price. Since both groups of believers belong to the Lord, a relationship that was above qualification or compromise, Paul can add, **Do not become slaves of men.** Paul's metaphor does not address the question of to whom the price was paid. Some interpreters argue that the price that Paul mentions was paid to God to appease divine wrath; others understand that the price was paid to the forces of evil to which the humans were in bondage. Paul's wording does not indicate to whom the price was paid, and since he offers no explicit remarks we may conclude that for Paul the issue was not important.

7:24 / Paul restates his overall concern and conviction, literally: "Each in whatever one was called, brothers and sisters, in this let one remain with God!" As before, the wording of Paul's Greek emphasizes the personal dimension and relational dynamics of Christian life. While the NIV's translation catches the general sense of the statement, it makes it sound more like a cold commandment than a word of comfort, assurance, and care. Paul's desire for the Corinthians is that they may be in such a relationship with God that they are about the work of God's mission. No matter what one's earthly status may be, if the believer's life is formed and directed in and out of a vital relationship to God, the believer's life will be one of faithful service.

Additional Notes §20

7:17 / Paul begins the verse with a Gk. phrase *(ei mē)* that normally introduces an exception to a previous negative statement: "Don't do this or that . . . *but* all the same. . . ." **Nevertheless** serves this rhetorical function in the NIV, although Paul's new introduction is only loosely related to v. 15b ("the brother or sister is not bound"). Perhaps the best paraphrasing translation of what Paul writes here is "Whatever the case" or "Be that as it may" or "At any rate."

Paul's verb, lit. "I direct" (Gk. *diatassō*), translated as **This is the rule I lay down,** is ambiguous. It is middle in form and could read, "I direct myself," so that Paul could be saying "This is the way I direct myself." At times, however, the middle is functionally active (cf. 11:34), although Paul knows and uses the active form of the verb elsewhere (9:14; 16:1). The middle form at least softens the force of the statement in comparison with the blunter active form.

Furthermore, while Paul refers in parallel phrases to both **the Lord** and **God** in this verse, his usages are not sufficiently distinct to determine whether he means to name Jesus Christ or God as "the Lord." A precise interpretation is impossible, although the spirit of Paul's remarks is both theological and christological.

Finally, it is possible, though perhaps not likely, that the last phrase of v. 17, "and thus in all the churches I direct," is not the conclusion to the foregoing statements in this verse. Rather, despite the versification, the words could be intended to function as the initial or introductory (paratactically formed: the run-on style of connecting phrases, clauses, and sentences with "and") phrase to the lines that follow in v. 18.

7:18 / Paul's Gk. for **circumcised** (Gk. *peritemnō*) and **uncircumcised** (Gk. *epispaō*); and then **uncircumcised** (Gk. *akrobystia*) and **circumcised** (Gk. *peritemnō*) is more complex than the English reflects and is graphic. The first reference to circumcision uses a verb *(peritemnō)* that literally means "cut round"; the first mention of uncircumcision also employs a verb *(epispaō)* that literally means "to draw over"—thus, "to obliterate the effect of circumcision." The second reference to uncircumcision is a noun *(akrobystia)* that means "foreskin" or "state of having the foreskin"; the second mention of circumcision repeats the initial use of the verb *peritemnō*. There is some evidence from antiquity that these terms and words were the language of racial slurs between Jews and Gentiles, so that Paul's discussion(s) of this issue are scandalous and perhaps trivializing (see J. Marcus, "The Circumcision and the Uncircumcision in Rome, " *NTS* 35 [1989], pp. 67–81, esp. p. 78 n. 1).

Both references to "being called" in this verse employ passive verbal forms, so that the unstated agent in the issuing of the call is understood to be God. Paul is fond of the use of the so-called divine passive as a way of thinking and talking about God and God's acts.

7:19 / Cf. Gal. 5:6; 6:15; Rom. 2:25–26; 3:1–2.

7:21 / The second portion of this verse is notoriously ambiguous. The NIV renders the line according to the understanding of the vast majority of scholars: **although if you can gain your freedom, do so.** Yet as the translation in the NRSV indicates, the words may also be read, "Even if you can gain your freedom, make use of your present condition now more than ever." Literally the line says, "But even if you are able to become free, rather make use [of it]." Many studies have tackled this difficult statement, but none has been more significant or influential than the work of S. S. Bartchy (ΜΑΛΛΟΝ ΧΡΗΣΑΙ: *Slavery and the Interpretation of 1 Corinthians 7:21* [SBLDS 11; Cambridge, Mass.: SBL, 1973]), who translates this line, "Were you a slave when you were called? Don't worry about it. But if, indeed, you become manumitted, by all means [as a freedman] live according to [God's calling]."

Whether Paul means "slavery" or "freedom" with the unstated "it"—i.e., "rather make use of slavery" or "rather make use of freedom"—he stresses the irrelevance or insignificance of such external conditions with a final call to doing something useful, not merely something for oneself. Fee (*Epistle*, pp. 315–18) argues extensively, vigorously, and persuasively for understanding Paul to say, *if freedom is gained, make use of freedom,* and the NIV seems to offer the best rendering of the phrase; yet one should still see that freedom per se is a secondary concern for Paul.

In this verse Paul uses the singular form of the pronoun **you** and the second person singular form of a verb **(you were called)**, although the references to "each one" and "a man" in the other sentences are generic singular forms of pronouns. Contrast v. 23, which is in plural forms.

7:22 / The NIV catches the precise sense of Paul's language with the word **freedman.** A freedman was a slave who had gained freedom after being born or sold into slavery, whereas a free man was one who was born free. See M. I. Finley, "Freedman," *OCD,* pp. 447–48.

7:23 / On the topic of slavery in antiquity, see the incisive essay by M. I. Finley, "Slavery," *OCD,* pp. 994–96.

7:24 / The phrase translated "with God" is subtle, for Paul could have used other words than the Gk. he employed here, *para theō.* The nuance of this phrase in Gk. means more than "in relation to" or "present with"; it also carries and communicates the sense of "from God's point of view." See Orr and Walther, *I Corinthians,* p. 215.

These verses are an alternating series of statements about virginity and marriage, the eschatological nature of the time, and the death of a spouse and remarriage. An amazing variety of issues is treated in rapid succession. Verses 25–28 are difficult, in part, because of the uncertain (for later readers) specific identity of the virgins. The virgin is an unmarried young woman, but other details of her status remain unclear. Paul's eschatology becomes explicit in verses 29–31, so that all of human existence is relativized in light of the conviction that God's work is bringing this world to its end. In turn, verses 32–35 are well-intended (v. 35) but one-sided advice. Then, the issue of the virgins comes around again in verses 36–38. Finally, Paul's logic extends itself to the matter of a woman losing her husband and the possibility of remarrying in verses 39–40, and his thought remains consistent to the end of the section.

7:25 / Paul clearly states that he is offering his own opinion, not a word from the Lord, but he suggests that his opinion is informed and valuable. Paul's thinking is determined both by the presence and power of the Spirit at work in his life and by his apocalyptically formed eschatological conviction that the future of the world as it now exists is to be but a brief span of time (see vv. 26, 31).

7:26 / Paul refers explicitly to **the present crisis,** using a Greek word that usually connotes "necessity" *(anagkē),* indicating that he is advising the Corinthians concerning what seems necessary under the circumstances. Therefore, Paul advises the virgins (the unmarried women) to stay as they are, unmarried—as should everyone, whatever their condition.

7:27 / Paul delineates the possible groups: **married** and **unmarried.** The rhetorical cast of his writing becomes pointed as he addresses the Corinthians with singular "you" forms, so that each one would feel addressed personally. Paul tells one group, first, **not** to **seek a divorce;** then, he instructs the other group **not to look for a wife.** The advice is male-dominant, as was the cultural setting of that day. Since the men were normally the initiators of the marital relationship, Paul naturally speaks to them at this point, advising against pursuing marriage or divorce.

7:28 / Nevertheless, having advised the Corinthians to remain as they were in terms of marriage, Paul adds that if someone marries—be that a single man **(you)** or a single woman **(a virgin)**—that person does **not sin.** The move to inclusivity is remarkable, especially given the cultural setting. Even having added this qualification and explanation, Paul offers further reinforcement for his original admonition, "Do not seek [to divorce or to marry]." Paul's motivation is to spare persons from the normal, natural, necessary concerns of marriage, which would distract them from devoting themselves to developing a deeper relationship to God.

Of course, commentators regularly note that Paul's perspective on marriage is slanted. He does say that avoiding marriage is a good way to avoid certain stress, and he does not ponder the positive dimensions of marriage that bring the partners in marriage to fulfillment and often make them better persons and stewards of God's grace. One should not be surprised by Paul's thinking. He is not necessarily antimarriage or negative about the value of such a relationship; he is merely unsympathetic and partially informed. Paul was not omniscient, although he was gifted with a capacity for celibacy, which gave him a particular point of view. Since he had no desire or need to marry, he could not fully appreciate the importance of such a life for those who are gifted for so living. Marriage would have been a second-best arrangement for Paul (perhaps worse for his wife!), but he musters empathy and compassion as best he can by saying, **if you do marry, you have not sinned ... I want to spare you** [many troubles in this life].

7:29–31 / Paul explains his reasoning in one long complex, compound sentence that makes up verses 29–31: **What I mean . . .** He explicates and illustrates by naming several groups: **those who have wives, those who mourn, those who are happy, those who buy,** and **those who use the things of the world.** The groups named are self-evident, although Paul attempts to create some pairs of contrasting groups as he uses rhetorical illustrations to speak to anyone and everyone at one level or another. Paul's point of view is unmitigatedly eschatological. All of human existence is relativized in light of the conviction that God's work is bringing this world to its end **(this world in its present form is passing away)**—an old world, infected with evil and disobedience, was dying, and in the power of the cross and resurrection of Jesus God was at work bringing a new world into existence through judgment and grace. Paul's words have been anticipated by many of his preceding remarks about Christian freedom and the aim of Christian life. His point is fairly simple: The time left is short (or, limited by God's current actions), so the believers are to live life fully for God. The passion of Paul's confidence in God and the urgency of his appeal for full devotion are still pertinent, even if one does not anticipate the imminent demise of this world.

7:32 / Paul's tone becomes more leisurely, and his sentence are briefer and at ease. He reiterates his motivation for advising the Corinthians, **I would like you to be free from concern** (as in v. 28); and then he adds his own positive, even optimistic position, **an unmarried man is concerned about the Lord's affairs.** Paul might have clarified himself even further had he added that "unmarried men *gifted with chastity and devoted to God* may be (or should be) concerned about the Lord's affairs." Failure is never in view in this motivational address.

7:33–34a / The focus shifts again to the married man and the reality that he will face in marriage (from Paul's point of view and in terms of his previously expressed understanding of the complexity of marriage—v. 28). Paul is concerned to warn those in Corinth away from unnecessary distraction in doing God's will. He might here have elaborated, however, "married men will (or should) be necessarily concerned about affairs of this world that are related to marriage." The issues with which Paul concerns himself in these lines and in the immediately preceding verses are focus, priorities, relationships—that is, putting the affairs or mission of God above all else.

7:34b / At last in this shifting discussion Paul turns to the **unmarried woman** or **virgin.** He comments on the advantage of her singleness in much the way he spoke to the unmarried man, and again his concern is that should she marry, she will be necessarily distracted from God's work by being concerned with the affairs of this world. This statement is remarkably balanced in terms of form, language, and concern in comparison with the foregoing words to unmarried men, so one sees that Paul's uniform concern is that the believer's first priority be the devoting of himself or herself to God's work. The explicit references to the unmarried woman's or virgin's **body and spirit** may reflect the concerns of those in Corinth, or these anthropological terms may result from the reality that in marriage, especially in giving birth to and rearing a family, the woman is subject to specific physical and spiritual demands.

7:35 / Paul reiterates his central concern with full devotion and a fulfilling relationship to God. The perspective is still apocalyptic-eschatologically formed: Christians either live for God or they don't. The ultimate importance of the call to devotion and mission is foremost in Paul's mind as he exhorts and pleads with those to whom he was writing. Still, Paul's attitude and understanding are ascetic, and there is a range of possibilities that do not seem to occur to Paul in this vigorous discussion. Paul seems capable of understanding marriage only as a responsibility that has the potential (or, certainty) of creating obligations. As he writes from his own Spirit-endowed gift of singleness with little understanding of the broad range of possible relationships in marriage, the idea that love and mutual support in a marriage might foster more effective Christian living does not appear to cross his eschatologically riveted thinking. Paul has said, however, and will repeat, that the advice here is his own as one devoted to and gifted with the presence and power of God's Spirit.

7:36–38 / These verses are remarkably obscure, a notorious problem for both translation and interpretation. Paul addresses a potential complication for those who may attempt to follow his advice to remain unmarried. His syntax is awkward, even clumsy, as generations of interpreters have noted. The translation in the NIV offers a resolution that reaches back at least to the KJV but that many recent commentators and translations have abandoned. The NIV does recognize the acute complexity of the verses and even offers an alternative translation to the difficult passage in the footnotes to the main text (see Additional Notes). Unfortunately, this other rendering does not fully expose and deal with several issues in the text any better than does the primary translation.

The basic problem for understanding these verses is that Paul seems to change the subject of his discussion (literally the subject of the verbs) from one sentence to another. Read in simplest, most straightforward fashion, verse 36 seems to refer to the man who is engaged to a virgin; whereas verse 38 seems to refer to the father of the virgin, although the reference to **the virgin** (lit. "your virgin") in verse 38 is an odd manner of referring to someone's daughter. Verse 37 is ambiguous as to its subject. Problems arise when translations, like the NIV, attempt to make Paul's words deal with a single subject, be that either the fiancé or the father of the virgin. Indeed, the attempt to read the lines as discussing the situation of a single subject (fiancé or father) produces strange, comical, possibly absurd results.

In any reading of the verses the **virgin** is to be understood as a young, unmarried woman. The NIV rendering in verse 36 suggests that the virgin **is getting along in years,** similar to the way the KJV translated the sentence; but this manner of translation ignores the syntax and the problem of the subject, for the words translated "is getting along in years" more likely means "is of strong passion" and almost certainly refers to the fiancé of the virgin rather than to the virgin herself. Thus, verse 36 seems to refer to an engaged man who had marked passion for relations with his fiancée.

Verse 37 is ambiguous and jumbled. Perhaps, even before this verse, Paul had created a significant twist with the words "let them marry" at the end of verse 36 (translated in the NIV as **They should get married,** a misreading of an impersonal verb). By saying "let them marry," Paul seems to begin to address the father of the virgin bride-to-be. Then, in verse 37, Paul may assume that he is reasoning with the father of the young woman, assuring him that in the correct circumstances discouraging or refusing marriage of his daughter is all right. Then in verse 38 Paul states the balance of the situation, again in relation to the father's point of view, "So that both the one marrying off his virgin does well, and the one not marrying does better."

Readers of this portion of 1 Corinthians may never know exactly what Paul intended to say and the issues he intended to address at this point. Was Paul addressing the fiancé, the father, both? All solutions have difficulties, although despite the obscure character of this text certain conclusions are beyond debate. First, Paul is once again speaking of the situation of persons who are unmarried, in this instance, those not previously married. His basic advice is that if they can refrain from marriage then they should, but if they cannot—having not been endowed with chastity, as a passionate desire reveals—then they are at liberty to marry. Second, Paul prefers the state of singleness, since he assumes it frees persons from marital and family matters that might distract them from fully attending to God's work. Third, Paul's ultimate concern is that God's mission be carried out faithfully and decently through the lives of men and women in the church. For Paul mission is more important than marriage, and marrying or refraining from marriage should facilitate God's purposes, not hinder the doing of God's will.

7:39 / With this verse Paul seems to shift back to the subject he originally addressed in 7:1–24, the situation of the married women and the nature of the marital bond for those who are already married. The position that Paul stakes out at the outset of the discussion, **A woman is bound to her husband as long as he lives,** is contrary to both pagan and Jewish practices in antiquity. This declaration is, however, consistent with the word of the Lord that Paul reported earlier in 7:10. Paul has already discussed the issues of divorce and remarriage, and here he does not elaborate that particular set of dynamics. Rather, Paul assumes the permanence of marriage (and the prohibition of divorce, although it may occur anyway) and in turn reflects on the situation of a woman whose **husband dies.** In such a situation, Paul's advice is clear: **she is free to marry anyone she wishes, but he must belong to the Lord.** In other words, Christian widows may remarry, but they are to marry Christian men. The further complication of a mixed marriage between believer and nonbeliever is not to be introduced into the life of the believer after the death of a spouse. The NIV once again gives an overly heavy tone to Paul's words, which literally say, "A wife is bound as long as her husband lives; but if he may sleep [a euphemism for dies], she is free to be married to the one she wishes—only in the Lord." Paul's admonition at this point assumes the word of the Lord and offers a common-sense reasoning to a related situation.

7:40 / What Paul says here comes as no surprise: He prefers the condition of singleness because it offers the potential for the believer to devote full energy and attention to the mission of God. Thus, if a Christian woman who becomes a widow can remain unmarried, Paul regards that as the best option. In the context of Greco-Roman antiquity, where women were often more vulnerable than men and dependent on others, some unmarried widows were in peril. Paul does not offer psychological or sociological analysis but once more demonstrates his conviction that the believers should avoid undue complications that might hamper their attention to God's will for their lives.

Paul's final word may be utterly serious or mildly sarcastic, and readers in Corinth might have heard him in different ways: **and I think that I too have the Spirit of God.** Those who recognized Paul's apostolic responsibilities would be comforted, while those who doubted Paul's spiritual gifts might feel confronted. In either case, Paul recognizes that his opinion and advice were formed in a theological matrix and not given off the top of his head or even from the bottom of his human heart.

Additional Notes §21

7:25 / This verse begins with the words **now about . . .** (Gk. *peri de . . .*), an apparent allusion to the letter and the concerns that the Corinthians had addressed to Paul. Therefore, scholars suspect and frequently suggest that some among the Corinthians were taking vows of celibacy, so Paul's discussion of the matter in this and the following verses has a more formal religious tone than may appear at the surface level of the words. This hypothesis about the situation may be correct, since Paul has already taken up the Corinthians' saying, "It is good for a man not to touch a woman [i.e., not to marry?]," in 7:1–7; and he refers again to the Corinthians' letter here.

7:26 / Conzelmann (*1 Corinthians*, p. 132) notes that the **crisis** (Gk. *anagkē*) is apocalyptic in nature, as the Gk. word indicates. D. J. Doughty ("The Presence and Future of Salvation in Corinth," *ZNW* 66 [1975], pp. 61–90) contends that the linguistic content of this section of the letter (vv. 25–40, esp. vv. 29–31) reveals not an apocalyptic outlook but a concern with the interaction and relationship of Christians and the world. The lordship of Christ over the lives of believers raises significant questions about how and why they relate to the structures of the present world. Thus, the issue is not merely one of the future but also, or especially, the presence of salvation in Corinth.

Watson (*First Epistle*, p. 75) observes an awkward repetitiveness about Paul's language in this verse and suggests that Paul is quoting a slogan from the Corinthians, who were stating their version of a line they had learned from or that agreed with Paul.

7:27 / Some commentators suggest that this verse is not focused on the **married** and the **unmarried,** but rather on the married and the widowed. Literally Paul refers to the "bound" (Gk. *deō*) and the "free" or "released" (Gk. *lyō*), so his language is ambiguous.

7:28 / **Troubles** (Gk. *thliphis*) is a synonym for "crisis" (Gk. *anagkē*) and is equally apocalyptic in its connotations.

7:29 / **Time** here is designated with the Gk. word *kairos,* not *chronos.* An old and sometimes artificial distinction between these words, where *kairos* means a significant moment and *chronos* means the duration of time, seems appropriate here from comparison with 7:39. Thus, some translations reasonably render the word *kairos* with "appointed time."

7:30 / Cf. Rom. 12:15.

7:31 / Conzelmann (*1 Corinthians,* p. 133) summarizes Paul's preference as "freedom in the midst of involvement," and explains, "Eschatology really determines the conduct of life."

7:32 / **Free from concern** (Gk. *amerimnos*) more literally connotes "free from distraction" and is sometimes rendered "carefree," which may be misunderstood to mean "happy-go-lucky" or "without a care." Paul is neither euphoric nor utopic. He is concerned with unnecessary or avoidable distractions, specifically from devotion and mission. L. Legrand ("The Spiritual Value of Virginity according to Paul," *Indian Ecclesiastical Studies* 1 [1962], pp. 175–95) argues that Paul's advocacy of virginity was noted by a desire for Christians to be freed from the world, but freed for spiritual progress. Moreover, D. L. Balch ("1 Cor 7:32–35 and Stoic Debate about Marriage, Anxiety, and Distraction," *JBL* 102 [1983], pp. 429–39) shows how Paul's language and logic would have gained a ready hearing from those familiar with Stoic contentions that marriage was advantageous for some and a hindrance for others.

7:34 / Paul's references to "being concerned" and to "interests" is not a discussion of good vs. bad; rather, he contrasts good and better at this point. Thus, attending to marital affairs is good, while attending to the affairs of the Lord is better.

7:35 / Cf. v. 32. Paul's effort to explain his concern is seen in the way he reiterates his point. This repetition is not typical of his normal style of writing. He states that he seeks **not to restrict you** (plural), a vivid and unusual choice of words that literally means "not to put a noose on you" (Orr and Walther, *I Corinthians,* p. 220).

7:36–38 / The NIV's alternative reading is:

(36) If anyone thinks he is not treating his daughter properly, and if she is getting along in years, and he feels she ought to marry, he should do as he wants. He is not sinning. He should let her get married. (37) But the man who has settled the matter in his own mind, who is under no compulsion but has control over his own will, and who has made up his mind to keep the virgin unmarried—this man also does the right thing. (38) So

then, he who gives his virgin in marriage does right, but he who does not give her in marriage does even better.

7:36 / Paul uses the Gk. verb *gameō*, meaning "to marry." Contrast v. 38, where he employs a related but different verb. The word translated **getting along in years** is *hyperakmos* in Gk. and takes its specific sense in relation to various subjects. The NIV reads the word in relation to an older virgin woman, although in the Gk. form and syntax this word relates more naturally to the man in this discussion (the fiancé of the virgin) and connotes "of strong passion" or "uncontrollably passionate." Barrett (*Epistle*, p. 182) suggests the rendering "over-sexed."

In addition to the interpretations that contend that Paul has either a fiancé or a father of a virgin in mind, K. N. Papadopoulos ("Sēmeiōma gia to 1 Kor 7,36–38," *Deltion Biblikon Meleton* 19 [1990], pp. 10–12) reads this passage in relation to Exod. 21:7–11 to argue that the man in Paul's mind at this point is a slave owner who could either marry his virgin slave girl or give her away in marriage to someone else; thus, the syntax is not so tortuous as translators and interpreters have suggested.

7:37 / **Control** here is the Gk. word *exousia*, most often rendered "authority," but here coupled with the preposition *peri* to indicate "control over" something.

7:38 / The verb here is *gamizō*, literally "to marry off" or "to give in marriage"; contrast 7:36, where Paul used *gameō*.

7:39 / Paul uses the word *chronos* in reference to "time," indicating the duration of time; thus, the NIV, **as long as** (Gk. *eph' hoson chronon*). Cf. 7:29.

7:40 / The form of the word **happier** is *comparative*, i.e., it states a comparison. Paul is not discussing "happy vs. sad," but "happy and happier." The word (Gk. *makariōteros*) is similar in its root form to the word most often translated "blessed" in the Beatitudes (Matt. 5:3–11); thus, Paul may wish to indicate or imply that such happiness is a state of grace, especially since one's marital status should result from the work of the Spirit in one's life.

§22 Contrasting Knowledge and Love
(1 Cor. 8:1–6)

At this point in the letter to Corinth Paul enters into the discussion of an issue that will engage him, in one way or another, through 11:1. While the concrete concern that calls for his attention is the issue of "food sacrificed to idols," at a theological level his focus is Christian rights and responsibilities, especially regarding "knowledge" and "freedom" in lifestyle practices. Interpreters trace the course of Paul's reflections in slightly different ways, for at one point Paul seems to consider the eating of foods that had originally been offered in pagan temple ritual, and at other places he seems to be commenting on the presence and participation of Christians at the sacrifices themselves. Some background information is necessary to comprehend this discussion that otherwise seems far removed from modern concerns.

Summarizing the general topic of sacrifice in antiquity, *The Oxford Classical Dictionary* reports:

> A sacrifice, according to Plato (*Euthyphro* 14c), is a gift to the gods, and this was the current view of antiquity.... Modern comparative method, however, combined with anthropological theory, has sufficiently shown the complexity of the problem. One ancient attempt to classify the mass of confused details [concerning sacrifices] ... distinguished offerings of praise, of thanksgiving, and of supplication. We may also distinguish between gods, daemones (heroes), and the dead as recipients of the offerings, and between private and public sacrifices. Finally, we may lay stress on the material of the sacrifice, the difference between vegetable and animal offerings, and on the way in which the offerings were made over to the supernatural powers (communal-sacrificial feast, holocaust, burial, libation, etc.). (S. Eitrem and J. E. Fontenrose, "Sacrifice," *OCD*, pp. 943–45)

In antiquity much meat and some other food and drink that was available for public consumption in urban settings was originally presented and processed in the context of pagan temple celebrations. A practitioner of pagan religion brought or

bought animals for sacrifice to one of the many pagan gods. After the sacrifice was made and the designated portions of the
sacrificial animal were presented to the gods, a further portion
was made available to the pagan temple priests for their use,
consumption, or resale. Yet another portion could be made
available to the person offering the sacrifice for a ritual meal in
the banquet facilities that were part of many temples. Meat that
was left over or that was initially designated for resale was
sometimes transported to the marketplace for purchase and private consumption.

In order to understand Paul's comments in this section of
the letter it is important to attempt to discern exactly which action or setting he is thinking about as he diagnoses the situation
and the problems that arose in the church in relation to these
practices. In chapters 8 and 10 Paul overtly addresses the matter
of idol meat, whereas in chapter 9 he indirectly focuses on the issue and is more generally concerned with the closely related and
foundational matter of Christian rights and responsibilities. In
10:1–11:1 Paul clearly takes up both the question of the believers'
involvement in the cultic aspects of sacrifice and consumption of
sacrificial foods in the temple (10:1–22) and the contention that
Christians may partake of food/meat that was originally from the
temple but then offered in the market for eating in private settings (10:23–11:1). Which of these settings and activities does
Paul have in mind in the discussion in chapter 8?

Traditionally the majority of scholars have understood
that in the present passage Paul is initially concerned with the
matter of eating foods sacrificed and then sold in the marketplace, as he is later in 10:23–11:1. But through the careful and
persuasive exegetical work of G. D. Fee, interpreters have come
to think that Paul begins a discussion in 8:1–6, 7–13 that he continues in 10:1–22 concerning Christian participation in pagan
temple cultic meals. However, this view and the traditional interpretation are difficult to maintain because of the complicated,
even contorted, discussion that Paul offers in 8:1–13. Moreover,
it may be that Paul is already thinking about both aspects of the
problem of idol meat and that he is mixing the concerns in this
chapter. Verse 10 of chapter 8 explicitly mentions the possible
presence of the Christian in the pagan temple environment, although it was an option in antiquity to dine in that setting much
as modern customers eat in restaurants without serious thought
about the preparation of the food. Paul's tone and emphases do

shift as he moves from 8:1 through 11:1, but as close reading reveals, Paul's primary concern in 8:1–13—with the possible exception of one illustrative reference in verse 10—is with the consumption of food that was originally offered to idols rather than with the participation of Christians in offerings to idols per se. Read from this vantage point, although the discussion deals with ancient and foreign matters for many of today's Western readers, Paul's remarks are fairly straightforward; with the assistance of rhetorical insights, the verses are comprehensible and even, by analogy, relevant for contemplating appropriate lifestyle practices for believers.

8:1 / As the opening words show, Paul is again responding to an issue brought to his attention by the Corinthians. The NIV presents Paul's introduction of the issues and then moves to state the Corinthians' position after punctuating with a colon. The NRSV goes further in suggesting that Paul is probably quoting the Corinthians' own position, perhaps from their letter to him, by placing quotation marks around "all of us possess knowledge." One may speculatively reconstruct the imaginary conversation Paul presents this way:

Paul: **Now about the food sacrificed to idols:**
Corinthians: **"We know that we all possess knowledge."**
Paul: **Knowledge puffs up, but love builds up.**

We have already explored Paul's response to and critique of the Corinthians' insistence on and preoccupation with **knowledge** and wisdom in the commentary on earlier chapters of this letter. At present, Paul's critique of the Corinthians' declaration follows in his sharp contrast between **knowledge** and **love**. Paul recognized the preferable character of love at 4:21, and in 13:1–14:1 he will elaborate the ultimate importance of love as the hallmark of Christian character and community. For now, he makes a play on the imagery of "increase" by saying that knowledge **puffs up, but** love **builds up** in order to expose the difference between that which yields arrogance or pride and that which produces positive, constructive results.

8:2 / Paul remarks that knowledge is of no value in itself. Knowledge for mere self-aggrandizement reveals a deeper ignorance, and preoccupation with self-glorifying knowledge is pretentious. Paul's choice of words, translated **as he ought to know,** can be misread. More literally Paul says, "as it is necessary to know," using an impersonal form of a helping verb (Gk. *dei*) that implies divine necessity. Thus, the gist of Paul's statement may be paraphrased, "as it is necessary to know according to God" or "as God requires one to know." What Paul states raises questions: What does God want the believers to know, and how do they know it when they do?

8:3 / Paul briefly states the answer to his implied questions. The appropriate criterion is not knowledge but love for God. To focus on knowledge demonstrates an inadequate understanding. What matters is to be known by God, and the evidence of God's knowing a believer is the believer's love for God. God's will and work, not a self-inflated estimation of the value of what one knows, must be the first priority of a believer. In other words, "God knows, and so we know; God loves, and so we love." To be known by God is to be loved, and to be loved by God enables the one who is loved to love God, not merely to pursue and to possess knowledge. Although he does not advocate any action explicitly, that "love builds up" indicates that the believers' love for God evinces itself in the constructive doing of God's work in the world.

8:4 / Again, Paul's rhetoric indicates that he is referring to, perhaps quoting from, the Corinthians' own thinking. The NIV, as usual, leads into Paul's citation or reference by punctuating with a colon.

Paul:	**So then, about eating food sacrificed to idols:**
Corinthians:	**"We know that an idol is nothing in the world and that there is no God but one."**

Some translations, among them the NRSV, indicate the Corinthians' thinking and slogans with quotation marks ("no idol in the world really exists" and "there is no God but one"). Either way, in verse 4 Paul is introducing and stating a logic and line of thinking that he will elaborate in the following verses. The only problem for interpretation in this verse is whether, when Paul writes, **We know,** he is in agreement with the following statements or is repeating the Corinthians' thinking. In 10:20 Paul will state his own clear conviction that behind the pagan idols is the reality of demons. Since this seems somewhat different from the assertion that idols are nothing in the world, it may be that his own thinking and teaching are not being presented in the statements recorded in verse 4.

8:5 / Paul starts to analyze and even to dissect the Corinthians' position. He does so carefully, taking phrases and offering his own commentary on them. First, he makes a general and uncommitted observation **(For even if there are so-called gods, whether in heaven or on earth)** that recognizes that people speak of and revere what they consider to be gods. Then, having allowed for this possibility, Paul seems to indicate that there is some reality to these so-called gods, saying, **as indeed there are many "gods" and many "lords,"** using plural forms (gods/lords) of titles he and the Christians attribute to the one true God who is the all-and-all of divine reality for Christians' faith and practice: "for us there is but one God."

8:6 / In this verse Paul makes a confessional statement that is creedal in character. This creed assumes a Christian perspective and focuses on creation, call, Christ, and redemption. From the discussion that follows in the remainder of this chapter one sees that the Corinthians had turned this central confession into a speculative thesis that led to a lifestyle that denied the reality of idols. Paul, by contrast, takes pagan gods and lords seriously. At 10:20, when Paul relates such gods and lords to demons, one sees that he considered such gods and lords to be dangerous entities.

The extraction of the beliefs that are stated in this verse and their abstraction into principles produced results (seen behind the controversies in Corinth) that Paul labors to critique and correct. In speaking of **one God,** Paul is not referring to a mere fact that, when known, sets one free; rather, the one God is **the Father,** the Creator who made **all things**—including humanity—so that the believers **live** in relation to this known God and devote life to doing God's will. God is the one **from whom** and **for whom** the believers **live.** Moreover, the **one Lord** is **Jesus Christ,** who is the one **through whom** both creation **(all things)** and those who are experiencing redemption **(we) live.** Jesus Christ is the Lord who mediates God's creative and redemptive power in such a way that God's will and way are made real in the lives of believers. The dynamics of such creative, redemptive, life-giving relations are the heart of Christian faith and living. In relation to the one God and one Lord the believer is both informed and formed; that is, the believer finds a new identity and a new way of life.

Additional Notes §22

8:1 / Paul begins this section with a phrase, now concerning . . . (Gk. *Peri*), that indicates he is focusing on a particular topic brought to his attention by the Corinthians—and almost certainly from the Corinthians' letter. The concern is with **food sacrificed to idols,** or idol meat (Gk. *eidōlothytos*). This rare term, perhaps coined for this discussion by Paul, has been found to be used for animal sacrifices that were presented and eaten in the pagan temples, not goods sacrificed and then sold or eaten elsewhere; B. Witherington III ("Not So Idle Thoughts about *eidolothuton*," *TynB* 44 [1993], pp. 237–54). See also G. D. Fee, "*Eidōlothyta* Once Again: An Interpretation of 1 Corinthians 8–10," *Bib* 61 (1980), pp. 172–97; and the critical reply to that work by B. N. Fisk, "Eating Meat Offered to Idols: Corinthian Behavior and Pauline Response in 1 Corinthians 8–10 (A Response to Gordon Fee)," *TJ* 10 (1989), pp. 49–70. The seminal study on idol meat is the monograph by W. L. Willis, *Idol Meat in Corinth: The Pauline Argument in 1 Corinthians 8 and 10* (SBLDS 68; Chico, Calif.: Scholars Press, 1985). Regarding 8:1–13, Willis contends that this chapter raises and presents the issue, which is more particularly treated in ch. 10.

Already at 4:6, 18–19; 5:2 Paul had used the verb translated here **puff up** (Gk. *physioō;* elsewhere English transl. = "go beyond," "become arrogant," "be arrogant," "be proud").

8:2 / Paul's rhetoric of anonymity establishes a fictional opponent's position, perhaps with sarcasm, for he writes literally, "If someone supposes to know something"—a position that Paul sets up to knock down. Moreover, in retort to the claim of any Corinthian who might allege spiritual insight, maturity, or perfection (an issue in earlier portions of the letter), Paul makes a pointed rebuttal, "Not yet!" (Gk. *oupō*).

8:3 / In juxtaposition to and as a replacement of the assertion of "knowledge" by "someone," Paul writes, "But if someone loves God!" The sense of Paul's contrasting declaration is this: It is what God does—God's knowing the believer, not the believer's knowing—that produces the worthwhile result: a believer who loves God.

8:4 / In 8:1 Paul made a general reference to idol food or idol meat. He uses the same term here, but it now qualifies the action of eating (Gk. *Peri tēs brōseōs oun tōn eidōlothytōn;* English transl. = **So then, about eating food sacrificed to idols**). Paul's phrasing indicates that his emphasis and concern are the action of eating, not the substance of the food per se.

8:5 / Paul's words *kai gar eiper* (lit. "for granted that" or "for although") are an indication of his purpose in v. 5, where he seeks to explicate the deeper issues inherent in the convenient, but possibly misleading, slogans of v. 4.

8:6 / The words of the confessional material in this verse are often set in poetic or creedal form in critical Gk. texts and in some English translations. Such schematization of Paul's words is the work of modern editors, although there is good reason to present the phrases in this manner. One way of arranging the lines that highlights the inherent theological dimensions and concerns of the verse is as follows (very literally rendered):

> But to us
>> there is one God, the Father,
>> out of whom are all things and unto whom we are;
>> and there is one Lord, Jesus Christ
>> through whom are all things and through whom we are.

Paul's opening words ("But to us") establish a Christian starting point for the declarations, much like a creed. Then, he makes a monotheistic declaration ("one God") after which he designates *Father*, a way of naming God that was practiced and taught by Jesus and that emphasizes relationship and most likely creation, as in the next words ("out of whom are all things"). The relational nature of Christian life is summarized with the recognition of calling and devotion ("unto whom we are"). In turn, Paul's words take a christological focus, a bold and mysterious declaration in the context of monotheistic faith: "and there is one Lord," for he names the Lord "Jesus Christ"—referring to the historical figure Jesus and identifying him as God's Messiah (Christ). Paul presents this one Lord as the agent of creation ("through whom are all things") and the agent of redemption and salvation ("through whom we are"), so that the lordship of Jesus Christ is thought of in terms of relationship to God, the doing of God's work, preexistence, and soteriology. The statement is heavily theological, although offered in relation to the stance of Christian faith ("but to us"); these theological convictions create a strong sense of identity and purpose for life.

§23 *Valid Christian Relations (1 Cor. 8:7–13)*

Two distinct groups emerge among the Corinthians as Paul continues, now more pointedly, to discuss the eating of food that had been offered to idols. Moreover, the basic issue of eating such foods becomes more complex as Paul mentions the practice of some of the Corinthian Christians' eating in an idol's temple. The matter is more than a question of customs and manners, as the overtly theological cast of Paul's language reveals.

Those who deny the idols insist their knowledge frees them to eat meat that had been previously sacrificed to idols (as most meat for sale had), despite the objections of other believers who associated idols with false deities or demons and were scandalized by the eating of idol meat. Paul teaches that freedom is not abstract, but concrete. Real freedom is being freed from the necessity to assert only, or primarily, one's own rights. Knowledge alone is dangerous. What ultimately matters is that believers desire the well-being of others rather than insist on their own rights and privileges.

8:7 / Paul bluntly refutes the claim of some of the Corinthians that they possessed special knowledge, saying, **But not everyone knows this** (referring to some Corinthians' denial of the relevance of idols). Paul refers to the pagan background from which certain Corinthian Christians came and indicates that every believer did not share the conviction that idols are not real. Paul's aim is to correct the arrogant behavior toward their fellow Christians of those denying idols. He labors in behalf of **weak** believers who assumed the idols were real and acted accordingly. Paul still does not concede the reality of these idols, but he makes plain that those who believe in such entities are bound by their convictions to act in a congruent way. His central concern, however, is the negative impact of the controversial behavior of the free ones on those who had religious scruples about so-called idol meat. While these weak people have the problem of defiled or defiling consciences, Paul does not address this group and suggest a remedy or cure. Rather, he takes the discussion to those who are eating idol meat and possibly encouraging others to do the same. The problem of the weak becomes a problem for Paul, and he takes the problem to their fellow Christians who apparently considered themselves to be above the matter.

8:8 / Paul offers a pair of statements that went against the contention of some of the stronger Corinthians. The ring of these lines is memorable, so Paul may have offered such remarks as counterslogans to the declared positions of some of the Corinthians. With all the uproar in Corinth over food, particularly over the eating of food sacrificed to idols, Paul states what should have been self-evident, **Food does not bring us near to God.** From the discussion of this topic in chapters 8 and 10, one suspects that some members of the Corinthian congregation thought that their cavalier disregard for what and where they ate demonstrated their superior knowledge and religious freedom. Such aims did not edify either the relationships among the believers or the relationships between the carefree diners and God.

In a balanced set of rhetorical phrases Paul makes and repeats one point: **We are no worse if we do not eat, and no better if we do** (lit. "neither by not eating do we lose, nor by eating do we gain"). These phrases underscore the last statement regarding being brought closer to God. Food does not do the job, because displaying or practicing this controversial freedom does not draw the believer closer to God.

8:9 / Paul turns directly to those insisting on eating idol meat and issues a strong directive, even an order, in the form of a warning. The NIV smoothes the statement, which more literally reads, "See that this right of yours doesn't become a stumbling block to the weak." Paul writes to the group in the community that was flaunting its freedom. By insisting on their liberty, they made the exercise of rights their ultimate concern. Paul perceives this insistence to be a threat, for it was self-serving and shortsighted. Nowhere in such exercise of personal freedoms is priority given to others over self. No consensus is sought in such arrangements. So Paul says that when one group's exercise of freedom or pursuit of rights becomes a scandal to another group's sensibilities, then the free people should be aware of the problem they are creating. His statement stings; it does not gently raise a hesitation. The force of the statement is so direct that no one should miss Paul's point.

8:10 / This verse creates complications for interpretation, because Paul specifically mentions the possible presence of believers in the temple of pagan deities. Whether Paul is discussing a possibility, a probability, or a reality is impossible to determine; he may be overstating the case to make his point with indisputable clarity. Interpretations that attempt to read the situation behind these remarks do not find sufficient evidence in the wording to make a definitive case. Moreover, a preoccupation with background can distract from the central concern Paul registers. Whatever kind of meat and wherever someone may eat it, Paul's point is this: if Christians give no thought to their actions when those actions are controversial, then although their actions are seemingly correct for them, others who do not share their convictions may misunderstand and be led astray.

Paul is not encouraging hypocrisy. Nor is he attempting to impose legalistic limits. By once again mentioning **conscience**, Paul deals with a concept of awareness that his readers would easily grasp and recognize as being emphasized. The ancient and the contemporary notions of conscience are different, however, and readers today may misunderstand Paul's argument (see Additional Notes for further information).

In essence, Paul's concern is that Christians give thought to others before they act in behalf of themselves, especially when they engage in activities that may produce needless controversy and undesirable results. According to Paul other believers are more important than the exercise of personal rights and freedom; thus, when pursuit of a supposed right becomes the first priority, then values have become imbalanced.

8:11 / The fire of Paul's rhetoric comes into full play in this declaration. The deep irony that Paul identifies is that **knowledge**, which some Corinthians contend produces freedom, can also destroy. By insisting on their rights because of knowledge, they may not only ignore but also harm the well-being of others. Paul reminds those who are in pursuit of their rights that the other believers—with whom they have a disagreement and for whom they may have mild disdain (calling them **weak**)—are those **for whom Christ died!** The believing community, with its various personalities, sensibilities, and disposition, is a community of persons for *all* of whom Christ died.

The believers, with their many differences, are alike in one way that should relativize their distinctions: each and every one of them are persons whose lives were given and sustained through Christ (8:6). The mention of the death of Christ serves to level the status and differences among believers by holding them together in the context of the gracious, mysterious, saving power of God at work in the death of Jesus Christ.

8:12 / Paul actually labels the behavior of those eating and scandalizing others who did not share their convictions as **sin**. To offend others through self-satisfying behavior is to **wound** them, to inflict harm. Yet the severity of the situation goes beyond even that level of gravity, for Paul writes that **in this way . . . you sin against Christ**. We see the corporate nature of Christian life. As Paul will later identify the body of believers to be the body of Christ, so here he recognizes that for one believer (member of the body) to harm another believer (another member of the body) is to inflict harm on Christ. Those insisting on their personal rights are in peril of violating the will and damaging the work of Christ in the world.

8:13 / Real freedom, Paul insists, is being freed from the necessity to assert only, or even primarily, one's own or a group's own rights. An ultimate concern for the well-being of others—here one's fellow believers—must inform and direct the behavior and practices of all believers. Thus, while Paul apparently had no problem with eating meat (**eat meat again** implies that he had eaten it already), he offers an illustrative personal example as the solution to the situation in Corinth, saying that he would refrain from eating meat (possibly idol meat) if his eating caused his **brother to fall into sin**. The sin mentioned here, in the context of the discussion of verse 12, is a violation of conscience, doing what others do rather than what one understands to be right.

While Paul's rhetoric is formed in negative statements (**I will never . . . I will not . . .**), his aim is a positive result: putting others before one's self or rights. While Paul never uses the word "love" in this portion of the discussion, the values and actions he encourages are the natural outcome of a life defined by love (see 8:1, 3; ch. 13). Finally the personal cast of Paul's language in making this argument leads to an even more personal and general discussion of rights and responsibilities in the next chapter of the letter. Remarkably, Paul seems to agree with the supposedly knowledgeable Corinthians about idol meat; however, he disagrees with the way they have been acting. Paul's comments reveal that he regards such behavior as misconduct both in and against Christ.

Additional Notes §23

8:7 / Paul's strong adversative opening, **But not** (Gk. *'All' ouk*) signals that he is taking exception to a previous statement. From context and content he is offering a correction to the claim in 8:1 that "We know that we all possess knowledge."

8:8 / Conzelmann (*1 Corinthians*, p. 148) observes, "The neutrality of food does *not* mean the neutrality of *conduct.*"

8:9 / The paragraphing of the NIV can be misleading. Neither the wording nor the grammar of Paul's Gk. gives reason to regard this verse as beginning a new segment of thought. In fact, the singsong sarcasm of v. 8 is extended in the poignant, passionate protest of this verse.

8:10 / Paul's reference to conscience *(syneidēsis)* is easily misunderstood by modern readers. A contemporary dictionary definition says,

> the sense or [awareness esp. of something within oneself] of the moral goodness or blameworthiness of one's own conduct, intentions, or character together with a feeling of obligation to do right or to be good. (*Webster's Ninth New Collegiate Dictionary* [Springfield, Mass.: Merriam-Webster, 1987], p. 278)

At the turn of the third millennium, however, conscience is understood in a remarkably introspective way. This understanding presents a problem for classical scholars, historical theologians, biblical scholars, and historians of psychology. Such interpreters of antiquity agree that ancients were not introspective in the sense that moderns (or postmoderns) are.

K. Stendahl makes and explains this point persuasively in his essay, "The Apostle Paul and the Introspective Conscience of the West," *HTR* 56 (1963), pp. 199–215; repr. in *Paul among Jews and Gentiles* (Philadelphia: Fortress, 1976). Ancients were egocentric, but they were not introspective. The Delphic inscription that reads "Know yourself" admonished ancients to assess their capacities with all possible objectivity; it did not direct them to look within to discover an inner self waiting to be actualized or to hear a voice registering the appropriateness or inappropriateness of their conduct. In Dio Chrysostom's Tenth Discourse, Diogenes says,

> it is difficult, nay rather impossible, to make use of god or man or one's own self if one does not know how. To make the attempt without know-

ing is an extremely harmful thing . . . in almost all cases where practical experience in "using" is lacking, it is difficult to be zealous . . . is there anyone, then, who can make use of himself who does not know himself? . . . Have you ever heard of the inscription at Delphi: "Know thyself"? . . . Is it not plain that the god gives this command to all, in the belief that they do not know themselves? (*Or.* 10.17–22, 27–28)

Thus, for the ancients self-knowledge and conscience were matters of assessing one's capacities and disciplining one's self with purposefulness.

8:11 / Paul signals the readers that he intends to give an explanation here by beginning the sentence with the explanatory postpositive (second word in the clause) *gar* (lit. "for," translated **So**).

8:12 / The word translated **wound** means "strike" or "beat" (Gk. *typtō*), so Paul is saying that the supposedly knowledgeable Corinthians strike a blow against the religious sensibilities of the weaker believers when they engage in their "enlightened" behavior.

8:13 / The Gk. word *dioper* **(Therefore)** that opens this statement shows that Paul is summarizing his conclusions from the deliberations in 8:7–12. He offers his conclusion in a conditional form: "if . . . [in that case] **I will never** . . ." Then, he adds another phrase in the form of a purpose clause, itself explanatory, "*in order that* **I will not cause him to fall.**" Thus, Paul delivers his advice and instructions in a nutshell.

§24 The Rights of an Apostle, Their Basis, and Paul's Practice (1 Cor. 9:1–18)

This chapter may appear to be an intrusion into the discussion of idols and eating foods that were sacrificed to an idol, but Paul takes himself and the matter of his rights as an apostle as an illustration of a proper demeanor for Christians. W. Willis ("An Apostolic Apologia? The Form and Function of 1 Corinthians 9," *JSNT* 24 [1985], pp. 33–48) is correct in observing that this section of the epistle is not about Paul's claiming of his rights as an apostle, despite the titles given to this portion of the letter in nearly every commentary and study Bible; rather, Paul explains the renunciation of his rights and, by example and implication, exhorts the readers to do the same for the benefit of others. Perhaps no major segment of any other letter is more rhetorical in form and force. Paul's style aims to engage, to persuade, and to motivate the readers toward doing God's will and work, not merely toward being religious—as they already are in very striking ways. In synopsis, Paul declares his own Christian freedom, then explains how and why he forewent his God-granted rights, and declares the motivation of his exercise of discipline. Paul vigorously presents a simple message that is easy to analyze but difficult to comprehend or embrace in life.

9:1 / Paul declares his freedom in a series of rhetorical questions. The queries are related; they build a case for the obvious freedom Paul enjoyed and examine the way Paul put that freedom into practice. Paul was **free** because of the grace of God in Jesus Christ. Yet, freed by Christ, Paul was commissioned or sent, **an apostle.** The outcome of Paul's exercise of freedom was faithful service to the Lord Jesus. That meant serving others in a way that produced dramatic results for their lives. Paul's founding of the Corinthian church is an example of this. In registering this logical sequence concerning freedom, Paul explains the real meaning of freedom in his own life.

9:2 / As Paul elaborates the meaning of freedom for his relationship to the Lord, he refers to his being an apostle. This contention seems to have been controversial. In verse 1 Paul appears to have stated one of the qualifications of an apostle: to have seen Jesus the Lord. Paul, of course, was not an earthly follower of Jesus, and so his experience of the Lord was distinguishable from the experience of those who were disciples during the course of Jesus' ministry and/or who were among the earliest members of the Jerusalem church. Paul's mention of any disputes related to the legitimacy of his apostleship is not his primary point, however, for his rhetoric aims at the Corinthians' remembering and affirming his work among them on behalf of the Lord. Their existence as a church is proof of his apostolic labor, and as an apostle he would have rights because of the freedom and commission of the Lord.

9:3 / If anyone questioned Paul's freedom, his apostolic experience, and attendant rights, all Paul needed to do was to point to the Corinthian congregation as evidence of God's work through him.

9:4–5 / Having reminded the Corinthians of their experience of his work and of their ability to affirm that he was the Lord's apostle, Paul next informs the Corinthians that he could make claims as others do. Paul mentions **the other apostles and the Lord's brothers and Cephas.** Paul's point in using this intriguing list of prominent persons (with whom the readers of this letter were most likely familiar) is to support his claims. Although the exact identities of those being named is not Paul's real concern, as a later reader one still wonders who these people were. "The other apostles" seems to refer to a broad group that included those who had seen the Lord Jesus and received a commission to ministry (see 15:3–11). The brothers of the Lord include James, whom Paul names explicitly later in the letter (15:7; also Gal. 1:19; cf. Mark 6:3). Cephas was the Aramaic form of the name Peter, meaning "rock"—a nickname given to Simon bar Jonah by Jesus in the course of his ministry (see 1 Cor. 1:12; cf. Mark 1:29–31; 3:16; Matt. 16:18–19).

Paul will elaborate the stated **right to food and drink** in more detail in verses 7–12; for now, he anticipates that discussion in order to create a contrast between his behavior and that of other leading figures in the church. The reference **to take a believing wife along with us** more literally reads, "to be accompanied by a sister as wife," although the NIV communicates the sense of Paul's words in a way that avoids unnecessary confusion. In the scheme of arrangements that Paul describes, the spouses of the traveling apostles were apparently also given hospitality by the churches that the apostles were visiting and serving.

9:6 / In contrast to the practices of those named in verse 5, Paul refers to himself and **Barnabas** in a way that indicates that they did not claim and accept food and drink, nor did they travel with the companionship of a spouse. Scholars often suggest that Paul is responding to some criticism of his habits of ministry, although if he is he does not elaborate the criticism here. In the writing of 2 Corinthians, this issue or one similar to it becomes explicit (see 2 Cor. 10–13, esp. ch. 11), but for now Paul's main concern is to recall the selfless, sacrificial pattern of his work in order to explain his motivation and to encourage the Corinthians themselves to be more concerned with others than with the exercise of their own rights. Moreover, Paul's rhetorical question shows further that Paul and Barnabas did **work for a living.** The practice of self-support and refusing the rights that were enjoyed by others set the pattern of ministry by Paul and Barnabas apart from the methods of others, but Paul merely refers to the methods of his and Barnabas's ministry to make a point about foregoing recognized rights. In the following verses (vv. 12–18) Paul further explains the motivation behind his particular practices.

9:7 / Paul mounts the rhetorical force of his case by referring to soldiers, planters, and shepherds. Paul forms analogies for the reasonableness of apostles' taking support from the congregations to which they ministered. The force of the logic in context, however, is not a comparison going from like to like, but a standard ancient argument that moves from lesser to greater, as becomes clear in verse 12. The language moves from everyday images to the level of remuneration for the labor of the apostles.

The choice of the images in the analogies is noteworthy. The **soldier** serves the commander; the vinedresser **plants a vineyard;** and the flock-herd **tends a flock.** In each instance some natural benefit is derived from the activity. Thus, from the by-product of the activities—warfare produced victory and booty; vineyards yielded fruit; flocks brought milk—the ones responsibly engaged in the activities educed an advantage without harm to the enterprise. In other words, Paul sees nothing wrong with taking support from the Corinthians, yet he refrains from enjoying the natural benefits of his labors.

9:8 / As Paul continues, he demonstrates that he recognized and agreed that God ordained that the apostles be able to derive their living from the work they did as ministers. He moves beyond a mere **human point of view**, as he documents his understanding by reference to **the Law**. Having laid out a logical, seemingly persuasive case, Paul does not leave the matter at that level; rather, he underwrites his reasoning with reference to the law, which was understood to be a definitive statement of the will and purposes of God.

9:9–11 / The mention of the law leads to a citation of Deuteronomy 25:4, in verse 9; and beyond this quoted material Paul builds a midrashic exposition in verses 9–11. That is, it is similar in form to the midrash, which freely retells a Bible story and makes applications of the lessons learned from the story to the situation of those to whom the midrash is addressed. In some critical editions of the Greek text, the words **when the plowman plows and the thresher threshes, they ought to do so in the hope of sharing in the harvest** are set as if they are also a quotation of Scripture. The style of Paul's words leading into these lines does seem to anticipate another quotation from the law. Although the maxim is similar to phrases in Deuteronomy 24:14 and Sirach 6:19, it does not exactly match any known text. The sense of the statement is plain, and Paul's exposition of the imagery in verse 11 is straightforward. Paul's use of Scripture is analogical, even semitypological, as he takes the references to **an ox** eating as it works and to agricultural activities as being indicative of God's will that the apostles take their sustenance from those among whom they ministered.

Paul's images and uses of illustrations at this point are occasions for some critics to accuse Paul of an abusive attitude toward the real elements of creation. Rather, Paul's style of exegesis is typical of his day. Philo of Alexandria, persherim (written interpretations of the Old Testament) from the Dead Sea Scrolls, and later rabbinical writings all engage in similar interpretations of texts. The idea was that God's will, as clearly revealed in simple matters, was to be applied to and understood as congruent with more complex issues. Mundane matters in relation to which God's will had been clearly revealed were taken as windows into the larger will of God and so treated as patterns for complicated situations. This kind of reasoning does not imply an inherent dismissal of the simple order of creation; rather, it recognizes the consistency of God's will in all levels of creation.

9:12 / Paul forms a rhetorical question to argue for his and Barnabas's right to **support from** the church to which they ministered. Yet he continues by bluntly stating that they did not use the right of support by the churches, lest their taking pay for ministry be misunderstood as fleecing the congregation. Paul's wording is circumspect; he does not want to cast aspersions on those who do claim support from the congregations or have their actions seen as inappropriate. Paul's aim was to avoid suspicion, to bypass potential misunderstanding, in order that no unnecessary objections be raised about the gospel itself because of the practices of Paul and his colleagues.

9:13 / Having explained the purity of his motives and the purpose of his practices, Paul elaborates the matter of his right to support by referring to the practice of supplying the needs of those in temple service from the proceeds given to the temple. This example is a fairly direct analogy that clarifies the previous models.

9:14 / Paul now builds on the picture he painted in verse 13 by saying, **In the same way.** . . . Then he cites a word from **the Lord** to the effect that **those who preach the gospel should receive their living from the gospel.** This command seems close to the words of Jesus in Luke 10:7 and does not appear to be a reference to an OT text.

9:15 / Still using a pattern of repetition to reinforce his argument, Paul states his position and practice, not in the form of another rhetorical question but as a direct statement, **But I have not used any of these rights.** Paul makes it clear that he is not asking indirectly for such support with his present discussion; then he proceeds to explain why he does not take his rightful support—although at this point his thinking anticipates what is to come and is not immediately clear to the reader.

9:16 / This verse lays out the situation Paul faced in preaching the gospel. He preached because God had commissioned or commanded him to do so. It is not to his credit that he preached; he would be in a deplorable situation had he not done so. God's commission made it necessary for Paul to preach the gospel, and for him to fail to fulfill that charge would be awful, unthinkable.

9:17 / Paul explains how he derives a benefit from his obedience to God's command to preach that he would not have received had he taken his rightful payment for his services. By not taking support, Paul did not claim his rights. He gave up his own rights for the benefit of being able to offer something to God and to others that he would not have had to offer otherwise. Paul's practice is simple, although it is so selflessly odd, so God-centered, and so much for the sake of others that we have difficulty grasping his line of thought. Above all, Paul aims to contribute something to the accomplishment of the mission that God gave him.

9:18 / As he concludes this section of the letter, Paul continues to explain why he preached without pay or support from the churches that he founded and to which he ministered. Amazingly, Paul's reward is that he takes no reward! Paul preached because he was commissioned to do so, and by not taking his due he gave up his own rights as an offering to God. Paul made an offering of his preaching to God, and in so doing he demonstrated his freedom (9:1) by providing his services freely to the church. By refusing to accept support, Paul preached according to God's commission, but he did not take advantage of the rights of support that God afforded him in conjunction with the command to preach. Paul gave his services to God **free of charge,** so that ironically his dividend was found in registering no charge.

Additional Notes §24

9:1 / When Paul declares his freedom in the rhetorical question, **Am I not free?** he names a standard theme of preaching among the wandering Cynics (so, Conzelmann, *1 Corinthians,* pp. 151–52). Examples of such thought and proclamation appear in Epictetus's *Dissertations* 3.2.48; 3.22.

By referring to seeing the Lord, Paul names only one element of the overall identity of an apostle. Above all, one must have received a commission to engage in gospel ministry—see 1 Cor. 15:5–8; Gal. 1:1.

The issue of being an **apostle** has been present in the background of the letter since 1:1.

The manner of naming **Jesus our Lord** is uncommon in Paul's writings, although one should be wary of making too much of such a stylized reference. See N. A. Dahl, "The Messiahship of Jesus in Paul," in *The Crucified Messiah and Other Essays* (Minneapolis: Augsburg, 1974), pp. 37–47.

9:2 / The matter of Paul's apostleship's being contested in Corinth is a crucial background issue for this letter. In ch. 1 Paul recognized the existence of factions that made special appeals to particular figures: Paul, Cephas, Apollos, and Christ (see the previous commentary). One should be aware, however, that as controversial as that issue may have been in relation to the writing of this letter, the situation changes for the worse in 2 Cor. Later, some seem vigorously to criticize, denigrate, and perhaps deny Paul's being an effective leader; although for the present context, one should not confuse the matter as Paul discusses it here with the more serious problem behind portions of 2 Cor.

9:3 / The NIV begins a new paragraph with this verse, although it is more likely that v. 3 is the final comment to the line of thought in vv. 1–2 rather than the initial thought of the segment that follows in vv. 4–6 or 4–7. In defense of the division into paragraphs between v. 3 and v. 4, see K. Nickel, "A Parenthetical Apologia: 1 Corinthians 9:1–3," *CurTM* 1 (1974), pp. 68–70.

9:4 / Paul writes with emphatic double negatives *(mē ouk)* here and in v. 5. The force of this construction is hard to translate into English, and the clear implication of the grammar is to assume a positive answer:

Stated question: "**Don't we . . . ?**"

Assumed reply: "Of course you do!"

The issues Paul names here, **food and drink,** may be loosely connected with the previous discussion of "food" and "eating," although the larger or central issue in Paul's discussion at this point is *the* **right** (Gk. *exousia*) and "the claiming of rights" (Gk. *chraomai tē exousia*).

9:5 / This fascinating verse provides a glimpse into the concrete practices of the early Christian communities. Beyond the clear insights and the probable implications of the lines, however, are many possible questions about the life of the early church. Many questions may be asked for which there may be no answers, although scholars have offered insightful and creative suggestions about elements of practice for which there is but little information (see Theissen, *Social Setting*).

9:6 / On the form and meaning that work took in Paul's world, and for a reminder of the humility (shame?) inherent in such work, see the stimulating and informative study by R. Hock, *The Social*

Context of Paul's Ministry: Tentmaking and Apostleship (Philadelphia: Fortress, 1980).

This reference to Barnabas is striking, for according to the account of Acts, Paul had already separated from Barnabas when he originally came to Corinth and worked there to found the Corinthian church. How the Corinthians knew Barnabas or about him is impossible to determine, although the positive way in which Paul mentions and associates himself with Barnabas at this point seems to indicate that the split that occurred in their pattern of ministry was not an ultimate undoing of their relationship or regard for each other.

9:7 / The NIV begins a new paragraph with this verse, which seems peculiar for a number of reasons. Critical editions of the Gk. text usually show a space, not a full paragraph, between v. 7 and v. 8, indicating a subtle turn in Paul's logic or point of view after, not before, v. 7. Moreover, v. 7 illustrates the point Paul has been making in vv. 4–6. The references to serving, planting, and tending are illustrative rhetorical reinforcements for the rights mentioned in the discussion of vv. 4–6.

The principle(s) behind the practices enumerated here are seen in Gen. 9:20–21; and esp. Deut. 20.

9:9 / The use of images in this verse borders on being allegorical, a manner of reading and interpreting the Scriptures that was common in Paul's day. Indeed, in Gal. 4 Paul specifically states that he is offering an allegory, although the method of interpretation does *not* move to the level of full allegorization here. Paul's exposition is creative, but it is not speculative. Furthermore, for a sharp critique of the argument of this use of Scripture as being allegorical, see D. Instone Brewer, "1 Corinthians 9.9–11: A Literal Interpretation of 'Do Not Muzzle the Ox,' " *NTS* 38 (1992), pp. 554–65.

The actual words of Paul and the line from the LXX (Deut. 25:4) are slightly different. Paul employs the verb *kēmoō*, translated **muzzle**, rather than the verb *phimoō*, a synonym that also means "muzzle." The nuances of the verbs may be slightly different, but in context no interpreter has been able to offer a sensible suggestion for Paul's alteration. Perhaps he was merely quoting from memory, or perhaps he knew a version of the LXX that was different from the one we possess; perhaps he had a purpose that escapes readers today. Moreover, the puzzle is compounded by the further citation of this verse of the LXX in 1 Tim. 5:18, where the words of the letter, though not the order, match the LXX wording.

The reference and use of the LXX at this point in the epistle has generated remarkable discussion in scholarly literature: e.g., G. M. Lee, "Studies in Texts: I Corinthians 9:9–10," *Theology* 71 (1968), pp. 122–23; and W. C. Kaiser Jr., "The Current Crisis in Exegesis and the Apostolic Use of Deuteronomy 25:4 in 1 Corinthians 9:8–10," *JETS* 21 (1978), pp. 3–18.

9:11 / Paul's image for ministry is remarkable, to sow spiritual things. The matter of spiritual things and what the Corinthians made of them is a part of the problem(s) Paul faced as he wrote this letter. From this reference we see that Paul understood spiritual things and the propagation of spiritual things to be real, so one may conclude that it is not the spiritual things per se but the bad theology of the Corinthians in relation to spiritual things that Paul sought to correct.

9:12 / Again, the NIV creates a paragraph in a questionable location that may affect one's reading of the text. Other currently available translations also break the paragraphing in the middle of v. 12, so the NIV is not alone in making this decision. Nevertheless, Paul's rhetoric at this point is vivid and spiraling, and he merely finishes the thought he began in the first part of v. 12. All of v. 12 may stand apart as a pair of direct observations about the topic being discussed in metaphorical terms in vv. 11 (sowing and reaping) and 13 (temple service).

9:15 / The decision to begin a new paragraph at this point once again suggests a sharper turn in Paul's writing than his Gk. grammar, rhetoric, and vocabulary admit. Nevertheless, Paul's grammar does break down in the middle of this verse. Having written, "But I made use of none of these [rights]; nor do I write these things in order that it may be so in my case—for it is better for me to die than—" Paul suddenly adds, "No one will empty my boast!" The awkwardness of these lines is indicative of the intensity with which Paul attempts to explain exactly what he is saying and why he is saying it. On the importance of maintaining the intensity of the statement in translation, see R. L. Omanson, "Some Comments about Style and Meaning: 1 Corinthians 9.15 and 7.10," *BT* 34 (1983), pp. 135–39.

Unfortunately the explanatory word "for" (Gk. *gar*) remains untranslated in the NIV before the words **I would rather . . . ,** so that the reader may not immediately see Paul's purposefulness in offering an explanation. Moreover, Paul writes "for" (*gar*) four more times in vv. 16–17, heaping explanation upon explanation. In all instances but one, the NIV smoothes out the wording unnecessarily and diminishes Paul's forceful, vigorous, deliberate style.

9:16 / Paul wrote, **for I am compelled;** more literally, "for a necessity has been laid upon me." His actual wording does not emphasize himself or his role in the action he describes; rather, he gives the primary weight to the charge that was given him and to the unspoken actor—God—who compelled him into action. Paul is describing not a psychological compulsiveness but a sense of God-directedness. Indeed, one should not even regard Paul's disposition as properly ethical. Focusing on 1 Cor. 9:14–18, E. Käsemann ("Eine paulinische Variation des 'amor fati,' " *ZTK* 56 [1959], pp. 138–54) critiques the understanding of Paul's purposefulness as noblesse oblige and demonstrates that Paul's perspective is a surrender in love of his genuine rights with a complete abandonment of expectation of reward.

9:17 / One reads of **the trust committed to me,** which places the emphasis on the correct subject (the trust) and implies God's activity. But one could more literally render the words "the commission I have been entrusted with," where the verb "entrusted" is *pisteuō*, connoting "to believe" or "to have faith in," so that one sees that

Paul's work is the result of God's "faith" in him and "faithfulness" through him.

9:18 / Paul poses a rhetorical question and then offers the answer. The answer comes with the final force of an explanation of purpose (Gk. *hina* + verb [*thēsō*, aorist active subjunctive or future active indicative]). Paul is drawing the lines of his argument together and making an important statement.

§25 Paul's Style of Ministry and Its Motivation (1 Cor. 9:19–23)

In verses 19–23 Paul describes the style of his ministry and its motivation. This segment of Paul's correspondence is challenging; it is clear at one level but sufficiently cryptic so as to invite a variety of understandings. The range of interpretations that has been suggested by commentators is remarkable, moving from an understanding of Paul as being totally selfless—perhaps in a psychologically unhealthy manner indicative of a loss of identity—to the contention that Paul was an opportunist in his dealings with potential converts. Careful reading of the text, however, indicates that such extreme interpretations are stereotyped, falling short of full comprehension of the subtlety of Paul's methods of mission and ministry. Although some interpreters think that the statements in these verses suggest inconsistency in Paul's patterns of behavior in conducting Christian missions, in fact one learns that for Paul all concerns were secondary in comparison with his all-consuming concern to be an accomplished agent of the propagation of the gospel.

9:19 / Paul reiterates his freedom and declares that while he is free from all, nevertheless he enslaved himself to all. The NIV translates these declarations with the words **Though I am free . . . I make myself a slave to everyone;** but more literally, Paul writes, "For being free . . . I enslaved myself to all." The opening of the line ("for") shows that Paul is offering a further explanation for his practice of foregoing his rights or freedom on behalf of others. Moreover, he says, "I *made* myself a slave" or "I *enslaved* myself," referring to the past stance he had taken in doing missions, not to a current and renewing practice as the tense of the verb ("I make") suggests in the NIV. Being free, having rights, Paul laid his rights aside in order **to win as many as possible.** Paul states that effective evangelization of others is more important than claiming, possessing, and preserving his own rights. The point of consistency in Paul's behavior was that he always put doing God's mission ahead of everything else.

9:20–21 / Paul reports that he varied his personal behavior depending upon his audience. Was this duplicitous? Was he a hypocrite? Certainly not if when he altered his behavior, he acknowledged it as openly and as freely as he does in these verses. There is no evidence in Paul's explanation that he did anything other than act in such a way as to better serve others by honoring their preferences and practices. In relation to **Jews** who were **under the law** Paul took on their law-observant patterns of living, although he himself was **not under the law.** Likewise, in relation to **those not having the law** he lived as they did; yet, he pauses at this point to explain that even when he was not being law-observant, he was **not free from God's law** because he lived **under Christ's law.** Paul does not elaborate his understanding of the law of Christ at this point, although from his subsequent discussion in chapter 13 one may suppose that Paul is talking about selfless love. Again, in a balanced set of statements **(so as to win those under the law . . . so as to win those not having the law)** Paul says overtly that he varied his behavior in order to win both law-observant Jews and those outside the law. Doing the mission to which God commissioned him and relating to all persons with as few unnecessary complications as possible—"putting up with anything rather than hindering the gospel of Christ" (9:12b)— was Paul's primary goal as he sought to make converts to the gospel.

9:22 / Paul relates the pattern of his ministry to the situation that existed in Corinth. There, some persons whose religious scruples precluded their eating idol meat were regarded as (and perhaps called) **the weak.** Paul explains how he behaved toward such persons in keeping with his selfless method of mission, and by implication he calls for those who were not weak to do the same. Paul declares that he sought to **become all things to all** people in all ways **so that** he **might** serve as God's agent in **all possible** circumstances in order to **save some.**

9:23 / As Paul continues, in a concise statement he shows that the power of the gospel presides over him as he does God's work. Paul says he served the gospel **(I do all this for the sake of the gospel)** and sought to participate or to **share** in its effective working **(its blessings).** The language Paul uses casts him in the role of a partner or a shareholder, so that one sees that the gospel is the senior partner in a partnership. Thus, the gospel is not relativized to worldly social conditions that are no more than contemporary social structures and sensibilities; rather, the apostle himself becomes relativized in order to preserve the integrity of the gospel. The outcome of this deliberate operation was the gospel's power at work blessing—endowing and transforming—the lives of those to whom and among whom Paul worked.

Additional Notes §25

9:19 / Paul literally writes, "For being free from all, to all I enslave myself in order that I may gain the more." Compare this declaration with 9:1; note here that Paul is freed *from* (Gk. *ek*) all, but he worked as a slave *to* all (Gk. *pasin*). The prepositional force of the language indicates the paradoxical truth of Christian freedom. P. Richardson and P. W. Gooch ("Accommodation Ethics," *TynB* 29 [1978], pp. 89–142) examine the ethical practice of accommodation in antiquity and in the life of the ancient church to expand the appreciation of readers for Paul's attitude and the way his practice would have been understood by his contemporaries.

Moreover, when Paul writes that he sought **to win as many as possible**, his choice of words is noteworthy. The verb "to win" carries the sense of "to gain" or "to win over"; the phrase translated "as many as possible" more literally reads "the greater part" (Gk. *tous pleionas*) and reveals the positive disposition of Paul's work. He is not passively taking whatever results ensue from his efforts; he is actively striving to gain the greatest number possible.

9:20–21 / In a seminal study that explores the complexity of Paul's statements and efforts, G. Bornkamm ("The Missionary Stance of Paul in I Corinthians and in Acts," in *Studies in Luke–Acts* [L. E. Keck and J. L. Martyn, eds.; Nashville: Abingdon, 1966], pp. 194–207) refers to "the life-situation in which the gospel is to accomplish its purpose dialectically, liberating here and binding there" (p. 196). He notes that Paul's "stance is rooted in the gospel and consequently—although the term is not used here—in the love which seeks not its own but the welfare of the other" (p. 197); and he summarizes Paul's method: "he calls on each to renounce for the sake of the other the use of his own *exousia*" (p. 203). More recently, D. A. Carson ("Pauline Inconsistency: Reflections on I Corinthians 9.19–23 and Galatians 2.11–14," *Chm* 100 [1986], pp. 6–45) offers a vigorous defense against the charge that Paul was inconsistent in his attitude and actions; rather, he asserts, there were definite limits to his principle of accommodation.

Moreover, focusing on the striking nature of Paul's flexibility in his ministry, which often is misconstrued as inconsistency, H. Conzelmann (*1 Corinthians*, pp. 160–61) observes that despite the neat form of Paul's rhetoric in these verses, "He *is* a Jew. To the Gentiles he must *become* a Gentile. The problem is not how he can live in Jewish fashion, but how he can live in Gentile fashion. Once again this lies not in his own arbitrary choice, but in his commission. He is free not in an abstract sense, but as an apostle." Somewhat similarly, K. V. Neller ("1 Corinthians 9:19–23: A Model for Those Who Seek to Win Souls," *ResQ* 29 [1987], pp. 129–42) relates Paul's taking on both Jewish and Gentile lifestyles as his "becoming weak" for the sake of others.

The phrase **under Christ's law** is *ennomos Christou* in Gk. and connotes being "subject to the law of Christ," although Paul offers no exposition of the phrase. Cf. Gal. 6:2, where Paul uses *nomos Christou* in reference to the entity of "Christ's law," as distinct from the idea of the state or status of being "under Christ's law."

9:22 / Orr and Walther (*I Corinthians*, p. 240) suggest that it is "intriguing" to compare this verse with 2 Cor. 10:10, in which Paul quotes his detractors, who say "His letters are weighty and forceful, but in person he is unimpressive and his speaking amounts to nothing."

Indeed, the last phrase **so that by all possible means I might save some** is ambiguous and may be read "so that 'at any rate' I might save some," although given the positive connotation of "the greater part" (NIV: "as many as possible") in v. 19, Paul is not likely indifferent as to the results of his execution of God's mission. In either case, however, Paul does not mean to suggest that he himself saves others, for he clearly and consistently argues throughout his epistles that only God saves! Thus, Paul speaks here of himself as God's agent for salvation as God works through his efforts. Cf. J. Lambrecht, "Universalism in 1 Cor 8:1–11:1," *Greg* 77 (1996), pp. 333–39.

9:23 / At the end of this verse Paul writes in a purpose clause to state his motive for conducting his mission as he did: "in order **that I may share** [the gospel's] **blessings.**" The manner of expression in the statement is concise, but in his choice of words Paul indicates that sharing in the blessings of the gospel is "participating in its furtherance" per se (Gk. *hina sygkoinōnos autou genōmai*), or as Fee (*Epistle*, p. 432) phrases it, "for the sake of *the progress* of the gospel."

§26 The Need for Discipline in Ministry (1 Cor. 9:24–27)

These verses form a transition in Paul's writing. In these verses, Paul brings his discussion of apostolic rights to a conclusion; at the same time, he begins to reorient the subject matter so that he may return to the issues related to idol meat—eating and participating in pagan temple cults—in chapter 10. The lines are vivid and for the most part clear. Yet, Paul's metaphors are inexact and should not, despite past practices in the life of the church, be allegorized or pressed beyond reasonable limits. In the context of this letter, Paul's images and instructions form a pointed polemic. In brief, Paul takes up a set of athletic images as metaphors, explaining and advocating discipline. The problem elements of the Corinthian congregation assumed they "had arrived" and that they were correct in their thinking, but to these people Paul writes using athletic images to tell them to "run" (or, "fight"—see below) and to stay focused.

9:24 / Paul takes the readers on an imaginary and instructive trip to the games, a popular setting in antiquity for both participants and spectators. The Corinthians were well-acquainted with athletics and high-level competition since the important Isthmian games were held in their city every other year. (See the discussion of the city of Corinth in the Introduction to this work, pp. 3–5.) In this imaginary context, Paul writes of runners. He recognizes that runners race for a prize; that is, they run for a purpose. Yet, despite the intensity and effort of all the runners, only one wins the prize. Using this picture, Paul admonishes the Corinthians to an active and disciplined life. This is not a simple motivational speech to encourage people to happier existence. Paul's call to purposefulness itself has a purpose.

9:25 / As Paul calls for the Corinthians to live purposefully, he moves back to the image of the race and recognizes how all those competing enter **into strict training** in preparation for competition and in hope of winning. Then, he turns the image to make an argument from lesser to greater: Athletes exercise discipline in their training and competing so as to win perishable crowns; Christians exercise discipline in the life of faith so as to get **a crown that will last forever.** In the ancient games, victors were awarded a wreath of leaves, pine, or celery to be worn as a temporary crown, and statuary from antiquity often presents persons wearing such an ornament and striking a victory pose. Paul's concern is elsewhere. The contrast he makes is obviously between simple prizes and life itself. To import a phrase into the interpretation, one may say that Paul is referring to eternal life. He will return to the topic of the resurrection and resurrection life in chapter 15, but in this verse he alludes to that issue as the goal of current Christian living.

9:26 / Paul shifts images, moving from the runner to the boxer and saying that he does not "fan the air" in the style of an untrained fighter. In other words, Paul's efforts are not aimless or futile. In their lives as Christians Paul's readers are not to waste time and effort. They are to act with purpose. Appropriate Christian living takes definite direction.

9:27 / As Paul develops the metaphor of boxing, he says that rather than box the air, he works like an expert pugilist whose punches count because they hit their mark. In the exercise of his God-given life and commission, Paul is focused through discipline. His images and metaphors are engaging for many. Nevertheless, Paul's final comments on boxing are almost shocking. He reveals that his opponent is himself. Surely this startling revelation is a lesson for the Corinthians, whose attitude leads to the kind of easy, self-indulgent living that merely presumes upon God's grace and does not relate in obedience to God's saving acts. Paul explains that he "blackens the eye of [his] body" lest he be disqualified himself—a sharp, strong word of warning to the readers about the necessity of devotion and steadfastness.

This tone of admonition and warning registers heavily at the end of chapter 9. Paul does not end his emphasis at this point, however, for the same tone and many of the same emphases reoccur immediately in the new images and lines of chapter 10.

Additional Notes §26

9:24 / The vocabulary of this verse and the accompanying lines is somewhat technical, coming as it does from the world of the games. The last phrase in this verse, translated in the NIV with the words **run in such a way as to get the prize**, is ambiguous in spite of the analogical nature of the sentence. The Gk. phrasing *(houtōs trechete hina katalabēte)* may be rendered either "run in the same way [as the athlete] in order that you may win" or "run in such a way that you may win." Whether they run like the athlete or with a purpose (the ideas are not antithetical), Paul wants the believers to conduct their lives with alacrity and deliberateness.

9:25 / Cf. 7:9, where one finds the only other NT occurrence of the verb *egkrateuomai*, translated here **goes into strict training** and at 7:9 as "control themselves." It is important and instructive to note that in Gal. 5:23 the noun form *egkrateia* ("self-control") appears in Paul's list of the fruit of the Spirit. Moreover, see R. Garrison, "Paul's use of the athlete metaphor in 1 Corinthians 9," *SR* 22 (1993), pp. 209–17.

9:27 / The verb translated **I beat** (Gk. *hypōpiazō*) is related to the word *ōps*, which names the part of the face under the eye. Thus the verb means "give a black eye," or when used metaphorically, "to deal a severe blow." Given the picture quality of Paul's language and discussion, perhaps one should translate with the English idiom "to beat black and blue" (so Orr and Walther, *I Corinthians*, p. 240).

The phrase translated **so that after** is also translated "lest after" in other versions; in any case the Gk. phrase *mē pōs* is strongly negative or prohibitive and should be understood to indicate strenuous objection. Moreover, the word translated **be disqualified** (Gk. *adokimos*) means "not pass the test"; such vocabulary and urgency suggest possible apocalyptic tone and emphasis for Paul's directions in these verses—much like the emphasis in 7:25–31.

§27 Pauline Preaching: Relating the Exodus to Christian Life (1 Cor. 10:1–13)

Having raised the serious, frightening prospect of disqualification at the end of chapter 9, Paul moves immediately to deliver a midrash on the exodus that is laced with scriptural allusions. The introduction of the story of the exodus wanderings of the Israelites in the wilderness may seem peculiar, but the development is logical; for as Paul used himself and the apostles as a personal lesson on Christian rights and responsibilities in chapter 9, and as he drew images from the athletic games to illustrate and register his teaching (9:24–27), now Paul takes up one of the best-known and most-loved stories from the OT to form analogies to the Corinthian situation in order both to document and to authenticate his instructions.

This section is a brief biblically-based expository sermon. In it Paul depicts Israel during the exodus in such a way as to emphasize the parallels with the situation of the Corinthians. Paul does this to expose and explain the true nature of the circumstances in Corinth: in their ignorance (which is, ironically, their arrogance) the Corinthians are dangerously close to repudiation through divine condemnation. The word "arrogance," encountered in chapters 4, 5, and 8, does not come up directly in this midrashic interpretation and teaching, but the portrait of the Israelites assumes their presumptuousness in relationship to God and forms a parallel to the attitude of the Corinthians that Paul has already named. Thus, in a manner that seems creative to us today, but that would have been familiar to many of his ancient hearers/readers, Paul applies the exodus story to the state of affairs in Corinth as a further, vivid word of illustrative warning. The particular manner in which Paul tells and retells the exodus events, especially in the way he relates the Corinthian situation to the text, is instructive concerning the character of Christian life.

10:1 / Paul immediately puts the Corinthians on notice with his opening address, **For I do not want you to be ignorant . . . , brothers, that. . . .** The implication of this statement is that the Corinthians are or at least are behaving as if they were ignorant. The word "ignorant" in Greek *(agnoein)* denotes a lack of knowledge (Gk. *gnosis*) and might be paraphrased with the word "clueless." Despite their concern with and claim of wisdom and knowledge, in Paul's estimation the Corinthians lack both. Even though gentle, this confrontation would be insulting and would cause any who took exception to listen carefully to what Paul was saying.

Then, Paul continues by retelling selected elements of the story of the ancestors of Israel during their wilderness wanderings: **that our forefathers were all under the cloud and that they all passed through the sea.** The repetition of "all" is the first pair of such all-inclusive references to the Israelites; Paul will continue in verses 2–3 by saying "they were *all* baptized . . . they *all* ate . . . and [they all] drank. . . ." Paul uses rhetoric to create a unified picture of Israel, where all equally enjoyed the benefits of deliverance and sustenance that were provided by divine grace. Moreover, by calling the ancestors of Israel "our forefathers," he connects the experience of the Corinthians with God's past saving acts throughout the history of Israel and forms the basis for the ensuing analogies that he will develop to instruct the Corinthians.

The references to the **cloud** and to the passing **through the sea** recall the story of the deliverance from Egypt in Exodus 13–14. At this point Paul is conjuring up images and the ideas of inclusivity and security in divine care before making creative interpretive use of the story in the verses that follow.

10:2 / Paul says **they were all baptized into Moses in the cloud and in the sea.** This statement is remarkable, for it interprets the deliverance of Israel from Egypt by acts of divine grace and power in explicitly anachronistic terms. Judaism knew the practice of baptism in various segments of its constituency: the Dead Sea Scrolls attest to the practice of ritual immersion for religious, ceremonial rites of cleansing in the Qumran community (1QS 3.5–9), and the NT records the ministry of baptism of John the Baptist in the Jordan River. Nevertheless, Paul makes an original set of connections, first, in unifying Israel's experience of the cloud and the sea; second, in referring to that experience as "baptism"; and, third, in referring to this "baptism" as being baptized into Moses. Paul's reshaping of the story at this point prepares the way for the dramatic connections he will make in the following verses between the experience of the Israelites, who had all been baptized into Moses, and the experience of the Corinthians, who had all been baptized into Christ.

10:3–4 / As Paul continues, he lays the groundwork for further analogies between the Israelites and the Corinthians by focusing on the eating and drinking of **spiritual food** and **spiritual drink** enjoyed by the Israelites in the wilderness (see Exod. 16–17; Num. 20–21). Paul recalls the experience of divine provision of food and drink in an unstated analogy to the Corinthians' own experience of partaking "spiritual food and drink" in the context of the Lord's Supper. The Lord's Supper will occupy Paul and the Corinthians explicitly in chapter 11, but for now Paul makes only an analogous reference to that particular portion of the community's life.

The implied analogies in these verses seem appropriate and defensible even to modern readers who might be unfamiliar with Paul's patterns of argument and reasoning, but as he continues to weave his elaborate web Paul offers a further image and commentary that may not make sense to readers at the turn of the twenty-first century: **for they drank from the spiritual rock that accompanied them, and that rock was Christ.** Paul has the story from Exodus 17 in mind, when God instructed Moses to strike a rock, and then water poured out for the people to drink. He may have combined that account with Numbers 21:16–18 (or perhaps he inherited an already amalgamated version of the story) before making his own creative use of the narrative: that rock was Christ. This claim strikes the reader of today as fantastic, although such connections were not considered odd or inappropriate in Paul's day. Targumic writings (*Tosefta Sukkah* 3:11; *Targum Onqelos* Num. 21:16–20), Philo of Alexandria, and Pseudo-Philo all make similar, though original, interpretations of the same OT account. Philo, a contemporary of Paul, interpreted the water-giving rock of the exodus story as the presence of preexistent Wisdom among the wandering Israelites (*Allegorical Interpretation* 2.86), so Paul's christological rereading of the story is but one interpretation of the "identity" of God's saving presence among the Israelites. Paul may be christianizing a standard theme of Jewish wisdom teaching, or he may be appropriating images and ideas from developed wisdom traditions in his own original way.

10:5 / The application of the exodus imagery is done through typological analogy (see *typikōs* in vv. 6 and 11). The typological analysis and application lay the foundation for the stark warning that comes in verse 5, where **Nevertheless** resounds with great force. The particular element that Paul emphasizes and develops at this point is perhaps surprising, if not shocking. Having highlighted the blessings of deliverance, sustenance, and divine presence, Paul bluntly states that in spite of the ancestors' having been "baptized into Moses" and having participated in an archetypal Lord's Supper and having had Christ among them in the wilderness, **God was not pleased with most of them,** and they were overthrown in the wilderness with **their bodies . . . scattered over the desert.** Thus, according to Paul, baptism, participation in the Lord's Supper, and even the presence of Christ are not unequivocal assurances against negative divine judgment. To those who might think otherwise, Paul plainly teaches that the sacraments are not magical charms that guarantee an absolute claim on salvation, and the saving presence of Christ is not to be taken for granted.

10:6 / The statements that follow in verses 6–13 work out further application of the midrash by adding and applying other exodus materials to Paul's basic exhortation. Now the story is brought to bear on the Corinthians in relation to the issues of idolatry and sexual immorality, themes that Paul dealt with explicitly in chapter 8 and in chapters 5–6. Moreover, Paul will return to the matter of idol meat in 10:14–11:1. Here, verse 6 introduces the application in a general manner, **as examples,** but already specifies the purpose of the lessons being taught through models: **to keep us from setting our hearts on evil things as they did.**

10:7 / This verse applies the scriptural lesson directly to the issue of idolatry: it denounces the **pagan revelry** of inappropriate eating, drinking, and sexual immorality by quoting a portion of Exodus 32:6 verbatim. As Paul develops this statement one sees that the false focus on the false god(s) results in erroneous behaviors. Relating to anything other than God as the ultimate concern of life will result only in problems.

10:8–10 / These three complementary verses form a trilogy of negative directions against sexual immorality, testing "the Lord," and grumbling. Paul considers all of these activities as the result of idolatrous concerns that make something other than God the central focus of living. He names these particular behaviors because they are relevant to the Corinthian situation as he has described it in chapters 5–6, 8, and perhaps in 9:3, 12.

Moreover, when these verses report the terrible results of such wrongful behavior, one sees that Paul is issuing a vivid warning, not giving a Bible-story lesson. The mention of the death of twenty-three thousand in a day (in Num. 25:1–9 one reads that twenty-four thousand died) is a graphic illustration of the peril of "idolatry." The reference is particularly appropriate for the situation in Corinth—with its idolatrous temptations—since the thousands of Israelites died after the men had immoral sexual relations with Moabite women who brought them to the altar of their pagan deity. The mention of the deaths by serpents refers to Numbers 21:4–9 and is explained in context by Paul's stating that the Israelites grumbled against God. Paul elaborates the matter of Israelite grumbling and divine retribution, however, with the mention of the **destroying angel,** a curious reference that seems to allude to the events of Numbers 16:46–50 using the language of Exodus 12:23. The implication of this ornamented analogy is that Paul deemed the Corinthians to be grumbling inappropriately as well.

10:11 / Paul explicitly details the application of the exodus story to the Corinthian situation. One should notice at least two significant elements of his explanation. First, Paul's exegesis of the OT clearly shows that he understands the Scriptures to be typological as a result of the Christ-event. Second, Paul locates himself and the Corinthians at the juncture of the ages, as the NRSV recognizes with the correct translation, "they were written down to instruct us, on whom the ends of the ages have come." The NIV translation, **on whom the fulfillment of the ages has come,** offers interpretation, not translation, although this imprecise rendering is not unique. This verse is generally mistranslated and misunderstood as a reference to either a general summary of all previous times or epochs ("end of the ages") or a general summary of all previous nonepochal time ("end of the age"). "Fulfillment of the ages" seems to fit the first category of comprehension, not the second.

Nevertheless, both of these understandings fail to take seriously Paul's apocalyptic-eschatological temporal dualism (see Introduction, pp. 12–15). From this particular perspective one sees that Paul himself understood that he and the Corinthians lived at the point where "the present evil age" (Gal. 1:4) and the "new creation" (2 Cor. 5:17; Gal. 6:15) were both already present and not yet present. Paul perceives that humanity is located at a time between the cross and the coming of Christ, when the old and new ages are mingled. In this interim the old is already dying and the new is already being born, though the old has not yet passed away and the new has not yet fully arrived.

10:12 / This verse is a summarizing sentence, as one sees from Paul's opening word, **So** (Gk. *hōste*), which is often translated "Therefore" to indicate that Paul is both summarizing and building upon what has gone before. Thus, he issues a sobering warning, probably because of his strong convictions about the danger of the volatile times in which humanity now lives—a time of tremendous importance because both God's work for salvation and the real and continuing threat of evil opposition to God are present, powerful, and at work in the world.

10:13 / More directly, verse 13 declares that the real crisis **(temptation)** that is besetting the community is manageable and conquerable. In fact, Paul declares the theological basis of such management: **God is faithful** (cf. 1:9). God provides the antidote to the reality of temptation that humans necessarily face at the juncture of the ages. There is no avoiding this temptation, but in this overlapping of times God's saving provision is mixed with the temptation. Paul is confident in God's sustaining grace. Although one can imagine different ways in which Paul would name this divine provision—the Spirit, Christ, the power of God—the apostle does not name God's grace at this point; rather, he declares God's faithfulness. In developing the argument as he does, Paul establishes the necessity of the Corinthians' being related to the God who saves.

Dealt with in isolation from the passage in which it occurs, this verse is sometimes turned into a quasitheological philosophical explanation of human suffering, evil, and divine will. The statement is elaborate and does perhaps invite such exposition and speculation. Yet, one must see that this verse is not an isolated philosophical statement that purports to delineate intricate facets of life. Paul speaks to the Corinthians in context: They are arrogant, overly self-confident, believing themselves to be "standing firm." But, Paul says, "Watch out!" The Corinthians are not above the unpleasant complications of normal human existence, and facing that fact they have one hope: the faithfulness of God. God is trustworthy, and even if the situation seems impossible, nothing is beyond God's power and grace. When the Corinthians confront times of trouble they should not deny their susceptibility to temptation or trust their own superspirituality to see them through. Rather, they need to remember, to know, and to act on the one ultimate assurance that is their real security: God is faithful. The tendency to overread this verse is a temptation within itself, but despite the mysterious matters that it raises, the plain sense of the verse is a call to recognize and to trust God.

Additional Notes §27

10:1 / Paul often introduces critical items of basic Christian belief and life with the phrase **I do not want you to be ignorant.** See Rom. 11:25; 1 Cor. 12:1; 2 Cor. 1:8; 1 Thess. 4:13. After this commanding opening the verses that follow in this section display a refined rhetorical character that indicates Paul's concern and magnifies his basic argument. On the structuring of the material in 10:1–13 as a subtle exegetical development of Exod. 32:6, see W. A. Meeks, " 'And Rose up to Play': Midrash and Paraenesis in 1 Corinthians 10:1–22," *JSNT* 16 (1982), pp. 64–78.

10:2 / The phrase **into Moses** (Gk. *eis ton Mōysēn*) is an apparent retrospective development of the standard Pauline phrase "into Christ" *(eis Christon)*—cf. 1:13, 15; 12:13; Gal. 3:27.

On baptism in general and in the context of the NT in particular, see L. Hartman, "Baptism," *ABD* 1:583–94. Furthermore, L. L. Grabbe (*The Roman Period,* vol. 1 of *Judaism from Cyrus to Hadrian* [Minneapolis: Fortress, 1992], §8.2.11.1, pp. 508–9) collects wide-ranging evidence for the practice of baptism in Judaism for ritual purification, initiation, or both. In no known source is there any indication of concern with the idea of being "baptized into Moses."

10:3 / Paul never mentions manna here by name, and he seems unconcerned with the exact details of the story that he is putting to typological use. The **spiritual drink** must be water, since that was what came from the rock in the original narrative, although Paul again makes no mention of the original substance by name. See further Exod. 16–17; Num. 20–21. Notice that in circumventing the explicit references to manna and water, Paul creatively connects the Corinthian circumstances with the original biblical text.

10:4 / On the targumic style and possible background in Judaism of Paul's exodus storytelling exposition of Numbers, see E. E. Ellis, "A Note on First Corinthians 10:4," *JBL* 76 (1957), pp. 53–56. One should note that the idea of Christ's preexistence is inherent in Paul's comments, although preexistence per se is not the focus of the discussion.

10:5 / The NIV translation abbreviates Paul's actual words in this verse and so obscures his explicitly stated purpose. The line literally reads, "**Nevertheless, God was not pleased with most of them;** for they were scattered about in **the desert.**" The NIV accurately explains the sense of the verb *katastrōnnymi*, "scatter about" or "spread around," since in the story in Exodus and Numbers (cf. Ps. 78:30–31) the bodies of the dead Israelites are strewn around in the wilderness. Nevertheless, Paul introduces the final phrase of this verse with the Gk. word *gar* ("for"), clearly indicating that he is offering evidence as explanation or in support of his contention that God was not pleased with most of the Israelites. No harm is done by the NIV rendering, but the basic flow of Paul's thought is broken down needlessly. Paul's contention that God was not pleased with most of them had at least as much to do with the Corinthians as it did with the Israelites.

10:6 / The phrase rendered **setting our hearts on evil** is much stronger in Gk. Paul writes of "lusting after evils" (Gk. *epithymētas kakōn*), using language that implies strong compulsive behavior under the influence of the power of evil. Moreover, the NIV rendering of the final words of the verse, **as they did,** is unjustifiably flat, for Paul repeats the verb "lust" (Gk. *epithymeō*) to create emphasis on the evil quality of the actions against which he warns, writing, "exactly as they lusted."

10:7 / The words translated **as it is written** are effectively a technical phrase in Paul's writings and signal his citation of (sometimes allusion to) portions of the Scriptures. The particular use that Paul makes of Scriptures is clear only in the immediate context, since he is capable of a variety of different styles of exegesis.

10:8 / Paul's Gk. at this point is vivid, filled with strong negatives and intense verbal forms (such as the use of the hortatory subjunctive, which makes this call not to commit sexual immortality a strong exhortation). The NRSV translation, "We must not indulge in sexual immorality," more accurately captures and communicates Paul's strong tone than does the relatively sterile rendering in the NIV.

10:9 / Behind the phrase translated **We should not test the Lord** is a textual variant that may cause different translations to read differently at this point. The NRSV, e.g., reads, "We must not put Christ to the test." The current critical edition of the Gk. NT accepts "Christ" as the original text of this verse. Unfortunately, the NIV does not offer a footnote to explain the decision to include "Lord" rather than "Christ" and to recognize that another reading is possible, even probable. Several studies have focused on this variant, and the scholarly consensus holds "Christ" rather than "Lord" to be the better reading. For example, see Fee (*Epistle*, p. 450 n. 2), who corrects the NIV at this point.

10:11 / Although Orr and Walther (*I Corinthians*, p. 246) recognize that "both words are plural in the Gk. text," they still translate "the end of the age." The failure to understand that the words "the ends of the ages" refer to two, distinct, overlapping, ultimately incompatible periods—marked out and distinguished by the active intervention of God—is unfortunately more often the rule than the exception. Nevertheless, our current worldviews should not determine the translation of ancient texts, especially when the imposition of an inappropriate understanding of Paul's view of the world causes the reader to fail to comprehend Paul's radical theological point of view and teaching.

For a careful look at how Scripture functions here and at other selected places in this letter, see R. F. Collins (" 'It was indeed written for our sake' [1 Cor 9,10]: Paul's Use of Scripture in the First Letter to the Corinthians," *Studien zum Neuen Testament und seiner Umwelt* 20 [1995], pp. 151–70), who analyzes the interface of Scripture and rhetoric to show how Paul creatively "discovered" the Scriptures in his rhetoric in order to do more than strict deliberation.

10:12 / The words **be careful** understate Paul's emphatic tone. He tells the Corinthians to "look out!" (Gk. *blepetō*), making the force of his warning even more intense by reducing the focus to a single rhetorical figure. In other words, the word "you" in this verse should be understood to address a single, ideal person. Paul is not speaking to all the Corinthians at once; rather, he singles out an imaginary Corinthian and warns that person (of course, in behalf of all) to "Watch out!"

10:13 / The mention of **temptation** (Gk. *peirasmos*) is telling in this context, for the idea of "temptation" is regularly associated with apocalyptic or eschatological moments in the entire NT and in portions of late OT writings. Moreover, in the context of this remark by Paul it is impossible to determine what—if anything—he assumes to be the origin of temptation, which is clearly not good.

Commenting on the phrase **he will also provide a way out,** Conzelmann (*1 Corinthians*, p. 169) makes the following incisive observations:

> this in itself can be a mere cliché. But in its Pauline context we have here a reference to the eschatological manifestation and liberation. Paul does not say that God helps again and again. He is speaking of the *one* eschatological act of salvation. . . . This comfort is genuine only when "God" does not remain a cipher, but is known through *demonstration* of his faithfulness.

For a limited but deliberate and explicit theological assessment of this verse, see the discussion of Armenian and Calvinist interpretations in D. M. Ciocchi, "Understanding Our Ability to Endure Temptation: A Theological Watershed," *JETS* 35 (1992), pp. 463–79.

§28 Directions against Idolatry (1 Cor. 10:14–22)

Paul returns here to the topics he dealt with in 8:1–13. There he touched on two related items, eating meat from idol sacrifices and participating in pagan cultic banquets. At this point, however, Paul reverses the order of his discussion and takes up the Christians' eating at the table in a pagan idol's temple in 10:14–22 before returning to the issue of eating idol meat per se in 10:23–11:1. In the present verses Paul elaborates and makes even more explicit application of his warning to the Corinthians. The argument is a pastiche of images and metaphors that challenges the imagination of the readers, although Paul's essential line of thought is unambiguous.

10:14 / As he begins this new segment of reflections, one sees in Paul's first word in this section, **Therefore** (or better, "On account of"; Gk. *dioper*), that Paul understands himself to be building on his preceding remarks and inferring conclusions in relation to them. He tells the Corinthians to **flee from idolatry.** This unequivocal instruction could stand alone, if the situation in Corinth were as clear as the injunction; but apparently Paul perceives confusion, for he continues to press his point with illustrative arguments from the life and the religious world of the community.

10:15 / This verse stands independently as an explanatory comment. One may read the remark in conjunction with what Paul has said to this point, or one may understand that he is indicating the reasonable nature of what he is about to say. Perhaps, however, the comment is a bridge that looks both backward and forward to all the elements of the current discussion that began in 8:1 and continues at least through 11:1. Paul's general contention is that sensible people ought to recognize and agree with his observations and instructions. (See Additional Notes on the word **sensible.**)

10:16–17 / Paul states in eucharistic metaphors (cup/ blood; bread/body; one loaf/one body) the unified nature of Christian life. The behavior of certain of the Corinthians relates to the religious reality that the entire community experiences. What some of the Corinthians do is understood by Paul to have implications for and an effect on the life of the congregation. Paul will discuss the problematic matter of the celebration of the Lord's Supper in detail in chapter 11, but here he refers to that practice and draws conclusions for the life of the community from the elements of celebration. There is no hint at this juncture of a problem with the community's observation of the Supper; rather, what Paul assumes that they all know and believe is the foundation of his corrections and directions to those who are stepping outside the boundaries of the life of the community to participate in pagan festivities. As the reader knows from Paul's letter up to this point, some of the Corinthians object to such participation in pagan ceremonies while others who join in the activities deny there is anything wrong with their actions.

Paul's eucharistic images argue for the unity of the community at both the vertical and the horizontal level of theological reality. First, the Christians in Corinth are united in a powerful and mysterious manner with their Lord Jesus Christ in the celebrations: **the cup of thanksgiving . . . participation . . . the blood of Christ** *and* **the bread that we break . . . participation . . . the body of Christ.** Paul declares rather than explains this union between the believers and the Lord, apparently underlining a conviction that would have gained ready acknowledgment from the Corinthians. Second, the Corinthians are united with one another through their mutual participation in the celebration: **one loaf . . . we, who are many . . . one body.** Thus, in and through and because of their collective observance of the Lord's Supper, the Corinthians are united with one another despite their very real human differences. In other words, because Christ is Lord— as the Lord's Supper celebrates—Christ's people are one in the power of his lordship.

10:18 / To further develop his objection against the inappropriateness of Christian participation in pagan cultic celebrations, Paul draws an analogy to Israel in order to identify the demonic forces associated with pagan religion and sacrificial food (vv. 18–20). This particular argument is a kind of historical proof for Paul's point. Because the modern reader may be unfamiliar with the practices Paul discusses, it is possible to miss his point. In brief, he observes that the priests of Israel partake of the substances sacrificed on the altar to the one true God; and so, in a real physical way they engage in a communion with God when they attend to his altar.

10:19 / Even Paul must recognize that the reader may fail to grasp his logic, for he asks literally, "What, then, do I mean?" (NIV: **Do I mean then that . . . ?**). Not wanting the readers to misunderstand, Paul provides a rhetorical question (v. 19) and an answer (v. 20) that make clear that an idol is not **anything.** Some in Corinth hold the gods to be real and for that reason object to the participation of others in pagan cultic meals. Those who eat justify their eating in pagan ritual settings because they think that the pagan gods are unreal. Paul steps into that debate at this point with rhetorical deliberateness.

10:20 / Paul answers his own rhetorical question, Is an idol anything? with a strong adversative, **No!** (Gk. *alla*). Yet, that answer does not lead him to take the side of those who see no harm in eating in pagan cultic locations. Apparently Paul thought that idol worship was not purely idle activity. He refers to the **sacrifices of pagans** to idols as being **offered to demons.** This comment is not a full-blown exposition on the demonic, nor is it possible to understand exactly what Paul believed a demon to be, although his thought here is in perfect line with OT passages that identify pagan gods as demons and condemn such sacrifices (see Exod. 22:20; 32:8; Deut. 28:64; 32:17; Ps. 106:36–37).

Paul's general perceptions and beliefs about the demonic are not clear from this statement, although there is no reason to conclude that he doubted the existence of demons. Nevertheless, scholarly discussions on this verse that enter into denial or defense of the reality of the demonic are off the point. Paul is juxtaposing two levels of concern, two loyalties, and two powers. One power is the power of **God** manifested in a clear and ultimate form in Jesus Christ, and the other is labeled **demons.** Paul states plainly that the Corinthian Christians are to be concerned with and involved with only God. There is no room for other affiliations, and the Corinthians are to avoid all possible compromises of their relationship to God.

10:21 / In turn, Paul forcefully declares the exclusive nature of Christian life in general images from the Lord's Supper. These images were introduced in verses 16–17 in Paul's argument concerning the union of the believers with Christ and with one another in Christ, but here Paul puts the figures of the **cup** and the **table** to another use. The Christians are confronted with an either/or: either they are going to be involved with and devoted to **the Lord,** or they are going to compromise themselves—no matter how innocently—with **demons.** As Paul reads the situation in Corinth, compromising concerns do not integrate well with total devotion to Christ; inappropriate actions jeopardize the believers' relationship to the Lord.

10:22 / Finally, Paul instructs the Corinthians through two rhetorical questions, informing them that their behavior—which is presented as an insistent practice of their personal freedom—may and does provoke God. In raising these questions, Paul contrasts human and divine strength in a way that issues an indirect threat.

Additional Notes §28

10:14 / While Paul's concern in this general segment of the letter focuses explicitly on idol meat—eating it privately and eating it in the context of the pagan cultic setting—he now declares his concern with **idolatry** per se. Paul crosses a line that he had not previously drawn, suggesting that his concern with idol meat in all contexts was that the Corinthians would lapse into idolatry. Otherwise, it is hard to comprehend this turn in the discussion.

10:15 / Paul's remark is not casual. The imperative form of this statement insists that the Corinthians examine and decide what is appropriate in their situation. Moreover, Paul plainly tells them what they should and should not do. By referring to the Corinthians as **sensible people,** Paul both confronts the members of the congregation and makes an appeal. The word "sensible" in Gk. *(phronimos)* connotes the ideas of "thoughtful" and "wise," and it occurred in the sarcastic comment in 4:10, "you are so wise in Christ" (see also Rom. 11:25; 12:16; 2 Cor. 11:19). Here the sarcasm is less pronounced, but given the pattern of Paul's usage of this word, probably present. Paul's declaration indicates that the wisdom he trusts is not merely human judgment, but the sensibleness of Christ. Pondering Paul's words "in Christ" will result in thoughtful decision and wise action among the Corinthians, who were failing in such activity at the time Paul wrote them.

10:16 / The way in which Paul constructs the lines of this verse is instructive. (1) The grammatical form of Paul's rhetorical questions—which are also real—assumes the answer "Yes!" (2) Paul assumes the communal nature of the traditional celebration of the Lord's Supper in v. 16 before dwelling explicitly on the unity of the community in v. 17. (3) The phrase **cup of thanksgiving** is sometimes translated "cup of blessing." Linguists identify these words as having a "clear Semitic ring" (Orr and Walther, *I Corinthians*, p. 25) and from this characteristic of the language suggest that Paul specifically had either the second, the third, or the final cup of the Passover meal in mind. The phrase does have a liturgical tone and may reflect traditional material from either Judaism or early Christian practice. Nevertheless, this vivid wording only colors Paul's remarks at this point; it does not communicate the substance of his concern. (Cf. P. Sigal, "Another Note on 1 Corinthians 10.16," *NTS* 29 [1983], pp. 134–39; and Fee, *Epistle*, pp. 467–68.)

Furthermore, the word translated as **participation** in this verse is the Gk. work *koinōnia*, which is often translated "communion" or "fellowship." This is noteworthy, since in the next verse the verb "partake" occurs, but it comes from a completely different root/stem in Gk. Thus, there is no verbal connection between **participation** in v. 16 and "partake" in v. 17, although in v. 18 a related form of the *koinōn-* word group lies behind the word "those who . . . participate" (Gk. *koinōnoi*—lit. "participating ones"). See W. A. Sebothoma, "*Koinōnia* in 1 Corinthians 10:16," *Neot* 24 (1990), pp. 63–69.

10:17 / The verb **partake** is *metechō* in Gk. and means "to have with" something. The language about the partaking of one loaf by the one body anticipates the careful reflections of Paul that will follow in chs. 11–12.

10:18 / Paul's words, **Consider the people of Israel,** are "Look at Israel according to the flesh" (Gk. *Blepete ton Israēl kata sarka*). Paul is fond of the phrase "according to the flesh," and while he uses it to speak of historic Israel at this point, he often sets *flesh* over against *spirit* or even *the cross* (see Rom. 1:3; 4:1; 8:4, 5, 12, 13; 9:3, 5; 1 Cor. 1:26; 2 Cor. 1:17; 5:16 [2x]; 10:2, 3; 11:18; Gal. 4:23, 29; and Eph. 6:5; Col. 3:22). In essence Paul is pointing here to the theologically correct practices of Israel in the context of the world (the present evil age) independent of the Christ event. His comments assume some kind of theological, though not practical, continuity between the altar services to God and the celebration of the Lord's Supper. The OT materials underlying Paul's discussion are found in Lev. 7 and Deut. 12–18, esp. 18.

The reference to participation **in the altar** is a typical, pious ancient Jewish circumlocution for God, whose name is avoided by mention of a clearly affiliated item. It is remarkable that Paul lapses into such circumlocutions when he enters into discussion of Jewish practices. This small bit of language is evidence of Paul's former life in Judaism.

10:19 / Regarding this verse and the following one, Conzelmann (*1 Corinthians*, p. 172) remarks, "The thoughts tumble over each other."

10:20 / Watson (*First Epistle*, pp. 105–6) offers helpful remarks about the difficult matter of "demons" and "worldviews." He recognizes contemporary authors who take various positions on the question of the demonic and correctly notes that such discussions are better conducted in another context than the reading of this portion of Paul's letter. Watson identifies different positions, but he does not venture one himself. One may wish for more, but Watson is wise not to clutter commentary on 1 Corinthians with a complex excursus on demons. An additional word of warning is necessary: Attempts to reconcile or harmonize first-century and postmodern worldviews are unwise and probably impossible. The right and wrong of the reality of demons ultimately has no effect on Paul's central theological contention that Christian faith and practice are incompatible with soft religious syncretism.

10:21 / When Paul writes, **You cannot drink . . . you cannot have a part,** he more literally and emphatically says, "*You are not able* to drink . . . to have a part . . ." (Gk. *ou dynasthe . . . pinein . . . ou dynasthe . . . metechein . . .*). Paul understands this behavior to be outside the boundaries of power granted to the believers by God; he is not simply concerned with can and cannot, but with may and may not. God does not authorize this activity.

10:22 / The grammatical form of Paul's rhetorical and real questions anticipates a resounding "No!" for an answer. The question itself reflects OT thought about idolatry and God's jealousy, e.g., Deut. 32 (see B. S. Rosner, " 'Stronger Than He?' The Strength of 1 Corinthians 10:22b," *TynB* 43 [1992], pp. 171–79).

§29 The Goal of Christian Life
(1 Cor. 10:23–11:1)

Once again Paul broaches the subject of merely eating idol meat, but now he seems concerned with the eating of such previously sacrificed foods outside the confines of the pagan temple. The section is challenging to translators and interpreters because Paul writes in a vigorous style that takes abrupt rhetorical turns that can be and often are lost in the reading of the text. Identifying Paul's line of thought is crucial to comprehending this otherwise confusing passage. Paul gives a helpful hint when he opens verse 23 with a near repetition of the slogan from the Corinthians that he quoted in 6:12. This quotation signals the dialogic nature and pattern of thought in the ensuing discussion and informs the reader to be alert for Paul's use of rhetorical devices. In essence, Paul introduces the subject of consuming idol sacrifices and offers his thinking about what should occur in Corinth. Then, he anticipates the objections of those who would differ with him, stating these objections in a diatribe-like fashion as an imaginary opponent might raise the objections. In turn, Paul formulates responses to his partner in debate and explains why his own understanding and instructions are preferable. Ultimately one sees the heart of Paul's concern—the Corinthian Christians' relations with God, with one another, and with those outside the church—that has guided all that Paul has written since he took up this general matter in chapter 8.

10:23 / Paul returns to the Corinthians' slogans about freedom and offers further rebuttal, clarification, and directions. This verse repeats the Corinthians' declarations in a form similar to that previously cited at 6:12, but now there is no "to me" restricting the words **Everything is permissible.** Rather than approach the matter at an individual level, as the Corinthians themselves seem to have done, Paul states and treats the issue at a general, congregational level. As he did in chapter 6, Paul states and qualifies this slogan twice. First, he repeats and reacts to it exactly as in 6:12, **but not everything is beneficial.** Then, he repeats the slogan and limits it in relation to edification or building up, **but not everything is constructive.** Paul's reasoning recalls the line he advocated at 3:10–15, so that one sees that Paul desires the unity and proper development of the church.

10:24 / Paul builds on these qualified statements by declaring a maxim, **Nobody should seek his own good, but the good of others**—literally, "Let no one seek that of the self, but that of the other." No briefer, bolder call to selflessness and service could be issued in this context. In other words, Paul teaches the Corinthians to live so that each may say, "Not my good but your good be done."

10:25 / This verse initiates an explicit discussion with simple, straightforward directions for action. The line of thought begun here runs through verse 30 and will take on weight as the argumentation proceeds. In general, however, Paul makes practical application of the principle that he declared in verse 24. In a creative turn of phrases Paul plucks the pronounced principle out of the thin air of abstraction and puts it into the Corinthian context with the power of particularity. In so doing, Paul maintains the principle of Christian freedom, but he treats the matter of conscience in relation to actions in a remarkably selfless fashion!

Paul simply says, **Eat . . . without raising questions,** but he qualifies the issue of questions with the phrase **of conscience** (Gk. *dia tēn syneidēsin;* lit. "through the conscience"). As was noted in relation to the matter of conscience in chapter 8 (vv. 7, 10, 12), ancient ideas about conscience were not the same as today's understanding of conscience (readers should see the discussion regarding conscience in ch. 8). In brief, Paul is saying, "Eat without thinking about the scruples you have been taught by tradition." In other words, the Christian does enjoy a freedom from mere social conventions and mere religious regulations. Freedom is found in relationship to God, and action is to be determined in the context of divine-human relations. To put Paul's point of view into paraphrase, "If you aren't worried about offending God, don't worry about other things."

10:26 / Paul cites Scripture—specifically the LXX text of Psalm 24:1—to verify his advice: **The earth is the Lord's, and**

everything in it. The position seems liberal, although this brief citation locates Paul in line with the thinking of Jesus when he said, "Give to Caesar what is Caesar's, and to God what is God's." Moreover, Paul's argument presents the same understanding that was given to Peter through a dream and an encounter with Cornelius in Acts, "Do not call anything impure that God has made" (Acts 10:15).

Paul's point of view is thoroughly theological: Humans live in a world of social relationships and conventions, but the ultimate concern that should form life is the relationship one has to God. Honest self-conscious behavior evolves naturally from a genuine relationship between a person and God, not merely from adapting behavior to social and religious conventions.

10:27 / Having stated his position and advised the Corinthians how and what they should do, Paul illustrates the applicability of the behavior that he is advocating by introducing an imaginary situation that could arise in Corinth. The reader sees that Paul addresses the entire congregation, as is evident in the plural "you" forms that he employs throughout this discussion. Initially, in this verse, he tells the Corinthians that in a typical, uncomplicated situation, they are to eat—even at the home of those who are not believers—without worrying about the source of the foods that are served. Apparently Christian freedom meant that Christians did not have to go out of their way to comply with particular socioreligious conventions.

10:28–29a / In turn, however, this verse introduces the idea of the conscience of others and relates it to the idea of one's own freedom. As the reader sees, Paul ultimately interprets freedom as an opportunity for putting others before one's self. Should someone, for whatever reason, inform the Christians that the food being served is from idol sacrifices, then the Christians should refrain from eating.

Paul is adamant, however, that the Christians do not refrain from eating such foods for their own sakes. Implicitly he agrees with those in Corinth who say that the food has not been tainted through association with idols and that they are free to eat it. Nevertheless, when a third party becomes involved, the Christians have a different set of responsibilities. As Paul said, Christians are to think of others, not of themselves (v. 24). Thus, when another person informs the Christians of the association of the food with idols—perhaps out of concern for the Christians, perhaps out of concern for themselves, perhaps because they are merely busybodies—the Christians are to refrain from eating because of the sensibilities of the person(s) who informed them concerning the food.

10:29b–30 / Paul poses a pair of rhetorical questions, apparently to bring additional clarity to the matter under discussion. Nevertheless, for many readers these verses throw sand in the gears of the argument's mechanism.

If one reads the two questions, which are formulated in a straightforward way in Greek, Paul seems to contradict the advice he gave in verses 27–28. That understanding is impossible, however, for Paul reiterates the same advice about selflessness and putting others before one's self in 10:31–11:1. Thus, many commentators sensibly suggest that in these lines Paul creates an imaginary dialogue concerning what he had said up to this point (in vv. 23–29a); verses 29b–30 are objections that Paul imagines might come from those in Corinth who would not fully agree with him. Paul has said, "Be selfless. Be more concerned with others than with yourselves." Now, in behalf of those who would disagree, he asks, "Why should I let someone else's scruples determine my lifestyle? If I have the right attitude, why should I worry about someone else?" This interpretive suggestion, that Paul is engaging in diatribe at this point, seems the best understanding of the passage. Otherwise, Paul's logic explodes on itself, and he contradicts his advice of the following verses with no indication of the reason.

One further, somewhat speculative observation may lend support to the foregoing exegesis. One should note that Paul writes to the Corinthians as a group. But when the objections come in verses 29b–30, one finds them in the first-person singular. This self-centered point of view is the perspective Paul is calling the Corinthians away from in the main lines of his argument. From a purely personal, self-centered standpoint, Paul's directions are objectionable, but that viewpoint is exactly the one that Paul directs the Corinthian church not to take.

10:31–32 / With two sets of imperatives Paul summarizes his position concerning the situation in Corinth, moving beyond the impression that he is concerned merely with foods and patterns of consumption. First, Paul mentions eating and drinking, but his next words supersede both of these activities when he writes, **whatever you do.** Paul's perspective on the life of the

Corinthian Christians is all-encompassing, and his concern is both uniform and universal: **do it all for the glory of God.** From what Paul advises, one sees that putting God above all else means putting others before the self; and with the self set in service to others, the Christian life aims to achieve the glory of God. Second, Paul states his position in the form of a negative admonition: **Do not cause anyone to stumble;** and he elaborates: **Jews, Greeks or the church of God.** Here one sees the missional concern of the apostle and the way that his interest in the well-being and life of the church focused on both those outside and those inside the congregation. Such was Paul's understanding of the purpose of Christian life.

10:33 / As he took a seemingly imaginary personal point of view in verses 29b–30 in objecting to the directions he had offered, now Paul takes a genuinely personal angle on his instructions. Paul's carefully crafted declaration tells the Corinthians that he lives according to the advice he is giving—he always puts others before himself. Literally and emphatically, Paul writes, "Exactly as even I myself in all things to all try to give pleasure, not seeking my own advantage but that of many—in order that they may be saved." The final clause, **so that they may be saved,** summarizes Paul's self-understanding and purpose in life. He lived so that God might work through him for the salvific benefit of others, because he understood that God acted through his (Christlike) selflessness and saved others in the operation.

11:1 / In 10:31 Paul began to bring the larger section of 8:1–11:1 to a consummated conclusion by again declaring the goal of Christian life to be the glory of God in all that believers do. Paul sought to make matters conclusive by referring to his own attitude, aim, and style of ministry. Here he calls specifically for the Corinthians to imitate him as he imitates Christ. Paul presents himself as a model for the church, because what he models in his lifestyle is the way, will, and work of Christ. According to Paul, the lordship of Christ determines his living, so that the reality of Christ manifests itself in the concrete matters of Paul's life and becomes a real presence that the Corinthians are able to see and, through imitation, themselves make real. In this way and for this reason, Paul issues a call to Christlikeness.

Additional Notes §29

10:23 / Some ancient manuscripts—not the most reliable—do read the Gk. word *moi*, "to me," at this point, but this variant is a scribal adjustment of the present verse to comply with 6:12.

10:24 / The statement is in the imperative verbal form. The NIV can be read as if Paul were offering polite advice (**Nobody should seek**); in fact, he speaks commandingly, "Let no one seek . . . !"

10:25 / The reference to the market is striking; Paul uses a Gk. word, *makellon*, that has a Latin origin, *macellum*, designating an area with enclosures where various merchants would offer a variety of food- and meatstuffs. The Latin ring of this term is highly appropriate for the city of Corinth, which was located in Achaia, but as a refounded, reconstituted Roman city. An article by H. J. Cadbury ("The Macellum of Corinth," *JBL* 53 [1934], pp. 134–41) discusses an inscription from Corinth that locates the market Paul has in mind at this point; see also J. Murphy-O'Connor, *St. Paul's Corinth: Texts and Archaeology* (Good News Studies 6 [Collegeville, Minn.: Liturgical Press, 1983]), pp. 24–25, 32, 37. More recently, see D. W. J. Gill, "The Meat-Market at Corinth (1 Corinthians 10:25)," *TynB* 43 (1992), pp. 389–93.

10:27 / In offering these instructions, Paul gives indirect evidence about the social life of the early church. He assumes the possibility of social interaction between Christians and non-Christians. The role of religion and religious differences is not at the front of the picture. Yet, the mention of the hypothetical **unbeliever** at this point is telling, for Paul designates such a person with the terms *apistos* (lit. "without faithfulness"), indicating a nonbeliever.

10:28 / The phrase rendered in the NIV as **"This has been offered in sacrifice"** reads, "This is sacrificial," referring to the character of the substance rather than to the action of the sacrifice. Paul's concern is with the offensive quality of the meat because of its association with pagan ritual. He is not commenting on sacrifice per se nor on the eating of meat. Moreover, when Paul adds the phrases **for the sake of,** his choice of words (Gk. *dia*) indicates that he is giving the reason he offers this advice.

For a detailed discussion of the ancient literary data pertaining to the social situation Paul assumed and addressed here, see M. Isenberg, "The Sale of Sacrificial Meat," *CP* 70 (1975), pp. 271–73.

10:29 / For a detailed rhetorical analysis of the materials in this segment of the letter, esp. at this point in Paul's discussion, see D. F. Watson, "1 Corinthians 10:23–11:1 in the Light of Greco-Roman Rhetoric: The Role of Rhetorical Questions," *JBL* 108 (1989), pp. 301–18. In particular, the negative particle here, **not,** is strong in form, so that one should hear Paul saying, "not at all." Compare this verse with Rom. 14:16.

M. E. Thrall ("The Pauline Use of *Synedēsis*," *NTS* 14 [1967], pp. 118–25) makes careful observations concerning how Paul's understanding of conscience fit and modified typical Hellenistic patterns of thinking; she demonstrates how Paul's usage might be understood and even misunderstood by Greco-Roman readers. The suggestion that **conscience** is effectively equal to condemnation may, however, overstate the nuance of Paul's usage.

10:30 / The word translated **denounced** means "vilified"; Paul uses a passive form of the verb *blasphēmeō*, indicating harsh criticism that was often religious in character.

10:31 / The statement begins with the Gk. word *oun*, "therefore," a stronger and more formal inferential particle than is suggested by the NIV's rendering, **So.** . . . Paul uses *oun* seldom and deliberately in this particular epistle (Fee, *Epistle*, p. 487). Conzelmann rightly observes the importance of this statement and summarizes Paul's argument poignantly:

> In a style characteristic of Paul (*eite . . . eite*, "whether . . . or"), freedom is declared: the criterion lies outside myself. It is an objective and at the same time also a historic criterion: the glory of God. *Oun*, "so," indicates the conclusion to be drawn from the now established possibility of freedom of action. (p. 179)

10:32 / Paul's triad, Jew/Greek/church of God, is remarkable; for it couples two ethnic designations that were oftentimes considered exclusive and comprehensive with yet a third category that is not ethnic in origin or nature, **church of God.** Paul does not develop the combination of these designations, although his delineation and juxtaposition of categories are intriguing.

10:33 / Paul completes this verse with a telling purpose clause, **so that they may be saved** (Gk. *hina sōthōsin*), which clearly states Paul's understanding of God's own ultimate aspiration and end; the passive verb assumes that God is the author and agent of salvation.

11:1 / In saying "Imitators of me become," Paul uses the Gk. word *mimētēs*, a term from the representative and performatory arts. In a negative usage the word connotes "fake," but in a positive usage the word seems to refer to a "representation." It is the representative aspect of behavior—the believers represent Christ—that Paul has in mind.

This section of the letter takes up a disruptive situation in the life of the congregation at worship. Paul addresses the men and the women in the congregation concerning their manner of dress, although he comes to that point via a complicated route. While the issues are practical—dress and behavior at worship—Paul frames the matters in genuinely theological terms, not only mentioning God and Christ but also bringing into consideration the meaning and implications of creation and nature.

In brief, Paul tries to say that men and women are different, that women and men are dependent on each other, and that in the Lord there is both a mutuality and a distinctiveness that results both from creation and from redemption. One hopes that the Corinthians had an easier time following Paul's logic than do modern readers who are not fully informed about the situation in Corinth that Paul is addressing. Through careful examination of the text, one infers that Paul's concern is with an obscure—to later readers—effort on the part of some women in Corinth to eliminate traditional dress codes or social norms in the context of Christian worship, although one sees this situation only dimly in and between all the lines that make up this section of the letter.

11:2 / The section opens with a word of praise from Paul. He offers a commendation that may or may not be in response to a claim the Corinthians have made about their own preservation of tradition as Paul delivered it. Since Paul does not refer to this matter with the words "Now concerning," the reader of the letter is uncertain whether Paul bases his affirmation on something the Corinthians had written to him or on something that he knew by word of mouth. However Paul knew what he knew about the Corinthians' attitude toward his teaching, he does **praise** them **for remembering** [him] **in everything and for holding to the teachings, just as** [he] **passed them on to** [them].

11:3 / No sooner has Paul praised the Corinthians than he begins to offer them further instructions that imply that what they know or think they know may have led them to inappropriate activities. In this verse Paul takes exception to a practice that he views as being outside the boundaries of normal church custom (see v. 16). Paul begins his argument in a striking way, by articulating a scheme of priority of relations, and he will continue in the verses that follow to approach the situation from additional angles. At this point there are three distinct and related statements. Viewing the pattern of Paul's presentation in a tabular form proves instructive. The reader should notice that the scheme that Paul registers is *not* a simple stepladder or hierarchy:

Christ	the head	of every man
man	the head	of the woman
God	the head	of Christ

Many interpretations of this scheme have been offered, but one should notice that Paul is not concerned with marriage or with the sheer nature of men and women in their sexuality; rather, he is concerned with the life of the community and the orderly conducting of worship among all the believers.

Above all, one should notice that the scheme begins with **Christ** in relation to **man** and ends with **God** in relation to **Christ.** The concern at the beginning and the end of Paul's remarks is with divine authority and the results of that identity coming to bear properly in human relations. While the traditional interpretation that holds to the notion of the man or husband having authority over woman or his wife may offend progressive sensibilities, Paul's concern is to recognize the divine authority of Christ over humanity and the ultimate authority of God. Other levels of concern are introduced to back Paul's basic point that humans under the authority of Christ and God do not behave in dishonorable ways.

The scheme that Paul sketches is a Stoic-like system of natural order that values order over chaos. Moreover, the inner framework of this system, focused on **every man** and **woman,** relates to the congregational worship in Corinth and the form or order that the worship took or was to take. Furthermore, verse 3 cannot be viewed in isolation as an absolute maxim; as Paul will note in verse 11, "in the Lord" there is a mutual relatedness or absolute interdependence between "woman" and "man" /

"man" and "woman" that means that neither is independent or autonomous.

The reader of the epistle must gain some general orientation before proceeding to read the particular elements of the remaining individual verses. Otherwise, logical coherence of the argument is lost to the reader. At this juncture in Paul's remarks, one should see that what is about to follow in verses 4–6 follows a line of argumentation concerning the scheme of authority laid out in verse 3 in specific relation to the worship activities of praying or prophesying, specifically focusing on the practice of women wearing head coverings.

Paul uses the word **head** repeatedly, but seemingly in both a literal and a figurative fashion. For the original readers, who had the data to distinguish what Paul meant to say, such a rhetorical ploy or device was creative and forceful, although for later readers it is confusing. (See Additional Note on v. 3 for more information on Paul's use of "head.") Thus, there are immediate problems for interpretation. Which instances of "head" are literal and which are metaphorical? Are all uses of "head" literal, all metaphorical, or is there some mix? Clearly the first occurrences of "head" in both verse 4 and verse 5 are literal because of the issue of covering and not covering. But what of the second use of "head" in each verse? Are they metaphors for Christ and husband respectively, or are they literal? (The third occurrence of **head** in verse 5 in the NIV was supplied by the translators.) From what follows in verse 7—where a man's not covering his head is explained in terms of his existing as the image and the glory of God and the woman's covering her head is explained in terms of her being the glory of man—one understands that the dishonored "heads" of verses 4–5 are metaphorical.

11:4 / Paul states that if a **man prays or prophesies with his head covered**, then he **dishonors his head.** How? Apparently by altering normal social practices or dress codes to show himself free from such conventions. Such a showing would make a spectacle of the man and, in bringing the attention to him, not bring the honor to Christ. Indeed, such a defiance of cultural norms, especially regarding something so superficial as a dress code, might imply that Christ was producing trivial forms of social discord.

11:5 / In a corollary fashion, this verse argues the converse for **every woman.** For women to alter dress codes in public worship drew attention to themselves, not to the Lord. What is important but often missed in this morass of reasoning is that Paul plainly assumes that properly clad women would be participating and leading in worship through the offering of prayers and prophecies. The problem here is with the alteration of dress, not with the utterance of prayers and prophecies. Genuinely Spirit-filled behavior is not to be subsumed under a self-aggrandizing show of personal freedom. Exactly the same is true for both women and men in worship.

11:6 / Paul offers a logical twist to his argument at this point, issuing a kind of *reductio ad absurdum:* If a woman is not veiled, then she ought to be shorn; but since it is a disgrace for a woman to be shaved, then let her be veiled.

Again one must step back from examining the elements of Paul's argument to see the general lines and connections of his thinking. A glance ahead is necessary. The strange sense of the argument begins to make sense when one sees that Paul understands nature (v. 14) to give indication of the God-ordained pattern of life. Nevertheless, several problems raised by Paul's statements are not easily resolved. (1) How can a woman, veiled or otherwise, pray or prophesy if she is to be silent in the church as 14:33–35 indicates? (2) Has Paul confused nature and humanly determined fashion? Are male and female hairstyles given by nature or set in style? (3) How is the reader to understand the amount of energy that Paul invests in this section (11:2–16)? Does the show of creative effort indicate the severity of the problem? Or is Paul simply at a loss? Or is he merely biased? (4) What kind of attitude do these lines reflect—Greek, Jewish, or Christian? It is easier to raise such difficult questions than to find gratifying answers related to these verses. Thus, one needs to return to the text and to follow the remaining course of Paul's presentation.

11:7 / Paul's bewilderingly difficult argument continues, assuming a knowledge of the situation in Corinth and now also assuming a knowledge of the creation stories of Genesis. In general, verses 7–12 continue to pursue Paul's point concerning appropriate and inappropriate behavior in worship from the perspective of a set of biblical texts. Specifically, in verse 7 Paul restates the idea with which he is working, bringing in the language of the Genesis account of Genesis 1:26–27—*the image* **and glory** *of God*. In the Judaism of Paul's day, the ideas of "image" and "glory of God" had become somewhat synonymous, so Paul's mentioning of "image" and "glory" may be complementary or compound rather than distinct. One must note, however, that Paul is not simply teaching Bible lessons; in fact, the situation in Corinth and Paul's desire for a resolution to the problems in worship clearly control his selection of texts and the exegesis or interpretation that he offers. Apparently Paul's logic runs this way: God brought forth man who now as the creature is explicit evidence of God's glory. Yet, woman was brought forth by God from man, so that if she is displayed explicitly, glory will go to man rather than to God. The point is that the creatures (man and woman) bring glory to the one from whom they come—man to God and woman to man. The argument is difficult, and all attempts at interpretation run the risk of misunderstanding Paul's thought. The argument, however, serves a clear point: the women should have their heads covered.

11:8–9 / These two verses extend Paul's argument by taking even more explicit recourse to the creation story of Genesis 2:18, 22. Paul declares that the order of creation, with man preceding woman, shows that woman is not independent from man and that man has a different status from woman because of his place in the order of creation. The statements in this verse are not, however, made for their own sakes, but as logical preparations for the ensuing explanatory declaration that Paul will make as he applies the facts of the creation story to the situation in Corinth.

11:10 / This verse begins simply, **For this reason**—literally, "Therefore" (Gk. *dia touto*). Nevertheless, verse 10 is an enigma. The opening words can relate either to previous or to ensuing comments. The phrase probably refers to what went before (vv. 8–9 or vv. 2–9), since still another phrase that begins with **because of** brings the line to its conclusion. In essence, Paul argues that because of the relationship of men and women at creation, women ought to have **a sign of authority** on their heads, and this wearing of a sign is related to **the angels.**

The allusion to the creation of man before woman may be clear, but what does Paul mean by "because of the angels"? The statement is obscure and theories abound. Two sensible suggestions merit attention. Perhaps the apostle is thinking of the fallen angels of Genesis 6 who took human women for wives; or perhaps he means the angels who were thought to be protectors of the order of creation and who were present, according to early Christian thought, in the assembly of Christians at worship (Rev. 2:1, 8, 12, 18; 3:1, 7, 14). The latter suggestion seems preferable because the discussion of behavior in worship directly relates to the idea of the assumed presence of the angels. Indeed the presence of the angels for the ordering of that worship would argue against any disorderly or unprecedented practices (men with coverings on their heads or women without). Moreover, the suggested connection to Genesis 6 would require considerable imagination and would still not be a clear argument. What is beyond dispute concerning this verse is that Paul means to mount still another line in his attack on disorderly innovations in worship.

11:11–12 / Verses 11–12 form a statement in peculiar juxtaposition to what Paul has said to this point. One should note the all-important phrase **in the Lord** in verse 11. By declaring this crucial theological/christological location Paul is able to make the clear and balanced statement that follows in verse 12. Now one sees that Paul understands the situation concerning men and women as he did the issues of circumcision and slavery in chapter 7. "In the Lord" one recognizes the eschatological abrogation of sexual distinctions, but as Christians await the Day of the Lord they are not to act as if the Day has already come. One remains in the state that one was called as the only valid demonstration of freedom. **God** stands over all, and in the Lord women and men are interdependent, even equal; but they are still as God made them in creation, men and women. They have not and they will not supersede their sexuality in this life, and showy attempts to rise above the God-given conditions of creation by doing such things as altering normal patterns of dress are inappropriate.

11:13 / This verse begins a final line of argumentation (vv. 13–16) that puts the issue with which Paul has been laboring before the Corinthians for a last time and from still another angle. Paul launches this last piece of ancient logic—a powerful appeal to recognized cultural standards that would have registered in a weighty way with the Corinthians—calling for the Christians in Corinth to **judge** the matter of a woman's being unveiled at prayer.

11:14–15 / Paul brings to the attention of the Corinthians **the very nature of things**. In so doing, he means to offer a kind of evidence—nature itself—that he intends for the Corinthians to use as the basis of their evaluation of the situation. Like other ancients, Paul and the Corinthians would have understood that "nature" indicates God's will, and so persons should style themselves according to the lines of nature as a copy of nature itself. Paul surely did not reflect on this relatively weak example or argument, for what he attributes to nature is merely human fashion, reflecting culture, not necessarily God—unless Paul thinks somehow that culture derives from nature and, in turn, that fashion ultimately goes back to God. Such thinking may well have been what Paul had in mind, and his advantage in using this argument would have been that the Corinthians probably thought the same way. Nevertheless, the argument strikes the modern mind as strange. Remarkably, in denouncing his opposition Paul cannot cite either revelation or the Lord; rather, he is reduced to custom for his standards and authorization. Indeed, this argument is a kind of natural theology that Paul uses rarely. Despite the peculiar quality of the discussion, however, Paul's general contention is simple: in worship members of the church are not to act in ways that draw attention to themselves rather than to God.

11:16 / In the end, the issues under discussion in this vivid section of the letter may elude resolution, although one should not fail to see that in verse 16 Paul himself recognizes the potential denial of his argument. Thus, he finishes his remarks on a weighty note: Should someone object to Paul's arguments, teaching, or reasoning; then that person must realize that Paul's position is a universal norm, for it is the **practice** . . . [of] **the churches of God,** and according to the practices of those churches, what was happening in Corinth was inappropriate.

In sum, at its root the alteration of custom often although not always stems from individualism, the claiming of personal rights in the name of the Lord—a problem already identified by Paul in the earlier sections of the letter. Christians, Paul tells the Corinthians, are "not to confuse a direct desecularization that is carried on by ourselves with the eschatological desecularization brought about by Christ, but to maintain the imperceptibility of this unworldliness—by dint of Christians wearing their hair normally and clothing themselves in normal ways" (Conzelmann, *1 Corinthians,* p. 191).

Additional Notes §30

On the general topic of the authenticity of these verses in Paul's original letter to Corinth, see the debate between W. O. Walker Jr. ("1 Corinthians 11:2–16 and Paul's Views Regarding Women," *JBL* 94 [1975], pp. 94–110), who argues that 11:2–16 is an interpolation into Paul's correspondence, and J. Murphy-O'Connor ("The Non-Pauline Character of 1 Corinthians 11:2–16" *JBL* 95 [1976], pp. 615–21), who critiques Walker and argues for Pauline authorship.

11:2 / Conzelmann (*1 Corinthians*, p. 182) wisely points to the "content of the commendation" as the point of continuity between 11:1 and 11:2. Initially Paul touches on matters he can affirm, although his commending of the Corinthians briefly precedes his turning to other issues that are impossible for him to laud. In what follows, both positively and negatively, the point of continuity is with 10:33–11:1, imitation of Paul and following his teachings. Moreover, D. K. Lowery ("The Head Covering and the Lord's Supper in 1 Corinthians 11:2–34," *BibSac* 143 [1986], pp. 155–63) finds connections between the two major portions of 1 Cor. 11 at the level of Paul's general discussion of Christian freedom, which he contends to be a dominant theme from ch. 8 through ch. 14.

11:3 / Orr and Walther (*I Corinthians*, p. 259) note, "Throughout this passage it is difficult to decide whether *anēr* should be translated 'man' or 'husband' and even more particularly whether *gynē* should be translated 'woman' or 'wife.' " Thus, the NRSV renders this verse in a paraphrasing manner, "Christ is the head of every man, and the husband is the head of his wife, and God is the head of Christ." The differences from the more literal translation of the NIV are immediately apparent. This "different" reading is possible, because the same Gk. word functioned to mean "man" and "husband"; and in a context where one would understand the topic to be husbands and wives, the same Gk. word that normally means "woman" can specify "the man's woman," i.e., the wife. The NRSV interprets this verse to refer to husbands and wives rather than to males and females in general, and the way the statements are written—particularly the use of the definite article in a restrictive fashion: literally "a woman . . . the man"—*may* indicate that Paul is discussing husbands and wives. Nevertheless, even that insight does not make the logic of this passage any easier to follow. Thus, one must remain close to the text to understand Paul's central concern.

N. Watson (*First Epistle*, pp. 111–12) succinctly summarizes much complex material and discussion of the idea and function of the word **head** in these verses in the following lines:

> It was commonly assumed by all commentators up to Barrett that the word was being used here to mean "ruler," so that the point of the verse

was that just as God rules Christ so Christ rules man and man rules woman. However, the use of *kephalē* to mean ruler is not a native Greek idiom. Liddell and Scott *[Greek-English Lexicon]* do not give the meaning "ruler" as a sub-category within the metaphorical usages of the word. The Hebrew word for head, *rosh,* is used in the Old Testament to denote a ruler, that is, the ruler of a community, but, when it is so used, the Greek translators of the LXX regularly render it by *archōn* or *archēgos* rather than by *kephalē,* the word they regularly use whenever the physical head is intended. Fee's judgment is that out of 180 occurrences of the word *kephalē* in the LXX there are only six in which it clearly carries the meaning "ruler."

There is, however, a common idiomatic use of *kephalē* in Greek to denote source. If the word is understood in this way, then Paul is thinking not of hierarchies of rulers and ruled but of a series of relationships of derived being. That is certainly the kind of relationship implied by the creation story of Genesis 2, which is clearly in Paul's mind in vv. 8 and 9.

The evidence and argument of Fee and Watson seem reasonable and persuasive. The noted connection between Gen. 2 and vv. 8–9 is beyond dispute, so the suggestion that Gen. 2 is the most logical background for understanding vv. 3–7 is exegetically sound and insightful.

Nevertheless, the interpretive debate is not settled. J. A. Fitzmyer ("Another Look at KEPHALĒ in 1 Corinthians 11.3," *NTS* 35 [1989], pp. 503–11) examines the LXX and Philo alongside Paul to argue that "head" could be understood as "authority over" another person; also J. A. Fitzmyer, *"Kephalē* in I Corinthians 11:3," *Int* 47 (1993), pp. 52–59. In a creative interpretive essay, S. E. McGinn (*"exousian echein epi tēs kephalēs:* 1 Cor 11:10 and the Ecclesial Authority of Woman," *List* 31 [1996], pp. 91–104) argues that the charismatic gift of prophecy gave the women who were endowed with this gift an *authority* over their heads—the men—because of the Spirit's presence and power at work in their contributions to the congregation's worship.

On the difficulty of this section and the awkwardness of Paul's logical development in argumentation, see the discussion of J. M. Bassler ("1 Corinthians," 326–27) in *The Women's Bible Commentary* (C. A. Newsom and S. H. Ringe, eds.; Louisville, Ky.: Westminster John Knox, 1992). For a more radical line of reinterpretation, see A. C. Wire, *The Corinthian Women Prophets: A Reconstruction through Paul's Rhetoric* (Minneapolis: Fortress, 1990).

11:4 / The statement is puzzling to many modern readers because they are familiar with the orthodox Jewish practice of men's wearing yarmulkes. Despite there being no OT text that requires such a covering, there is no prohibition. The practice of Jewish men wearing religious headgear is a later rabbinic development that has no bearing on Paul's discussion. Moreover, Paul does not seem very concerned with this matter in the context of this discussion; rather, he raises the issue as part of his argument against the women going without a covering in worship.

11:5 / As noted above in relation to v. 3, the third occurrence of **head** in the English translation of the present verse is a word that is

supplied by the translators. In fact, in Gk., the perfect passive participle "having been shaved" (Gk. *exyrēmenē*), translated here **were shaved**, is preceded by the definite article "the" (Gk. *tē*) probably meaning "the woman," not "her head"; so that the line reads "for it is one and the same thing as her having been shaved."
     With regard to this verse and others J. Murphy-O'Connor ("St. Paul: Promoter of the Ministry of Women," *Priests & People* 6 [1992], pp. 307–11) argues that Paul was bothered in this particular instance by the blurring of sexual distinctions in Corinth, although he was supportive of women's ministry. See also J. Murphy-O'Connor, "Sex and Logic in 1 Corinthians 11:2–16," *CBQ* 42 (1980), pp. 482–500.

11:7 / See Conzelmann, *1 Corinthians*, pp. 187–88 for more on the synonymous understandings of image (Gk. *eikōn*) and glory (Gk. *doxa*) of God. Cf. Gen. 1:27.

11:8 / Cf. Gen. 2:22 LXX.

11:10 / The phrase **sign of authority** in the NIV is a translation of the single Gk. word *exousia*, which normally means "authority." The NIV paraphrase is an attempt to make sense of this obscure statement. As Orr and Walther note, "There is no other occurrence of *exousia* with *epi* ["over," NIV = **on**] and the genitive in Paul" (*I Corinthians*, p. 261); thus, Fee (*Epistle*, pp. 512, 518–22) corrects the translation to read, in part, "the woman ought to have authority over her head." As Fee recognizes, the plain sense of Paul's words is that "the woman ought to have freedom over her head to do as she wishes"; but "the problem with that, of course, is that it sounds so contradictory to the point of the argument to this point" (p. 520).

11:11 / This verse begins in Gk. with the strong conjunction, "nevertheless" (Gk. *plēn*), which the NIV renders as the postpositive, "however." In fact, this conjunction often breaks off one line of discussion and passes on to another subject (LSJ 1419). Moreover, Paul actually holds the words "in the Lord" (Gk. *en kyriō*) until the end of his clause to create strong emphasis on the phrase: *in the Lord!*

11:12 / The NIV and other translations seem to miss Paul's very deliberate use of prepositions in this verse. He writes lit., "For exactly as the woman [is] *out of* [Gk. *ek*] the man, thus also the man [is] *through* [Gk. *dia*] the woman." Paul refers to the creation story in the first part of the statement and to birth in the second. He recognizes a distinction in terms of order or creation, but he parallels man's birth from woman as a complementary condition that means the equality of the sexes despite their real differences.

11:14–15 / The grammatical form of this question in Gk. *(oude)* is unusual, but "it is fairly certain that it introduces a question expecting affirmative answer . . ." (Orr and Walther, *I Corinthians*, p. 261).
     Regarding these verses C. L. Thompson ("Hairstyles, Headcoverings, and St. Paul: Portraits from Roman Corinth," *BA* 51 [1988], pp. 99–115) examines artifacts to suggest that Paul was affirming short

hair for men, long hair for women, and the right of the women to make decisions concerning head coverings. D. W. J. Gill ("The Importance of Roman Portraiture for Head-Coverings in 1 Corinthians 11:2–16," *TynB* 41 [1990], pp. 245–60), however, argues that Paul's concern is twofold: to warn men away from wearing head coverings in worship so as to draw attention to social status, and to admonish women not to abandon veils in worship as an act of contentiousness. Both Thompson and Gill agree that Paul is concerned above all with orderly worship through the practice of acceptable social conventions.

11:16 / This verse summarizes and looks back to the discussion from 11:2–15. Paul has been discussing the local congregation in Corinth, and now he places that group in the context of the entire church, a connection and identity he established explicitly and originally at 1:2. Recognizing the difficulty of this verse and the section to which it is related, J. C. G. Greig ("Women's Hats—1 Corinthians xi.1–16," *ExpT* 69 [1958], pp. 156–57) suggests the following paraphrase of this verse, "However, we have more to do than to argue. Rather than provoke contentiousness, we have no custom *the one way or the other*, either personally or as churches." J. Nolland ("Women in the Public Life of the Church," *Crux* 19 [1983], pp. 17–23) finds a larger following with the understanding that Paul is concerned that the women practicing ministry in Corinth give honor to their sex and not attempt to be pseudomen; thus, Paul was not a radical feminist, nor was he bound to defending conventional hierarchy.

§31 Problems in the Assembling
(1 Cor. 11:17-22)

These few lines are vitally related to the verses that follow, verses 23-26 and verses 27-34, although the weighty traditional nature of the ensuing verses distinguishes verses 23-34 from verses 17-22 and suggests the separation of the discussion of the Lord's Supper into smaller, more manageable parts. Paul's words and his concerns are straightforward, nearly self-evident, although the energy of his argument causes the discussion to shift about in a way that might be difficult for some readers to follow.

11:17 / Paul identifies and criticizes a problem or problems related to when the Corinthians come together. He takes a point of departure from the beginning of the previous section (11:2), where he had praised the Corinthians; now he says by contrast that he is unable to praise them for what they are doing in their **meetings.** Paul literally writes, "But this charging I do not praise." This introductory line is transitional and, at a glance, ambiguous in point of reference. The NIV rightly recognizes that Paul is looking forward at this point rather than back to the previous lines, so one reads, **In the following directives.** The subject that Paul is about to address is the meetings of the Corinthian congregation. In what follows he will take up a sequence of unpraiseworthy activities that include behavior at the Lord's Supper (11:17-34) and the use of spiritual gifts in worship (12:1-14:25); he corrects the various misunderstandings and misbehaviors as he discusses these problems and then sets out guidelines for orderly worship (14:26-40).

There is an undertone of irony when Paul says that he is not able to praise the Corinthians at this point, because his readers would not have felt particularly flattered by Paul's remarks in the previous section of the letter (vv. 2-16). In this section Paul is even more blunt. He says the Corinthians' gathering is not for the better but for the worse; the results of the congregational assembly are negative. To paraphrase sensibly, one might say that the congregational assembly did more harm than good.

11:18 / Paul explains why he is unable to praise the Corinthians in their assembling. He has heard particular information about their gatherings. Although he names them as a **church** (see 1:2), he immediately recognizes **divisions** that exist **among** the members. Moreover, he says **to some extent I believe it**, implying in a slightly sarcastic way that he is not surprised by the problem of factions. In part, Paul's concern with divisions may go back to the discussion of factions in chapter 1, but at this point Paul does not make that connection explicitly.

11:19 / Oddly, Paul offers a rationalization for this problem. He explains that factions are necessary in order that those who are approved may be recognized. The reader is left to wonder whether Paul is being sarcastic or whether he discerns God creating confusion in Corinth—or both. When Paul says, **No doubt there have to be differences among you**, the reader wonders how forceful Paul means for this observation to be. He uses the Greek impersonal verb *dei*, which normally means "it must be" or "it is necessary," and which, in the vast majority of NT occurrences means "it must be" or "it is necessary" because of the presence, action, and will of God.

The NIV translation is near paraphrase, though probably accurate, at this point. The words **to show which of you have God's approval** more literally say, "in order that those who are approved may become manifest among you." Implicit in this statement is the notion that some are approved while others are not; from Paul's wording the reader is to understand that God does the approving and disapproving, although the behavior of the Corinthians is the key to distinguishing the groups.

11:20 / Paul explicitly raises the matter of the Lord's Supper, declaring that the meal the Corinthians eat at their assemblies cannot be so named. The Greek text indicates that Paul is still explaining his understanding of the situation, although the way Paul words the statement—he begins, "Thus" or "Therefore" (Gk. *oun*)—is lost in the NIV. Indeed, the translation **it is not the Lord's Supper you eat** is problematic, since Paul actually writes, "It is not the Lord's Supper to eat." The wording of this remark may indicate that Paul meant to say that the problem lay with the purpose of the gathering or the motivation that was brought to the assembly, rather than with the course or nature of the events per se. It is not the Lord's Supper they eat, because they do not gather to eat the Lord's Supper. Inappropriate aims make even appropriate actions unacceptable.

11:21 / In sharp juxtaposition to "the Lord's Supper" Paul states here that **each of you goes ahead without waiting for anybody else,** which literally reads, "for each one starts her or his *own* supper to eat." In other words, self-interest colors the eating from the outset. Paul contrasts "the Lord's Supper" with "the [Corinthians'] own supper" and in the comparison reveals that a primary focus on the self is the problem with the Corinthians' eating.

In this and the following verse Paul identifies that he opposes individualistic self-gratification in the extreme. Moreover, he gives a theological force to his denunciation by showing that self-interest undermines community. That is, self-interested activity breaks down the unity of the church that God has brought into being. Each person or group goes an individual way, without concern for others. Thoughtlessness toward others causes humiliation and, as becomes clear in what follows, is antithetical to love.

Commentators rightly suggest that differences in the social status of believers in Corinth lie behind the formation of groups where some remain **hungry** and others get **drunk.** Some apparently had more means, time, and goods than others, and distinctions were made. This insight is helpful at a sociological level and assists modern readers in understanding the practical dimensions of the problems in Corinth, although Paul does not address the situation on that plane (pace Watson, *First Epistle,* pp. 117–19). Indeed, Paul does not say to wait for others and then to distribute the goods more equitably, although in one way that might have pleased him (see 10:33). Simply altering the activity will not correct the true problem in the Corinthian church. Rather, Paul addresses this problem as a theological issue: persons are focused on themselves rather than on "the Lord" and others who are part of the community of faith that God has called into existence. Paul gives no sociological pep talk; rather, he moves ahead with his argument and recalls the Corinthians to a proper theological point of view (vv. 23–34).

11:22 / Paul issues a series of remarks, including four rhetorical questions and a final declaration. He uses these to provide a forceful explanation of his inability to commend the practices of the Corinthians. The tone of the lines is telling. The first question is as a double negative in Greek and amounts to stinging sarcasm, **Don't you have . . . ?** (*contra* Conzelmann, *1 Corinthians*, p. 195). The second question exposes the real results of what was happening in Corinth, **Or do you despise . . . ?** The third question is neutral and open, **What shall I say to you?** And the fourth question is also genuinely deliberative, **Shall I praise you for this** [the way they are behaving]? Finally, Paul bluntly says, "I do not praise you!"—a declaration in direct opposition to the first words of 11:2, "I praise you. . . ."

The grammar of the last question and the concluding statement is ambiguous; so that one may read the lines as the NIV: **Shall I praise you for this? Certainly not!** Or, one may understand the phrasing to be slightly different: "Shall I praise you? In this I do not praise!" The question is a minor matter of punctuation, and while Paul's rhetoric is unclear, his force and meaning are unequivocal.

From the way Paul frames these questions one must ask whether the Corinthians are interpreting divisiveness as a pluralism that deserves praise. If so, Paul's remarks indicate that unity is essential and unity without diversity is meaningless. To bring shame to those who have nothing is to express disdain, even if unintentionally, for the church of God. One might conclude by contrast that to cherish God's church would lead one to honor the less fortunate or that to bring honor to those who have nothing would be an expression of concern for God's church. As Paul compares and contrasts matters in Corinth, the reader finds him teaching that an interest in God's work may be seen in concern for others, and that concern for others may be the best indication of genuine concern for God's work. In the end, as he repeats himself ("Shall I praise you for this? Certainly not!"), Paul expresses his basic disapproval of the gatherings in Corinth. Self-serving activity, even when religious in nature, is not God's will or the purpose for the church.

Additional Notes §31

For a creative and insightful reading of this passage that identifies the missional character of the early church's eucharistic practices, see S. H. Ringe ("Hospitality, Justice, and Community: Paul's Teaching on the Eucharist in 1 Corinthians 11:17–34," *Prism* 1 [1986], pp. 59–68), who relates the celebration of the Lord's Supper to the Christians' participation in God's own eschatological drama. The attempt by J. A. Gibbs ("An Exegetical Case for Close(d) Communion: 1 Corinthians 10:14–22; 11:17–34," *Concordia Journal* 21 [1995], pp. 148–63) uses exegesis but needs more hermeneutics in drawing out a case for contemporary practices from the passages in Paul's letter. The concerns Gibbs attempts to address in this work may never have entered Paul's mind.

11:18 / The word Paul uses for the **divisions** in Corinth is *schismata* in Gk., from the Gk. verb *schizō*, which means "to tear." By naming the groups in Corinth in this way Paul recognizes tears or ruptures in the life of the congregation.

11:19 / Paul refers to the groups in the church using the Gk. word *haireseis*, translated **differences**, a noun related to the Gk. verb *haireomai*, "choose." He recognizes that the differences are the result of *choice*, as in joining a particular party or belonging to a specific school of thought.

On this difficult issue of interpretation, Conzelmann writes,

> The question is how strictly *dei*, "must," may be taken: Does it refer to a "necessary process, namely, one determined by an apocalyptic plan? It is more natural simply to take *dei* with the appended *hina*-clause ["in order to"]: the objective fruit of the divisions is the visible separation of wheat and chaff.

Nevertheless, Conzelmann also recognizes that "in favor of the 'sharp' view [the apocalyptic understanding] is the similarity with the eschatological logion ['there will be dissensions and squabbles']." Conzelmann, *1 Corinthians*, p. 194.

Perhaps there is sarcasm or bitter irony in Paul's observation. It is doubtful, given his comments in 1 Cor. 1:10–17, that Paul thinks either that factionalism is good or that God would author such divisions as an end in themselves. Nevertheless, Paul may mean to say that given the problems in Corinth, God must be at work to differentiate those who are faithful from those who are behaving inappropriately.

The reader has seen repeatedly that the apostle thought and taught from an apocalyptic-eschatological point of view. If he writes in that vein at this point, he understands God's power to be at work in the separation of the Corinthians into groups **to show which of you have God's approval** (lit. "in order that those who are approved may become known among you"). For a forceful interpretation of vv. 18–19, see

H. Paulsen ("Schima und Häresie: Untersuchungen zu 1 Kor 11,18.19," *ZTK* 79 [1982], pp. 180–211), who examines extrabiblical early Christian literature to demonstrate that the early church understood rifts and divisions among the members to be evidence of necessary eschatological activity. Paulsen shows that Paul's phrase "it is necessary divisions and factions to be" (Gk. *dei schismata kai haireseis einai*) was a well-known saying in the early church. The attempt by R. A. Campbell ("Does Paul Acquiesce in Divisions at the Lord's Supper?" *NovT* 33 [1991], pp. 61–70) to read Paul's teaching merely at the level of social discrimination is typical of current trends in interpretation, but nevertheless it is anachronistic and insufficiently alert to Paul's genuinely theological concerns and perspectives.

11:20 / The reference to this activity as **the Lord's Supper** is the only NT designation of this event in the life of the early church. The Gk. phrase *kyriakon deipnon* is difficult to render in English, since the Gk. word *kyriakos*, which is an adjective, has no direct parallel in English idiom. The only other use of this adjective in the NT is in Rev. 1:10 in reference to "the *Lord's* Day." In secular usage during the NT period this same word meant "imperial." The phrase in this verse might be paraphrased, "the Lord's own supper," to emphasize the qualifying nature of *kyriakos*. The idea is that the supper belongs to the Lord.

11:21 / For an interpretation that attempts to fuse the current trend toward sociological exegesis and theological interpretations, see P. Lampe, "The Eucharist: Identifying with Christ on the Cross," *Int* 48 (1994), pp. 36–49.

§32 Recalling the Origins of the Lord's Supper (1 Cor. 11:23-26)

These four verses recapitulate the early Christian tradition concerning the institution of the Lord's Supper. They are the earliest preserved description of this central event in the life of the first believers. Paul reiterates this tradition as the foundation of his ensuing teaching in 11:27-34. In light of the Corinthian situation he explicates matters related to the tradition, but he does not explain or theologize the tradition directly. Commentators are almost certainly right to assume that basic teaching about this practice would have been done at an earlier time when Paul was personally present among the Corinthians, although Paul makes no overt reference to his elaboration or interpretation of the tradition of the Lord's Supper.

Despite their brevity, verses 23-26 are enormously important for the church in both belief and practice. Full-scale comparative analysis of this passage in relation to parallels in Mark 14:22-24; Matthew 26:26-28; and Luke 22:17,19-20 is imperative for development of theology of the eucharist, but that larger project is both unnecessary and impossible in the context of this commentary. What seems most important in Paul's representation of the tradition of the Lord's Supper is that he emphasizes that the supper is the Lord's and that he calls the Corinthians to an involvement with the Supper that will take any inappropriate focus off themselves as they remember that their participation is done in remembrance of the Lord and as an act of proclaiming his saving death and his anticipated coming. As the Corinthians participate in the Supper, Paul insists that the reality and the meaning of the death of the Lord are to take hold of their lives and, as they celebrate the Lord's Supper, the truth of Christ's death and the promise of his coming are to shape and direct their living as a community. Thus, the Lord's Supper embodies or actualizes in a celebratory way the reality, as well as the theological and subsequent social implications, of the truth of Jesus' saving death.

11:23 / Verse 23 claims **the Lord** as the ultimate source of this tradition, since the words Paul is about to recite concerning the elements of the Supper go back to the Lord whom Paul understands to be raised and who is alive in the Spirit. Whether Paul means to claim a more direct or independent revelatory experience in relation to his knowledge of this tradition is impossible to determine from what he writes at this point. While his use of words is concise, the selection of terms and the form of the phrases is important.

The way Paul refers to receiving and passing on tradition occurs again at 15:1–8, where he recounts the resurrection appearances of the Lord. Paul's manner of phrasing the way he knew and taught traditional materials does not explain the source of his information or the circumstances of his reception of the material. Attempts to rationalize Paul's knowledge as coming from other Christians and attempts to defend the supernatural revelation of the tradition are equally speculative and indefensible. With regard to another context, however, see Paul's explicit statement at Galatians 1:12.

Paul's language concerning receiving and passing on the tradition was technical vocabulary in both Greek schools and Jewish synagogue thought. Ancients understood the reception and the handing on of tradition to imply several important points. First, lines of authority were established and recognized in the transmission of tradition. Authoritative teachers instructed recognized students who in turn became authorities in their own right. Second, the transmission of tradition through selected channels of communication guaranteed the veracity of the tradition that was passed along from one person to another. Thus, in saying, **I received from** the Lord **what I also passed on to you,** Paul establishes both the authority and reliability of the teaching.

As he continues, Paul alludes to **the Lord Jesus,** a frequent manner of reference that here has the concrete, historic effect of recalling the historical Jesus and a specific time in his life. Paul does not belabor this point, however, although the way he continues indicates that he intends to renarrate a set of past events that were fixed in the memory of the early church. Moreover, it is remarkable that nothing in the tradition of the Lord's Supper as Paul presents it in this verse or in the lines that follow necessitates the Passover setting found in the Gospels. It is true, however, that the Passover setting in the Gospels is not in the words of institution, but in the narrative, so perhaps it is not peculiar that the Passover setting is absent in 1 Corinthians. Nevertheless, the simple mention of **the night he was betrayed**— referring to a particular time and a particular act that need no explanation—shows the fixed nature of this tradition and points to its association with the larger passion narrative.

The verb "was betrayed" (Gk. *paredideto*) is passive and may be translated "was handed over." Thus, the reader is uninformed as to who handed over Jesus. Interpretations that understand this passive to be a divine passive (God is the one who handed over Jesus) are grammatically defensible, but the range of NT texts concerned with the handing over make it clear that Judas Iscariot (unnamed in any Pauline writing) betrayed or handed over Jesus. Divine passives occur throughout the NT, but when a plausible nondivine actor is well-known in relation to a particularly infamous act, there is no reason to overread the text.

11:24 / The last words of verse 23 recount that Jesus took bread, and verse 24 narrates the first act of the Supper in relation to that bread. In their original Jewish context thanksgiving and breaking of bread were table customs that were performed by the head of a household or a host. The words **this is my body** refer to the bread alone. Brokenness is not in view in this traditional line; rather, the emphasis is on the phrase **which is for you,** words that recognize the vicarious nature of Jesus' death. Some interpreters contend this clause is inherently sacrificial in focus, but that view is not necessary.

The following words, translated **do this in remembrance of me,** are ambiguous in Greek in terms of their point of reference, though they clearly interpret the ritual. In Greek the phrase literally says, "Do this unto my memory." Does this mean that as Christians do and remember what Jesus said, they perceive the power and presence of Christ, or that as Christians do these things, God's memory of Christ or Christ's own memory of his disciples is jogged toward realization of the Parousia (or both)? Both interpretations are suggested by scholars, although the first option finds by far the most support.

The determination of the original meaning of the Lord's original words is an important matter, both historically and theologically. Paul's understanding of these words and the interpretation of the sayings that he taught the members of the congregations he founded are also significant subjects. Nevertheless, because Paul is not interested at this point in expounding such topics, the reader of the letter cannot discern Paul's deeper levels of understanding and teaching regarding the Lord's Supper from this text. (For further discussion, however, see the Additional Notes below.)

11:25 / Paul moves to the narration of the second, similar act. In saying **in the same way,** Paul recognizes that Jesus gave thanks over **the cup.** One should notice particularly that the focus of this statement is the cup, not its contents. This observation helps the reader to understand that the interpretation **(the new covenant in my blood)** attaches to the administration of the element (the content of the cup), not to the element itself (the drink). Moreover, the two acts stand separately as well as together as sacramental communications. One should notice that the covenant is related to the cup as Paul recalls the tradition in these verses. The blood defines or establishes this new covenant. Unfortunately, the type of covenant that Jesus or Paul had in mind is not indicated by these statements, though the relationship of the covenant to blood recalls, in the context of 1 Corinthians (see 5:7), the motif of the Passover lamb. The language of new covenant does, however, bring the text of Jeremiah 38:31 LXX (NIV: Jer. 31:31–34) to mind and signifies the eschatological significance and nature of the events around Jesus' death.

Nevertheless, the repetition of the words of the Lord Jesus end on the same note that concluded his words concerning the bread: **do this, whenever you drink it, in remembrance of me.** Whatever this ambiguous reference to remembering means, there is no question that the motif of remembrance anticipates repetition of the acts.

11:26 / In bringing this formal, traditional segment of his teaching to a conclusion, Paul extends the repetitive theme and brings together the bread and cup in the declaration **you proclaim the Lord's death until he comes.** In referring to the Lord's death in this way, Paul connects it with God's future in the Lord's coming. In the context of this discussion, particularly in the framework of this letter, this concluding note places the observation of the Lord's Supper in the larger conceptual framework of apocalyptic eschatology. It takes the Supper as a prescribed celebration that is essential for the time between the cross and the coming of the Lord Jesus Christ. Paul has already dramatically registered the importance of the cross as the foundation of God's salvation in chapter 1, especially 1:17–25. In turn, in chapter 15 he will take up the eschatological issues of resurrection and "the end"; but at this point, he is focused on the present as a concrete form of life that finds its shape and direction from Christ's cross and God's ultimate reign over all.

In reminding the Corinthians that they are proclaiming the Lord's death until he comes, Paul highlights the essentially missional nature of even so congregationally oriented a ritual as the celebration of the Lord's Supper. The participation in the Supper was to have an evangelistic cast, for one was not merely receiving the elements for one's own sake (or the sake of the community). The believers gave themselves to the celebration as a means of proclaiming the death of the Lord, a death that yielded mysterious salvific benefits for all who heard and believed the proclamation. Note, the Supper is not presented as a means of strengthening believers so that they could proclaim the Lord's death; rather, participation in the Supper is understood to be that proclamation itself. By manifestly observing Jesus' self-giving death and the formation of the new covenant, the believers made known a christological truth of eschatological importance.

Additional Notes §32

11:23 / For a different opinion, see L. Luke, " 'The Night in which He was Delivered Up' (1 Cor 11:23)," *Biblebhashyam* 10 (1984), pp. 261–79.

11:24–25 / Two elements of the Gk. text require observation. First, Paul refers to Jesus' act of giving thanks using the Gk. verb *eucharisteō,* from which the church derives the designation for the Lord's Supper as the Eucharist. That title gives emphasis to the celebratory nature of the entire Lord's Supper. Second, the words **do this** (Gk. *poieite*) may be rendered "you are doing this," and in translating in this fashion, Orr and Walther (*I Corinthians,* p. 267) suggest, "[The verb] can ... be either imperative or indicative.... It seems better ... to take *poieite* as an interpretive instruction than as a command for future repetition." Nevertheless, Paul and the early church did not read the verb this way. One sees from Paul's phrasing of vv. 24–25 that he meant to inform the

Corinthians that every time they celebrated this Supper, it was for remembrance of the Lord.

Attempts to reconstruct the original words of Jesus from the lines
of this tradition, usually read in conjunction with the parallel materials
in the Synoptic Gospels, have produced a wide variety of results and
conclusions. (Consult B. D. Smith, "The More Original Form of the
Words of Institution," *ZNW* 83 [1992], pp. 166–86; and for an exercise in
skepticism and pessimism, see H. Maccoby, "Paul and the Eucharist,"
NTS 37 [1991], pp. 247–67.) On one extreme there are those who deny
that Jesus uttered any words of institution over the elements at table
with his disciples, and on the opposite extreme there are elaborate har-
monizations of the differing canonical accounts that argue that Jesus
said each and every word exactly as it was recorded in Scripture, although no one account preserves the full record of his sayings; rather,
all accounts must be taken together to know all that he said. Comparative analysis of the four (three, since Matthew is so close to Mark) canonical versions of Jesus' words at the Last Supper is helpful, since such
comparison allows the reader to perceive the particular emphasis that
each author brings to the individual accounts of the words. For two different attempts to do such comparison, see Fee, *Epistle*, pp. 545–47; and
M. L. Soards, *The Passion According to Luke: The Special Material of Luke 22*
(JSNTSup 14; Sheffield: JSOT Press, 1987), pp. 28–30.

Reconstructions that go beyond comparison are highly speculative. They are attempts to discover and recapture a history behind
the texts rather than attempts to understand the texts themselves. Although such studies are not pointless, they produce dubious results.
One example (with brief critique) of such work suffices to show why
such reconstruction is avoided here.

Many scholars contend that the words **do this in remembrance
of me** are a later addition by the church to specify Jesus' intention in
speaking about the bread and the cup. "The main argument for this
view is that the words are absent from Mark's account" (Watson, *First
Epistle*, p. 122). Even so, some of the same scholars argue that "the
words, 'Do this in memory of me,' can be accepted as a guide to Jesus's
intentions at the Last Supper, even if they do not represent his actual
words" (Watson, *First Epistle*, p. 122). Counterarguments prove nothing
about the authenticity of these words, although they may address the
matter of the probability of the authenticity of the lines. One should
note that Paul's account in 1 Cor. is probably fifteen years older than
Mark's version of the Supper; Luke's version of the narrative is probably older than Mark's as well. Both Paul and Luke know and include
the words "Do this in remembrance of me." Paul's "older version" and
Luke's "correcting hand" might be taken to imply that Mark left these
words out, deliberately or accidentally. Moreover, when Paul (or the
earlier church) wants to clarify the meaning of Jesus' actions and statements in this context, one finds such interpretation from a third-person
perspective—as in v. 26, "For as often as you eat this bread and drink
the cup, you proclaim the Lord's death until he comes"—not in the first
person, **in remembrance of me**, with Jesus as the speaker. The text itself
shows that when interpretation was needed it was offered from a later

point of view, not that explanatory words were written onto Jesus' lips. Furthermore, attempts to reconstruct what Jesus "really" said in Aramaic are even more speculative and ultimately imply that what is important for true comprehension is something other than the text of the biblical materials. However, whatever Jesus said—probably in Aramaic—the texts that preserve his words are all written in Gk. Since we have only the biblical texts, I have restricted the work in this commentary—except for this explanatory disclaimer—to commenting on the text that lies before us.

11:26 / The grammatical form of the words **until he comes** in Gk. *(achris hou elthē)* both gives a future cast to the coming, lit. "until he may come," and implies that the matter of the Lord's coming is an eschatological issue open to the Lord's own discretion. Yet, while Paul looks and points toward the future, his focus on **the Lord's death** is the strongest point of emphasis in relation to the situation in Corinth.

The temporal aspect of this verse runs deep and takes important turns. The eating and drinking, which are present actions, look back to the death of the Lord, a past event; but the eating and drinking make that past death present in and through proclamation, thus qualifying the present in relation to the past so that those in Corinth look forward to the future (when the Lord will come) from the vantage point of the cross.

§33 Proper and Improper Attitudes at the Supper (1 Cor. 11:27–34)

In essence, Paul's reflections in this section are concerned with one's attitude toward the Supper. He gives advice for eliminating an improper disposition at the celebration. The final lines, verses 33–34, are practical and elucidate the more abstract materials that comprise verses 27–32.

Some preliminary comments on this section are in order. First, Paul is not directly or indirectly concerned with the nature of the sacramental elements; second, the matter at hand is not the issue of one's personal piety or lack thereof; third, Paul's concern is for believers to have an appropriate attitude that fosters appropriate behavior.

After the rich, complex verses of the earlier portions of this chapter, these tightly focused verses may seem related to merely mundane matters in the past. The verses, however, are filled with concrete issues that cause Paul to make remarks that have been applied to many different, later contexts. The verses are specific, but there are important implications for all Christians. Thus, elements of these verses have been given significant weight and demand careful attention.

11:27 / The opening word of the line, **Therefore** (Gk. *hōste*, "so then" or "and so"), indicates that Paul is drawing a conclusion from what he has said and giving an explanation to his teaching. Despite the way that this sentence is bound to its context, this verse has been used for an unbelievable number of reasons to keep people from participating in the Lord's Supper. For example, in certain periods of church history people would refuse to participate in the Lord's Supper after taking their first communion (if they took even that) until they were on their deathbeds and had received ritual absolution from all the sins of a lifetime. Such hypersacramentalism and hypersensitivity to Paul's warning against participating in the Lord's Supper **in an**

unworthy manner is not grounded in a sensible reading of Paul's statements.

At the outset, the reader should notice that in this section, in distinction from the vast majority of the rest of the letter, Paul is addressing each of the Corinthians as individual persons. The matters under discussion are personal, but in the context of an address to the body of believers, the issues are not private. Moving from a concern with the general life of the congregation, Paul turns to the members as believing persons. The issue he discusses here is so serious that he writes to gain every person's attention.

In the context of this letter and in the light of the discussion he has offered the Corinthians up to this point, one should see that, for Paul, to eat **the bread** and to drink **the cup of the Lord** in an unworthy way is eating and drinking with an attitude of self-centeredness, of individualism or arrogance. As Paul has presented the situation in Corinth, with one person or group attempting to prove personal spiritual superiority, even hyperpious individualism would fall under the rubric "unworthy." Unworthy participation amounts to coming to the Supper without regard for the result of Christ's reconciling work that draws the Christian community into a new selfless relatedness. Paul insists that such an attitude makes one **guilty of sinning against the body and the blood of the Lord.** In other words, to live in such a way—even religiously—as to deny the reconciling, unifying effects of Christ's death casts one into the company of those who crucified Jesus.

11:28 / Because of the importance of the celebration, with its capacity to proclaim Christ's death in anticipation of his coming (11:26), Paul insists that one must **examine** one's self to ensure the appropriate Christlike attitude and then, in a spirit of self-giving and interrelatedness with the other believers, one may eat and drink. The qualifying phrases **of the bread** and **of the cup** show that Paul is concerned with participation in the activities of the Supper, not with the elements that are being used in the course of the celebration. The admonition of this verse is about attitude, not about the substances that are being consumed.

11:29 / Without the proper attitude, Paul says, one participates in the Supper unto **judgment;** that is, one casts one's self outside the pale of redemptive reconciliation into the context of

God's eschatological wrath. Verse 29 mentions **recognizing the body of the Lord.** This statement should not be reduced to an abstract level. Rather, Paul speaks metaphorically about the concrete nature of the celebration, so that to recognize or discern the body (notice the absence of blood) means to comprehend and appropriate into one's own life the transforming significance of Christ himself. "Body" metaphorically identifies the Christ event with its power to transform lives and create the new Christian community of reconciliation. The mystery of the Lord, his presence and relatedness to the congregation, lends its hue to the color of this mysterious line. To discern the body in the context of the Lord's Supper is to see the reality of Christ in each and every other member of the "body" (ch. 12) and to value each person for the part played and the place given by the Lord whose body all the believers now constitute.

When we contrast the mention of "the body of the Lord" here with the previous reference to "the body and blood of the Lord," we see that Paul is not writing in shorthand; his choice of words clarifies the level of his real concern. The language is metaphorical, referring not merely to the Lord himself or even to "the body of Christ" that will be a topic of discussion in chapter 12; rather, Paul uses this picture language to signify the presence of the Lord in the life of the church and the relationship of the Lord and the believer that forms the foundation of the relationship(s) between the believers themselves. One should evaluate the motives and aims of one's participation in the life of the church by determining if that participation focuses on the Lord's real presence and the real relationship that forms human existence as a result of his presence.

Fee (*Epistle,* p. 564) is typical of commentators who, even after examining the complex theological character of Paul's metaphors, then write, "To fail to discern the body in this way, by abusing those of lesser sociological status, is to incur God's judgment." One understands this conclusion, especially when Paul's enigmatic lines lie so close to verses 33–34. Nevertheless, this conclusion is a reduction of the gospel to a moral maxim: because of God's judgment, be nice, especially to those less fortunate than you. Paul is not so trite. The gospel calls the believer beyond himself or herself into a new and radically freeing relationship to Christ, so that in that relationship one may put others—no matter their social status—before one's self. This is Christlikeness: freedom from the self and freedom for God and others. One should notice that Paul says, "Eat at home"; he does not say, "Bring more food and pass it around." True freedom is charismatic in quality, often unpredictable and even offensive in the way it alters human life and reorients living. Paul's metaphorical language seeks to speak of that charismatic quality of life without pressing it into a set of ways to be nice. Believers live in relationship to Christ and out of that relationship into relationship with others.

11:30 / Furthermore, Paul offers his own startling interpretation of troubling developments in the Corinthian church. He opens this line with the words *dia touto* ("Because of this" or "Therefore"; translated **That is why** in the NIV) and then explains the illness and death of some of the members, saying, That is why **many among you are weak and sick, and a number of you have fallen asleep.** In other words, the failure of certain Corinthians to discern the body of the Lord in an appropriate way (v. 29) had—because they arrogantly and self-centeredly focused on themselves—already produced terrible results.

Paul's troubling statement is open to misunderstanding and abuse. He is explaining that he perceives God to be at work disciplining the members of the Corinthian church. Whether or not he was right in his conclusions, he does not say that all sickness and death are the result of inappropriate behavior. Paul's analysis at this point is concrete and historical in nature and should not be treated as an observation on all of life and the difficulties that are encountered in daily living.

In giving this explanation Paul speaks from the perspective of his belief in Christ's real presence in the "remembrance" of the Supper. Because the Lord is present in the remembrance of the Supper, his powerful presence produces dramatic effects on the lives of the believers. Thus, according to Paul, those who come to the Lord's Supper with inappropriate motives are vulnerable to the Lord's power, which in their particular circumstances brings judgment. One should see that this explanation is descriptive and dramatic, not a declaration. He is not issuing a threat so much as offering a passionate warning. He is not condemning but informing, although he understands that judgment has already come to bear on certain members of the church.

11:31 / In turn, verse 31 speaks again of **judgment.** From the cast of the remark this reference to judgment is not eschatological but, as in verse 30, present judgment in this world. In combination with verse 30 this additional statement explains why it is so important that the Corinthians heed Paul's directions. The statement is cryptic, but Paul seems to be saying that humans are in no position to make a valid judgment about themselves in terms of the way God evaluates their lives. To make a play on Paul's wording, the Corinthians have not been judging themselves adequately, as is seen in their experiencing divine judgment; if they had judged themselves appropriately, they would not have experienced judgment.

11:32 / Lest Paul end this discussion of judgment on a totally negative note, he steps back from the experience of the judgment to explain why such judgment is a benefit to those believers who receive it. Apparently Paul means for this verse to offer sober comfort to the Corinthians in the face of undeniable problems. He says the judgment that the Corinthians have experienced is to their benefit, for it is the Lord's discipline, not an end in itself, but the difficult means to a better end. Through divine discipline the believers are brought to a place where they will not be doomed to be judged with **the world.** Even in judgment, Paul perceives that the believers receive a divine benefit.

11:33–34 / Verses 33–34 begin, **So then,** and in a summary fashion that builds on everything said up to this point they aim at correction or circumvention of the previously named problem(s). Note the three-part advice that Paul gives, or restates, here. (1) **When you come together to eat, wait for each other.** From 11:21 one knows that the Corinthians individually or in small groups are going ahead with their meals. (2) In verse 34a, Paul parenthetically separates satiation of hunger from the community meal or celebration, saying, **if anyone is hungry, he should eat at home** (cf. 11:22). (3) Paul's advice aims at preventing condemnation **(judgment)** that would necessarily ensue from a continuation of the inappropriate gathering in which the Corinthians are already engaging (cf. 11:17–19).

From this analysis one sees the repetition of concerns between 11:33–34 and 11:17–22. Indeed, as commentators interested in the literary quality of the letter notice, the two sets of verses form a bracket or an inclusio around Paul's reflections on the Lord's Supper in the material found in 11:23–32. The nature of repetition is to create emphasis, both by repeating the information itself (vv. 17–22; 33–34) and by highlighting the material that is surrounded by the repetitive two parts (vv. 23–32). Thus, verses 33–34 both bring the final segment of Paul's discussion (vv. 27–34) to a conclusion and help focus and hold the entire reflection from 11:17–34 together.

Paul's directions assume a fairly free-flowing, charismatic fellowship. His advice is practical and rather minimal given the seriousness of the situation as he seems to have understood it. When Paul tells the Corinthians to **wait**, he instructs the congregation as a whole to put both others and the whole church before their individual desires. As he did earlier in the letter, Paul calls for the Corinthians to forego or perhaps even to use their rights for the responsible execution of God's will. Cliques in the congregation meant catastrophe for the celebration of the Lord's Supper, which itself signified and actualized the new patterns of relationship that were being created in the Christ-centered and Christlike lives of believers. Thus, Paul said, wait.

At the conclusion of this series of directions, criticisms, comments, explanations, and warnings, Paul offers a promise: **when I come I will give further directions.** Such a statement serves both to assure any Corinthians who have additional questions regarding the Supper and worship that Paul will provide them with an opportunity for further conversation, and to let the believers know that Paul has not exhausted his instructions at this point.

Additional Notes §33

11:27 / Although the explicit mention of "judgment" occurs for the first time in v. 29, v. 27 is typical of the majority of the verses in this section in using terminology associated with or connoting judgment. Note the pattern throughout this section: an unworthy manner, guilty (v. 27); to examine (v. 28); discerning, judgment (v. 29); judged ourselves, come under judgment (v. 31); judged, are being disciplined, be condemned (v. 32); judgment (v. 34). The judgment that Paul speaks of in this and the following verses is both present and future; the two are intimately related. Paul understands that the future, final judgment of God is at work in the present, placing God's eschatological standards before the believers and holding them accountable. One sees a complex vision of eschatological judgment that perceives that the ultimate purposes of God are at work in the lives of believers at the present time. Thus, Paul does not know a separate realized and future eschatology;

rather, he speaks of one divine reality from two distinct, related temporal angles.

One should note and contrast the mention here of **the body and blood of the Lord** with the similar phrase "the body of the Lord" in v. 29. See the comments on v. 29 above.

11:28 / The word translated **to examine** (Gk. *dokimazetō*, from *dokimazō*) is related to the word translated "approval" (Gk. *hoi dokimoi*, from *dokimos*) in v. 19. Thus, Paul's language makes a connection that shows that the examination to which one is to submit oneself is to be done in terms of the standards of approval that God sets for life. God's will, not human opinion, is to be the measure of one's attitude and behavior.

11:30 / Another way that one might understand Paul's point in this verse is that since the body of Christ in Corinth is sick with controversy, the people who are members of the body are sick as a symptom of the body's condition.

11:31 / The verbs that speak of judgment in this passage are generally passive, i.e., humans are judged in an eschatological sense by God. The reality of God's judgment, however, and the revelation of God's will in the life, work, and message of the Lord are understood by Paul to be available to believers so that they may make worthy decisions and conduct themselves in a worthy way—worthy of the gospel.

11:33–34 / Concerning the practical dimensions of the Lord's Supper, C. H. Talbert (*Reading Corinthians: A Literary and Theological Commentary on 1 and 2 Corinthians* [New York: Crossroad, 1987] pp. 74–75) asks the sensible questions, What was eaten? Where was the meal eaten? When was the meal eaten? In answering these questions, he consults ancient literature from the period to offer a helpful picture of the typical banquet situation. He portrays a gathering of thirty to fifty persons of diverse social standing at the home of a well-to-do person whose dining room and atrium were both used for the supper. Groups arrived and stayed as they were able, with the better-off members having more leisure than the lower social classes. In the extended and informal atmosphere of such a gathering, the purpose of the meeting could be lost and the convocation could devolve into a mere social occasion with one group or another having little to do with the rest of the assembly. As Talbert concludes, "The problem in Corinth, then, was that cultural norms took precedence over Christian distinctives at the meal."

§34 *The Nature of Enthusiasm (1 Cor. 12:1–3)*

This section addresses a new topic, namely, spiritual gifts (or the spiritual gifts of the spiritual ones). The modern reader of this passage may miss simple elements of Paul's discussion because of the distance between the worldviews of the first century and the present day. No matter what one thinks about such matters at the turn of the twenty-first century, from what Paul wrote, it is clear that he assumed the reality of extraordinary spiritual experiences and understood that his readers would agree. If later readers have difficulty making this assumption, they should recognize that the difficulty is a hermeneutical problem for themselves, not for Paul and his original readers.

At this point in the letter, Paul battles a particular theological explanation that is given to the experiences, not the experiences themselves. The situation seems to be that the Corinthians are taking spiritual gifts as the grounds for comparison among themselves, and that is leading to ranking of gifts and boasting. Among the Corinthians the flamboyant gifts are more cherished and more highly esteemed. Remarkably, some people in Corinth seem to have become so elevated in their spirituality that they had no use for, and even expressed disdain for, the all-too-human Jesus who suffered the disgrace of dying on the cross. Paul will have none of this kind of spiritual expression; he disavows such activity and tells the Corinthians how to distinguish between legitimate and illegitimate demonstrations of spiritual power.

12:1 / Verse 1 shows that the Corinthians brought this topic to Paul's attention. The Greek word translated **Now about** (*peri*) has already introduced material at 7:1, 25; 8:1; and will recur at 16:1. In response to whatever question(s) the Corinthians directed to him, Paul states his wish that they **not . . . be ignorant,** which implies that the Corinthians do lack adequate information regarding the subject of **spiritual** matters (see 10:1).

Remarkably, it is not a lack of experience that may make the Corinthians ignorant. From Paul's discussion one can see that spiritual gifts were manifested abundantly in the Corinthian congregation. The problem that Paul's remarks reveal was the result not of a lack of experience, but of a lack of proper theological understanding and a lack of spiritual discipline. As Conzelmann remarks, "In the *conception* of the Spirit they [Paul and the Corinthians] are at one. The point at issue is the theological existence of the believers, their concrete determination by the Spirit" (*1 Corinthians*, p. 204).

12:2 / The way that Paul addresses the Corinthians, especially in conjunction with the misunderstanding and misappropriation of spiritual gifts, may indicate that he has a particular segment of the congregation in mind. He writes, **when you were pagans**, recalling a time and experience to which ethnic Jewish Christians would not relate. Paul's statement accomplishes two things. He gives his readers an indirect but sarcastic reminder that they had been wrong before, and then, on the basis of this image of past pagan experience, he is able to form an analogy to the patterns of behavior in which they are currently engaged. Thus, interpreters often suggest that the difficulties that Paul is about to discuss in chapter 12—perhaps also regarding earlier and later matters in the letter—are the results of Christians who were previously pagans bringing patterns and attitudes from their former religious experiences into the life of the church. Such wholesale importing of pagan understandings and activities would cause serious lapses in Christian faith and practice.

Speaking of that former time, Paul highlights the uselessness or futility of pagan religious experience by saying, **somehow or other you were influenced and led astray to mute idols.** Paul's recollection of the Corinthians' pre-Christian activity is not flattering. He is not concerned, however, with assessing that former religious life; rather, he is concerned to criticize problems in the life of the church and introduces non-Christian religious life only to form an analogy between it and the behavior in the church that he wants to bring to an end.

12:3 / This verse builds on the foregoing lines, looking back and moving forward with the word **Therefore** (Gk. *dio;* lit. "this is why"). Thus, after recognizing the topic brought to his attention by the Corinthians (v. 1) and conjuring up images of past pagan religious life (v. 2), Paul identifies the problem in even more specific terms. From the way that he describes and responds to the situation, the reader can infer that the problem in Corinth was the result of the practice of ecstasy. The Corinthians were getting caught up in the thrill of the emotional experience, rather than seeking to glorify God.

Ecstasy should be contrasted with enthusiasm to grasp Paul's point. The issue is more than a matter of linguistic nuance; rather, the matter pertains to the genuine difference between two distinct forms of religious practice. While neither term ("ecstasy" or "enthusiasm") occurs in Paul's text, for theological purposes in understanding this passage, it is helpful to use that language in reflecting on Paul's statements. Ecstasy is the effort to "stand outside" oneself (English from Gk. *ekstasis* = "displacement"), to grasp onto a vital power that provides one with an extraordinary experience. Enthusiasm is the result of one's being indwelt by the power of God (English from Gk. *enthysiaō* = "to be inspired by a god"), so that one's quality of experience is transformed. Paul realizes that it may be difficult or impossible to distinguish the frenzy of ecstasy from the empowering of enthusiasm. "Therefore," he offers a criterion for making a valid distinction. According to Paul genuine enthusiasm affirms the lordship of Jesus, whereas the practice of ecstasy generates behavior contrary or hostile to the affirmation of Jesus' lordship. The recognition of the lordship of Jesus is the criterion that forms the parameters of legitimate enthusiasm. The **Holy Spirit** moves the one under the power of the Holy Spirit to declare, **"Jesus is Lord"**!

Other NT authors and writings faced this same dilemma in the life of the early church, and while patterns of language vary in response to each distinctive situation, the solutions offered by the NT authors are remarkably consistent: see Mark 9:38–40; John 15:26; 1 John 4:1–3.

Additional Notes §34

12:1 / The language at the outset of the discussion is ambiguous in Gk., but the basic sense of Paul's remarks comes through however one decides to translate the Gk. word *pneumatikoi*—either "spiritual gifts" as in the NIV or "spiritual ones" as some commentators argue. One should notice that throughout the remainder of the section Paul continues the discussion by referring to *charismata* (translated "gifts"), clearly his own preferred manner of designating spiritual gifts. Some commentators argue that the difference in the words *pneumatikoi* and *charismata* reflects the language used by the Corinthians on the one hand and Paul on the other. Still other interpreters suggest that Paul used *pneumatikoi* pejoratively and *charismata* in a positive way. Yet others argue that *pneumatikoi* means "spiritual ones" whereas *charismata* means "spiritual gifts," so that Paul subtly and shrewdly shifts the grounds of the discussion in the course of his correcting the Corinthians' thinking—i.e., Paul takes the spotlight off the people and puts it on the gracious gifts of God. Conzelmann's observation, however, is insightful: "In itself the translation 'spiritual people,' 'men of the Spirit,' is also possible, cf. 2:15; 3:1; 14:37. Yet, despite 14:37 the theme is not types of men but gifts" (*1 Corinthians*, p. 204 n. 1).

Whatever his meaning or motivation, Paul refers to the *pneumatikoi* only once in this chapter, and he continues the discussion using the word *charismata* in 12:4, 9, 28, 30–31. At a minimum, the use of *charismata* emphasizes that whatever spiritual gifts occur in the Corinthian congregation, those gifts are by God's grace *(charis)*.

12:2 / Cf. 10:19–20 to see that Paul is not brushing pagan belief and practice aside as mere illusions.

12:3 / The interpretation of Paul's comment, **no one who is speaking by the Spirit of God says, "Jesus be cursed,"** produces vigorous debate. To capture the sense of the statement in contemporary idiomatic English, one should understand the line to say, "To hell with Jesus!" Did Paul mean to suggest that someone said this, or is he only illustrating the absurdity of inappropriate behavior? Commentators disagree. Moreover, even among those who argue that Paul's statement assumes the reality of the activity and does not speak of it as potential behavior, there is further disagreement. If there are those in Corinth who are saying this about Jesus, who are they? Are they non-Christian pagan ecstatics? Are they non-Christian Jews? Are they early Christian docetists? A definitive answer is impossible, but it is also unnecessary for following the main positive lines of Paul's observations concerning the disposition of genuinely Spirit-inspired behavior. For further discussion, compare the essays by B. A. Pearson ("Did the Gnostics Curse Jesus?" *JBL* 86 [1967], pp. 301–5), N. Brox ("ANATHEMA IĒSOUS [1 Kor 12,3)," *BZ* 12 [1968], pp. 103–11), J. D. M. Derrett ("Cursing Jesus [I Cor. xii.3]: The Jews as Religious 'Persecutors,' " *NTS* 21 [1975], pp. 544–54), and J. M. Bassler ("1 Cor 12:3—Curse and Confession in Context," *JBL* 103 [1982], pp. 415–18).

The Gk. word *anathema* that is translated **be cursed** is a startling term. The word becomes "anathema" in later church usage, although at this time it would have been recognized as a compound noun from *ana* ("up" or "again") + *tithēmi* ("to put"), connoting something set aside—usually for a deity—and especially something cursed. An essay by R. Scroggs ("The Exaltation of the Spirit by Some Early Christians," *JBL* 84 [1965], pp. 359–73) notes resemblances between Paul's observations here and the discussion of blaspheming the Spirit in Mark 3:28–29, suggesting that the Corinthian phenomenon was not an anomaly.

§35 Unity and Diversity of Gifts (1 Cor. 12:4–11)

Paul makes a crucial point at this juncture in his argument: There is a unified purpose in the truly varied expression of the Spirit in the life of the church because of the common divine origin of each believer's gift. Moreover, although he is not in this first-century correspondence doing full-blown fourth-century Trinitarian reflection—such as was done later in great church councils and christological discussions (e.g., Nicea and later still at Chalcedon)—Paul makes a remarkable statement about the diversity in the unity of the divine in order to underscore the godliness of diverse expression of God's gifts in the life of believers in the church. As Paul writes generally about **gifts**, one can see that he is thinking of concrete manifestations of the Spirit and not of natural, birthright propensities. Gifts and talents may ultimately be related, but they are not one and the same thing. In the present discussion Paul has special or extraordinary manifestations of the presence and power of the Spirit in mind as he reflects on spiritual gifts in the life of the Corinthian congregation.

12:4–6 / In verses 4–6 there are three parallel statements based on an underlying triad of **Spirit/Lord/God**. In relation to each of these three persons Paul recognizes variety and sameness. There are varieties of **gifts** of grace and there is one Spirit; there are varieties of kinds of **service** and there is one Lord; there are varieties of activities **(working)** and there is one God. Paul almost creates a chant with the repetitive quality of his language, which literally says:

There are different kinds of gifts	**but the same** Spirit;
and **there are different kinds of** service	and **the same** Lord;
and **there are different kinds of** working	**but the same** God who **works** everything **in all**.

Paul's point is driven home through declarations about the reality of God and the gifts, service, and work that manifest God's own rich, complex, diverse, and unified presence among the believers. Diversity in the human sphere exists, relates to, and is unified by unity in the sphere of the divine. By drawing these phrases together Paul creates the theological matrix for valid interpretation of the phenomenon of spiritual gifts. Ultimately all gifts extend from God and are given for the good of the church. These gifts are not rendered to the disposition of the ones who receive them. They are given and established under the rule of Jesus the Lord. Variety exists in the unity of the church because of the reality of the divine that is manifested in such complex coherence.

As Paul's discussion creates a coherence between the same Spirit and the same Lord and the same God, recognizing the oneness of God in the reality of God's diverse manifestations, so the clustering of phrases "different kinds of gifts" and "different kinds of service" and "different kinds of working" communicates the unified aim of the diverse gifts working in service. These lines of the letter reveal careful rhetorical crafting, not casual forming of phrases; thus, in the triadic rhetoric one sees both Paul's purposefulness and his purpose in writing.

12:7 / This simple sentence states the truth that Paul most wants the Corinthians to realize. Paul coordinates the beginning of this sentence with the foregoing verses through the contrasting conjunction **now** (Gk. *de*), so that the verse fits as a summarizing conclusion to the complementary lines of verses 4–6. Whatever spiritual gifts are being manifested in Corinth, they are not for personal privilege or glory, but **for the common good.** The good of others, not merely the good of the self, is the purpose of the Spirit's giving anything to anyone and everything to everyone. The unifying purpose of the manifest diversity of the Spirit in the life of the church is the well-being of all those called by God to be a part of the church. The divine giving of spiritual gifts is the concrete outworking of God's own saving mission to the world, and those gifted by God for that mission become agents of God's working for the common good of the fellowship of believers in the world.

12:8–10 / In three verses Paul catalogues gifts without offering an exhaustive inventory of the manifestations of the Spirit. The list seems representative and particularly relevant to

the situation in Corinth. Paul repeats the phrases **the Spirit** . . .
the same Spirit . . . **that one Spirit** to reemphasize the unity of the
diverse gifts in their being manifestations of the single, unified
Spirit of God. Paul mentions nine particular gifts (see Additional
Notes below). His phrasing, **to one** . . . **to another** . . . **to another** . . . , recognizes diversity among the recipients' gifts; and
the repeated qualifiers **through the Spirit** . . . **by means of the
same Spirit** . . . **by the same Spirit** . . . **by that one Spirit** ". . . all
these are the work of one and the same Spirit," declare the unity
of the divine that holds the operation of the gifts together.

In the overall context of Paul's discussion in this chapter of
distinguishing between speech inspired by the Holy Spirit and
speech that finds its origin elsewhere (vv. 1–3), one should notice
that in this list of nine gifts, **distinguishing between spirits,** that
is, the capacity to judge rightly that Paul calls for throughout the
letter, is itself recognized to be a charismatic reality.

Paul lists nine manifestations of the Spirit (Gk. *hē phanerōsis
tou pneumatos*). These phenomena are offered in this context as illustrative examples of the gifts of the Spirit that Paul has been
discussing to this point. Among the items mentioned are the
following:

(1) **The message of wisdom,** literally "a word of wisdom"
(cf. 1:17–2:16, esp. 1:24; 2:4–6). From Paul's earlier discussions
one understands that the gift of the message of wisdom is a God-
given insight into the mysterious purposes and workings of God
in and through Jesus Christ.

(2) **The message of knowledge,** literally "a word of knowledge" (cf. 1:5; see 13:2–12; 14:6). The wording of this reference
makes it a parallel to the preceding mention of the message of
wisdom. It is perhaps necessary to understand the message of
knowledge as a synonymous phenomenon, since Paul's other
references to such knowledge do not make it clear whether he
means a supernaturally given piece of information or a Spirit-
given discernment concerning the reality of God and human
life. The way Paul clusters wisdom, knowledge, revelation, and
teaching suggests some relationship and similarity among these
phenomena, although the exact nuance that Paul intends to impart by the use of these different words is not recoverable from
his letters.

(3) **Faith** (cf. 2:5; see ch. 13). Interpreters debate whether
Paul means to name the faith that is a basic element in the life of
all believers by virtue of the work of the Spirit (as in Gal. 5:22) or

whether he is referring to "faith that can move mountains" (as stated in 13:2). Since Paul understands that one and the same Spirit brings faith as a foundation and faith as an extraordinary working of divine grace into the lives of believers, it is not necessary to distinguish precisely what Paul has in mind. In context this remark lies in proximity to 13:2, so that Paul may be anticipating that more explicit description of the manifestation of faith. In any case, Paul understands that faith constitutes the basis of all believers' relationship to God and that the Spirit is the source of every believer's standing with God. Nevertheless, for some Paul's implication here is that the Spirit's gift may be so great as to bring about extraordinary results even for the believers. Although he is correct in one way, Conzelmann exaggerates the distinction between Paul's use of *pistis* ("faith") at this point and other occurrences of the same word: "*Pistis* is here a special gift alongside others, and accordingly not faith, but apparently the ability to perform miracles" (*1 Corinthians*, p. 209).

(4) **Gifts of healing,** literally "gifts of cures" (see 12:28–30). In naming this manifestation of the Spirit, Paul uses the plural form *charismata* ("gifts"), which he qualifies with the words "of healing" (Gk. *iamatōn*). Paul's language indicates the manifestations of the Spirit through the lives and ministry of believers so that others experience divine healing. The focus is on those who are gifted with such acts of ministry. Paul does not have in mind the persons who experience healing from maladies, nor does he seem to refer to a capacity that some specially gifted believers would possess. The plural ("gifts") indicates manifestations of grace that work, from time to time and from place to place, through certain members of the church. As always in Paul's thought, humans being do not have and manipulate God's power, but they are selected as agents through whom God works extraordinary deeds (cf. 2 Cor. 4:7–18).

(5) **Miraculous powers,** literally "workings of power" (see 12:28–30). The NIV's introduction of the word "miraculous" is unfortunate, for that word carries philosophical connotations about so-called natural law and breaches of natural laws that would be foreign to Paul and the first readers of his letter. According to the Synoptic Gospels and Acts, Jesus and certain members of the early church did "powerful acts" that were believed to be extraordinary manifestations of God's power. Such acts were not normal, in the sense of being everyday occurrences; but Paul and other early Christians did not see God as

having established a world that ran by natural law until God reached in and altered the course of events. God was transcendent, but his presence was immanent and his power was constantly at work—only sometimes the manifestations of that power were out of the ordinary and so especially remarkable. To be simplistic and a bit sarcastic, it took later philosophers to reason God out of the workings of the everyday world and into a realm of transcendence so that only by interrupting events or violating the laws of nature could God do miracles. Such a world and such a God were unknown to Paul. As in the case of gifts of healing, God works through specially gifted persons to achieve God's will in sometimes marvelous ways.

(6) **Prophecy** (see ch. 14). Theories about the nature and practice of prophecy in the early church abound, as does the scholarly literature on this subject. In antiquity, and especially in the history of Judaism, a prophet was a Spirit-inspired speaker who revealed or declared God's will to the people. At times prophets spoke symbolically or metaphorically, but in general their message was plain, "Thus saith the Lord." While prophecy was understood to be a gift of God's Spirit, a special anointing unto inspired proclamation, Paul presents prophecy in such a way that the believers are encouraged to pursue and to desire this particular gift. Paul's explicit references to prophecy in chapter 14 make his understanding of the shape and scope of this particular gift clear. Prophecy was deemed especially desirable because it edified, encouraged, and consoled. Prophecy was a genuinely missional activity that brought the one blessed with the gift into the service of others.

(7) **Distinguishing between spirits,** literally "discernings of spirits" (cf. 12:1–3; see 14:29). Again, this reference has generated considerable discussion among interpreters. Among others, Fee (*Epistle,* pp. 596–97) notes the subsequent statement in 14:29 and the similar admonition to examine prophecies in 1 Thessalonians 5:20–21 to argue that Paul has in mind the gift of making inspired assessments of inspired utterances. This understanding is exegetically grounded and judicious.

(8) **Speaking in different kinds of tongues,** literally "kinds of tongues" (see chs. 13–14). As will be clear from the lengthy and vigorous discussion of this topic in the next two chapters of the letter, this gift was causing a disproportionate number of problems among the Corinthian Christians. This gift is a special form of Spirit-inspired utterance, distinguishable from proph-

ecy, that aims toward God rather than comes from God through the speaker to the people. The person who was so gifted was privileged to talk to God in different kinds of tongues. This reference itself generates debate, but from Paul's comments one can see almost certainly that Paul does not have in mind the speaking of other known, human languages that the speaker had not studied in a normal fashion. In fact, such speech is thought to be unintelligible both to the one speaking and to the majority of those who might hear the speaker. Such Spirit-filled talking might appear to be mere gibberish if it were left uninterpreted. Thus, this gift required a special complement that Paul names as the last of the manifestations of the Spirit enumerated in this list.

(9) **The interpretation of tongues** (see ch. 14, esp. vv. 5, 13, 26–28). This special gift is an ancillary manifestation of the Spirit that was given and used in conjunction with the previously named speaking in different kinds of tongues. Tongues required explanation in order to be edifying for anyone other than the speaker, so along with the gift of utterance was given the gift of elucidation and clarification, in order that tongues might serve a missional purpose for the sake of others than the speaker. Noticeably, the speaker of tongues is not the one gifted with the interpretation of his or her own utterance.

12:11 / This verse is a summary statement. It "takes up vv. 6–7 and rounds off the section" (Conzelmann, *1 Corinthians*, p. 209). Paul again articulates his central conviction, which is the key issue he wishes to register with the Corinthians: **All these are the work of one and the same Spirit.** He states his point, however, with the addition of the recognition of God's Spirit's sovereignty or freedom (**just as he determines**), repeating the basic thoughts about diversity and unity for the fifth time in the span of eight verses while nudging the reflection along with the mention of the Spirit's determination of the allotment of gifts. Paul will elaborate and explain his convictions about God's will or determination of the composition and complexion of the church in the remainder of chapter 12, but for now he only mentions that topic in passing. Nevertheless, the subject has been implicit in the discussion of spiritual gifts from the outset of the conversation.

Additional Notes §35

12:4–6 / The word translated as **gifts** is *charismata,* from *charisma* ("gift"), a word that by root is related to *charis* or "grace." The idea behind this word is that it names a "gift of grace," here clearly God's grace. One understands the gifts being discussed to be God's gifts or spiritual gifts, but as the name indicates, these gifts are God's gifts through the Spirit for the working of grace.

12:7 / The passive form of the verb **is given** (Gk. *didotai,* from *didōmi*), expresses the explicitly stated divine origin of the gifts Paul is discussing. This statement anticipates the more overt expression of divine origins and sovereignty in the administration of gifts that comes in v. 11 and in the remainder of the chapter.

12:8–10 / In general cf. 1:7, where Paul offered an initial affirmation that the Corinthians were not "lacking in any gift" (Gk. *charisma*); see Gal. 5:22–23 for Paul's well-known list of the "fruit of the Spirit." Regarding prophecy, articles in the *TDNT, EDNT, IDB/IDBSup,* and *ABD* are all informative and helpful. The work of David Hill (*New Testament Prophecy* [Atlanta: John Knox, 1979]) and David Aune (*Prophecy in Early Christianity and the Ancient Mediterranean World* [Grand Rapids, Mich.: Eerdmans, 1983]) are thorough. See G. D. Fee ("Toward a Pauline Theology of Glossolalia," *Crux* 31 [1995], pp. 22–23, 26–31) for an attempt to grasp the theological sense of Paul's statements about tongues by relating them to Paul's understanding of God's own principle of power made perfect in weakness (2 Cor. 12:9).

12:11 / The polished grammatical sequence of Paul's statement, captured well in the NIV, first recognizes the variety of all these things—the manifestations of vv. 8–10—and then focuses on the oneness and the deliberateness of the operation of the Spirit. In summing up his teaching, Paul's line of thought runs from variety to unity to purposefulness.

§36 The Body of Christ (1 Cor. 12:12–31a)

In three striking movements these verses introduce (vv. 12–13), develop (vv. 14–26), and apply (vv. 27–31) Paul's best-known ecclesiastical metaphor: the body of Christ. Scholars debate the exact background from which Paul may have drawn inspiration for developing this memorable image for the church. Paul is likely to have encountered the thinking of Stoic philosophers, some of whom spoke of the cosmos in its unity as a body, and Jewish wisdom thinking, which often reflected upon the idea of corporate personality among a whole people. Nonetheless, Paul's thinking has unique elements, and his use of the image of body is extraordinary. One should notice that Paul uses this metaphor both of the local church and of the church universal (see Rom. 12). Furthermore, in the philosophical view of antiquity, being a body was the concrete basis of all human relation. In the context of this letter to Corinth, as Paul refers to the body, he employs a term that formed the platonic antithesis to that with which many of the Corinthians were obsessed: "spirit."

12:12 / Paul starts with a simple statement that a **body** is a unified entity. He recognizes the complex make-up of the body with its **many** and various **parts**, but he points above all to the oneness of the body. Thus, he establishes an initial point of reflection for the use of the ensuing metaphor, "body of Christ." By referring to the body as a **unit**, Paul forms an image that serves to explicate a powerful theological thesis, **So it is with Christ!** Christ means variety, but more importantly Christ means essential unity. Paul's theme becomes "diversity in unity, and unity over diversity." Modern interpreters sometimes read Paul's vision in an artificially balanced way, so that "unity in diversity" and "diversity in unity" become equal and synonymous statements. They are not. According to Paul, in Christ unity dominates diversity and makes diversity genuinely meaningful and constructive. The problem in Corinth was diversity run wild.

12:13 / From the outset of this discussion it is clear that this metaphor is possible because of the unifying work of the Spirit. The emphasis on unity cuts sharply across all social boundaries. Then, as Paul develops the metaphor, he ponders the significance of "body" from alternating points of view.

Paul expands, or perhaps even mixes his metaphors, with the additional reference to being **baptized by one Spirit into one body.** Nevertheless, this expansion of the basic image of the body makes it clear that the power of the Spirit is at work, so that one sees that God creates the unity of the body despite the original complexity or even seeming incompatibility of the constituent parts. Ethnicity **(Jews or Greeks)** and social class **(slave or free)** are superseded and even consolidated by the power of the Spirit at work among humanity. In Christ, as a body, believers may come from one group or another—and in worldly terms those origins might be irrelinquishable or irrevocable—but in Christ such diversity finds meaning (or is made meaningless) as believers are unified despite differences. Paul's ultimate concern is to emphasize unity.

12:14–19 / In verses 14–19 Paul returns to the more direct reflection on the image of a body and approaches the metaphor from the perspective of differentiation of body members. Paul develops this perspective and argues for the necessity of differences. He states that such differences are by divine design and volition. Then he concludes by summarizing the purpose of differences.

Paul contrasts specific parts of the human body, personifying the anatomical members in a playful but serious way: **foot, hand, ear, eye.** He paints a pair of absurd pictures by asking rhetorical questions: What if the whole body were an eye? There would be no hearing. But, what if the whole body were an ear? There would be no smelling. The point is plain: diversity is necessary because of the diversity of functions that are necessary.

Over this whole picture, Paul makes a crucial theological declaration: **God has arranged the parts of the body, every one of them, just as he wanted them to be** (v. 18). This assertion returns to the thought that was expressed briefly in 12:11—"one and the same Spirit . . . gives them to each one, just as he determines." Having made the point about the necessity of diversity in the body, Paul declares the differences to be God's will and work. At this point, Paul argues for the sensible necessity and divine purposefulness of diversity.

12:20–26 / Paul's perspective shifts in these verses, refocusing on his principal theme of unity. As important as the recognition of diversity is for the life of the church, Paul still wants to emphasize the overall or transcending purposeful unity of God's activity: **there are many parts, but one body.** Therefore, as he continues, Paul again develops his thinking about this subject as he declares that unity reflects divine design.

Paul develops the assertion that unity is necessary by relating his thought to the motif of mutual care in the church. One part of the body cannot say to another, **I don't need you!** Paul makes this point in a striking way. He writes of **parts of the body that seem to be weaker** that **are indispensable,** most likely meaning to refer to internal organs. Then, he refers in an indirect way to the sexual organs, when he says, **the parts that we think are less honorable we treat with special honor** [and] **the parts that are unpresentable are treated with special modesty.** This situation is the result of the way in which **God has combined the members of the body.** The goal of God's work was that **there should be no division in the body.**

Implicit in this verse is a foundational assumption. Not only has God enriched the unified body by granting distinctive gifts to the diverse parts of the body, but also God created the unified body per se, and the deliberate arrangement of the diverse members of the body. In other words, not only has God brought the richness of diversity to the coherence of unity, but also God created unity through the deliberate arrangement of diversity. Unity prevails and makes diversity meaningful. Remarkably, God's authority and purposefulness lie behind both unified diversity and diversified unity.

Still working from the metaphor of the body, Paul concludes this phase of the reflection by summarizing the value of relatedness in the church. God arranged the members of the body with all their diversity so that there was a mutual dependence and a harmonious unity, the result of which was that **its parts should have equal concern for each other.** Thus, in their necessary diversity and in their mutually dependent unity, all parts of the body suffer, experience being honored, and rejoice together—exactly because of God's design and exactly as the members of the body of Christ should also.

12:27 / Verses 27–31a apply and explain the metaphor of the church as **the body of Christ** in relation to the Corinthians' situation. Verse 27 begins with the bold declaration, **you are** the body of Christ. This statement means there is diversity among the Corinthian Christians in terms of their gifts, although they are united by God's design and work among them. Despite the differences, **each one . . . is a part** of the body, and each and all are necessary for the good of the whole.

12:28 / Paul delineates the godly order of spiritual gifts, probably placing speaking in tongues last in order to devalue the desirability of this flamboyant gift. He names eight specific members of the "body." As he begins, Paul counts the first three members that he names, **first . . . second . . . third . . . then . . .** Commentators disagree whether Paul meant to rank certain gifts. The form of the Greek words (ordinal numbers: first . . . second . . . third) is not indicative of Paul's intention, despite declarations by interpreters to the contrary. It is true that in the earlier chapters of the letter Paul has recognized that the Corinthians are all too eager to rank gifts and make comparisons. In this context, the act of ranking would seem to play into rather than correct the problem that Paul is facing. Perhaps what would be most surprising to the Corinthians is exactly which gifts Paul ranks first, second, and third.

The list given in this verse is similar to but not exactly the same as the nine gifts mentioned in 12:8–10: some points are parallel and others are not. In both lists Paul mentions those with gifts of healing, miraculous/mighty powers, prophecy/prophets, and speaking in tongues. In the initial listing at verses 8–10 Paul referred to messages of wisdom, messages of knowledge, faith, distinguishing spirits, and interpreting tongues, none of which is explicitly repeated here. And, in this verse Paul writes of **apostles**, teachers, those able to help others, and **gifts of administration**—all listed for the first time explicitly. This variety in listings probably indicates that Paul's references to gifts are illustrative, not exhaustive. Moreover, one should note that the lists are remarkable combinations of forms of service and functions in the life of the early church. Everyone and everything mentioned are assumed to be charismatic in character, not static in the sense of possessing status, office, or power. Paul's conviction and contention is that the Spirit endows believers—as God pleases—with various gifts of grace for the good of the entire church. Nevertheless, the items that are mentioned repeatedly gain prominence through the repetition and may be of special concern in relation to the Corinthian situation.

12:29–30 / Paul pursues the theme of the necessity of differentiation or variety of gifts in a series of rhetorical questions. He takes selected ones of the parts (persons or gifts) enumerated in verse 28 and asks repeatedly, **Are all apostles/prophets/teachers,** etc.? The grammatical form of the questions assumes the answer will be no.

The specific items about which Paul inquires are striking. First, from the list of parts delineated in verse 28, Paul again recognizes apostles, prophets, teachers, miraculous/mighty powers, gifts of healing, and speaking in tongues. Here, however, he does not mention those who are able to help others or those with gifts of administration. He does reintroduce those who were gifted to interpret tongues, a gift or part originally recognized at 12:10 but not mentioned in verse 28.

Through repetition and reintroduction, Paul creates emphasis and gives focus to his discussion. One should notice that only three gifts or parts are mentioned in all three of Paul's listings: miracle workers, those with gifts of healing, and those speaking in different kinds of tongues. Commentators are right to recognize that these three gifts would be the most flamboyant and probably the most valued by the members of the Corinthian congregation.

12:31a / Having worked through his complex discussion of the body of Christ and the necessary diversity and absolute unity of the members of that body through God's will and work, Paul concludes this section with an admonition: **But eagerly desire the greater gifts.** Even though all gifts are granted by God, it is still appropriate for the Corinthians to aspire toward the greater gifts! Ironically, what they might consider these to be and what Paul will tell them they are in the following chapters prove to be quite different.

Additional Notes §36

12:12 / This sentence begins with the Gk. word *kathaper*, "for as," which signals a rhetorical turn in Paul's reasoning that is lost in the NIV translation. Paul's language clearly informs the reader that he is building a dramatic metaphorical analogy that will carry weight in the argument he is mounting.

12:13 / This line also begins in such a manner that the reader understands Paul to be issuing an emphatic explanation. The Gk. text reads *kai gar*, best understood as "for indeed" rather than merely "for." This is a minor point, but Paul is offering rhetorical signals to his readers that should not be ignored.

Paul's introduction of ethnic **(Jews or Greeks)** and social differences **(slaves or free)** in this verse is problematic. Up to this point he has been recognizing and explaining differences among the believers that exist because of their different spiritual gifts. Now, however, with the introduction of these new issues, the argument about diversity in unity takes on a different cast. One wonders whether Paul is attempting to address two simultaneous problems at once and has conflated lines of thought. How can spiritual endowments, race, and social status be equated in one reflection? In the ancient world race and social standing were both given at birth. The gifts of the Spirit were not. Commentators suggest that Paul may have introduced an unnecessary, even confusing line into his argument with the references to Jews, Greeks, slave, and free. Perhaps, as in Gal. 3:28, having focused on unity and having mentioned baptism (a means of unification), Paul is drawing on a baptismal confession or liturgical refrain at this point. If so, Paul's concern with diversity in unity brought to mind an established statement of unity in Christ. The remark, then, is tangential and illustrative, not truly suited to the central matter of reflection, but loosely related and so brought into play.

Moreover, Paul further expands the images associated with the gifts by referring repeatedly to baptism or being baptized. That allusion is puzzling, so that interpreters debate what use Paul wished to make of the phenomenon of baptism. R. E. Cottle (" 'All Were Baptized,' " *JETS* 17 [1974], pp. 75–80) reads the references first **(we were all baptized)** in relation to conversion, not water baptism or baptism in the Spirit, and then **(we were all given the one Spirit to drink)** in relation to a second baptism in the Spirit. It is not clear, however, that Paul knew such distinctions. Through repetition, these enigmatic statements serve, no matter what their point(s) of reference, to underscore the common bond and experience of all members of the church.

The exact details of Paul's purpose may not be clear or recoverable at this point, but his basic emphasis remains the same, and through the oddity of the references to race, social status, and baptism in this verse becomes even more emphatic: Unity in Christ! Nevertheless, as

Conzelmann aptly remarks concerning this verse and the introduction of these new elements, "For here Paul speaks only of the *unity* which is brought about by the abrogation of the (physical and social) difference between believers. This idea is not derivable from the figure of an organism [a body]" (*1 Corinthians*, p. 212).

12:14 / Still another verse begins emphatically, *kai gar*, "for indeed." Logically, however, this verse seems connected with v. 12 rather than v. 13 as Paul returns to the images of the body parts in forming his analogies and arguments.

12:15–18 / The NIV translation of vv. 15–18 is accurate in its colloquial and vivid style of rendering Paul's lines at this point. Paul's energy and wit are both evident in his imaginative illustrations that the NIV brings over into excellent English translation. In this vein, the NIV correctly conveys the importance of Paul's declaration in v. 18 by rendering *nuni de* (lit. "but now") **But in fact.**

12:18 / There is a striking linguistic similarity between the statement here, which is in the context of a discussion of God's will in endowing members of the church with selected spiritual gifts, and the statement in 15:38 concerning God's giving a body to "seed" according to God's own will. Although Paul's vocabulary and theology are similar and consistent, these images and metaphors are unrelated, if not incompatible. This point of continuity was noted by Conzelmann, who writes in relation to the metaphor of the "body" that "the figure has for [Paul] no importance on its own account" (*1 Corinthians*, p. 213).

12:20 / The paragraphing of the NIV includes v. 20 with vv. 14–19 as a unit of thought. Nevertheless, this line seems better fitted to vv. 21–26, since this verse begins Paul's shift in focus from considering the necessity of diversity back to the essential nature of unity— a theme that immediately follows rather than immediately precedes v. 20. The logic of this line and the following verses brings to mind the popular maxim "One for all, and all for one." Moreover, the opening words of the line are the same as those in v. 18, *nun de* ("But in fact"; NIV: **As it is**). These words introduce a conclusion that takes a degree of exception to foregoing reasoning as they introduce a new angle in logic. In agreement, see Conzelmann, *1 Corinthians*, p. 213.

12:21 / Notice that in this imaginary dialogue, **the head** is but a part—though prominent—of the body. **The head** is not identified in any special fashion with Christ himself. Compare the similar images and uses of this metaphor in Rom. 12:3–8; Eph. 1:15–23; 2:15–16; 4:3–4, 11–12, 15–16, 25; 5:23, 29–30; Col. 1:18, 24; 2:9–10, 19; 3:15. The images are distinct in their various locations: 1 Cor. and Rom. understand that the church is the body of Christ, whereas Eph. and Col. present a development of that basic image so that Christ is the head of his body, which is the church. Distinctions exist and developments have occurred, so readers should perceive and take into account the nuances of the metaphors of the body, no matter who wrote the canonical letters attributed to Paul.

12:23 / The NIV loses something of the continuity of Paul's Gk. cognates with the translation sequence **less honorable . . . special honor . . . unpresentable . . . special modesty.** Trying to find appropriate English words to reflect and to preserve the integrity of Paul's language is difficult, but Orr and Walther propose the following sequence: "greater honor . . . less honorable . . . unpresentable . . . greater presentability" (Orr and Walther, *I Corinthians*, pp. 283–85). The connections are clear and deliberate in Paul's own choice of words, *atimotera . . . timēn perissoteran . . . aschēmona . . . euschēmosynēn.*

12:25 / Cf. 1:10–12.

12:27 / This verse functions as a bridge from Paul's metaphorical analogy to his more functional summation or conclusion (Orr and Walther, *I Corinthians*, p. 287).

12:28 / In this list of gifts or parts, Paul uses image-laden language to name certain phenomena: **those able to help others** is *antilēmpseis* in Gk., a word normally indicating a "helper," "protector," or "supporter" that can be used metaphorically in relation to cultivated plants to mean "giving a return." Similarly, **those with gifts of administration** is *kybernēseis* in Gk., a word meaning "guidance" in the sense of "steering" or "piloting." A form of the same word can indicate a helmsman, and the word is sometimes used metaphorically in relation to city government.

12:31a / In this concluding admonition Paul says, "But you be zealous for the more important gifts [of grace]!" In turn, v. 31b leads into the poetic meditation on "love" that follows in ch. 13. Prior to ch. 13, where he will advocate the supreme way of love, Paul's remarks on gifts have been essentially restrictive. In fact, by consulting the canons of ancient rhetoric, J. F. M. Smit ("Two Puzzles: 1 Corinthians 12.31 and 13.3: A Rhetorical Solution," *NTS* 39 [1993], pp. 246–64) has argued that even 1 Cor. 12:31 is ironic, so that in this admonition Paul is ridiculing the Corinthians because they are obsessed with pursuing spectacular forms of charismatic gifts. This conclusion seems to exaggerate Paul's tone, although it is a reminder that Paul is not swept away with the Corinthians in the pursuit of self-aggrandizing spiritual activity. Rather, Paul's concern to this point has been to check the Corinthians' misunderstanding and misappropriation of God's gifts. Now, however, "he directs their attention to higher gifts, ones that allow no self-development and no self-contemplation on the pneumatic's [ecstatic's] part" (Conzelmann, *1 Corinthians*, p. 215).

§37 The Superlative Way of Love (1 Cor. 12:31b–13:13)

These verses are often referred to as an excursus on love, and there are good reasons for this description. Remarkably, in this extended meditation on love Paul does not write about loving: there is no statement here that X *loves* Y. Love itself is the actor or the object of reflection. This beautiful passage never attempts to offer an abstract definition of love; rather, Paul rehearses critical characteristics of love and states in practical terms what love is and isn't or does and doesn't do. The verses of this deliberation describe rather than define, for love is cast as a capacity rather than a commodity. From Paul's admonition to aspire for the greater gifts—literally, he says, "Earnestly seek the higher gifts of grace" (12:31a)—the reader finds him promising to show the Corinthians "a still more excellent way" (12:31b).

The transition from 12:31a to 12:31b is awkward, and the material that follows in chapter 13 is unusual. First, it intrudes. First Corinthians 12:31a flows well into 14:1, and the theme of love in chapter 13 relates only indirectly to the particular situation being addressed to this point in the epistle. Second, the material on love seems to be a self-contained, quite polished unit. Third, there are comparable Greek and Hellenistic Jewish parallels to this meditation on love found in such diverse materials as Tyrtaeus, Plato, Maximus of Tyre, and especially 1 Esd. 4:34–40; cf. also the analogous meditation on "wisdom" in Wisdom 7:22–30. Fourth, the chapter seems unconcerned with Christ. This array of observations produces a variety of suggestions, but in any case the material seems to be an originally independent piece (or originally independent pieces) of developed tradition that Paul inserted into this context and applied to the Corinthian situation. Paul is likely to have worked minor adaptations on this material in order to fit it into this letter, and it is not impossible that the piece was originally composed as an independent one by Paul himself.

12:31b / Paul calls for and attempts to turn the thinking of his audience in a new, positive direction with the rhetorical declaration, **And now I will show you the most excellent way.** The words imply that the way Paul is about to reveal is "incomparable" or "all surpassing" (Gk. *kath' hyperbolēn*). His readers might recognize that in this statement Paul is claiming to present the highest form of Christian faith and practice. The word "way" (Gk. *hodos*) functioned as a euphemistic technical designation for Christianity in the early days of the church. At points in the NT one finds simple references to Christian belief and life as "the Way" (Acts 9:2; 19:9, 23; 22:4; 24:14, 22). Whether Paul intends to play on that image here is uncertain, but by claiming to show the Corinthians the most excellent way, he is nevertheless purporting to inform them of the essence of Christian living.

13:1–3 / Verses 1–3 establish the necessity of love, for love alone confers worth to all other spiritual gifts. The mention of **tongues** has immediate relevance to the Corinthian situation, and the **gong** and **clanging cymbal** are items naturally associated with pagan religious ecstasy, so that Paul's words form a poetic critique of the Corinthians' behavior as one knows it from the previous chapters. Yet in the next lines **the gift of prophecy** names a Christian phenomenon highly regarded by Paul. Thus, Paul makes a startling point in unambiguous fashion: Manifesting spiritual gifts, even a gift that Paul values, is useless without **love.** Paul is not merely issuing a condemnation of those who have religious values that are different from his own or those of his cohorts; he is stating the essential underlying motive or actuality that must influence and even control all spiritual realities. Moreover, the mention of **mysteries** and **knowledge** sounds a note about concerns that the Corinthians have demonstrated, and as Paul refers to such issues in this context, the first-century readers would naturally associate these matters with apocalyptic writings and the eschatological age of the end times because of Paul's imposition and use of this perspective throughout the letter.

In turn, the reference to **faith** in verse 2 seems peculiar. In this statement, faith appears to be something akin to miraculous power, which might be a traditional definition rather than Paul's own understanding of faith as "fruit of the Spirit" (Gal. 5:22; cf. 1 Cor. 12:9). The phraseology is more reminiscent of the images introduced by Jesus in Mark 11:23 and Matthew 17:20; 21:21 than of Paul's own perspective on faith. Paul makes it clear that even extraordinarily powerful faith, which can accomplish great feats, is of marginal value or even useless if the one with such faith has no **love**. Through a series of dramatic images, Paul makes his understanding of the "most excellent way" quite clear. Paul's twin verdicts in these verses are that without love **I am nothing** and **I gain nothing**. According to Paul's teaching about Christian belief and practice, human lives and achievements are ultimately judged by the presence or absence of love.

13:4–7 / A change of style occurs in verses 4–7. The content and style are those of Jewish parenesis, or concrete directions, and the form is didactic (instruction) rather than hymnic (praise). The English phrase **love is** supplies the verb "to be," which is absent in Greek, but the translation accurately captures the descriptive intention of the lines. In brief, verses 4–6 create a listing of the characteristics of love that is epitomized in verse 7. Love is presented as the essential Christian attribute: Love is selflessness and is not self-centeredness. Love is **patient** and **kind.** It is "not jealous, boastful, arrogant, rude." Then, with a shift from the nature of love to the activities of love, Paul declares that "love does not insist on its own way" nor, then, is it "irritable or resentful," nor does it "rejoice at wrong." Rather, love "rejoices in the right" (NIV: **it does not envy . . . boast . . . is not proud . . . rude . . . self-seeking . . . easily angered . . . keeps no record of wrongs . . . does not delight in evil . . . rejoices with the truth**). The reader of this letter would naturally associate the way that love does not act with Paul's earlier references to the very behavior of the Corinthians in their gatherings for the Supper (ch. 11).

Paul's language concerning love is crisp, and in rendering his words the NIV is more explanatory than succinct, although judicious and accurate. The NIV's style is more verbose than Paul's own diction, and while the translation provides important insights into the sense of Paul's concise wording, it loses something of the vigor of Paul's poetic style. The NRSV or even the KJV may be less immediately clear for contemporary readers, but Paul's poetic style shines through in these versions. The lines critique the Corinthian situation elegantly but abstractly.

Paul summarizes the character of love, although he has already stated its traits, now saying that it "bears all things, believes all things, hopes all things, and endures all things" (NIV:

always protects, always trusts, always hopes, always perseveres). In short, love defines and directs Christian life, although Paul's meditative mood is too poetic to allow him to make such a conventional declaration. The problem with Paul's own elegant description of love is that later misreadings and misuses of this contemplation reinterpret **love** as if it were being gullible or welcoming abuse. In fact, the description Paul gives in verses 4–7 is of God's love, which transcends the boundaries of selfishness or self-centeredness in the righteous pursuit of reconciliation and redemption (chs. 1, 4). The call to Christians is to live by the grace and power of God in such a way that God's own love forms and directs life so that God's love becomes the Christians' love. Spiritual gifts must function in service to the aims of God's love, or Paul says they are, despite their sometimes extraordinary effects, dead ends in themselves.

13:8–10 / Once again the style shifts at verse 8. Instead of the pithy wisdom sayings of the foregoing lines one encounters more elaborated arguments. The preceding verses of this meditation on love assert that charismatic gifts are worthless without love. Now Paul further promotes love by establishing the temporal quality of the gifts and the enduring, eternal, eschatological nature of love. Thus, verse 8 opens with a contrast between **love** and **prophecies, tongues,** and **knowledge**—declaring that love will endure and that prophecy, tongues, and knowledge will come to an end (or will cease). This turn of thinking should cause alert readers to recall 1 Corinthians 7:31, where Paul said "the present form of this world is passing away," so that now one encountering Paul's statements may infer that prophecy, tongues, and knowledge belong to this world, not to God's new creation. Moreover, and in further pursuit of the dramatic contrast between love and gifts, in verse 10 Paul identifies the basis for the cessation of knowledge and prophecy—they are **imperfect.** Finally Paul promises the survival of that which is perfect and declares the eschatological end of imperfection. Again, the statements should cause the attentive reader to recall Paul's statements in 1 Corinthians 3:10–15 concerning what kinds of things will survive God's scrutiny on the Day of final judgment.

13:11–12 / To make his point concerning the passing away of imperfection (that is, the gifts) and the eternal nature of love, Paul offers a dramatic metaphor in regard to the putting aside of **childish ways.** Immaturity gives way to maturity, so that a childish concern with flamboyant gifts should run its course and end with the advent of a mature concern for love. Moreover, with the ensuing metaphor of seeing in a mirror dimly Paul articulates a contrast between current existence and the promised eschatological vision of seeing **face to face**. The pattern of Paul's logic is the contrast of lesser with greater, so that through these images he admonishes the Corinthians to have less concern for spectacular spiritual gifts and a greater concern for the reality of love, God's own love.

From these metaphors Paul takes up the idea of knowledge that occupied his reflections in earlier chapters. Current knowledge is labeled partial, whereas eschatological knowledge is promised to be full. Current Christian knowledge, though valuable, is of limited importance in comparison with the full knowledge imparted by God in an eschatological form. Paul writes that all full eschatological knowledge, as well as current partial knowledge, is based in our being **fully known** by God, so that the reader learns again of God's genuine priority in life and in the experience of salvation. As Paul made clear in chapter 1, what matters is not what humans know but what God has done, is doing, and will do.

13:13 / This concluding verse heightens the previous lines of thought and argument. Paul creates a slight contrast between what he says in these statements and what went before, for now the readers hear of the **three** highest gifts—**faith, hope and love**. Faith was mentioned in 13:2, but it is not clear that the same sense is intended here (see esp. Paul's "faith-talk" in Romans and Galatians). Nevertheless, faith becomes the foundation for Christian life. In turn, hope emanates from faith (13:7), but as the lines continue one sees that Paul's purpose in developing his argument in this manner is to establish the superiority of love, as he already stated in 12:31b.

Interpreters debate whether 13:13 means that faith, hope, and love are valid and remain valid eternally or that faith, hope, and love are now valid, but only love will endure eternally. From Paul's wording it is impossible to make a final decision, although in context the second option may be preferable. In either case, one should see the superior and eternal character of love. The supreme characteristic and motivation for Christian life—now and forever according to Paul—is nothing other than love.

Additional Notes §37

These are among the most quoted verses in all of biblical literature. In fact, Paul's words are so well known in Western culture that
they require practically no technical explanation. Even the figures of his
metaphors have become standard images in secular speech among
most literate people. The logical lines of Paul's argumentation were
examined above, and the basic metaphors are either classic or self-
evident. Thus, in the Additional Notes that follow, there are primarily a
series of words from the NIV that are first given in their Gk. lexical form
and then explained briefly in an effort to provide more than a superficial acquaintance with the elements of the substance of Paul's thought.

The classic study of love, which has undergone much refinement
through criticism, is A. Nygren's *Agape and Eros* (rev. ed.; London:
S.P.C.K., 1953). More recently, J. G. Sigountos ("The Genre of 1 Corinthians 13," *NTS* 40 [1994], pp. 246–60) shows how recognizing the form
of ch. 13 as an encomium assists comparison and interpretation in relation to both Plato and 1 Esd. 3; cf. J. Smit, "The Genre of 1 Corinthians
13 in the Light of Classical Rhetoric," *NovT* 33 (1991), pp. 193–216;
and furthermore, see J. O'Brien, "Sophocles's Ode on Man and Paul's
Hymn on Love: A Comparative Study," *Classical Journal* 71 (1975/76),
pp. 138–51.

On 12:31b–13:13 as an originally independent Pauline writing,
see E. L. Titus, "Did Paul Write I Corinthians 13?" *JBR* 27 [1959], pp.
299–302.

12:31b / Paul writes in reference to **the most excellent way**
(Gk. *eti kath' hyperbolēn hodon*), a phrase that essentially indicates "still a
way better than any" or "yet an incomparable way." The language is not
extravagant exaggeration, despite the use of *hyperbolē*. Paul wants the
reader to understand that this is an extraordinary path of life that goes
beyond all others discussed up to this point. The claim may strike some
as arrogant, but in a letter in which Paul has been concerned to curb
the artificial, inappropriate arrogance of the Corinthians, the phrase
should be taken as a sincere declaration of Paul's conviction that he is
about to portray the extraordinary essence of Christian life to the
readers.

13:1 / The reference to **tongues of angels** (Gk. *glōssais tōn ag-
gelōn*) recalls the discussion at 12:10 and may provide insight into the
Corinthians' practice of and fascination with tongues. Paul contrasts
human and angelic tongues, perhaps indicating in the latter reference
the understanding of tongues that was prevalent in Corinth. When certain Corinthians spoke in tongues they may have understood that they
were being gifted with angel speech, a privilege that would distinguish
those endowed with such a capacity.

Moreover, in the context of this letter Paul's mention of a **re-sounding gong** (Gk. *kalkos ēchōn;* lit. "brass sounding") and a **clanging cymbal** (Gk. *kymbalon alalazon;* lit. "cymbal tinkling") would conjure familiar images in the minds of his readers. Such instruments were common in pagan worship, and in Corinth, where there was a vital brass industry, these would have been common implements for making noise and getting attention. See W. Harris, " 'Sounding Brass' and Hellenistic Theology," *BAR* 8 (1982), pp. 38–41; W. W. Klein, "Noisy Gong or Acoustic Vase? A Note on 1 Corinthians 13.1," *NTS* 32 (1986), pp. 286–89. Furthermore, the mention of the cymbal may be related to the language of Ps. 150:5.

13:3 / A minor textual problem makes it uncertain whether Paul says that without love it is no gain to hand over one's body "in order to boast" or "in order to be burned." Most interpreters prefer the plain sense of the notion of Paul's hypothetically surrendering his **body to the flames**, although the other reading is difficult to account for if it is not original. Whichever reading is authentic, the sense of Paul's statement is that either the pride or the selflessness of sacrifice is worthless without the authorizing motivation of love. See J. K. Elliott, "In Favour of *kauthēsomai* at I Corinthians 13:3," *ZNW* 62 (1971), pp. 297–98; J. H. Petzer, "Contextual Evidence in Favour of *KAUCHĒSOMAI* in 1 Corinthians 13.3," *NTS* 35 (1989), pp. 229–53.

13:4 / Paul's description of **love** is complex. When he lists the positive aspects of love he uses stylized Gk. that is vivid with images. Concerning love he says it is **patient** (Gk. *makrothymos;* lit. "long-tempered"); **kind** (Gk. *chrēstos;* lit. "useful" or "mild"). Then, Paul uses negative definitions to describe aspects that are not love: **envy** (Gk. *zeloō;* lit. "to be zealous"); **boast** (Gk. *perpereuomai;* lit. "to put oneself forward" or "to show off"); **proud** (Gk. *physioumai;* lit. "to be inflated" or "to be full of one's own importance").

13:5 / In this verse a series of verbs continues to expand the negative definition of love by stating explicitly what love is not and what it does not do: **rude** (Gk. *aschēmoneō;* lit. "to behave dishonorably or indecently"); **self-seeking** (Gk. *zēteō ta heautēs;* lit. "to seek the things that are its own"); **easily angered** (Gk. *parozynomai;* lit. "to be hot-tempered" or "to be sharp"); **keeps record of wrongs** (Gk. *logizomai to kakon;* lit. "to reckon the evil").

13:6 / Paul shifts the perspective slightly by offering an illustrative contrast that probably can be understood to summarize all the negative activity that he mentioned overtly in the preceding verses; moreover, in case he left anything out of the account, he offers a comprehensive summary of what love does not do: **delight in evil** (Gk. *chairō epi tē akikia;* lit. "to rejoice over unrighteousness [or wrongdoing]"); then, he states the opposite explicitly, saying what in fact love does: it **rejoices with** (Gk. *sygchairō;* lit. "to rejoice with" or "to congratulate") **the truth.** The phraseology of this last positive declaration demonstrates love's positive disposition in recognizing and celebrating "the truth" (God's truth).

13:7 / Paul's positive description of love's activities continues with a series of verbs that name what love does. He qualifies the statements by saying that love **always** (Gk. *panta;* lit. "all things") acts in this manner, or better, that the action of love is for the good of "all things." Specifically, Paul recognizes that love **protects** (Gk. *stegō;* lit. "to bear" or "to cover"); **trusts** (Gk. *pisteuō;* lit. "to believe" or "to trust in"); **hopes** (Gk. *elpizō;* lit. "to hope"); and **perseveres** (Gk. *hypomenō;* lit. "to endure"). On the particular character of Christian hope, see E. Wong, "1 Corinthians 13:7 and Christian Hope," *LS* 17 (1992), pp. 232–42.

13:8 / In contrast to what love always does, Paul gives another negative definition by saying that **love never fails**—a statement wherein the verb **fails** (Gk. *piptō*) means "to fall down."

13:10 / The absolute character of the contrasts between the positive and negative features of love serves a rhetorical function and is a vivid illustration of what Paul means by love. The pattern of contrasts probably reflects Paul's apocalyptic-eschatological worldview, as becomes evident in the references to **perfection** (Gk. *to teleion;* lit. "the complete/perfect thing") and **imperfection** (Gk. *to ek merous;* lit. "the partial thing"). Paul is contrasting the temporal with the eternal. He has said that the form of this world is passing away (7:31), and in listing the qualities of love he declares what will pass away (the negative) and what does and will characterize the eternal (the positive). In meditating on love Paul reveals what he understands to be the character and the goal of the eschatological work of God.

13:11 / Paul adds to the images by offering a metaphor to drive home his basic line of thought. He refers to being **a child** (Gk. *nēpios;* lit. "infant" or "toddler"), a negative status in the way he states it and in the NT world. In the minds of most ancients, children were little unbridled bits of chaos, whose only hope was to grow into adulthood. Thus, Paul says he **put . . . behind** (Gk. *katargeō;* lit. "to have finished with"—here, perfect = "to have been finished with" or "to be completely done") the things of that undesirable time. In ch. 3 Paul had confronted the Corinthians with their spiritual immaturity, so that this image resounds that note of criticism and reemphasizes the importance of their growing into spiritual adulthood.

13:12 / Paul's second metaphor focuses on the use of a **mirror**. The mirror (Gk. *esoptron;* lit. "polished metal") would have been a well-known commodity in ancient Corinth. Looking in a mirror had associations with vanity, so that Paul may be implying that the best one can do in the context of this world that is passing away is somewhat in vain. In any case, the metaphor is awkward, for one sees oneself in a mirror and one looks at another face to face. Paul's chief concern, the future and direct encounter of humanity with God, directs his selection and combination of imagery in this statement. Cf. F. G. Downing, "Reflecting the First Century: 1 Corinthians 13:12," *ExpT* 95 (1984), pp. 176–77; R. Seaford, "1 Corinthians XIII.12," *JTS* 35 (1984), pp. 117–20. In fact, Paul is attempting to make a connection between seeing poorly in a reflection and knowing God poorly when a child (or knowing God poorly before "we" see him face to face).

Other elements of Paul's comments were pertinent to the situation he confronted in Corinth. (1) At best, an ancient mirror gave **a poor reflection** (Gk. *en ainigmati;* lit. "in a riddle"). (For an intra-biblical reading of Paul's image see M. Fishbane, "Through the Looking Glass: Reflections on Ezek 42:3, Num 12:8 and 1 Cor 13:12," *Hebrew Annual Review* 10 [1986], pp. 63–75.) (2) The idiom of seeing **face to face** (Gk. *prosōpon pros prosōpon,* translated literally) is Semitic in character and may reflect the story of Moses' seeing God directly. (3) Three verbs offer a concise theological assessment of the situation in Corinth as Paul saw it and as he has described it in this letter. The Corinthians are concerned with knowledge, but they only **know in part** (Gk. *ginōskō ek merous,* translated literally). Only as God wills and works for the completion of God's own purposes will humans ever **know fully** (Gk. *epiginōskō;* lit. "to know thoroughly"). Indeed, whatever humans know that matters at all is the result of their being **fully known** (Gk. *epiginōskō,* "to be known thoroughly") by God. Paul applies this paradigm of knowledge, knowing, and being known to himself, but his implications for the Corinthians are evident. This use of himself as an example is consistent with the previous references to Apollos and Paul in ch. 4, where Paul explained that he engaged in such "personal" deliberations for the benefit of those in Corinth to whom he wrote. (For a highly debatable interpretation to the contrary, however, see E. Stuart, "Love is . . . Paul," *ExpT* 102 (1991), pp. 264–66.)

§38 The Practice of Prophecy (1 Cor. 14:1–5)

The discussion returns to the direct consideration of spiritual gifts that was the explicit focus of Paul's remarks up to 12:31a. One should notice at the outset that Paul's general concern is with orderly worship, but there are bends and turns to the argumentation that are hard to follow and highly debated. Moreover, as later readers turn to this passage they sometimes forget the concrete historical circumstances that lie behind Paul's remarks, but to do so is a disaster. Paul faced a complex, problem-laden congregation that had disruptive behavior of nearly unimaginable proportions at work in it. The severity of the situation brings Paul to argue with a vigor that can seem overbearing from afar, although one should recognize that Paul apparently thought such elaborate and forceful discussion was needed at the time. Indeed, students of the Corinthian church's history can develop a deep sympathy for Paul's difficult situation when they read *1 Clement*, a letter from a later church leader in Rome, written in the last decade of the first century A.D., some forty years after Paul's own letter. This later letter shows that many of the problems Paul faced in Corinth in the 50s still existed in the 90s. Knowing the severity of the problems Paul faced makes it easier to understand his energy, tone, and even aggravation with the Corinthians.

At the outset (vv. 1–5) Paul compares and contrasts only two of the gifts: tongues and prophecy. His discussion makes clear that so-called tongues are unintelligible assertions (glossolalia), not foreign languages. Paul's concern is not so much with the content of tongue speech and prophecy as with the mode and orientation of these utterances. Paul declares the superior merit of an utterance that is oriented away from one's self over speech—even if it is spectacular spiritual speech—that merely serves one's self.

14:1 / In 14:1a Paul opens this segment of the letter as he ended a previous section at 12:31a—with an admonition, **Fol-**

low the way of love! Then, as Paul launches into his discussion of the disorderly circumstances that apparently characterized the Corinthian church at worship, he urges the readers to **eagerly desire spiritual gifts,** but he makes his own preference clear by adding **especially** (lit. "rather"; Gk. *mallon*) **the gift of prophecy.** "Prefer prophecy" becomes Paul's thesis for all that will follow in chapter 14; he even repeats this admonition in 14:39, "Be eager to prophesy." These twin declarations in 14:1 and 14:39 form a literary inclusio, which emphasizes the material it surrounds. From this insight one gains a solid footing for attempting to follow Paul's thought as he winds his way through the rest of this discussion.

14:2 / Verses 2–5 develop the thesis that was stated in verse 1. Having declared his own strong preference for prophecy over tongues, Paul offers a reflection on these two gifts that informs the readers that **anyone who speaks in a tongue** does not address people but God, and no human understands because the speaker **utters mysteries with his spirit** (lit. "but in spirit speaks mysteries"). According to Paul's teaching, there is a clear point and a clear audience for tongues, but other humans are not the intended recipients of the message and so they do not comprehend the substance of the speech in tongues or benefit from it.

14:3 / Paul pursues the same objective from another point of view. By contrast to the tongue speakers, those who prophesy speak to humans for the edification, encouragement, and consolation of their hearers. As one can see from nearly everything that Paul writes in this letter, the building up of the church and the well-being of the whole body of Christ are his principal concerns. In fact, Paul borders on saying that the value of any gift or action is the same as its value for edification of the church.

14:4 / Paul analyzes the meaning of the contrast he has painted between prophecy and tongues. He tells the Corinthians that tongues edify the one speaking and prophecy **edifies the whole church.** In verses 5, 12, 17, 26, Paul will return explicitly to the importance of practicing spiritual gifts for the good of the church.

14:5 / Paul's prejudice is clear, but it could be misunderstood. Therefore, he states that he wants all to speak in tongues, but even more he desires that all prophesy. Both gifts have true value, but as Paul will explain, there are fewer potential complications with prophecy than with tongues; so prophecy is preferable.

One might think at this juncture that Paul has made himself clear, but he is not finished. He will now undertake a series of arguments that illustrate and support his contention. Moreover, he will do so in two segments of discussion: verses 6–12 and verses 13–19.

Additional Notes §38

14:1 / **Follow the way of love** (Gk. *Diōkete tēn agapēn;* lit. "you [pl.] pursue love"). Having said that the Corinthians should be zealous for the greater gifts of grace (12:31), now Paul is more specific in this new declaration. He tells them to "pursue love." The NIV's paraphrase is sensible. Love sets the path or charts the course, and the Corinthians are challenged and privileged to follow that path in pursuit of God's own end. In brief, after 14:1a admonishes the Corinthians to "pursue love" (reiterating the theme of ch. 13), at 14:1b Paul employs the postpositive conjunction "but" (*not* **and** as in the NIV; Gk. *de*). This word indicates Paul's moving in a related but different direction in this particular phrase of the verse. The words of 14:1a prepare the way for 14:1b, where Paul dives into the discussion of ch. 14 with the words, "But, be zealous for the gifts [of the Spirit], but especially in order that you may prophesy."

14:2 / The Gk. word *glōssa* means **tongue** or "language," but its use here refers to spiritual utterance. From Paul's discussion of this phenomenon one finds that to speak in a tongue was a supernatural gift. It was not speech in an unstudied human language or dialect. This gift was bestowed on an individual (14:4, 16) and had a spontaneous quality (14:15) that was at least in part under the will of the speaker (14:27–28). Even the speaker did not necessarily understand the utterance (14:2, 13). In order to impart an intelligible communication, the gift of tongues required the practice of a complementary spiritual gift of interpretation (14:2, 5, 13). Tongue speaking benefited the speaker as a direct spiritual communication to God (14:2, 16–17), but without interpretation it had no capacity for benefiting the congregation, even when spoken in the assembly (14:17, 27–28).

In setting the word **spirit** with a lower case "s" and in rendering the phrase "with his spirit" rather than "in the spirit," the NIV interprets Paul's use of the word (Gk. *pneuma*) to refer to the spirit of the human speaker. This reading is possible, perhaps correct; yet, Paul's ambiguous phrase in Gk. contains the possibility that Paul meant to indicate that a tongue speaker spoke "in the Spirit of God," so that the unintelligibility of the speaking was because of the divine origin of the language. A final decision for this question of translation is impossible and not crucial for grasping the basic sense of Paul's statement.

14:3 / Paul's description of the effects of prophecy is instructive; the words he chooses to explain prophecy are image-laden: **strengthening** (Gk. *oikodomē*; lit. "building up," from the language of construction or household management), **encouragement** (Gk. *paraklēsis*; lit. "invitation, exhortation," from the language of the courtroom or debate wherein one "appealed" to another for a decision), and **comfort** (Gk. *paramythia*; lit. "encouragement, consolation" from the realms of education and friendship). Together these words impart the picture of a rousing address meant to motivate, to enable, and to bring results.

14:4 / In a incisive essay, E. Schweizer ("The Service of Worship: An Exposition of I Corinthians 14," *Int* 13 [1959], pp. 400–408) makes clear that the character of Christian worship is found only in congregational togetherness where each and every member participates in the worship to the mutual upbuilding of the entire church. Such a situation was assumed and encouraged (because of problems in the realization) by Paul. The way Paul phrases the juxtaposition of speaking in a tongue over against prophesying names two kinds of speaking—one taking an obscure form (tongues) and the other imparting content (prophecy). Both kinds of speech have value, but of very different quality with very different results.

14:5 / Paul's grammar forms an elaborate, unnecessary purpose clause. He writes, *thelō hina prophēteuēte* (lit. "I wish in order that you [pl.] may prophesy"); whereas, as Zerwick and Grosvenor observe, he could have more easily and more normally written, *thelō hymas lalein* (lit. "I wish you [pl.] to speak"). The awkwardness of the phrasing anticipates the even more forceful concluding, contrasting declaration, *mallon de hina prophēteuēte* (lit. "but rather in order that you [pl.] may prophesy"). The rhetorical deliberateness of the lines is part of Paul's ploy to emphasize the importance of prophesying over speaking in tongues.

§39 The Advantage of Intelligibility (1 Cor. 14:6–12)

Here is the first of Paul's two complex, imaginative deliberations in support of his thesis in 14:1–5, which describes the crucial value of prophecy and the proper role of tongues. Paul shifts into a diatribe style of disputation, issuing a series of rhetorical questions followed by illustrative analogies and a concluding exhortation.

14:6 / Paul begins with a hypothetical false first-person statement: speaking **in tongues** precludes one from speaking in sensible, understandable expressions. Should he come speaking in tongues, he will not be able to offer other kinds of utterances that would be useful: **revelation, knowledge, prophecy,** and **word of instruction.** The exact sense of the beneficial messages that Paul describes with these words is hard to determine, but the further mention (see 13:2) of prophetic powers and revelation or knowledge brings an apocalyptic-eschatological tone to the discussion, suggesting that there is a special urgency that demands clarity and intelligibility in communication.

14:7–9 / Paul's second illustration refers to musical instruments. In verse 7 he mentions the **flute** and the **harp,** and in verse 8 he adds the **trumpet.** His point is simple: The muted or jumbled playing of such instruments cannot be comprehended, so there is no benefit from such noise. In verse 9 Paul makes direct application of this image by saying that tongues are no more useful than is indistinct music, for one not speaking in **intelligible words** is as helpful as one speaking into the air.

14:10–11 / Paul continues in a third analogical argument to illustrate his point about the liability of tongues by reminding the Corinthians of the pointlessness of speaking to foreigners in a language they do not understand. Foreign sailors and tradespersons were always passing through Roman Corinth, and a common language (Greek) was required for people to communicate with one another.

14:12 / Paul draws his arguments to a conclusion. He redirects the energies of the Corinthians and calls for them to excel in edification—**gifts that build up the church**—as the genuine manifestation of the Spirit alive and at work among them. He reiterates his earlier point (see 12:31a) that the Corinthians are to seek the preeminent gifts, not merely the flamboyant or unusual ones. While Paul's point is clear, his grammar and style are not. This sentence could mean either "Seek spiritual gifts that edify the church in order to excel" or "Seek to excel in the spiritual gifts that edify the church." Given the thrust of the general argument against self-directed spiritual practices, the NIV's choice of the second option, **try to excel in** gifts that build up the church, is probably correct.

Additional Notes §39

14:6 / Paul's address takes a rhetorical form, beginning **Now** (Gk. *nun de;* lit. "But now"), followed by a direct address, **brothers** (Gk. *adelphoi*), a masculine plural form that would be understood to address both the brothers and the sisters in the church. With this attention-getting salutation, Paul then asks a rhetorical question in a conditional form that poses an informal riddle to the audience: . . . **if I come . . .** , **what good . . . ?** But, without giving the Corinthians an opportunity to formulate an answer, Paul offers another conditional statement that answers the question: . . . **unless** (Gk. *ean mē;* lit. "if I don't" or "except that"). Paul leads his audience from problem to solution with this style. Clearly, Paul is not conducting a neutral discussion.

One may infer what kinds of utterance Paul has in mind when he names **revelation or knowledge or prophecy or word of instruction** by studying these same words in a variety of contexts in Paul's letters; but the way Paul lists the words in a running fashion ("or . . . or . . . or . . . or") seems to form a conceptual cluster naming forms of intelligible speech rather than indicating distinct kinds of addresses.

14:7–10 / Watson (*First Epistle,* p. 146) notes that what holds the three analogies (**flute or harp; trumpet;** and **languages**) together is the idea of sound. The Gk. word *phōnē* serves in all three analogies to mean "sound," but ultimately Paul's emphasis is on sensible or intelligible sound. Sound requires patterning to be understood; clarity, purpose, and meaning must be present if the gifts are to edify the congregation.

14:12 / The beginning of this verse indicates that Paul is applying or interpreting his analogies in relation to the Corinthian situation, **So it is with you.** The application of the analogies is made with great force, **Since you are eager to have spiritual gifts . . .**, with Paul literally saying, "Since you are zealots *of spirits* [Gk. *pneumatōn*], be zealous in order that you may abound to the upbuilding of the church!" Paul's phraseology is peculiar, and Fee (*Epistle*, p. 666) suggests that rather than indicating a zeal for spiritual gifts, Paul's choice of words indicates the Corinthians' singular pursuit of one particular gift to be manifested in their diverse spirits, viz., tongues.

§40 The Desirability of Intelligibility (1 Cor. 14:13–19)

This is the second of Paul's two deliberations in support of his thesis in 14:1–5. Paul explains that tongues should be interpreted and that prophecy is to be preferred over tongues, since prophecy benefits others whereas tongues edify only the person speaking.

14:13 / Paul bluntly, in an explanatory rhetorical style, introduces his ensuing argument against a sheer enthusiasm that would be indistinguishable from self-serving ecstasy. The verse functions to serve notice to the readers to listen: **For this reason.** Then comes the advice: tongue speakers should pray for the power to understand what they are saying. The implications of this advice are that it is possible that the one speaking in tongues does not understand what is said and that God may grant the tongue speaker the ability to interpret the otherwise unintelligible but divinely inspired speech.

14:14 / Paul backs his advice with a first argument that is essentially negative reasoning: Tongue speaking releases the **mind** from full control of the self so that the **spirit** (the spirit of the person) **prays** in a direct address to God that God will understand. At the same time, Paul says, this means that the mind of the one praying is **unfruitful.** Paul's statement is clear, although his reference to this practice is mysterious because of the mystical disposition of the practice. To restate the matter positively, Paul assumes that in typical prayer one's mind stays engaged, but in tongue speaking one moves to a level of religious experience closer to ecstasy where the mind is "standing outside."

14:15 / Paul now asks about the value of such religious practice. He challenges the readers to decide the matter through a rhetorical question: **So what shall I do?** Then, he immediately answers to avoid a wrong conclusion: Paul will do both! He **will**

pray and **sing with** his **spirit, but also** he will pray and sing with his **mind.** The believer is not confronted in Paul's deliberation with a strict either-or decision. The matter is more complex, and so Paul continues to explain.

14:16 / In a second argument, Paul pictures an imaginary situation to make the point that the concern for others, both Christians and non-Christians, orients the practicing Christian enthusiast and grounds enthusiasm in sensible reality. Paul refers to the other person, who in his imaginary situation is not a practicing charismatic Christian, with the words, **one who finds himself among those who do not understand**—more literally, "the one holding the place of the uninitiated" or perhaps "the one occupying the place of the inquirers." This designation can refer to laypersons, of undefined status, who are not a full part of the Christian worship. Paul's point is this: such persons cannot and will not understand tongue speaking.

14:17 / Paul's ultimate missiological attitude shines through in an unambiguous statement of concern—and the need for concern—for others. There is a certain sarcasm in his statement, **You may be giving thanks well enough,** which comes from the frustrating results of such spectacular practice of spiritual gifts, **but the other** [person] **is not edified.** Religious practice that serves only the self is not inherently wrong, but in certain circumstances it is not the best activity.

14:18 / In a third argument, Paul uses his own religious practice as an example and in support of his argument for the appropriate practice of **tongues** *and* prophecy. He reports his own practice of tongues in a bold way, **I speak in tongues more than all of you;** but he makes this statement as a backdrop for once again stating his clear preference for prophecy (v. 19). He speaks in tongues and is thankful to God for it; moreover, he is vigorous in his practice. This report might lead the reader to expect Paul to place a high value on tongues, but as he clearly indicates, he prefers the value of prophecy in the church.

14:19 / Despite the avid tongue speaking that Paul reported in verse 18, he now enters an all-important qualification: **But in the church.** Although Paul did engage in speaking in tongues, he says in church he preferred that which makes clear sense to **others.** From these statements one infers that Paul practiced glossolalia privately, though he does not impose such a restriction on the Corinthians' speaking in tongues. Nevertheless, the degree of Paul's preference of prophecy over tongues is clear from the numbers he articulates: five intelligible words (lit. "five words with the mind") are better **than ten thousand words in a tongue**—odds of two thousand to one!

Additional Notes §40

14:13 / In 14:12 Paul had admonished the Corinthians to "try to excel in gifts that build up the church." Now he writes directly in relation to that admonition, indicating his purposefulness in explaining the ensuing specific instructions by beginning this verse, **For this reason** (Gk. *Dio*). Thus, the reader knows clearly that Paul is about to inform the Corinthians about excelling in edification. Paul gives instruction to the one speaking in tongues in a combined imperative and purpose clause, lit. "let him pray in order that he may interpret."

14:14 / Paul's phrase, **my spirit** (Gk. *to pneuma mou*), generates discussion among interpreters concerning his point of reference. Fee (*Epistle*, pp. 669–70) notes and discusses this verse as "a very difficult sentence in the middle of this argument." As Watson (*First Epistle*, p. 147) observes, "The expression . . . is sometimes used by Paul in an inclusive sense to refer to my whole being, being equivalent to 'me' (see e.g. II Cor. 2.13; cf. Gal. 6.18). More fundamentally, however, it refers to myself as capable of relationship with God (see e.g. Rom. 1.9; 8.16)." Both observations are correct, but Paul is not likely trying to make a self-revelatory declaration. Thus, the reader should not take Paul's example at this point in reference to himself with utter literalness. Paul can and does use references to himself in an illustrative fashion that does little more than set up an idealized or exemplary figure. The reference here is not concerned with Paul's own practice except as it illustrates a general truth that he is attempting to teach the Corinthians.

14:15 / The reference to praying and singing is the result of Paul's concern with worship; he is naming two prominent activities that typified the worship of early Christianity wherein one might expect to encounter a manifestation of God's Spirit in the spirit of the worshipers. Paul's own enthusiasm and mysticism still escape the reflection of some theologians who insist on reducing Paul's spirituality to something more rational and less genuinely charismatic than Paul himself describes his religious experience to be: e.g., G. J. Sirks ("The Cinderella of Theology: The Doctrine of the Holy Spirit," *HTR* 50 [1957], pp. 77–89), nearly equates prophecy with christological exegesis of the OT. Sirks's emphasis on the reception of the Spirit in the congregation as a whole, not merely by individuals, is itself a helpful corrective to overemphasis on individual spirituality.

14:16 / In Gk. this verse begins with the word "otherwise" *(epei)*, which the NIV leaves untranslated. This small omission obscures the easy recognition of Paul's logical turn back to the problem with uninterpreted tongues in order to advance the argument that the mind of the worshipers should preferably remain active for the benefit of the full congregation. There is a real danger that a worshiper lost in the Spirit/spirit may lose the capacity to communicate to others the significance of the presence and the power of the Spirit at work among them. That Paul intends to address the Corinthians as individuals at worship in this and v. 17 is clear, for he writes to **you** (sing. pronoun Gk. *sy*) and uses the second-person singular forms of the verbs.

Interpreters debate to whom Paul is referring with the word *idiōtēs* (NIV = **who do not understand;** lit. "unlearned, uninitiated, outsider, nonexpert, ordinary person"). Does he mean to name inquirers who are not Christians, or does he refer to nontongue speakers? Part of the complication is the appearance of the word in the larger phrase, **one who finds himself among those who do not understand.** Fortunately, the word *idiōtēs* occurs again in v. 23, and in the context of this overall discussion, the two uses of the word suggest that Paul means to refer to other Christians who hear the tongue speaker but do not understand the speech. Thus, the NIV wisely translates here and at v. 23 **who do not understand** (cf. the marginal note recognizing that "among the inquirers" may be another translation). This rendering expresses Paul's own ambiguous usage but leans toward recognizing the other Christians at the point of reference.

14:17 / Paul continues to address the Corinthians as individuals at worship, **you** (sing.). The combination of Gk. words *men gar . . . alla* ("for . . . no doubt, but") is cavalier in tone, slightly disdainful or sarcastic. The language confronts the Corinthians in their individualistic spiritual self-satisfaction. By contrast, Paul speaks of the edification of **the other,** using a representative male-singular form that would have been understood to refer to others, both men and women.

14:19 / When Paul states that he would **rather speak five intelligible words,** he writes, "I wish five words with my mind to speak." This mentally aware or engaged speaking is not devoid of the Spirit, however; rather, one should understand that Paul is referring to Spirit-inspired, mindful speech such as prophecy (see 14:14–15).

§41 The Effect of Intelligibility (1 Cor. 14:20–25)

Paul advances the discussion of the value and liability of the practice of tongues, marshaling a consistent case for the Corinthians to cultivate and consummate the gift of prophecy in the life of the church. The language and concerns in verses 20–25 are reminiscent of those in 2:6 and 3:1. Readers of the letter and expert interpreters alike find this portion of chapter 14 difficult to follow, however, and various scholars have offered a variety of interpretive suggestions concerning the logic of these lines.

There are two basic schools of thought on how best to interpret verses 20–25. C. H. Talbert (*Reading*, pp. 87–91) is at the forefront of those commentators who have argued that Paul begins these lines by referring to a statement by the Corinthians. He explains this first in their own terms and then refutes it in his own language. According to this solution, Paul first cites an assertion in verses 21–22 that the Corinthians themselves are making. The Corinthians have cited selected verses from Isaiah in defense of their practice of tongues; then, they have interpreted the OT text to mean that tongues are a sign (i.e., something meant to convince them) for unbelievers, not believers, whereas prophecy is a sign for believers, not unbelievers. Paul himself responds to this Corinthian argument in verses 23–25, where he reverses their logic: Tongues in the assembly will not point unbelievers to God but will baffle them. It is prophecy that will convince them of the presence of God.

This solution is based on observations and hypotheses about Paul's rhetoric, which at best is not fully clear. Talbert's reading of this problematic passage is both attractive and useful, but it presupposes a mental and rhetorical dexterity of which many readers (including the present one) would be incapable, especially given that the text does not contain clear rhetorical signals.

Thus, while Talbert's reading is possible, the following commentary takes another interpretive line and focuses on the meaning of "sign." The understanding or misunderstanding of this word in verse 22—"sign" (Gk. *sēmeion*)—determines the sense of this section. Readers of the NT are familiar with the references to "signs" in the Synoptic Gospels as well as the Gospel according to John and perhaps with other uses also. In John in particular, there is a significant positive meaning for this word: Jesus did signs, and through those signs his disciples came to believe in him. Other uses of the word "sign" are not so purely positive—Mark 8:11 states that "the Pharisees came and . . . asked for a sign from heaven" to test Jesus, not necessarily a noble cause. In Mark 8:12 a rather disgusted Jesus sighs and says, "Why does this generation ask for a miraculous sign? I tell you the truth, no sign will be given to this generation."

Paul himself seldom uses the word "sign." The readers of Paul's letters encounter the word only at Romans 4:11; 15:19; 1 Corinthians 1:22; 14:22; 2 Corinthians 12:12; and 2 Thessalonians 2:9; 3:17. In every place other than this passage, Paul's use of the word "sign" seems neutral. It refers to a clear indication of God's presence, power, and will. Nevertheless, exactly what such a "sign" means is determined only in context. One can find "signs" (NIV: "distinguishing mark") or indicators of God's approval and disapproval, of salvation and wrath—as one would expect in Paul's apocalyptic-eschatological point of view. Thus, it is best to allow the text of 1 Corinthians 14 to inform us of the meaning of the word "sign." According to the line that Paul cites from Isaiah, God speaks "in other tongues . . . of other ones . . . to this people, and even so they do not hear. . . ." Paul says this line explains the sign: Speech in other tongues produces no hearing or comprehension! The sign is the failure to hear—an odd notion, but no odder than Jesus' words in Mark 4:12, also citing Isaiah, " . . . so that they may indeed see but not perceive, and may hear but not understand; lest they should turn again, and be forgiven" (Mark 4:12 from Isa. 6:9–10). The conclusion is that in the context, Paul means for "sign" to name a clear indication of God's power at work through the failure to comprehend what is spoken through tongues.

14:20 / Paul calls the Corinthians away from childishness—perhaps meaning a fascination with things that dazzle—to maturity. The reader can recall Paul's own idealized first-person statement in 13:11. Here he literally calls for them to "become perfect" or "complete ones," although the plain sense of the admonition is "Grow up!" Moreover, in an aside that may be an indirect comment concerning his opinion of what all the problems in Corinth amount to, Paul expresses his desire that they be naive in terms of evil.

14:21 / Paul refers to "the law" (Gk. *nomos*), a designation most often applied to the books of Moses, and then quotes Isaiah 28:11–12 LXX as a text on the topic of tongues. The citation is a very loose paraphrase that alters vocabulary, word order, subjects, and verbs alike, since the original passage in Isaiah referred to foreign languages, not to glossolalia. The alterations are typical of the way Paul cites Scripture on occasion, probably from memory, and the slight changes are sensible tailoring of the text to the Corinthians' context. Above all, one should see that Paul finds in Isaiah a scriptural precedent for his position, and the citation leads into his next statements. In Isaiah the **strange tongues** were a sign of God's judgment against the people because of their disobedience in ignoring Isaiah's own intelligible words; for Paul the problem with tongues is that they are unintelligible and so obscure God's clear message. The text of Isaiah becomes the groundwork for Paul's comments, which are offered as exegesis of the text, but more, an explanation of the situation in Corinth.

14:22 / Verses 22–25 are difficult, as noted above. The wording and grammar of Paul's lines are clear, but many readers find that the content of the statements is itself hard to follow. Verse 22 states a principle and claims to exegete the cited biblical passage by beginning with the explanatory word **then** (Gk. *hōste*, lit. "so then"), which the NIV obscures by placing it as the second word in the sentence. Working from the citation Paul concludes that **tongues . . . are a sign, not for believers but for unbelievers;** whereas **prophecy . . . is for believers, not for unbelievers.** The way forward in this application is clear only when one recognizes that the sign or the indication of God's work here is the negative effect of the people's not hearing God's message (since it is hidden in the strange tongues), just as they did not hear God's message in the passage from Isaiah. The sign shows that God's message was not heard: the people are baffled. It is not necessary, and Paul does not understand, that a true sign must produce some purely positive effect. In Isaiah God declared that people would speak in strange tongues and those hearing would not listen to or understand the tongues. For Paul, when the

Corinthians spoke in tongues, it produced a sign consistent with the words of Isaiah. In both instances people heard others talking and did not understand and were not persuaded. Paul's argument seems odd only if one takes sign in the sense of a positive outcome where those hearing understand and believe.

14:23 / Paul develops the picture he is painting by building on the lead he established in verse 22. Now, he says, given that the whole church assembles and all speak in tongues and the uninitiated or unbelievers enter, what should one expect to occur? In keeping with the sense Paul made of Isaiah, he explains that the uninitiated will say that the tongue speaking believers are raving mad.

14:24 / In turn, he takes the imaginary scenario even further. Introducing a shift of focus with the words **but if,** Paul begins to recount a new and different development. This scene and the results of what takes place are not the direct outworkings of the text of Isaiah, but Paul uses his imagination in relationship to the circumstances in Corinth to show how the converse situation would appear. He proposes that all the Corinthian believers are prophesying and the uninitiated enter. Then the uninitiated **will be convinced by all that he is a sinner and will be judged by all** (lit. "is convicted by all and held accountable by all").

14:25 / Paul elaborates the result of this hypothetical turn of events in dramatic, energetic, descriptive phrases. The unbeliever who is moved by the practice of prophecy among the believers will, first, be stripped of all pretense and shame **(the secrets of his heart will be laid bare)** and, second, will **worship God** and say that **God is really among** the believers.

In seeking to understand 14:20–25, readers have to make a decision between the line of reasoning offered by Talbert and the understanding of the passage suggested in the commentary above. (It is even possible to conclude that Paul misstated his thinking or that his secretary misheard him.) While either reading makes plausible sense of the text, my contention is that the difference between the straightforward sense of verse 22b (read without my proposed interpretation of v. 22a) and verses 24–25 is problematic. If one reads the passage in line with my suggestions—that for Paul, "sign" in verse 22a means "that which is (positive or negative) evidence of the power, will, and work of God"—one sees some sense emerge from this strange sequence of statements. In any case, however, the general sense of Paul's remarks in the letter makes it clear that at this point he is marshaling still another argument for the preferable nature of prophecy in comparison with tongues in the context of worship.

Additional Notes §41

Talbert (*Reading*, p. 89) offers a most helpful analysis of the constitution of prophecy. His summary is as follows:

> This early Christian prophecy was not just preaching and teaching but was regarded as a supernatural gift. According to Paul, it was a gift given to an individual (1 Cor 14:30); it had a spontaneous quality (14:30); it did not force one to speak against one's will (14:30, 32a); it enabled the prophet to know something from a divine perspective (14:24–25); it functioned for evangelism (14:24–25), for upbuilding, encouragement, and consolation of the church (14:3), as well as for learning (14:31); it was to cease at the parousia (13:8, 10).

Moreover, in his treatment of this passage, Talbert acknowledges the insightful work on these verses of ch. 14 by B. C. Johanson, "Tongues, a Sign for Unbelievers? A Structural and Exegetical Study of I Corinthians xiv.20–25," *NTS* 25 (1979), pp. 180–203.

14:20 / Paul's call for the Corinthians to be **adults** employs the Gk. word *teleios*, which occurred in 2:6 and 13:10. The word functions to mean "adult" as compared with the **children** who are also mentioned in this verse. The connotation of the Gk. word is "maturity, completion, wholeness" and sometimes "perfection."

14:21 / Paul's citation of a text from the OT, Isa. 28:11–12, becomes the basis for a brief expository sermon that follows in vv. 22–25. Verse 22 seems to state the interpretation of the quotation that then leads into the observations and directions that Paul issues in vv. 24–25. In citing Isaiah, however, Paul does work small changes, paraphrasing the original text. The liberties Paul seems to take with the text of the OT are apparently the result of his applying the text to the particulars of the Corinthian situation.

14:22 / The way Paul refers to **believers** and **unbelievers** is remarkable, since he uses a participial form *(hoi pisteuontes)* meaning "the ones believing" for **believers,** but he names the **unbelievers** with an adjective *(apistos)* that means "unbelieving [person]." There is a hint of an action in the way Paul refers to **believers,** while there is recognition of a characteristic in the reference to **unbelievers.** This pattern of reference may be purely incidental or even traditional; nevertheless, the method of naming the two groups is not directly comparable. In paraphrase one might compare "the ones having faith" and "the ones without faith."

Another slant on reading this seemingly confusing passage attempts to make sense of the issue of believers, unbelievers, and the relationship of the two: W. Grudem, "1 Corinthians 14.20–25: Prophecy and Tongues as Signs of God's Attitude," *WTJ* 41 (1979), pp. 381–96. Grudem contends that Paul understands tongues to be a sign of God's judgment on unbelief, but Paul does not want the Corinthians to give this discouraging sign to the unbelievers in their midst.

14:23 / Paul paints a vivid picture of unbelievers concluding that tongue speaking Christians **are out of** [their] **mind;** the form of the words means "you are raving mad."

14:24 / At this point in the translation of Paul's letter, the NIV introduces the words **that he is a sinner,** apparently from the theological imagination of the translators. Nothing in the text or in any variant warrants this addition. Fee tries to explain the presence of these words by suggesting that "lying behind the word 'convicted' is the OT view that one is exposed before the living God through the prophetic word; inherent in such 'exposure' is the call to repentance, the summons to have one's exposed sins forgiven by a merciful God" (*Epistle,* p. 696). Be that as it may, one can see that Paul's statement is **judged by all** implies some diagnosis and prescription. Even so, the addition of whole interpretive phrases is not precise translation. It is possible that Paul meant to say that the unbeliever would be positively convicted by the real presence of God among the Christians at worship.

14:25 / Orr and Walther (*I Corinthians,* p. 304) suggest that the statement **"God is really among you!"** is probably Paul's adaptation of similar declarations found in Isa. 45:14; Dan. 2:47; Zech. 8:23.

§42 Protocol for Practicing Spiritual Gifts (1 Cor. 14:26–33a)

Paul steps back from a strict focus on prophecy and tongues in verses 26–33a as he considers more generally the practice of Christian worship. Essentially, Paul delineates regulations for orderly assembly and worship. Behind all the particular instructions about worship practices, however, is the basic theme Paul sets out at the end of verse 26, "All of these things must be done for the strengthening of the church."

14:26 / The modern reader of Paul's letter gains a glimpse into the worship of the early church in the initial lines of this verse. Paul refers to specific elements of early Christian worship: **a hymn, or a word of instruction, a revelation, a tongue or an interpretation.** Paul's Greek is telling at this point: **Hymn** is *psalmos,* perhaps a reference to the use of the Psalms in the life of the early church; **instruction** is *didachē,* indicating teaching of all kinds; **revelation** is *apokalypsis,* a form of eschatological teaching that implied a special communication from God and that some scholars suggest may have included the phenomenon of prophecy; **tongue** is *glōssa,* in this context a reference to inspired speech that was directed from the speaker to God but that was unintelligible to other human listeners; **interpretation** is *hermēneia* (as in Hermes, the message-bearing god), a gift that complemented tongues by explaining the tongue speaking for the edification of the church.

Paul's encouraging words are not complete without important qualification. In fact, the principle he articulates validates the activities of worship. All of these worshipful activities must produce edification for the entire congregation.

14:27–28 / Having called for active participation in worship and for all worship to contribute to the strengthening of the church, Paul issues further, specific regulations that restrict the practice of tongues. According to his directions, tongue speaking was to be limited to two or three tongue speakers per assembly. He insists that there must be someone present who can interpret the tongues for the benefit of the congregation. Furthermore, Paul adamantly adds that when no interpreter is present, the ones gifted with tongues must restrict themselves to practicing tongues only in private communication with God. Without interpretation glossolalia is unintelligible and therefore useless, and, as he described in the previous verses, uninterpreted tongues in a disorderly presentation might cause observers to think that the congregation is crazy.

14:29 / By this point in the correspondence, Paul's preference for prophecy over tongues in the setting of worship is indisputable. Nevertheless, he regulates the practice of prophecy in worship in much the same way that he regulates the practice of tongues. Two or three prophets may speak in a single assembly, and when listening to the prophecy **the others should weigh carefully what is said.** But who are the others? Paul may mean that the other prophets are to evaluate the words of the prophets who speak, or he may mean that the rest of the congregation should assess what the prophets bring to the worship of the congregation.

Since in this letter Paul exhorts the entire congregation to desire to practice the gift of prophecy, it is unlikely that he assumed prophecy to be the strict prerogative of a special group. Prophecy was for the good of the whole church, so it seems most likely that Paul is telling the entire church to practice active listening when the prophets speak. The prophets do not speak as tongue speakers, primarily for themselves; and their words do not await an interpreter to make them meaningful for the other members of the church. Thus, it appears that the whole church is to be involved in discerning the message(s) of the prophets.

14:30–31 / Curiously from what Paul writes in these verses, some prophecy is recognized to be more urgent than other prophecy, since at times one speaker is to yield to another. The prophets are assumed to be in control of their minds and their actions to the point of responsibility. Exactly how this process would have worked in practice is lost to later readers of the letter, although in other ancient Christian literature there are many more and more explicit regulations for the critique of prophets and prophecy. Paul is not concerned at this point with the problem of false prophecy, which occupies him in other contexts and which so bedeviled the early church that prophecy came under general suspicion and fell almost completely out of practice.

Paul is concerned with order. More than one prophet can be in communication with God at a time, and in the context of worship more than one prophet may have something to say. Paul calls for the responsible execution of decision making with regard to prophecy, exactly as he had called for the congregation to evaluate the messages brought to them (v. 29). Prophecy was prized, but it did not have a privileged status that put it beyond sensible standards for the general life of the church. Verse 31 extends the direction of the previous lines. Nevertheless, in elaborating this point, Paul specifically reiterates his ultimate concern for the Corinthians: **so that everyone may be instructed and encouraged.**

14:32 / This verse is also difficult to grasp on a first reading. Paul means either "each prophet controls the spiritual gift he or she possesses" or "one who prophesies is subject to evaluation by other prophets who are present." Given that 12:10 recognizes discerning the spirits as an identifiable gift of the Spirit and Paul's emphasis in 14:13–19 on the importance of mind and spirit working in conjunction with each other and Paul's stated assumption (and expectation) that tongue speakers can limit their expression to instances when interpreters are present, the first option seems most likely. That is, a prophet is to assume responsibility for the legitimate use of the gift of prophecy. The prophet is not assumed to be in a trance, and Paul has encouraged congregational reaction to the prophecies, probably including discussion, so that the prophets are to govern their employment of the gift they have been given for the good of the congregation.

14:33a / This verse both forms a summary of all that Paul has been saying about worship and serves as a bridge to what is about to follow. Paul articulates the central or most important theological conviction that underlies everything he has said and will say: **for God is not a God of disorder but of peace.** Order is understood by Paul to be the very nature of God, and so whatever God is doing should result in order; humans should be aware of this reality.

Additional Notes §42

14:26 / The form of Paul's sentence, indeed the opening phrase that forms the question **What then shall we say?** is the same as the opening phrase of v. 15, which was translated, "So what shall I do?" In both cases the Gk. *(ti oun estin)* means, "How therefore is it?" The NIV applies the sense of this question to the different verses in light of the particular subjects of the ensuing sentences. The parallel form of the question does make a rhetorical connection between the questions and forms a kind of refrain as Paul pursues his complicated arguments.

The manner in which the NIV proceeds after this point is questionable, although not an issue of enormous weight. The NIV's rendering of Paul's words **When you come together, everyone has . . .** is confusing. Does everyone do everything? Paul's Gk. is much clearer, saying, "When you [pl.] come together, *each one* has . . ." Paul expects that one by one each person will contribute one item to the worship.

14:28 / Paul's statement **If there is no interpreter . . .** is stronger in Gk. than the NIV's translation indicates. Paul uses the mildly adversative conjunction "but" (Gk. *de*) at the beginning of this statement to coordinate and juxtapose the remarks in vv. 27–28.

14:29 / Paul's concern, expressed in the form of a double command, is that **prophets should speak** and **the others should** discern or **weigh carefully.** The identity of the others was discussed in the commentary above, but what should be seen in this compound command is that prophecy, a matter of supreme importance and divine inspiration, should not drop into the middle of the life of a congregation as an unquestioned word of God. Paul insists that those hearing the prophets listen and evaluate what they hear. This dynamic operation of prophecy in the life of the church precludes some special persons assuming an authoritative role and requires responsibility of those to whom the prophets speak.

14:30 / The translation **And if a revelation comes to someone . . .** roughly captures the sense of Paul's own words, which more literally say, "But if to another a revelation is made." Revelation is not, despite the NIV, an independent operation. Someone—God—makes a revelation or reveals something to someone. Divine initiative is in Paul's mind as he makes this statement; the initiative of God in working with the one who receives the revelation demands the attention of the others, who should honor God's work and make way for it. For Paul, one's getting a revelation is not as important as God's giving the revelation.

14:31 / The degree of concern in the early church with prophecy and with discerning authentic and inauthentic revelation is seen in the *Didache*, a second-century church handbook that claims to be a collection of teachings by the twelve apostles on issues of relevance to the ancient church. In chs. 10–13 of the *Didache* there are extensive observations and elaborate instructions for dealing with prophets and prophecy. Paul's words here are the earliest preserved discussion of this phenomenon in the life of the church, but the topic became a matter of importance as prophecy flourished and was badly abused. Paul's letters and Acts all demonstrate that there were false prophets and bogus prophecy from the very first years of Christianity.

14:32 / The verb translated **are subject to the control** (Gk. *hypotassō*) is the same as the verb translated "be in submission" in v. 34. Here, Paul is explicit that **the spirits of the prophets** are in submission to the **prophets.** For a helpful comparative description of Greco-Roman, Hebrew, and early Christian prophets and prophecy that sets 1 Cor. 14 in its own rich historical context, see T. Callan, "Prophecy and Ecstasy in Greco-Roman Religion and in 1 Corinthians," *NovT* 27 (1985), pp. 125–40.

14:33a / The reason for breaking this verse at this point is explained in the materials that follow on v. 33b.

§43 Women and Order at Worship (1 Cor. 14:33b–36)

These verses follow the summary or bridge statement that Paul made at the beginning of verse 33, a declaration that looks back to the previous discussion of Christian worship and probably looks ahead to this next section of the letter. The traditional versification of the text is a problem, for the majority of contemporary English-language translations understand that the concluding words of verse 33 should be read as a phrase leading into the next portion of Paul's reflection, whereas the verse numbers suggest including the words "as in all the congregations of the saints" with the immediately prior phrase, "For God is not a God of disorder but of peace. . . ." The commentary below will deal with the matter of the versification, but prior to that detailed analysis, one should recognize that verses 33b–36 must be among the NT verses that have caused the most difficulty at the turn of the twenty-first century. Several basic exegetical issues inherent in the verses pose difficult problems for skilled interpreters, but these complex interpretive issues are exacerbated and at times superseded by equally complex religious and sociological factors. Thus, some preliminary observations are in order. Any discussion of women's participation or speaking in the course of worship must take into consideration comments that already occurred in chapter 11, even though the concerns of chapter 11 are somewhat different in focus than those of chapter 14. In general, in chapter 11 the focus was on men and women, whereas here, as verse 35 indicates, the issue almost certainly concerns husbands and wives. In particular, at 11:6 one finds that it is "a disgrace" (Gk. *aischron;* lit. "shameful") for a woman to be shorn, but in 14:35 it is "disgraceful" (Gk. *aischron*) for a wife to speak in church. Nevertheless, how can a woman or wife pray or prophesy in church when veiled (11:6) if she is to remain silent in the church? Other issues of language and textual criticism (treated below) make the interpretation of this section even more complicated!

What can be made of the evidence? Although there have been literally dozens of suggestions concerning the interpretation of these verses—ranging from the sensible to the silly—there are four options for understanding the lines. The first explanation could be that Paul wrote these lines as they are and that these verses are meant to be taken at face value. Indeed, the shift of focus from men and women to husbands and wives may provide a key, indicating that Paul is advocating the preservation of traditional Jewish patterns of family relations, although this understanding is problematic since Paul writes to Corinth, which is not a Semitic social context. Thus they would be expressing a timeless principle correctly applied to all women in all churches. The problem with this conclusion is that it fails to grapple with the incompatibility of the plain sense of these lines and other statements made by Paul in this and other undisputed letters.

The second explanation, increasingly popular among both conservative and radical scholars, is that 14:34–35 is an interpolation, that is, material accidentally inserted into Paul's original text by a scribe. Perhaps this was originally an early scribe's comment in the margin. A strong case for this option can be based on the unusual character of the language and the textual problems associated with these verses: verses 34–35 are transposed to a position after 14:40 in some few and inferior manuscripts. While the manuscript evidence is not strong, it does show both some scribes dealing with the illogical intrusion of these verses in the discussion of worship from the perspective of tongues and prophecy (two specific forms of verbal expression) and the scribal recognition of a naturally smoother transition from 14:33a to 14:36. The burden of proof for omitting these verses lies with those making such an argument (e.g., Fee), and C. H. Talbert shows the problems with attempting to omit the lines from Paul's letter to Corinth. While this position resolves the difficulty of fitting these lines with other statements by Paul in this letter (ch. 11), it falls short of dealing with the position stated in these lines and elsewhere in the canonical NT (1 Tim. 2:11–12).

A third, creative, sophisticated, and responsible attempt to make sense of these perplexing verses is Talbert's reading (*Reading*, pp. 91–95), which starts by contending that in verses 34–35 Paul is quoting the Corinthians' own sayings in order to refute those declarations. Thus, Talbert's argument is that the rhetorical form of the material in 14:34–35, 36 is dialogical. Talbert contends that these lines offer a position derived from general cultural values of the Greco-Roman era and the position taken in these verses runs counter to the explicit teaching of Paul elsewhere, e.g., Gal. 3:27–28; 1 Cor. 11:5, 12, including this letter. Additionally, Talbert sees Paul himself replying to, refuting, and rebutting the logic of verses 34–35 in verse 36, thus challenging and denying the view that the women should be silent in the church. A critique of Talbert's suggestion could be that Paul's rhetoric in these lines is not so clear as to signal and promote the recognition of the conversational or dialogical character of the text that Talbert suggests. In general, though, this interpretation is sensible and attractive. It deals with the text as we have it and makes sense of it in relation to other passages that Paul wrote in his letters.

A fourth explanation is that these lines come from Paul but are not meant as a universal directive. Rather, Paul is writing in relation to a specific practice that is disrupting the worship of the Corinthian congregation; the exact circumstances are obscure, although Paul and the Corinthians know precisely to what he refers. The verses may refer to disruptive behavior that resulted from pagan ecstasy being imported into the context of Christian worship. If Paul is writing to address such a specific problem, then his advice applies only to this situation and is not meant to be followed elsewhere. There are other statements in Paul's correspondences that assume first-hand knowledge of a situation and require later readers to infer and even to speculate to understand (see 5:1–5, 9–11; 15:29 in this letter, or 2 Cor. 2:5–11; 11:12–15; 12:7–8; Gal. 5:11–12; Phil. 3:2; Phlm. 18).

The lack of specific information about the situation(s) Paul faced in Corinth may make it impossible for later readers of the letter to determine conclusively the meaning of these lines, even if they do come from Paul. Paul's rhetoric could be much clearer if he intended for the verses to function as a timeless principle for how women are to behave in worship settings. The only way to progress toward Paul's meaning is by tracking the path set by the passage itself.

14:33b / Problems for interpretation begin with the basic issue of recognizing which words are parts of which sentences. At the beginning of verse 33 one finds an explanatory phrase, **For . . .** (Gk. *gar . . .*), which follows the preceding statements about prophecy and order in verses 29–32, perhaps even relating to the full discussion of tongues and prophecy from verses 27–32. After the words **For God is not a God of disorder but of peace,** one encounters a phrase beginning with the word **as** (Gk. *hōs*), which is normally used to form or to introduce a comparison, As **in all the congregations of the saints.** Taking this phrase with either the preceding line about God (v. 33a) or the following statement about **women** (v. 34) is somewhat awkward. The traditional versification results from the understanding of verse 33a and verse 33b as a complete sentence, "For God is not of confusion but of peace, as in all the churches of the saints." Nevertheless, the NIV (in agreement with NA[27]; see also the RSV, NRSV, REB, and other contemporary translations) connects the phrase in verse 33b with the following lines: **As in all the congregations of the saints, women should remain silent.** Both readings are possible. As Orr and Walther (*I Corinthians*, pp. 311–12) note, however, "custom is directly applicable to the activity of women in the church but is more difficult to relate to God's peace role." Ambiguity is certain, and a decision about coordinating the phrase **(As . . . saints)** with either verse 33a or verse 34 alters the nuance of Paul's remark, but ultimately how one reads the phrase does not determine the understanding of the overall sense of the passage. The phrase does seem to fit less awkwardly with verse 34, so that one finds a reference to church custom and then an example of it in the mention of women's silence.

Another problem for interpreting this section is that the phrase "the churches of the saints" in verse 33b is peculiar. There is no such designation in the context of the undisputed Pauline letters. Rather, churches are referred to as the church(es) of God or Christ and as the church(es) of a region or city. Thus, divine proprietorship and geographical setting are the normal ways of identifying Pauline congregations. The peculiarity of the statement in verse 33b complicates decisions about the origin and purpose of both these particular words and other statements made in connection with this phrase. No ready solution for the full range of problems is at hand, so verse 33b remains a problem in its own right.

14:34–35 / These two verses are distinct sentences in Greek, but for a number of reasons it proves expedient to treat the statements in the verses together in commentary. Above all, the coherent command to silence in verses 34–35 seems to contradict the expectation that women would be praying and prophesying, albeit while veiled, in chapter 11. Interpreters attempt to minimize or eliminate this problem in various ways. There is a great deal of speculation about the kind of speech that Paul is forbidding in verses 34–35. Some suggest that he opposes only idle chatter or gossip. However, the verb **to speak** (Gk. *lalein*) is not, as some commentators suggest, equivalent with "to chatter." The verb does not name an activity that is distinct from other sensible speech or prayer or prophecy. Through the rest of chapter 14 "to speak" clearly and consistently refers to inspired speech (see vv. 2, 3, 4, 5, 6, 9, 11, 13, 18, 19, 21, 23, 27, 28, 29, 39). The vocabulary employed in these verses does not distinguish this reference from all other mentions of speaking in this and other chapters.

By observing the focus on women in chapter 11 in contrast to a proposed focus on wives in chapter 14, some commentators suggest that Paul's remarks here apply only to wives, not to all women. This reading is possible as the argument develops in the middle sections of verses 34–35, **. . . but must be in submission as the Law says. If they want to inquire about something, they should ask their own husbands at home . . .** ; but it ultimately makes little sense to suggest that Paul divided women into two classes and discriminated between them in his treatment of the groups. Nothing in Paul's discussion of marriage and remaining single in chapter 7 prepares for such a division and such differentiation.

Moreover, the reason given for the silence of the women, that they should be "in submission, as the Law says," is problematic. There is no such prescription or prohibition in the law, and no text is cited here from the OT as is the case in all other Pauline references to the law in his letters. As Fee (*Epistle,* p. 707) notes, the appeal by some interpreters to Genesis 3:16 is not persuasive, since that text does not say what is argued, even in the most indirect way, in verses 34–35. Other attempts to argue from either materials of later rabbinic Judaism or references in Josephus are equally problematic to reconcile with Paul. One can only wonder which law is the point of reference here; perhaps Paul is not referring to the OT at all.

In turn, the directions for women or wives to ask their husbands at home should they desire to inquire about something is odd. One can only wonder why that domestic environment takes precedence over being **in the church,** which is the one place about which Paul cares most. Read one way, this piece of instruction puts a private human domain above the new corporate spiritual realm that Paul understands to be the locus of God's Spirit's most powerful presence and action. One wonders if there is an unseen, irrecoverable issue at work that prevents later readers from clearly comprehending these remarks.

As was mentioned in the introduction to this section, there are a number of options to understanding 14:33b–36. All of these hinge on various interpretations of verses 34–35. This could be an instruction from Paul to women to avoid a certain type of speech in the church. Perhaps verses 34–35 are a non-Pauline scribal interpolation into this part of Paul's letter to Corinth, although it is difficult to see what would have brought this obscure remark into this otherwise focused discussion of tongues and prophecy. Perhaps Paul is awkwardly quoting and responding to a position that the Corinthians had developed; perhaps they distinguished between wives and other women in worship. Or, it is possible that Paul was addressing a specific problem in Corinth that has no real application today. One finally cannot decide from the evidence available which of the several suggestions for interpretation is absolutely correct.

14:36 / The lines of verse 36 become all the more important in trying to understand the previous statements because of the significant uncertainties inherent in verses 34–35. Here at least, Paul's words and rhetoric are clear. The verse comprises two rhetorical questions, and in tone the questions are emphatic, even sarcastic. The form of both questions indicates that they could be answered either positively or negatively, but the telltale word **only** indicates which answer Paul expects. Quite literally Paul writes, "Did either the word of God go forth from you? Or, did it reach you *alone* (NIV: only)?"

The only sensible response to both inquiries is no, an emphatic no! Thus, one thing is clear: the Corinthian congregation is not alone in receiving and hearing God's word. They should not attempt to stand alone in trying to bring God's will into reality. This fact requires the reader to cast whatever this passage means into the broader context of the revelation and reception of the gospel. Taken in that way, there is but one sure conclusion to be drawn about these verses. The arguments in verses 33b, 34–35, and verse 36 are—whatever they mean— based purely on custom and the law, not on revelation or a word of the Lord. The character of the remarks gives the statements a restricted force. Thus, of our four options for understanding these verses, the first option—that these verses limit the speech of all women in all churches—is unviable. It is astounding that this particular reading of these difficult, enigmatic verses, coupled with one reading of 1 Timothy 2, became the church's norm. In contrast to this reading one finds both declarations and assumptions about women (some of whom were wives, e.g., Prisca) taking active roles of leadership in the life of the early church (in 1 Cor. 11:11–12; Gal. 3:28; and in the regular mentioning by Paul of prominent Christian women ministers in his letters).

Additional Notes §43

14:34–35 / The range of suggestions for interpreting these lines was generally covered above, although Watson (*First Epistle,* p. 154) adds another often-encountered twist to the problem of dealing with these verses with the following observation:

> If [the verses] are the work of Paul, then we must decide which position is truer to the gospel of Jesus Christ, the position stated in these verses or the position affirmed in Gal. 3.28, according to which there is in Christ *no such thing as Jew or Greek, slave and freeman, male and female.* We cannot have it both ways, and neither can Paul.

This noble-sounding declaration may be short-sighted in that it does not really present the options available for understanding these lines, even if they did come from Paul. Given Paul's more normal pattern of writing, one can say with certainty that Paul did not restrict the role and activity of women in all the churches he founded and with which he worked. If Paul did write these lines, in light of everything else he communicated in his letters, one would probably be more prudent to assume that Paul is speaking directly to a particularly problematic group of women in a particularly problematic situation that is beyond our ability to comprehend. The situation in Corinth was dire, and Paul takes some extreme measures in this letter (cf. ch. 5). Perhaps he had no other alternative than to give harsh and abnormal directions in an aberrant situation. That we do not know all that we need to know in order to understand these lines should lead to a degree of humility in light of the limits of our knowledge.

A challenge to the traditional understanding of these lines that puts the problem of interpretation in a helpful light comes from J. M. Bassler ("1 Corinthians," pp. 327–28), who asks the following questions:

How can women like Euodia and Syntache (Phil. 4:2–3), Prisca (Rom. 16:3; 1 Cor. 16:19), Mary (Rom. 16:6), Junia (Rom. 16:7), and Tryphaena and Tryphosa (Rom. 16:12) function as co-workers in the churches if they cannot speak in those churches? How can Phoebe fulfill the role of deacon (Rom. 16:1–2) if she cannot speak out in the assembly?

As Bassler continues, "Something is seriously amiss here." The inconsistency of the collected elements of the total picture causes Bassler to conclude the words on women in vv. 34–35 are most likely a later (anonymous) marginal gloss incorporated into the words of the text of Paul's letter by a copyist.

Finally, two other contributions merit mention. One by C. Vander Stichele ("Is Silence Golden? Paul and Women's Speech in Corinth," *LS* 20 [1995], pp. 241–53) suggests reversing the dynamics by which this passage is often read. Rather than understand the speech of women in church referred to in ch. 11 as the norm and the silence of women in ch. 14 as the exception, Vander Stichele suggests that the silence should be understood as the norm and the speech, under the power of the Spirit, as the exception. The second work, by L. A. Jervis ("1 Corinthians 14.34–34: A Reconsideration of Paul's Limitation of the Free Speech of Some Corinthian Women," *JSNT* 58 [1995], pp. 51–74) contends that theories of an interpolation at this point in Paul's letter are unpersuasive, but the real sense of Paul's statement is to ensure the peaceful practice of prophecy, not to limit the speech of women in general; thus, the problem was not that the speakers were women, but that the type of speech in which the women were engaging was counterproductive.

14:36 / The assertive tone of Paul's two questions in this verse is immediately apparent from the emphatic position of the first words of the verse, "From you . . . ?" (Gk. *aph' hymōn . . .*) and the portentous placement of the initial words of the second part of the challenge, "To you . . . ?" (Gk. *eis hymas . . .*).

Some translations imply that v. 36 is attached to vv. 37–38 rather than to vv. 34–35. As Watson (*First Epistle*, p. 155) observes, however, "If vv. 34f. are accepted as a genuine word of Paul, then v. 36 is perhaps more naturally attached to those verses than to those that follow." Since Watson doubts the authenticity of vv. 34–35, his commentary associates v. 36 with the verses that follow in the letter; nevertheless, most translations and most commentators find the attachment of v. 36 to either v. 33 (omitting vv. 34–35) or vv. 34–35 to be most likely given the manner in which Paul's questions seem to take exception to a previous point. Both questions literally begin with the word "or" (Gk. *ē*). D. W. Odell-Scott ("Let the Women Speak in Church. An Egalitarian Interpretation of 1 Cor 14:33b–36," *BTB* 13 [1983], pp. 90–93) makes much of the particle *ē*, taking it as an indication that Paul is refuting the men in Corinth and what had been said as reflected in vv. 33b–35.

§44 Confrontation and Advice (1 Cor. 14:37–40)

Paul concludes his discussion of the problems in worship in Corinth with a direct challenge in verses 37–40. Paul states his point of view through the rhetoric of conditional sentences: "If this . . . then that." His language is mildly insulting both in the choice of words and in the tone. Thus, there is a confrontational character to the statements in verses 37–38, although Paul's concluding admonitions (vv. 39–40) are more neutral in expression.

14:37 / In the first conditional statement, **If anybody thinks he is a prophet . . . ,** Paul states a criterion that puts the burden of proof on anyone wishing to disagree with him: **let him acknowledge that what I am writing to you is the Lord's command.** Agreement, by contrast, would verify one as a prophet or a spiritual one. It is not clear how Paul relates his teaching to a command of the Lord, but it is clear that the point of discussion is the issue of prophecy and spiritual gifts, not the immediately preceding matter of wives speaking in church (see v. 39).

Paul's declaration that what he is teaching is the Lord's command is a bold claim. Readers should recall that in chapter 7 and in other places in his letters Paul does not hesitate to distinguish his own words from those of the Lord, even when he is facing very difficult circumstances. It is unlikely that Paul claims this authority for his teaching on prophecy and the use of spiritual gifts lightly. Thus, the readers in Corinth would understand the seriousness of Paul's point and would be forced to make a decision about the appropriateness of certain behaviors that had cropped up among them. Paul's conditional challenge forces the readers to practice spiritual discernment and recognize the validity or invalidity of particular practices of and teachings about spiritual gifts in the life of the congregation.

14:38 / In this verse, as in the preceding one, Paul issues a conditional challenge to certain members of the Corinthian congregation. His method of formulating the confronting statement is telling. He writes to an indistinct imaginary individual: "If any-body . . ." (v. 37); **If he . . .** (v. 38). The Corinthian congregation was not large, and Paul had spoken with Chloe's people and with the persons who brought the letter from the Corinthians to him. Paul could easily have ascertained the name of the person or persons who were causing problems or who were likely to resist his directions. Nevertheless, Paul writes obliquely of "anybody" and "he," not calling specific names. The effect is threefold: (1) By not singling out any one person explicitly, Paul avoids forcing anyone toward a position of shame; (2) by refusing to cite anyone specifically, Paul is also using a typical rhetorical tool employed by ancient speakers to show disdain; and (3) the passive form, **will be ignored,** suggests God's involvement in the life of the church. In other words, should someone resist or deny Paul's teaching as coming from the Lord, that person is in danger of being ignored by God because it is God whom that one is ignoring!

14:39 / Ultimately, tongues are permissible but prophecy is preferable. There is no new information here, although the way Paul explicitly forbids the forbidding of tongues may indicate his desire to preclude any further misunderstanding. Paul does not oppose tongues; rather, he wants them used in a constructive fashion. Although such religious practice was apparently highly prized by the Corinthians, Paul states and encourages a preference for prophecy because of the immediately edifying potential of such sensible communication. The good of the whole congregation sets Paul's overall priorities and causes him to see the value of one spiritual gift or another. Implicit in this value system is a profound theological truth: God is not merely redeeming the world by blessing individuals. God is at work to redeem the world by calling individuals into a new humanity, where persons find their special places as God sees fit among those whom God is calling into a new relationship with himself and with other persons.

14:40 / Thus, Paul finally states the point that he has made repeatedly and in several different ways: **Everything should be done in a fitting and orderly way.** A pedestrian reiteration of Paul's point would be: contributions to worship fit as they are complementary and edify the whole congregation; they are orderly as they bring order, not disorder, and contribute to the patterned upbuilding of the church. Such are God's ways and such is God's will (see 14:4–5, 12, 19, 26, 31, 33a).

Additional Notes §44

14:37 / Paul's claim is significant; he insists that should one regard oneself as a **prophet** or a spiritual person, then that person should recognize that Paul's message is **the Lord's command**. The gift of prophecy has been discussed throughout the chapter, and here Paul apparently has in mind a prophet's power of spiritual discernment, which he mentioned in vv. 30–31. Moreover, the word translated **spiritually gifted** in this verse is the same basic word that occurred at v. 1 in the neuter plural form, "spiritual gifts." Inherent in Paul's forthright challenge is another level of confrontation. The special spiritual gifts that are being sought by some Corinthians are evinced by the recognition that what Paul is saying is from the Lord. According to Paul's declaration, to differ with Paul would be proof that one was not a prophet or spiritually gifted. Paul places potential opponents who might claim special spiritual powers in a double bind—to disagree would be to call one's gifts into question, and to agree would be to take Paul's position as inspired and correct. This assertion is a rhetorical trap, designed to win a full hearing and compliance with the directions given, although the challenges fall in line with the directions he gave in 14:29.

Saying that his directions are the Lord's command seems clear on the surface, but what Paul means, where he received the decree, and how, are all open questions. Watson (*First Epistle*, p. 155) states that "Paul now claims for himself the right to speak for God," but that is wrong. Paul may demonstrate a sense of authority here, but he claims no rights. The exercise of a genuine responsibility is not the same as the assertion of a right. Moreover, the form of this statement by Paul is much firmer in tone and grammar than is his more modest claim at 7:40b; and one should not confuse the character of the two remarks. Perhaps Watson is correct, however, when he writes, "Although there is no explicit appeal to apostolic authority here, such a claim is probably implicit (cf. 12:28)." Unfortunately, Watson's additional comments on Paul's authority go beyond the boundaries of exegesis.

14:38 / This is disdainful dismissal of anyone who might disagree with Paul: "But if anyone fails to acknowledge [what Paul has delivered as the Lord's command], let that one fail to be acknowledged." By whom the one resisting Paul's teaching will be unacknowledged is open to speculation. The congregation? Paul? God? All of these? The comment is too cryptic to allow one to infer an answer to this intriguing question.

14:39 / This verse is a final piece of rhetorical summary. The first word of Paul's statement, **Therefore** (Gk. *Hōste;* lit. "So then" or "So as"), indicates a significant conclusion, and the accompanying direct address, **brothers** *(adelphoi),* would summon the attention of the members of the congregation. The language of this verse echoes 12:31a, and even more the language and theme of 14:1. Through such repetitious rhetoric Paul creates continuity in his lengthy and complicated argumentation and brings clear emphasis to his primary position.

14:40 / Paul concludes this discussion by appending another summary slogan, probably to the whole discussion: "But *all things* [the first word of the Corinthians' own slogan from 6:12] well-fittingly and according to order let it be!" The comment applies directly to prophecy, tongues, and the other spiritual contributions to worship. Unfortunately, the phraseology of the NIV softens the mettle of Paul's pronouncement.

§45 Back to the Basics (1 Cor. 15:1–11)

The letter moves toward its conclusion with a long, crucial defense of the truth of the resurrection of the dead and its intrinsic importance for all of Christian faith and living. The length and complexity of this reflection, coupled with its subject matter, make this portion of the letter important for understanding early Christian belief and practice, the foundational nature of resurrection faith for all of Christian theology, and the reconstruction of Paul's overall understanding of God's work in and through Jesus Christ. Interpreters have given this material extensive attention, making much of this discussion of resurrection faith because of its position, length, and subject matter. An unbelievable number of interpretations has been the result.

Paul has held this discussion until the end of his letter. Since he did not launch into this particular area at the outset of the correspondence it seems that this subject was not the central difficulty that he had to oppose and correct. The positioning of these remarks does give them a certain penultimate, perhaps even ultimate, importance, but Paul's tone is more neutral in these lines than in his previous more caustic comments and emphatic directions.

Without denying the absolute importance of the material that Paul offers in chapter 15—this is a discussion of the very basis of all of Christian faith and practice—the following commentary will take a rather simple line in attempting to read what Paul is saying to the Corinthians. He seems to be concerned that some in Corinth deny the resurrection of the dead. It is clear from his comments that not all of the Corinthians are engaged in a full-scale denial of life after death (see 15:29). In fact, it may not be necessary to understand that anyone in Corinth denied the resurrection altogether; rather, what they held to may have been a particular understanding of life after death that Paul now finds it imperative to correct.

Many commentators argue that some of the Corinthians are focused on an overly-realized eschatology that insists they already have experienced or are experiencing the resurrection; thus, there is no future dimension to their belief in resurrection. Verse 19 is often the key element in such a line of interpretation and will require careful attention. Yet, while there are undeniable evidences of an overly-realized eschatology at work among some of the Corinthians, Paul's text does not support this interpretation of the Corinthians' contentions about the resurrection having already occurred. One does find such a problem overtly in the Pastoral Epistles (2 Tim. 2:17–18; perhaps 1 Tim. 1:6), but the materials here are not so explicit and do not support the weight of such an interpretive suggestion. What some of the Corinthians seem to be denying is a resurrection of the dead—they may believe in life after death, but they do not expect that life to take form in and through God's raising the dead to new life. Life continues after death, but there is no need for the dead to be raised for such an afterlife.

Given the specific contents of Paul's comments, the situation—as complicated as it has been understood to have been—seems simple. *Some of the Corinthians believe that there is life after death without a resurrection of the dead.* The simplest, most sensible solution to understanding what some of the Corinthians were saying is to see them affirming a continuation of life after death through the survival of the spirit of the persons who have died, but not through an act of new creation by God in resurrection of the dead. The early chapters of the letter revealed a concern in Corinth with a kind of dualism between body and spirit. The Corinthians behaved in bizarre ways to demonstrate the freedom of their spirits. They engaged in both licentious actions and ascetic practices to show their spiritual status and freedom. The status of the spirit was assumed to be independent of and superior to the reality of physical life. Paul argues for the absolute dependence or relatedness of all aspects of human life. The creature has no independent existence apart from the Creator and the gift of life from God. Humans are not independent spirits trapped in material bodies.

The following commentary pursues this line of interpretation: for some of the Corinthians, there is no need of a resurrection of the dead, for the dead live as being truly freed spirits. The dead have superseded mundane physicality by leaving their dead bodies behind. There is no need for a resurrection of the dead; such a notion is abhorrent, since the body has been left behind in death—and that for the better. Paul opposes this line of dualistic thinking. Note the odd comment in verse 46, where Paul argues for the necessity of the physical—for its priority and for its actual redemption and transformation in resurrection. The Christian does not begin a superior spiritual life in the context of this world that simply continues after death; the believer has a new relationship with God through God's work in Jesus Christ, and based on that new relatedness the believer anticipates God's gift of a new life after death through the resurrection (of the dead). This whole chapter is Paul's argument against the Corinthians' misunderstanding of resurrection, or life after death, as a simple freeing of the spirit through death. Paul insists that humans are creatures whose lives are created by God. If there is a life beyond this physical world, it is life as new creation because God who gave a first physical life now redeems that corrupt existence in a new, incorruptible gift of (spiritual) life through the resurrection of the dead. The Corinthians deny the reality or necessity of bodily resurrection—it is a disdainful notion to those who consider themselves to be liberated in the spirit and from the body by death. Paul insists that the resurrection of the dead, the granting of a new transformed life as a new creation, is not only true; indeed, it is the key to comprehending the reality of God's saving work.

Thus, to make his critique and teaching clear, Paul takes the Corinthians back to the foundation of their faith. It is helpful to sketch the lines of Paul's materials before examining the details of his remarks. First, verses 1–2 declare the absolute bedrock importance of the basic gospel message for Christian faith and life. Then, verses 3–8 restate the foundational teaching Paul had done in Corinth. The lines are rich and complex, so that interpreters generally recognize that in these tradition-laden verses there are one or two early Christian confessional formulae to which Paul adds his own commentary. As he writes, Paul recalls the substance of his primary teaching in a series of statements that finds its structure in a sequence of "that" (Gk. *hoti*) clauses: "*that* Christ died . . . *that* he was buried . . . *that* he was raised . . . *that* he appeared." These phrases form the backbone of the confessional material in verses 3–5, and there is additional information both embedded in this basic framework and attached to it in verses 6–8. Thus, some interpreters suggest that two *competitive* confessions are amalgamated and adapted by Paul, although no polemical note occurs in the lines, and the phrase "that he appeared" is merely explicated through the ensuing series of statements in verses 6–8.

In turn, verses 9–11 explain Paul's point so that there is no need to speculate about the sense of his metaphorical language. Specifically, Paul tells of his earlier, pre-Christian behavior that should have disqualified him as an apostle. Then, he grounds the reality of his calling in the reality of God's transforming grace. The degree of the power of God's grace is clear in that Paul was not merely redirected, so that his own zeal took new directions; rather, God's grace grasped his life and made it into something new and different. Throughout this section, Christ's death, burial, resurrection, and appearances are taken in their full soteriological force; they are not reported as isolated propositions.

15:1–2 / In verses 1–2 Paul identifies what follows in verses 3–11 as **the gospel** [that] **I preached to you,** and he qualifies this gospel with the phrases **which you** [in turn] **received and on which** [in turn] **you have taken your stand,** and "through which also" **you are saved.** The verbs Paul employs are similar to those at 11:23, where he referred to the authoritative transmission of oral tradition, as he does here by using the same technical terms. This set of descriptive phrases makes it clear that Paul preached a definite message and that the Corinthians accepted that message in the specific terms of Paul's presentation. In other words, at the outset of their belief, the Corinthians were in agreement with Paul concerning the substance of the gospel. Moreover, that message as preached and believed had the saving effect of bringing faith to the members of the church in Corinth. As Paul recalls the origins of faith in Corinth, he highlights that there was a definite foundation to the church's beginning.

Then, Paul recognizes the troubling possibility that the Corinthians may **have believed in vain.** It is impossible from this conditional comment to determine whether Paul meant to refer to a frightening possibility or merely to state a shocking absurdity in order to gain the Corinthians' attention. As one can see from the correspondence, the Corinthians have not abandoned belief, but apparently Paul regards them as having altered the content of the basic message that they heard and believed. Clearly they have gone too far, but exactly how far Paul estimates them to have gone is impossible to determine.

15:3–5 / Paul continues to recall the original message that he preached in Corinth by saying that he delivered that particular gospel tradition **as of first importance** (Gk. *en prōtois*). He may mean either that he delivered the teaching logically "above all" or temporally "in the first instance," or both. In either case the words state Paul's starting point in proclamation to the Corinthians. Thus, the material that follows this comment is of great interest and importance.

Verse 3 tells of Christ's vicarious, sacrificial, atoning death **(for our sins)** that occurred as part of God's will and work **(according to the Scriptures)**. This description of Christ's death solicits reflection and requires explication. Paul's allusive references to the death do not specify the mechanics of *how* **Christ died** for our sins or according to *which* Scriptures his death took place. Paul simply states that Christ's death had purpose and that it fitted with the Scriptures. Nevertheless, an informed early Christian reader might have associated the vicarious, even saving, significance of Jesus death with Isaiah 53 LXX, Zechariah 12:10, or any of several of the psalms. Moreover, the reference to the slaying of the paschal lamb in 1 Corinthians 5:7 already highlighted the connection between the early Christian understanding of Christ's death and the Passover and exodus. Thus, Paul does not need to elaborate what he has in mind, for his readers would know certain Scriptures that were read in relation to the interpretation of the meaning of Christ's death.

Verse 4 tells of the burial and the timing of Jesus' resurrection **(on the third day)**, which also occurred as part of God's will and work **(according to the Scriptures)**. The mention of the burial almost certainly is not intended to be associated with the reference to the Scriptures, although one might find a point of correlation between the burial and Psalm 16. Again Paul seems to assume a certain knowledge on the part of his audience, for he has no need to issue specific citations. The exact texts that Paul and the Corinthians might have brought to mind with regard to the raising of Christ are indeterminable, although Hosea 6:2, Jonah 2:1 (cf. Matt. 16:21), Isaiah 52:13; 53:10–12; or Psalm 15:8–11 LXX (Ps. 16:8–11 in the NIV; cf. Acts 2:25–28) are likely connections that would have been made. Indeed, the rhetoric of Paul and other NT authors concerning the scriptural bases of comprehending Christ, his death and resurrection, is often sufficiently general to support the suggestion of some commentators that Paul and other early Christians thought of Christ as the fulfillment or key to understanding all of the OT in and for the life of the church.

Paul's recollection of tradition moves in verse 5 into the realm of historical memory. One learns of the initial appearance to Cephas (NIV, **Peter**), a partial explanation of the prominence of Peter in the life of the early church. This reference is similar to the mention of such an appearance in Luke 24:34. The interpretive problem with Paul's statement, however, is more with what he does not say than with what he recalls. There is a strange, disturbing absence of reference to the appearance of the risen Jesus to the women at the empty tomb. The lack of this record leads to all kinds of speculations and interpretations. All these arguments, however, are from silence.

One does also learn of the subsequent appearance to **the Twelve,** an odd note given that for a time there were only eleven disciples in the inner group after the demise of Judas Iscariot; indeed, Acts records the addition of Matthias as a replacement for Judas among the Twelve (Acts 1:15–26) after the risen Jesus' appearances and ascension into heaven (Acts 1:6–11). Nevertheless, one sees in Paul's remark the early presence and importance of "the Twelve." Thus, one finds in verses 3–5 clear evidence of the early interpretation of Jesus' death and resurrection and an indication of the early church's recognition of authorizing appearances that identified and formed the structures of the church. One could not ask for more in the space of three verses.

15:6 / Paul refocuses his report at the beginning of verse 6 with the temporal qualifier **After that** (Gk. *epeita;* lit. "afterward"). The additional information in verses 6–8 reports the subsequent appearance of Christ to **more than five hundred** believers **at the same time** and declares that most of them were **still living** at the time Paul wrote. Paul adds that **some have fallen asleep,** a common ancient euphemism for "died." The overall report communicates a complex of important information in the discussion of the resurrection of the dead. Paul's statements both document the reality of the appearances of Christ "from the dead" by taking them out of the realm of private hallucination and also register the undeniable point that even those who saw the risen Lord died.

15:7 / Paul begins still another additional sentence with *epeita,* translated in the NIV with **then.** The rhetorical pattern makes parallel statements of verses 6 and 7. In turn, the mention of **James,** the brother of the Lord, recognizes and perhaps explains his prominence in the early church; indeed, the remark may explain his being a believer, since he was no disciple of Jesus. Orr and Walther remark, "James' new status as a believer offers an indirect proof that there was nothing he could remember from his acquaintance with Jesus in the family that would make such belief impossible" (*I Corinthians,* p. 322). But the facts of James's coming to leadership in the early church cut two ways: That James did not believe before and without this appearance is a direct proof that there was nothing he knew from the family or from his acquaintance with Jesus that compelled him to believe in Jesus! Moreover, the reference in verse 7 to the appearance **to all the apostles** seems to name a central criterion, perhaps *the* criterion, for apostleship from Paul's perspective. Those who saw the risen Lord were ultimately those who were "sent out ones" (apostles).

15:8 / Paul moves to yet another moment of past time. He begins verse 8 literally, "But **last of all,**" telling of the final such appearance of the resurrected Lord, this one to Paul himself. At the time of Paul's writing of this letter to Corinth, that last appearance had taken place approximately twenty years earlier. Nevertheless, Paul's words are vivid, even shocking. He literally says he was born as of an "abortion" (Gk. *ektrōma*), a word that sometimes indicates a stillbirth or an untimely birth. The metaphor is not only violent and perhaps offensive but also odd. Paul experienced his encounter with the risen Christ *after,* not before, the others, so that the vivid birthing image does not fit precisely, for it suggests an early or a short-term delivery. The point of the image, however, seems to be the violent intervening character of the call that Paul experienced, a discontinuous development that produced unforeseen results. Thus, Paul aims at communicating the abnormal manner in which he became an apostle, although in this context his chief concern is to underscore the validity of the reports of the encounters of the apostles with the resurrected Christ. The Christ who was raised was the Christ who was seen in his risen form by a great variety of witnesses.

15:9–10 / Having mentioned the encounter with the risen Jesus that constituted his call, Paul goes on to explain the significance of God's grace as he knew it from that experience. He understood grace to be unmerited and transforming. Grace characterized the power of God as it had moved in Paul's life; but as one looks back through Paul's references to tradition, one sees that grace characterized the appearances to the apostles, James, the five hundred, the Twelve, and Cephas; and even the resurrection of Christ himself. The power and continuity of God's grace were Paul's main concern, and his determination to allow the magnificence of God's grace to be manifested in his own life was a sign of his genuine appreciation of the unmerited transformation by grace that he received in conjunction with the appearance and commission of Christ. For Paul the reality of the resurrection was but a manifestation of the reality of the power of God's grace, and he was so persuaded of the ultimate importance of God's grace that he lived his life to show **the grace of God that was with** him. Paul contends that God's grace grants what cannot otherwise be had, as in the resurrection of the dead.

15:11 / Paul reminds the Corinthians that no matter from whom they heard the gospel, the message that they had heard was the one he had briefly reiterated in verses 3–8 and to which he had added his own adamant testimony in verses 9–10. Paul clearly expected no one to take exception to this teaching, for as he knew it and as he described it, this message about God's work in Jesus Christ united and held together the entire work of the early church.

Additional Notes §45

15:1 / Talbert (*Reading*, p. 96) notes the manner in which vv. 1–11 are held together by the verbal repetitions **preached** and "believed," in both vv. 1–2 and v. 11, so that the parameters of this particular section of the passage form an inclusio. Moreover, what Paul says he preached that the Corinthians **received** he also "delivered," having himself "received" the tradition (v. 3). For a more detailed analysis of the logic of 15:1–11 as a whole, see J. Lambrecht ("Line of Thought," pp. 655–70), who treats vv. 1–3a, 3b–5, 6–8, 9–10, 11 as a sequence of reasoning that begins and ends with the statement of Paul's thesis.

Furthermore, Paul's manner of addressing his audience is deliberate in rhetorical form. First, he states his objective, **I want to remind you;** lit. "I make known to you." Then, he addresses the Corinthians with a formal salutation, **brothers,** which as a masculine plural form the Corinthians would have understood to indicate both men and women, brothers and sisters. Conzelmann describes this beginning with the words "considerable ceremoniousness" and later summarizes the gist of Paul's ensuing statement saying, "Hearing the message of faith and understanding oneself on the basis of this message are not to be separated" (*1 Corinthians,* pp. 248–49). Moreover, in a brief but stimulating article, M. C. Tenney ("The Essence of the Gospel," *Christianity Today* 3 [1959], pp. 9–12) suggests that Paul's implied definition of the gospel was a combination of history, theology, and divine power.

15:2 / The NIV translates in order to bring clarity to Paul's idiomatic Gk. First, the words **By this gospel** are lit. "Through which." The phrase clearly refers to the gospel mentioned in v. 1, translating the Gk. preposition *dia* as "by" rather than as "through" and supplying "this gospel" for the pronoun "which." In English "by" implies that the gospel does the saving, but Paul's statement indicates that "through" the gospel the Corinthians are saved—apparently *by* the power of God (see 1:18). Furthermore, the Gk. verb *sōzesthe,* translated **you are saved** in the NIV, is passive in form, but the present tense may be rendered "you are being saved."

15:3 / The combination of verbs, **received . . . passed on** (Gk. *paradidōmi* with *paralambanō*), is regarded as technical terminology "for reception and transmission of church doctrine" (Zerwick and Grosvenor, *Analysis,* p. 528). For one influential examination of the traditional material in vv. 3–5, see H. Conzelmann, "On the Analysis of the Confessional Formula in I Corinthians 15:3–5," *Int* 20 (1966), pp. 15–25; in complement consult J. Kloppenborg, "An Analysis of the Pre-Pauline Formula [in] 1 Cor 15:3b–5 in Light of Some Recent Literature," *CBQ* 40 (1978), pp. 351–67.

15:4 / The verbs in this verse and the last phrase of v. 3 are remarkable. Paul states that Christ "died," **was buried,** and **was raised.** The verbs "to die" and "to be buried" are aorist in form, indicating simple past action without expressing an interest in the particularity of the time or its ongoing significance (if any). Yet, the verb "to be raised" occurs in the perfect tense, a way of indicating completed past action that presents ongoing significance in its completion or "which denotes a present state resulting from a past action. The implication is therefore that Christ, having been raised, is now risen Lord" (Watson, *First Epistle,* p. 159).

In turn, the phrase **on the third day** was itself a fixed part of early Christian tradition as one sees by comparing Mark 8:31 ("after three days") with the parallels in Matt. 16:21 and Luke 9:22, which also refer to the raising of Jesus "on the third day." On the possible relationship of the phrase "on the third day" to Hos. 6:2, see H. K. McArthur, "On the Third Day," *NTS* 18 (1971), pp. 81–86.

15:5 / The verb translated in the NIV and most other translations as **he appeared** (Gk. *ōphthē,* from *horaō*) is passive and means "was seen." The verb recurs in vv. 6–8 in relation to those whom Paul names as having seen the raised Christ. Commentators argue that it is preferable to render the verb "appeared" since the experience is clearly one in which Christ took the initiative to reveal himself to those who saw him. Furthermore, the LXX refers to God's appearance with the passive form of "to see" = "to be seen," where it seems clear that God *appeared*. Yet, Paul's use of the passive form and the possible preservation of that verbal voice in the tradition that Paul recalls may originally have indicated that God showed Christ to those who saw him. This arrangement is what Paul reports in Gal. 1:15–16, and the logic of such revelation fits well with the report of Christ's being subjected to God at the end (1 Cor. 15:24–28).

Much has been made of Paul's failure to refer to the appearance of the resurrected Jesus to the women at the tomb. E. L. Allen ("The Lost Kerygma," *NTS* 3 [1957], pp. 349–53), however, raises an equally problematic silence that is normally ignored: the lack of reference to the appearances Paul recalls here in the narratives of the Gospels and Acts.

15:6 / Following v. 5, vv. 6–8 continue with a series of temporal references to distinct appearances of the resurrected Christ to groups and individuals. Although the appearances are independent in occurrence, Paul lists these events in a cumulative sequence that documents the reality of Jesus' resurrection from the dead.

The wording of the phrases is clear, although once again (cf. 7:39; 11:30) Paul refers to people's having fallen asleep, a euphemism for died that has led to unfortunate misunderstandings about the NT understanding of the fate or state of the dead. The euphemism "fell asleep" in no way indicates that the body stopped working and the soul went on hold in slumber.

15:8 / Paul's language is colloquial as he writes, "**and last of all,** as if it were," so that the NIV leaves the casual remark "as if it were" untranslated. This minor omission is, however, insignificant compared to the way the translation of the remainder of the verse obscures the violent and distasteful character of Paul's actual statement. P. R. Jones ("1 Corinthians 15:8: Paul the Last Apostle," *TynB* 36 [1985], pp. 3–34) has even made a vigorous case for understanding the phrase **last of all** as a deliberate theological (possibly polemical) claim to be *the* final apostle.

The NIV softens Paul's tone and language. Despite its shortcomings, the translation **as to one abnormally born** is an improvement over many other translations of this verse. Nevertheless, Paul's language is still more vigorous, violent, and startling—not merely puzzling. Paul writes (lit.), "and last of all, as if it were to one aborted (or, to a miscarriage) he was seen also by me." Paul's call was not a smooth operation; it was disruptive, untimely, irregular, invasive, and personally transforming! For an excellent analysis of this passage in conjunction with Paul's complementary statement in Gal. 1:15, see G. W. E. Nickelsburg, "An *ektrōma*, Though Appointed from the Womb: Paul's Apostolic Self-Description in 1 Corinthians 15 and Galatians 1," *HTR* 79 (1986), pp. 198–205. See also H. W. Hollander and G. E. van der Hout, "The Apostle Paul Calling Himself an Abortion: 1 Cor. 15:8 within the Context of 1 Cor. 15:8–10," *NovT* 38 (1996), pp. 224–36.

15:9 / Paul's apparent modesty shines through in this statement, although the declaration is ambiguous and may say more than straightforward translation of the words suggests. Paul's literal words "to be called apostle" could mean "to be called an apostle," or they could assume the supplying of the verb "to be," thus, "to be called to be an apostle." One cannot discern from the words alone whether Paul meant to refer to apostleship as a designation or as a function. Perhaps he meant both. In commenting on the phrase "last of all" in v. 8, F. F. Bruce (*1 and 2 Corinthians* [NCB; Grand Rapids, Mich.: Eerdmans, 1987], p. 142) observes, "**last of all** among those entitled to be called apostles," but this exposition may place the emphasis on the wrong nuance in Paul's declaration. Cf. 1:1; 3:5–23; 4:14–16; 9:1–6; 11:1–2.

15:10 / Paul writes explicitly of **grace**, God's grace. As he elaborates on the foundational tradition of Christianity, Paul declares enthusiastically that he was what he was as a result of **the grace of God**. Moreover, Paul insists that God's grace worked through him and brought about whatever results came through his being an apostle. This verse provides a brief but fundamental insight into Paul's understanding of God, grace, and Christian life.

15:11 / When Paul concludes this verse saying, **you believed**, he speaks to all the Corinthians, recalling the act of their belief, not merely the content of their belief. The focus is on the relational dimensions of belief between God and humanity through the gospel, not merely on a body of doctrine that was embraced. The way in which Paul and the other early Christian preachers proclaimed the gospel was by the grace of God, and by that same grace—declared in v. 10—the Corinthians believed what they heard preached.

§46 Controversy in Corinth (1 Cor. 15:12–19)

These verses move from the foundational issues to a controversy in the Corinthian church, and the verses articulate a tough-minded logic that proves the error of the position taken by some of the Corinthians. The problem was that some of the Corinthians said there is no resurrection of the dead. The statement as Paul reports it could mean that they said there is no resurrection at all, or they advocated "immortality" (survival of the spirit) rather than "resurrection" (new creation), or they denied a future resurrection and claimed a fully realized this-worldly resurrection (as in 2 Thess. 2:1–2; 2 Tim. 2:17–18). Option one makes the plainest sense of the words, but there is no indication in general that the Corinthians denied life after death. In fact, 15:29 speaks clearly against the idea that the Corinthians were unconcerned with life after death. Option three makes sense given the Corinthians' penchant for ecstasy and sacramentalism, but Paul's statements do not explicitly refute the claim that the resurrection had already passed. Thus, option two seems most likely given the full discussion by Paul: the Corinthians denied that the dead would be raised. Life went on after death, but through the survival of the person's spirit. Note the tone of Paul's argument. He is correcting a misunderstanding and a misappropriation, not a major distortion or denial of the truth. Paul argues at length and in a gentle but firm and thorough fashion to redirect the understanding and the actions of the Corinthians.

Nevertheless, whatever understanding of the Corinthians' beliefs one adopts for making sense of this part of the letter, this section resists viewing Christ's resurrection in isolation as a mythic theme or an eternal timeless truth. Christ's death and resurrection have a definite, determinative role in both the beliefs and the actions of members of the church (see 15:58). Paul's argument exposes the errors of the Corinthians' denial of a resurrection of the dead. In so doing, Paul argues a tight logical loop: *Christ is raised* → the gospel is preached → the Corinthians have

faith → the dead in Christ are raised → *Christ is raised.* As Paul
presents the connections, to falsify one element of this loop is to
invalidate the whole, and to invalidate the loop exposes the testimony of the apostles as false testimony about God. If, moreover,
the testimony about God's gracious saving work is false, then the
dead are lost and Christians have no hope but are to be pitied as
deluded.

15:12 / Paul launches his discussion with a conditional
sentence **(But if . . . how can . . . ?)** in the form of a question that
creates a logical connection between the resurrection of Christ
from the dead and the resurrection of the dead per se. Christ has
been preached as having been raised from the dead, and the Corinthians believed this proclamation. Therefore, for them to believe that Christ is raised is for them to believe that there is a
resurrection of the dead.

15:13–14 / Paul shifts points of view to the position that
the Corinthians have taken, which he wants to refute and correct. Again, he writes in conditional sentences to force the readers to draw particular conclusions. Paul stands the faith of the
Corinthians on its head: If there is no resurrection of the dead,
then Christ cannot have been raised, because he was dead. Paul's
rhetoric indicates an assumption that such a thought is possible
and true, although he does so only to force a further undesirable
conclusion. If Christ is not raised, then the apostolic proclamation is false and the Corinthians' faith is without foundation.

Someone could agree, although Paul does not assume this
as he makes and continues this line of argumentation. To agree at
this point would mean that the entire life of the Corinthian
church was a foolish mistake or a bogus operation. As Paul's letter has indicated, the Corinthians have an experience with the
presence and the power of God's Spirit that informs them of the
real, even divine, substance to the life of their congregation.
Thus, while some could agree with Paul's present logic as he pursues an absurd end, Paul does not seem to think that they will argue with his true line of reasoning.

15:15 / The statement in this verse complements and
particularizes the logic of verses 13–14. If what the Corinthians
are saying is true (that there is no resurrection of the dead), then,
Paul argues, the preachers lied about God; God did not raise
Christ, because dead persons are not raised by God. Again, Paul

does not mean for the Corinthians to agree with this argument that he intends to be patently absurd. The form of the argument is a grand *reductio ad absurdum.*

15:16–18 / Paul draws tight the links of his logical chain: the dead in general, Christ in particular, the Corinthians, dead Christians. One may see how these elements are related in the argument, although at the outset one should recognize that Paul's statements assume some knowledge about the relationship of sin and death, which he does not offer at this point (see Rom. 3–7). According to Paul, the general denial of the resurrection of the dead means the particular impossibility of Christ's having been raised. In turn, that Christ was not raised means that the faith of the Corinthians was unfounded and that the death of Christ (which was not overturned by God in resurrection from the dead) did not deal with the sins of the Corinthians. Thus, anyone **in Christ** who died simply perished. Paul's argument has led the Corinthians to an undesirable conclusion, quite deliberately.

15:19 / One can read this verse as Paul's response to or rejection of a statement that the Corinthians made **(only for this life we have hope in Christ),** but in the wake of the argument generated in verses 16–18, it is more likely that Paul is driving home the unacceptable nature of the conclusions that he reached through his foregoing (false) reflections. Thus, from the discouraging imaginary scenario of the previous verses, Paul makes a conditional statement that, in its first part, summarizes the whole matter as the readers should see it from the position at which they arrived by following Paul's argument ("we have hoped in Christ in this life only"). Then, the second part of the verse states Paul's verdict on this obvious but fully unacceptable conclusion. If the dead are not raised, Christ is not raised, faith is nothing, and the dead perish, then those in the church who might try to find some hope in Christ for this life are a truly pitiful, misguided, deluded group. Paul reduces to nothing the hope of those who would deny the resurrection of the dead as an act of divine transformation and creation. To deny the resurrection of the dead is to misunderstand the grace of God, and for Paul, God's transforming grace is the basis of all valid Christian hope. The Christians do not have an essential existence that is their guarantee of passage to a life after death. All rests with God. If there is no resurrection of the dead, if God's gracious power did not raise Christ from the dead, if there is no gracious divine dealing with sin, and if the dead have perished, then there is no point to Christian existence in the context of the present world. In other words, if the form of this world is not passing away (because it is being superseded by God's new creation that is already revealed in the resurrection of Christ from the dead), then so what? Or, if "this is as good as life gets"—even if it goes on forever—so what?

Additional Notes §46

In general this section of the letter is a grand conditional discussion. Paul makes a series of seven conditional statements, real and unreal, that then generate a series of results of the stated conditions, again real and unreal. The argumentation can be tricky, but fortunately English grammar and idiom function similarly to the norms of koine Gk., and so the English reader can follow the discussion by instinct without having to analyze and classify the forms of the various conditional statements—protases and apodoses. Fee offers an elaborate outline that may prove helpful, although the analysis presses for a degree of precision that Paul may not have intended (*Epistle*, pp. 739–40).

In general, Paul's seven conditional statements may be viewed and understood as follows:

	IF (condition):	THEN (coordinate):	
v. 12	if it is preached that Christ has been raised from the dead		*real*
		some of you say that there is no resurrection of the dead	*real*
v. 13	if there is no resurrection of the dead		*unreal*
		not even Christ has been raised	*unreal*
v. 14	if Christ has not been raised		*unreal*
		our preaching is useless and so is your faith	*unreal*
v. 15	if in fact the dead are not raised		*unreal*

	we are . . . false witnesses . . . God did not raise [Christ]	*unreal*
v. 16 if the dead are not raised		*unreal*
	Christ has not been raised either	*unreal*
v. 17 if Christ has not been raised		*unreal*
	your faith is futile; you are still in your sins	*unreal*
v. 19 if only for this life we have hope in Christ		*unreal*
	we are to be pitied more than all [others]	*unreal*

Paul effectively stands theological reality as he knows it on its head and proceeds to declare the consequences. Coupled with the unreal conditions of the six unreal conditional statements are sets of most undesirable circumstances. Having flipped from reality to irreality after v. 12 because of the illogical and undesirable denial of the resurrection of the dead, Paul proceeds to demonstrate how pointless Christian faith and life are without the real foundation of Christ's resurrection, itself an indication and a promise of the resurrection of the dead. Paul winds on into absurdity from v. 13 through v. 19. Then, remarkably, in v. 20, after having taken the readers on this trek through the land of undesirable irreality, he returns directly to a discussion of reality, declaring, "But Christ has indeed been raised from the dead"—exactly as he was proclaimed according to v. 12!

15:12 / Talbert (*Reading*, p. 97) identifies an assertion by the Corinthians embedded within this verse that Paul quotes in order to discuss and refute: **there is no resurrection of the dead.** Talbert is suggesting, not merely that this is Paul's summary, but that this is a kind of motto that some in Corinth have articulated. The attitude behind such a statement, whether a quotation or not, is analyzed and termed "spiritual elitism" by R. A. Horsley (" 'How can some of you say that there is no resurrection of the dead?' Spiritual Elitism in Corinth," *NovT* 20 [1978], pp. 203–31), who examines the dualism of immortal soul and mortal body that was common in the first-century Greco-Roman world, a dualism that produced spiritual elitism wherein the elite denied the resurrection of the dead body.

15:19 / Talbert (*Reading*, p. 98) also argues that in this verse there is another citation by Paul of a Corinthian declaration, "If in this life in Christ, we are *hoping only*, we are of all men most pitiful." Whether or not one perceives a Corinthian motto in this material, the phraseology of Paul's statement is ambiguous. The adverb **only** may be read with the words **this life** or the words **we have hope.** Thus, Paul could have made two possible and quite different statements: "in this life we have only hope," i.e., in life the believers have nothing but hope; or "in this life only we have hope"—i.e., only in this life is there hope. The NIV translation, "If only for this life we have hope . . . ," agrees with most contemporary renditions in understanding Paul to refer to Christian hope that is limited to earthy life. Whatever Paul said, he said it to demonstrate that the position was wrong.

§47 Christ, the Resurrection, and the End (1 Cor. 15:20–28)

These verses form a remarkably rich section of Paul's reflections and teachings about resurrection. One encounters quotations of and allusions to several passages from the LXX, and Paul employs other traditional materials in formulating his argument. Despite the seemingly straightforward nature of the lines, they are subtle. In verses 20–22 Christ is presented as the one through whom there is a resurrection of the dead. Verses 23–28 delineate the events of the end, though Paul is probably not concerned here with a strict chronological ordering. Rather, all Paul's teaching follows from Christ's having been raised by God from the dead.

15:20 / Paul sets this line in firm juxtaposition to his previous comments with the initial words "**But** now" (Gk. *nyni de*). In declaring a fresh starting point, Paul abandons imaginary rhetorical conditions and proclaims his essential conviction, which is to be taken as the foundation of the faith and understanding of the Corinthians: **Christ has indeed been raised from the dead.** Paul explains this basic conviction and its implicit meaning for Christian life in a biblical metaphor: **the firstfruits of those who have fallen asleep.**

The declaration of Christ's resurrection required explanation in part because its occurrence defied expectations. In Judaism the resurrection was thought to be future and corporate. All those who would be raised were expected to be raised together at some future time that God would determine. This pattern of expectation was developed in Judaism in a dialogue with the Scriptures. Thus, to claim that Christ was raised from the dead—before all others and before the end—seemed to go against the biblical perspective. Paul's metaphor of "firstfruits," however, demonstrates that the reality of Christ's resurrection is not contrary to the teachings of Scripture, but in keeping with the biblical patterns of thought. In Judaism, the firstfruits were the first portion of the new crop that were taken as a sign and a promise of the remainder of the crop that was to come. By faith the Jewish farmer took the firstfruits and offered them to God in honor of God's promise, and so the entire crop was consecrated to God.

In referring to Christ as the firstfruits of those who have fallen asleep, Paul indicates that he understood the resurrection of Christ as an anticipatory promise of the general resurrection of the dead and as a consecrating reality that signaled the devotion of the remainder of those who were to be raised to God. This rich biblical metaphor ultimately sets and states Paul's understanding of the meaning of Christ's resurrection from the dead in more specific terms than did the complex arguments of verses 12–19.

15:21 / No sooner has Paul made his thinking clear through the employment of a precise biblical image than he moves on to complicate his reflections with additional materials. In vague terms this verse prepares for the overt comparison of Adam and Christ that follows in verse 22. Paul anticipates the comparison in a reasonable way. He writes in the form of a conclusion: **For . . .** (Gk. *epeidē gar;* lit. "For since . . ."); although he is introducing a new line of thought. The declaration falls into two balanced clauses:

> through a man, death
> and
> through a man, resurrection of the dead.

The statements are general, undefined, and apparently universal in their outlook. One man introduced death, and another man introduced the resurrection of the dead. Fortunately, Paul elaborates and interprets his statement in the next verses.

15:22 / Paul signals that he intends to explain by beginning this verse with the words **For as** (Gk. *hōsper*) and continuing in mid-sentence, **so** (Gk. *houtos*). Paul specifically names **Adam** and **Christ** and refers to them so that one sees clearly that they are the two of whom he wrote in verse 21—**in Adam all die . . . in Christ all will be made alive.** Paul's rhetorical contrast is simple and clear, "For as in Adam . . . so in Christ." One should notice, however, that all *will* be made alive in Christ. Resurrection is reality for Christ, but Paul casts the resurrection of others—dead or living—as a future phenomenon.

Commentators debate who the "all" of verse 22 are. The "all who die in Adam" refers to all humanity; but does "all who will be made alive in Christ" indicate all humans or merely all believers? The matter cannot be settled simply from the words in this verse or even from examining these lines in the context of 1 Corinthians 15. Paul's remarks in 1 Thessalonians 4:13–18; 5:1–11; Philippians 2:5–11; and Romans 9–11 are critical parallels for interpretation, but even when those passages are taken into account, interpreters still debate the sense of this statement in verse 22. Nevertheless, Paul is addressing the church and is speaking about matters pertaining to their understanding of the life of the congregation, although that area of interest nearly always has broader implications for humanity at large. Paul uses the word "all" a total of twelve times in this discussion, with most references occurring in verses 24–28.

15:23–24 / In rapid succession these lines tell of the dramatic events of **the end,** or the Day of the Lord as Paul names it elsewhere. In turn, Paul recognizes Christ's own coming, the larger event of the Parousia (Christ's so-called second coming along with those who **belong to him**), the destruction of the forces set in opposition to Christ, Christ's delivery of the kingdom to God, and Christ's reign, which is future in its full form but now underway as Christ labors against his enemies. The language of this portrayal is highly traditional, fully informed by the literature and thought of Jewish and early Christian apocalyptic eschatology. Paul means what he writes, but one never knows how literally he intended for the standard apocalyptic images to be taken.

15:25 / The language of Psalm 109:1 LXX (Ps. 110:1 NIV) comes through in this verse. Readers should note that this is the most cited psalm in all the NT. Literally the verse declares, "For it is necessary for him to reign until *he may put* all *the enemies under* his *feet.*" (The italicized words reflect the original text of the psalm.) Despite the simplicity of the language, there are complications for interpretation because of grammatical ambiguities and because of Paul's alterations to the psalm. To whom "him," "he," and "his" refer is not immediately clear. In context all these pronouns seem to refer to Christ, although the ensuing discussion, particularly in verse 27, clouds the matter.

In any case, Paul offers a messianic interpretation of the psalm in order to make his argument concerning the reality of the resurrection of Christ and of the dead. There is a grand scale to the picture presented in this verse, although Paul's particular argument about the situation in Corinth is still the central concern that is driving his reasoning. When read in relation to Christ, the psalm text implies his resurrection, exaltation, ongoing reign, and ultimate victory. Paul's real interest, however, despite all the fascinating details of this verse with the cited psalm text, is to authenticate the resurrection of Christ from the dead and the general resurrection of the dead in the future.

15:26–27 / As Paul explicates the psalm and the meaning of the current reign of Christ, he states that **death** is the **last enemy** of Christ. The implication of Paul's scenario is that Christians necessarily face death as an inevitable foe until Christ's reign achieves the end toward which it is working. Thus, according to Paul, though Christ reigns and defeats his foes, including death, the ongoing work of the reign is not complete, and death is still active, although death's end is already sealed.

In reading these verses, one should not miss the thoroughly theological cast of Paul's teaching. There is a powerful, all-encompassing concern with christology in this vision of the end; but as verse 27 makes clear, God and God's power are active in Christ's accomplishing the good and final result of which Paul writes. Thus, Paul cites Psalm 8:6 LXX in verse 27a to indicate God's role in achieving the final victory of Christ over the enemies, including death. The citation again refers ambiguously to "he" who **put everything under his feet,** although now Paul explains that God put Christ's enemies under Christ's feet and is not himself (God's self) under Christ.

15:28 / Finally, verse 28 clarifies the ultimate purposes of God's power at work in Christ. Paul elaborates the particulars of the arrangements so that there can be no confusion or misunderstanding. When all is subjected to Christ, Christ will be subjected to God. Paul formulates the final portion of the verse as an unmistakable purpose clause: **so that God may be all in all!** The statement is clear, unambiguous, and undeveloped, so it generates vigorous interpretive debates and raises irresolvable questions.

Additional Notes §47

15:20 / The combination of Gk. words, *nyni de,* at the outset of this line is rhetorically forceful, noting an intensive reversal of what had been said between v. 12 and this point in the argument. The sense of the phrase in Gk. is "But now . . . ," although Zerwick and Grosvenor (*Analysis,* p. 529) prefer the rendering of the words as "But the fact is." Moreover, the reference to Christ as **firstfruits** presents an image that may be unfamiliar to many modern readers. The festival of "firstfruits" was a holy convocation that included thank offerings and sacrifices at the time of the completion of the barley harvest, seven weeks after the Passover. The operation of the firstfruits offerings is detailed in Exod. 22–23; 25; 29; Lev. 2; 23; and Deut. 26.

15:21 / Orr and Walther (*I Corinthians,* p. 328) judge Paul's rhetoric at this point to be "almost cryptic," because his manner of expression is succinct, even terse. There is an effectiveness in brevity, although the bare statement in this verse begs for elaboration. A brief explication follows, but for greater detail in terms of Paul's understanding of this juxtaposition of Adam and Christ, see Rom. 5.

15:22 / On **Adam** and Adam typology in antiquity, see R. Scroggs, *The Last Adam: A Study in Pauline Anthropology* (Philadelphia: Fortress, 1966); and L. Goppelt, *Typos: The Typological Interpretation of the Old Testament in the New* (German original, 1939; Grand Rapids, Mich.: Eerdmans, 1982). More particularly, on this use of the OT in this passage, see J. Lambrecht, "Paul's Christological Use of Scripture in 1 Cor. 15.20–28," *NTS* 28 (1982), pp. 502–27.

15:23 / The focus shifts again at this point and continues to pursue a new line through v. 28. The essence of the section that begins here is a presentation of traditional apocalyptic ordering of the end as yet another argument for the reality of the resurrection of the dead. Paul's language is vivid. When he writes of **each in his own turn,** the word translated **turn** is a Greek military term indicating "rank" or "order." Paul perceives, anticipates, and reveals that the resurrection of the dead proceeds according to a divine plan. Note, however, that Paul's concern and focus in this section are primarily **Christ** and **those who belong to him.** He is not giving a detailed account of the events of the end. Rather, he is telling just enough of the story to make his point forcefully that the resurrection of the dead is a reality that will take place according to God's will and work in God's own time.

15:24 / The opening phrase of this verse reads **Then the end.** The words **will come** are supplied by the translators of the NIV. The brevity of Paul's phrase in this context has generated debate, for some scholars try to read "the end" as if it meant "the last," in reference to the ranks or orders ("turn") mentioned in the previous verse. The NIV translation moves to paraphrase in agreement with the interpretation of the vast majority of scholars who understand the Gk. words *to telos* to refer to **the end,** as in *THE END*. Normally, *to telos* refers to "the end" in the sense of a consummation or completion of an ongoing process.

The readers of this text should recognize that the language of this passage is deliberate and revealing in Gk. Paul signals the future quality of these reflections by using a series of verbs in the subjunctive mood in vv. 24, 25, 27, 28: somewhat lit. "he shall abolish" (v. 24), "he shall put" (v. 25), "he shall say" (v. 27), "all things shall be subjected," and "God may/shall be" (v. 28).

15:25 / The temporal qualifier **until** (Gk. *achri hou*) that occurs here is the same temporal designation that was used in 11:26 in reference to the period of time "until" the resurrected Christ may come. The importance of these apocalyptic images for Paul's understanding of God's will and work should never be underestimated in reading his letters or in assessing his thought.

15:26 / The Gk. verb *katargeitai* that is translated **to be destroyed** (here and in v. 24) more exactly means "to be brought to nothing, to be rendered useless, to be abolished, or to be canceled." Paul knows and frequently uses the simple verb for "destroy" (Gk. *apollymi*) elsewhere; cf. Rom. 2:12; 14:15; 1 Cor. 1:18–19; 8:11; 10:9–10; 15:18; 2 Cor. 2:15; 4:3, 9. Paul has already used forms of the verb *katargeō* at 1:28; 2:6; 6:13; 13:8, 10–11; 15:24. The nuance connoted by this verb outside this chapter has consistently been "to nullify" or "to bring to nothing," and that sense of action is almost certainly what Paul wished to communicate here.

15:27 / The phrase translated **when it says** is ambiguous in Gk. Paul's words may intend to say "whenever *he* shall say . . . ," referring to Christ's own future declaration of victory over **"everything."**

15:28 / In completing his reflections, Paul does not attend to the fate of the opposition, nor does he indicate a concern with the details of Trinitarian relations; rather, he presents a final theological vision centered on God as in Isa. 9:7 and Rom. 11:36.

§48 Arguments against Misunderstandings (1 Cor. 15:29–34)

Paul offers another set of arguments against the Corinthians' denial of resurrection of the dead. He makes statements and asks questions in a loose sequence, and all he says is aimed to refute and reverse the Corinthians' position. In form and thrust the argument is similar to verses 12–19. In these lines Paul works through rhetorical questions to bring the thinking of the Corinthians into proper line.

15:29 / Having reviewed the anticipated events of the apocalyptic end, Paul remains concerned with the denial in Corinth of the resurrection of the dead, but in this verse he shifts the point of view and the method of argument dramatically. In fact, verse 29 is almost free-standing, although it relates intimately to the current context of discussion. The opening word **now** (Gk. *epei;* lit. "otherwise") signals a new level of reflection. Paul drops back and takes a look at the denial of the resurrection of the dead in relation to a new item of evidence. He uses two rhetorical questions to ask about an apparently real practice of the Corinthians that exposes the inconsistency between what they were doing and what they were saying in relation to the resurrection of the dead. Unfortunately, the translation of the NIV moves past careful paraphrase at this point and introduces phrases that have Paul writing more clearly than he did. A much better English rendering of Paul's words is found in the NASB: "Otherwise, what will those do who are baptized for the dead? If the dead are not raised at all, why then are they baptized for them?" Exactly what Paul means by referring to people **who are baptized for the dead** is not clear. Dozens of theories have been proposed, and none is fully satisfactory. Whatever Paul means, we should note that he does not criticize or deny the practice but uses it to score his own point that the dead will be raised; and we should resist any interpretation that bases its understanding on either the idea of baptism of the dead or a doctrine of baptismal regeneration, since these topics are not in view here, and even elsewhere Paul demonstrates no such thinking (cf. 1 Cor. 1 and Rom. 6).

In brief, Paul refers to the practice of some in Corinth of being baptized in behalf of the dead. Whether this means they were baptized for their own dead bodies, or for the saints of the OT who died before Christ, or for family and friends who were on their way to being baptized because they believed in Christ but died before baptism, is impossible to determine and irrelevant for grasping Paul's point. He registers the inconsistency of denying the resurrection of the dead and then being baptized in behalf of the dead. Baptism symbolized death with Christ to the power of sin, and it was done in hope and in anticipation of experiencing the power of God's resurrection (see esp. Rom. 6). If there were no resurrection of the dead, then being baptized in behalf of the dead made no sense. Paul means to imply that by their actions some of the Corinthians indicate a concern with or belief in the resurrection of the dead.

15:30–31 / Paul again shifts the point of view in formulating a string of arguments in favor of the reality of the resurrection of the dead. Now he speaks from a personal point of view in reference to his work as an apostle, writing of **we** and **I,** apparently referring to his and the other apostles' common experiences. Thus, verses 30–31 pose another question and adamantly state its answer: Why would Paul jeopardize himself for a hopeless lie? He would not, but he declares that he did risk his very life for the sake of calling the Corinthians and others to believe the gospel truth of Jesus Christ's death and resurrection from the dead. Thus, given the reality of Paul's personal sacrifice, the Corinthians should see that the message he preached of the resurrection of the dead was not a lie.

15:32 / This verse issues another question that functions to illustrate the serious degree of Paul's perils in ministry. Thus, the rhetoric specifically extends the point of verses 30–31. Unfortunately, from this intriguing statement one cannot know whether Paul's reference to fighting with beasts is literally true or a hyperbolic metaphor, although the difficult phrase **for merely human reasons** (Gk. *kata anthrōpon*) probably signals the metaphorical nature of the remark. Nevertheless, even if he speaks in picture language Paul means to identify the seriousness of the threat he faced in Ephesus. Therefore, Paul cites Isaiah 22:13b to establish the necessity of the truth that the dead are raised: **Let us eat and drink, for tomorrow we die.** The apostle's remarks have been labeled opportunistic, but when read in their specific context, the statements are in no way unscrupulous. Paul's mild sarcasm should not obscure his sincerity; he means to use the reality of the hardships he was willing to suffer to certify the truth of the teaching about the resurrection of the dead. So Paul believed and so Paul behaved.

15:33 / Paul quotes a well-known Greek proverb from the poet Menander in verse 33 to make the point that association with those in Corinth who deny the resurrection of the dead presents a danger to those forming such affiliations. This citation forms yet another volley in Paul's campaign against the denial of the resurrection of the dead. By quoting this popular maxim Paul puts the discussion on the level of common sense, Christian common sense, as he makes explicit in the following lines.

15:34 / The foregoing proverb leads into a blunt upbraiding in verse 34. Paul's language is plain, and he openly states his purpose. Paul has already indicated when he did not (4:14) and when he did (6:5) mean **to shame** the Corinthians. When the members of the congregation were actively responsible for a needless problem, Paul used the powerful social phenomenon of shame to attempt to correct problems. As noted earlier in this commentary, shame was a different social reality and worked in distinct ways in the ancient world; nevertheless, even given the distance between antiquity and the present day, Paul's methods of persuasion, even when honestly acknowledged, do not fit neatly with today's more therapeutic and tolerant patterns of interaction.

The call to sobriety is straightforward (**come back to your senses as you ought**), and such language was standard rhetoric for urgent eschatological exhortations in early Christianity; literally Paul says, "Sober up righteously and by all means don't sin!" Moreover, he asserts that some are *agnōsian*, usually translated "lacking knowledge" and rendered **ignorant** in the NIV but best understood to refer to an active lack of knowledge about God. There is a difference between ignorance that actively disregards the truth and naiveté that is as yet uninformed. Paul charges the Corinthians with active ignorance; thus he sees himself naming their shame.

Additional Notes §48

15:29 / The practical nature and logical tone of the series of illustrative arguments in vv. 29–34 are much closer to the style of vv. 12–19 than the materials in vv. 20–28. Paul seems to have come back to earth from his sighting of the end. The word "otherwise" signals this transition.

The tense of the verb in Paul's query is, however, striking: **what will those do.** The point of this question is to recognize the senselessness or pointlessness of the practice of being baptized in behalf of the dead if there is no resurrection of the dead. The aim and function of Paul's argument are clear, although there is no sure way to determine what kind of practice he refers to in this statement. One is tempted, nevertheless, to create a mirror reading of Paul's reference to the Corinthians and thereby understand that some of the Corinthians were saying, **The dead are not raised at all.** Whether or not Paul exaggerates the position of the Corinthians is also impossible to determine. In turn, archaeological data that shed light on the concern of citizens of Corinth—not merely the Christians—with the dead and the world of the dead are examined in helpful detail by R. E. DeMaris ("Corinthian Religion and Baptism for the Dead [1 Corinthians 15:29]: Insights from Archaeology and Anthropology," *JBL* 114 [1995], pp. 661–82), who suggests the practices of the Corinthian Christians were a facet of the local preoccupation with the underworld.

For an idiosyncratic but influential reading of this verse, see J. Murphy-O'Connor (" 'Baptized for the Dead' [I Cor. XV,29]: A Corinthian Slogan?" *RB* 88 [1981], pp. 532–43), who takes the phrase "baptized for the dead" to be a Corinthian gibe at Paul's apostolic sufferings that Paul in turn used against the Corinthians. Or, for the suggestion that *hyper* in the phrase "baptized for the dead" means "because of"—i.e., because of the influence on the lives of those being baptized of Christians who are now dead—see J. D. Reaume, "Another Look at 1 Corinthians 15:29, 'Baptized for the Dead,' " *BibSac* 152 (1995), pp. 457–75.

15:30 / Paul makes yet another emphatic declaration in this verse that should have struck his readers forcefully, saying, "Why *indeed* are *we ourselves . . . ?"*

15:32 / As noted above, the Gk. phrase *kata anthrōpon* is practically a simile, and there are multiple suggestions for translation/interpretation. The same phrase occurs in 3:3 and 9:8, although there are differences in the contexts of the discussions in which Paul uses the words. The observation by interpreters that Paul's Roman citizenship would have precluded his being subjected to combat with wild animals is perhaps correct, should Paul have provided proof of his status.

15:33 / Orr and Walther (*I Corinthians*, p. 336) suggest that the popular maxim found here may come from Euripides. Nevertheless, it is preserved through a line in Menander's *Thais* 218 (itself a lost comedy). Paul is not necessarily offering a conscious citation or quotation, as the line was apparently a cliché.

15:34 / This is the only place in which Paul uses the verb *eknēphō*, connoting "come out of a stupor"; it is the only occurrence of the word in the NT. In secular usage the verb means "to sleep off a drunken fit." Paul's choice of words is not particularly flattering, and his rough imperative is compounded by the striking adverb *dikaiōs*, "righteously." By implication Paul charges the Corinthians in their denial of the resurrection of the dead with being "under the influence" of something that needed to be overcome with "righteousness." On Paul's intent to shame, cf. 6:5.

§49 Comparing Bodies and Seeds
(1 Cor. 15:35–44)

These ten verses assemble a wide variety of materials as Paul continues to argue in behalf of the reality of the resurrection of the dead. Here, Paul offers a collage of data as he quotes the LXX, alludes to stories from Genesis, and develops analogies related to seed, flesh, body and glory, and Adam. The lines of the discussion open in the style of a diatribe with a dialogical argument, leading to Paul's central point in verse 38, "God gives . . . as he wishes." Above all, Paul's point in relation to the issue of the resurrection of the dead is that the resurrection or spiritual body is a kind of its own. The bodies of those who are raised from the dead are as unique as are other bodies, but the spiritual body is like all other bodies in that it is given by God.

15:35 / Verse 35 opens this complex of data, facts, and figures with a pair of questions from an imaginary inquisitor (as Talbert [*Reading*, pp. 100–103] observes). The questions form a sequence: **How are the dead raised?** and **With what kind of body will they come?** In the verses that follow, Paul takes up these question in reverse order, answering the query concerning what kind of body in verses 36–44, with addenda in verses 45–49. Then, in verses 51–57 (or, 50–57) he addresses the issue of how the dead are raised.

15:36–37 / Paul begins by issuing an initial, scoffing reply to the question about the kind of body that the dead will have in resurrection. **How foolish** renders Paul's more direct and offensive address, "Foolish one!" (Gk. *aphrōn*). Then, he begins an analogy on seed to contrast what is sown with what subsequently grows. Paul's lesson is not concerned with horticulture, although that is the realm of his illustration. He suggests that a sown seed **dies** (a parallel to burial) and then it will **come to**

life. Paul points out that the "death" of the seed is necessary and precedes the emergence of new plant life.

Furthermore, he observes that the one sowing does not sow a plant to grow a plant; one sows a seed. The body (form) of the seed and the body (form) of the plant are different, but the sower plants the seed in order to grow the plant. Paul's point is that there is anticipation of difference and transformation from the seed to the plant.

15:38 / Paul engages in the agricultural metaphor in order to make the point that he declares in this verse: God is sovereign and supreme in relation to all creation. The form of the seed does not to the human eye show forth the form of the plant that will grow from the seed. The plant takes a form that results from the theological fact that **God gives it a body as he has determined.** From this statement, Paul elaborates on the notion of God's giving the body according to God's will: **to each kind of seed he gives its own body.** This additional observation in verse 38b sets up the following analogies in verses 39–41.

15:39–41 / In one way the argument in these verses is simple and clear, and in another way the line of thought strikes many readers as being strange. In essence, Paul refers to a variety of entities: humans, **animals, birds, fish, heavenly bodies, earthly bodies, the sun, the moon,** and **the stars.** He claims the plain, observable truth: each of these elements of creation has a distinct form, be it flesh or splendor. Indeed, the different forms of these items make them both what they are and distinguishable from one another. This long series of observations works out the point that Paul made in verse 38b, "to each kind of seed" or to every part of creation "he [God] gives its own body." The elaborate and gentle flow of this illustration does not suggest that Paul is operating in utter frustration, even though he regards the problem in Corinth concerning the resurrection of the dead as "foolish" (v. 36).

15:42–44 / Paul draws a conclusion by interpreting the picture he painted in the previous verses. At this point, he combines his interpretation of the analogy of the seed and plants with the references to different kinds of bodies throughout created order.

The theme of the exposition is announced with the declaration, **So** also **the resurrection of the dead.** Paul takes up the contrast of the form of the sown seed and the grown plant. Now, however, Paul expands the contrast by introducing the categories of **perishable** and **imperishable,** or as the terms are more literally rendered in some translations, "in corruption" and "in incorruption" in verse 42; **in dishonor** and **in glory** as well as **in weakness** and **in power** in verse 43; and finally, **natural body** and **spiritual body** in verse 44. In each of these pairs of contrasts, Paul uses the first-named characteristic in reference to the body of a human in this present life—perishable, dishonorable, weak, natural; the second characteristic in each pairing describes the body of those who are resurrected from the dead—imperishable, honorable, powerful, and spiritual. These lists are not exhaustive, though they briefly create a vivid contrast. Above all, in the list of characteristics, one should notice the final pair of contrary characteristics: **natural body** and **spiritual body.** As N. Watson notes,

> the expression, "a spiritual body," would certainly have shocked the Corinthians, for whom body and spirit were clearly antithetical . . . [moreover,] the two adjectives used here to describe the two kinds of body are the same adjectives as used in 2.14f to differentiate unbelievers and believers . . . [so one sees that] the spiritual body is not composed of spirit but a body appropriate to life in the new age under the rule of the Spirit. (*First Epistle,* p. 176)

With the contrasts stated and the argument made, Paul summarizes his conclusion, which is the point for which he seeks to win the Corinthians' agreement: **If there is a natural body, there is also a spiritual body**—after all, a seed becomes a plant by God's determination.

Additional Notes §49

On the significance of bodily resurrection of the dead, see R. J. Sider, "St. Paul's Understanding of the Nature and Significance of the Resurrection in I Corinthians xv 1–19," *NovT* 19 (1977), pp. 124–41.

15:35 / The theme of this section is the resurrection of the dead, not merely resurrection or even the resurrection of Christ. Paul's concern is focused specifically as he opens this section with a diatribe, presenting an imaginary opponent in debate **(someone)** and quoting that one. The NIV translates this dramatic introduction, **Someone may ask,** but more literally Paul states in good form, "Someone will say." Interpreters debate whether Paul means to quote a slogan or question he knows from Corinth, although he means to anticipate the potential objection(s). The future cast of the opening ("will say": Gk. *erie*, third-person sing. future of *legō*) suggests the debate is hypothetical rather than real.

The phrase **what kind of body** pinpoints the crux of the dispute or disbelief. The notion of a body was antithetical to the ideas of superior spirituality that were current among many of the Corinthians. Nevertheless, Paul gives his own theological prejudice when he phrases the opponents' question, **How *are* the dead *raised?***—employing a passive form of the verb (Gk. *egeirontai* from *egeirō*) that indicates or assumes that God is the unnamed agent of the action in raising the dead.

15:36 / Paul's rhetoric in response to the inquisitor is forceful. After explicitly calling the opponent **foolish**, Paul emphatically addresses the imaginary figure saying, "**What you** yourself **sow** is **not** made alive except that **it dies.**" Paul adds emphasis with the emphatic second person sing. pronoun "you/yourself," and then he uses another passive verb, "is made alive" (Gk. *zōopoieitai*, from *zōopoieō*), that assumes the activity of God. The force of this rhetoric is to introduce a theological discussion through examples and an appeal to the experience of the imaginary partner in the discussion.

15:38 / The sequence and the tenses of the verbs in the statement **God gives . . . as he has determined** are striking. The first verb (Gk. *didōsin*) is present tense, and the second verb (Gk. *ēthelēsen*) is aorist or simple past. As Orr and Walther recognize, God gives what God already determined—a statement of confidence in the idea of a "divine plan" (*I Corinthians*, p. 342). Paul's assumption is that God is sovereign in deciding and acting in relation to raising seed into plants, and by implication, in relation to the resurrection of the dead.

15:39 / Commentators frequently note the extremely awkward construction of Paul's statement(s) in this verse. The phrases are repetitious and clumsy, obscuring the plain sense of the idea being expressed. The NIV offers an excellent translation at this juncture with the small problem of continuing to render the Gk. *anthrōpōn* as **men** rather than as the more natural and neutral and accurate "humans."

15:40–41 / The language of these verses is reminiscent of the material in Gen. 1 LXX. Paul's introduction of this imagery seems purely illustrative, for he merely extends the argument in progress and does not develop it through the references to heavenly and earthly bodies, sun, moon, and stars.

15:42–44 / The initial words of v. 42, *houtōs kai*, translated **So,** are a rhetorical signal to indicate that Paul is drawing a conclusion or forming an important comparison. The entire introductory phrase, **So** [also] **the resurrection of the dead,** emphasizes the gravity of the ensuing comments in these verses. The entire argument amounts to this: The body raised is different; the body raised is real. By implication, Paul recognizes that there already **is** (**it** *is* **raised,** not "will be") evidence of the reality of the different, raised spiritual body in Christ himself.

The paragraphing of v. 44 in the NIV is debatable at this point, as it breaks the verse into two segments and locates the first part of the verse with the previous paragraph and then uses the last phrases of the verse to lead into vv. 45–49. Actually v. 44b serves better to conclude the discussion from vv. 42–44 than to initiate the reflection that follows in vv. 45–49.

§50 The First and Last Adam (1 Cor. 15:45–49)

Paul completes his arguments concerning the question "what kind of body" (from v. 35b) in another form of argument in verses 45–49. Paul concludes this discussion by using Adam *typology*. Paul takes this new line of reasoning and introduces still another illustration to reemphasize three ideas: (1) The spiritual body will be distinctive; (2) God gives the spiritual body; and (3) those who are raised from the dead *will* have or be or get their bodies in the future as they are transformed by God from being like Adam to being like the risen Christ. Paul is both countering the claims of some of the Corinthians and clarifying the understanding of the resurrection of the dead as it relates to the lives of the Christians in Corinth. Verse 46 is a crucial statement that both puts the Corinthians on notice about the resurrection of the dead and gives them a proper understanding of their current status in the world: **The spiritual did not come first, but the natural, and after that the spiritual.** In other words, the Corinthians have not arrived at their final calling through Christ. They are only in transit, although God has set a destination for them and they are being called toward it.

15:45 / As in verse 42, Paul's opening words here indicate that he is forming a comparison to draw a conclusion or to make a point, **So** (Gk. *houtōs kai;* lit. "And thus"). Paul probably intends to look back and comment further on the discussion of verses 42–44, that there are two distinct kinds of bodies, natural and spiritual. As is clear from what follows, Paul insists that there is a divine order to the sequence of these bodies. Here Paul refers to **Adam** to illustrate and to prove his point.

The reference indicates that Paul is citing Scripture, specifically Genesis 2:7, although he offers a version of the text that is slightly different from the LXX: *The* **first** *man* Adam *became a living being.* (The italicized words reflect the original text.) This scriptural reference, however, is cited to provide a firm antithesis to the statement that follows: **the last Adam, a life-giving spirit.** These are Paul's own words, not a quotation from the Scriptures, despite the careful way in which Paul set up these balanced, contrasting declarations. The crafting of the lines into such sharp rhetorical contrast raises the profile of both statements but brings the main weight to bear on the second declaration, which comes as if it were a statement "greater than" the first.

The force of Paul's observation and the purpose of the contrast is partially lost in translations. The word translated **living** in reference to the first Adam is *psychē* in Greek and comes from the same root as the word translated "natural" in verse 44; likewise, the word translated **spirit** in reference to the so-called last Adam (Christ) is *pneuma* in Greek and comes from the same root as the word translated "spiritual" in verse 44. In forming this contrast, Paul is arguing that humanity inherits one kind of body and life from Adam and a new, different body and life from Christ— through faith and the resurrection of the dead. Moreover, Adam was a living being, as are all humans, but Christ is a life-giving spirit, something that neither Adam nor any other human can be. In this verse Paul uses the idealized figures of Adam and Christ to represent humanity in this ("natural") life and in the ("spiritual") life to come through resurrection of the body. But the readers should note that humans are indeed like Adam, living beings; unlike Christ, they are not life-giving but rather receive life through him.

15:46 / This concisely written statement makes the central point that Paul is attempting to register, saying literally, "But not first the spiritual but the natural, afterward the spiritual." The Corinthians cannot know the reality of the spiritual body until they experience receiving it as God determines in the resurrection of the dead. Paul insists that the life granted through the resurrection from the dead is real, but it does not precede the transformation of life in the context of this world; rather, that transformation is an indication and an anticipation of the final reality of new, unexperienced existence through the resurrection of the dead.

15:47 / Paul restates the same point in both more mundane (**the dust of the earth;** Gk. *ek gēs choikos*) and more exalted (**from heaven;** Gk. *ex ouranou*) terminology. The language of both phrases is highly reminiscent of the LXX account of creation in Genesis 1–2. Interpreters debate whether Paul meant to indicate the distinct origins of the two Adams or whether he meant to create a contrast between their natures to illustrate his basic argument in this section. A final decision is impossible, but the thrust of the passage makes it far more likely that Paul is creating contrasts in illustration of his discussion of different natures of bodies rather than attempting to comment on the cosmic origins of the first and second Adam.

15:48–49 / The argument in verse 48 is like by like: as was the **earthly man,** so are humans of the earth, and as is the **man from heaven,** so are the ones of heaven. Verse 49, however, makes a crucial point about Paul's understanding of the resurrection of the dead: in the present life humans bear the likeness of the human Adam, and in the future **(so shall we)** believers will bear the likeness of the one from heaven who has already been raised from the dead when they too experience the resurrection of the dead.

Additional Notes §50

15:45 / Paul's introductory phrase, **So it is written,** contains formulaic language recognizing and leading into a citation of Scripture (here, Gen. 2:7). The simple word **so,** however, is an ambiguous reference in Gk. *(houtōs kai),* best translated "and thus" or "so also." This manner of reference can look either backward or forward, although the occurrence of the same phrase in v. 42 probably indicates that at this point in his argument, Paul intends to draw a conclusion from what had been said, not what he was about to be stated. Moreover, the Gk. word *prōtos,* translated **first,** is introduced by Paul for two apparent reasons: (1) it anticipates and sets up a contrast to the subsequent reference to **the last Adam;** and (2) it prepares for the repetition of the word "first" in v. 46 in Paul's declaration of sequence—"first . . . not spiritual . . . but natural." Furthermore, this verse is another way of saying what Paul had said in v. 22.

15:46 / This simple-seeming verse is quite complicated. First, Paul is unusually adamant in making his statement, which the NIV renders into smooth English. Paul actually employs two strong adversatives, "But . . . but . . . ," both the Gk. word *alla.* Literally Paul wrote, "But not first the spiritual, but the natural; afterward, the spiritual." Second, in arguing for this particular sequence, Paul vigorously reverses the order advocated by the Hellenistic Jewish philosopher Philo of Alexandria, whose own neoplatonic outlook colored his reading of the OT so that spiritual things were prior to and greater than natural or material things. Third, in using the language of **spiritual** (Gk. *pneu-matikos*) and **natural** (Gk. *psychikos*), Paul reintroduces vocabulary used both in the last segment of his discussion (see 15:44) and earlier in the letter in reference to the ability or inability of "spiritual" and "natural" persons to receive "the things that come from the Spirit" (see 2:14). If Paul's choice of words is indicative of his concerns, part of the problem in Corinth is that some of the Corinthians are carried away with an unacceptable, self-centered, self-aggrandizing, so-called spirituality.

15:48 / This verse is the first of a pair of neatly balanced statements made by Paul in his defense of the reality of the resurrection of the dead. The language used of "the second man" (v. 47) echoes the discussion of "heavenly bodies" in verses 40–41. Remarkably, in that previous reflection, Paul talked almost exclusively of "glory" as the character of heavenly things.

15:49 / This verse is also a beautifully balanced rhetorical construction. Paul refers to the **likeness** of both the **earthly man** and the heavenly **man**. The word **likeness** is *eikōn* in Gk., the same word used in the creation account of Gen. 1:26–27 LXX; thus, Paul's meditation is likely built on or related to that part of the OT. In relation to the likenesses of these two archetypal figures, Paul says that believers **have borne** the earthly man's "image," using an aorist to indicate simple past occurrence; and he declares that they **shall bear** the image of the heavenly man, using a future tense. There is a serious textual variant for the second of the verbs in some old and reliable manuscripts; it reads, "let us bear," using an aorist subjunctive (or hortatory aorist) rather than the future tense verb. The matter is far from certain, though it is not a major theological problem; nevertheless, the future form of the verb fits Paul's normal pattern of reference to the resurrection of the dead, and *"the likeness of the heavenly one* is hardly to be achieved by exhortation"— see Orr and Walther (*I Corinthians,* p. 344), who cite the fifth-century Christian writer Theodoret, who wrote, "He [Paul] has said 'we shall bear' in a predictive, not a paraenetic, sense." If Paul uses the future tense here, he once again makes the point that the resurrection of the dead is real and in the future, as God wills.

Paul completes this long and complicated discussion of the resurrection of the dead with these nine verses. Verse 50 is a significant declaration that forms a bridge from the preceding analogies and arguments to the question that was posed and left unanswered in verse 35a, "How are the dead raised?" Then, verses 51–57 speak of the "mystery" of the resurrection of the dead and the end. Finally, verse 58 issues a concluding exhortation that extends from the full range of eschatological teaching that Paul offered in chapter 15.

15:50 / Verse 50 introduces a new idea or line into the reflection. In a sense, the concern is the same as that named explicitly in verse 35a. Now, however, as Paul re-presents the issue, quite naturally, from Paul's statement that **flesh and blood cannot inherit the kingdom of God,** one would ask, "Then how? How are the dead raised?" Paul assumes that unstated question and uses the following lines to answer the query.

In this verse Paul's subtle point about the unsuitability of that which is **perishable** for that which is **imperishable** is lost in the ring of his bold and poetic declaration at the outset of the verse. Nevertheless, this more subdued statement registers Paul's conviction of the incompatibility of the form of this world and God's new creation or kingdom. The transformation that Paul is about to discuss, the resurrection of the dead, is both necessary because of God's incomparable goodness and made real by God's gift of grace in Jesus Christ.

15:51–52 / The anticipated transformation of "flesh and blood" into the God-given spiritual body is a **mystery.** As Paul tells it, this mystery is known, not by reason but, if at all, by God's revelation of this truth. Thus, in the very presentation of the account of the "mystery," told as it is in dramatic apocalyptic-eschatological terminology and images, Paul scores the point that the transformation of earthly existence into spiritual reality is purely God's work. In turn, as Paul writes in traditional terms and language of divine transformation, he uses mysterious images designed to inspire awe and confidence. One may compare his similar teachings at 1 Thessalonians 4:13–18; 5:11. He continues by extending his reasoning in a didactic fashion, never afraid to repeat himself, "We shall be changed!"

15:53 / Verse 53 offers a prophecy that will be fulfilled at an appointed time in God's future, again repeating the language and the logic of the discussion in verses 35–49.

15:54–55 / Paul looks to the time of the resurrection of the dead, and as he does so he offers a prooftext for his point from Isaiah 25:8. The victory is God's, through Christ, and this divine victory has implications for Christian hope and life (v. 54). To amplify his position Paul adds the words **in victory** to Isaiah's phrase **death has been swallowed up.** Then, Paul continues in verse 55 with a quotation from Hosea 13:14, which he again adapts, tailoring the language of the biblical material to suit the context.

One sees the intricacy of Paul's logic throughout this chapter, but especially by noticing that Paul introduces both quotations from the LXX at this point in relation to the statement he made earlier in 15:26, "The last enemy to be destroyed is death." In declaring the inevitable demise of death, Paul originally quotes the OT (see v. 27) to validate this message of hope. Here again he issues a scriptural warrant to assure the readers that God's word is trustworthy.

15:56 / Verse 56 is Paul's own exegesis of the quotations from the prophets in the previous verses. One sees his hand clearly in the mention of **law** at the end of the line. This concern of Paul's, well-known from other letters and in other heated discussions, is not a concern for Paul in this conversation with the Corinthians. This mention of the law does not reveal the depth of Paul's reflection on the topic that can be seen in Galatians or Romans, where Paul wrestles with the issues and implication of the law for Christian life. Here he only mentions the law somewhat unfavorably, associating it with death and the sting of death, which is sin; indeed, he says the power of sin is the law. To restate the declaration that Paul never elaborates or explains, the law is the power of sin, which is the sting of death, which is the final enemy of Christ. One may infer that Paul did not see a place for the law in the reality of the resurrection of the dead. In brief, however, verse 56 is a concise attempt to state the magnitude and reality of God's future resurrection of the dead.

15:57 / Lest the readers become uneasy by the future cast of Paul's discussion of the resurrection of the dead, in this verse he continues with a doxological declaration of the meaning of all that he has written, especially in relation to the present. In the resurrection of Jesus Christ from the dead and in the establishment of his lordship in the context of earthly existence, God had already anticipated and actualized in an anticipatory form the ultimate victory that will come in the mysterious end about which Paul has been writing.

This energetic word of thanksgiving to God for the victory given through the Lord Jesus Christ recognizes the present significance of what God is already doing and mitigates against the misperception that what God is doing in Christ has little to do with life in this world. Yet, the dominant future bent of Paul's reflections is an important corrective to the denial of the resurrection of the dead.

15:58 / At last, verse 58 follows, issuing a final admonition **(therefore)** that Paul appears to base on the traditional materials he presents throughout this chapter. The command is not a mere work ethic. Rather, Paul once again calls for action and issues an assurance of the Lord's preserving of vital Christian efforts (cf. 3:10–15). Thus, Paul argues for the reality of resurrection, basing his argument on God's work in Christ and calling for the Corinthians to embrace his teaching as the basis for their future hope and current living. Paul's use of eschatological materials is remarkably similar in 1 Thessalonians. There, in two dramatic segments of apocalyptic teaching, Paul informs the readers about the truth of God's future and directs them to action. Here he says, **Always give yourselves fully to the work of the Lord;** and he explains that the Corinthians are able to do so, because they know that their **labor in the Lord is not in vain.** They have such knowledge from what Paul has told them about God's resurrection of the dead. Similarly, in 1 Thessalonians 4:18, Paul admonishes, "Therefore encourage each other with these words"; and in 1 Thessalonians 5:11, he advises, "Therefore encourage one another and build each other up, just as in fact you are doing." Paul consistently moves from eschatological teaching to ethics, from instruction about God's future and its meaning for believers to directions for the shape and substance of life in the Christian community.

Additional Notes §51

15:50 / Paul uses good rhetorical form to draw attention to the significance of the pronouncement that he is about to make. First, he explicitly refers to the forthcoming remark, saying, **I declare to you** (lit. "This is what I mean"); then, he salutes the audience, "**brothers** and sisters" (understood in the form of the address). To paraphrase Paul, "This, brothers and sisters, is what I mean." Such an introduction captures attention and directs it to the statement that follows immediately.

In somewhat formal tones and metaphorical language, Paul declares that **flesh and blood cannot inherit the kingdom of God.** Paul's use of the phrase "flesh and blood" here and in Gal. 1:16 shows that he is speaking metaphorically of human beings, not the literal substances of flesh and blood (although he might mean this literally as well). In turn, the second part of the formal declaration, **nor does the perishable inherit the imperishable,** repeats the language of Paul's discussion in v. 42, although now Paul introduces the further metaphor of inheritance, still another way of trying to speak intelligibly of the reality of the resurrection of the dead.

15:51 / In grand rhetorical fashion, **Listen** (lit. "Behold"; Gk. *idou*), Paul now states his intention to **tell . . . a mystery.** The words **I tell** introduce the following words of explanation concerning the **mystery.** Paul does not use the word **mystery** often or lightly (cf. 2:1 [in some translations and texts]; 2:7; 4:1; 13:2; 14:2); rather, he uses it to refer to the eternal will and work of God that is ultimately inscrutable to humanity. The explanation begun in v. 51b continues through v. 52 before returning to commentary on the mystery.

There is a critical problem with the text of v. 51. The difficulty relates to the number and the placement of negatives in the statement. There are a striking variety of other possible readings, e.g., "We will not all sleep, nor will we all be changed" or "We will all sleep, but we will not all be changed." Nonetheless, the NIV follows the most reasonable text-critical solution in reading and translating this verse. Scribes clearly found this particular declaration concerning the mystery of God intriguing and made various kinds of sense of the facts of the future resurrection of the dead.

15:52 / The word translated **flash** is often rendered "moment" in other translations. The Gk. word at this point is *atomos,* from which English derives "atom." In Greek thought, the *atomos* was regarded as the smallest or indivisible particle. Cf. this verse in general with 1 Thess. 4:16–17.

15:53 / Paul again offers commentary and explanation concerning the declared mystery. The English translation of Paul's language does preserve something of the similarity at the root level of the words he sets in opposition to each other: **perishable** and **imperish-**

able; **mortal** and **immortality;** although the Gk. words translated with the prefix **im-** in English begin with an *a-* (alpha privative). The real sense of Paul's statement is that the new form of resurrection life is without the character or capacity of perishability and mortality. If one could translate "perishable-less" and "mortality-less" one would be closer to the sense of Paul's statements.

15:54 / Paul uses a stock formula to introduce the citation of Scripture, although nothing in the formula signals that Paul intends to blend different texts in the quotation. Here, he refers to Scripture, and he begins to quote Isaiah.

15:55 / Paul continues to quote Scripture, but now turns to Hosea. How he knew or produced this harmonized, blended quotation is uncertain, although the two original prophetic words are made closer by the alteration of the wording of Hosea. The word **victory** (Gk. *nikē*) is an original element of Isaiah, but Hosea reads "judgment" (Gk. *dikē*), which has been changed to **victory** so that the texts blend smoothly. This doubling up of questions produces great rhetorical force and dramatizes the point.

15:56 / Paul's commentary on the citation(s) in vv. 54–55 is not completely pertinent to the context of the discussion of the resurrection of the dead in which he offers the current comments. The material of Rom. 5–7 takes up the themes that are mentioned here briefly, but the context of the discussion in Rom. is different from that of 1 Cor. 15. Nevertheless, Paul offers these explanatory words in anticipation of the joyful outburst that will follow in v. 57.

15:57 / This verse is purely doxological in nature, although the language fits the context of the discussion and the christological and theological emphases of the thanksgiving-praise focus the reflection in a way that Paul has been advocating throughout the letter: on God's work in and through Jesus Christ. Cf. Rom. 6:17; 1 Cor. 15:57; 2 Cor. 2:14; 8:16; 9:15 to note the range of Pauline *charis*-formulas (see R. Banks, "Romans 7.25a: An Eschatological Thanksgiving?" *ABR* 26 [1978], pp. 34–42).

15:58 / The language of this final "ethical" admonition is weighty in tone and in Paul's choice of words. One should see, however, that despite the seriousness of this exhortation, Paul's genuine affection for the Corinthians shows through in the statement: **my dear** (Gk. *mou agapētoi;* lit. "beloved of me"). Paul's words call for action and inspire confidence, ultimately grounding all effort and all security in the reality named in the final (his word order, not the NIV's) phrase of the verse: **in the Lord.** Paul calls the Corinthians to do **the work of the Lord** with full confidence because of their standing in the Lord; in other words, they stand in the Lord and do the Lord's work because they are secure in the Lord. Such a lifestyle is the result of the confidence acquired in knowing that the future is God's. As always for Paul, eschatology means ethics.

Paul almost certainly is responding to a pair of inquiries at this point, since the words **now about** (vv. 1, 12) identify topics that were brought to Paul's attention by the letter or the delegates from Corinth. Paul discusses the collection he was assembling. He states some guidelines that the Corinthians may follow, and the principles inherent in his directions provide theological insight into Christian life. In turn, Paul mentions his future travel plans to inform the Corinthians of his situation and anticipated movements. His specific remarks may seem cryptic to later readers, but they are related to the seasonal conditions of travel in the first-century Mediterranean world. Finally, Paul refers to Timothy and Apollos. The statement about Timothy is apparently designed to provide the Corinthians with information that Paul believes they need, but the references to Apollos seem to be in response to an inquiry from the Corinthians to Paul about that highly regarded preacher.

16:1 / Paul answers a questions from the Corinthians concerning his taking of a collection among the members of the churches he had founded in Asia Minor and Europe. The same collection is mentioned in 2 Corinthians 8–9; Galatians 2:10; and Romans 15:24–33. The NIV translates in a paraphrasing fashion at this point. The designation of those for whom the collection was intended as **God's people** more literally in Greek names these people as "the saints" *(toi hagioi)*. This collection is best explained by Paul in Galatians 2:1–10 as something he wanted to do as a result of the conference in Jerusalem. Luke presents a secondary account of this meeting of the early church in Acts 15.

On the surface this assembling of an offering can be understood as a good-will or relief effort, but consideration of the full dynamics of the project indicates that the collection was a great deal more than mere charity. Paul's purposes, as noted in the several mentions of this collection (esp. Rom. 15), reveal the real importance and theological significance of this act of Christian benevolence. Remarkably, Paul saw the difficulties suffered by members of the Jerusalem church as an opportunity to break down the wall of hostility and skepticism between conservative Jewish and less law-observant Gentile Christians, for in the giving and in the receiving of the collection both the givers and the recipients were mutually acknowledging the bond that existed between them in Christ. Differences in culture and practice could perhaps be minimized as love was expressed in Christian charity. Thus, Paul attempted to use generosity and caring to build bridges across gulfs of suspicion that earlier dialogues had not spanned.

16:2 / One sees from Paul's remarks that giving in the church had not yet been systematized. There was no standard timetable and there was no formula for how much one should give. Tithing apparently was not yet an idea in the church. Paul says, however, that he does not wish to do fund raising when he arrives in Corinth; indeed, he desires the giving to be done naturally and willingly, so that generosity is more charismatic than duty-bound. He does, however, sketch a procedure for the gathering of the collection. As Talbert (*Reading,* p. 105) has noticed, by focusing on the phrases in Paul's directions, one may identify the principles that lie behind or in the activity of the collection:

> **On the first day of every week**—regularly;
> **each one of you**—comprehensively or universally;
> **should set aside a sum of money ... saving it up**—systematically;
> **in keeping with his income**—proportionately; and
> **so that when I come no collections will have to be made**—freely, not under pressure.

16:3–4 / Paul's plans for delivering the collection were open to development or, better, to the guidance of the Spirit. One element of the arrangements seems definite: representatives that the Corinthians themselves were to select would bear the gift to Jerusalem. This aspect of the delivery serves a practical purpose. Someone has to transfer the funds from the givers to the recipients, and by asking the Corinthians to choose delegates, Paul ensures their participation and sets himself and his colleagues above any possible suspicion in the handling of the purse. Moreover, there is another possible dimension to the direct involvement of the members of the Corinthian congregation. In their taking the gift to the saints in Jerusalem, Paul is

engineering a meeting of the Jerusalem Christians and representatives of the predominantly Gentile churches, who were sometimes subject to skepticism by the believers in Jerusalem. The
Corinthians' active role would necessitate a summit of sorts between the ethnically diverse members of the universal church of
Christ. Thus, the love of the Pauline congregations would be
physically represented in Jerusalem by real persons as well as by
the material elements of collection itself.

Paul's own plans for participation in the delivery of the
collection were unformed. He indicates an openness to direction
(from the Spirit?) as he says he will also go **if it seems advisable.**
Advisability is not to be equated with prudence, however; for
later, in writing Romans he indicates that he had found it fitting
to go to Jerusalem, although he perceived difficulty and peril in
making the trip (Rom. 15:23–28; Acts 20:22–24; 21:10–13).

16:5 / Paul sketches his future itinerary, indicating the
intention to pass through **Macedonia** on the way to Corinth,
which was in Achaia. This particular route meant that Paul did
not plan to sail directly from Ephesus to Corinth, and from 2 Corinthians 8–9 one learns of the Macedonian Christians' participation in the collection.

16:6 / Paul's reference to a possible stay in Corinth is
simple. He intended to spend the winter, the season when travel
was impossible, in Corinth; then, when spring came he could go
either east or west as the Spirit directed. The winter season was
not fit, or at least safe, for sailing the west-east corridor from Corinth to Asia Minor or Palestine, so Paul planned to avoid unnecessary dangers. Moreover, as some commentators point out, the
Greek verb (*propempō*) underlying **you can help me on my jour-
ney** is nearly a technical term for supply assistance or physical
support for someone engaged in traveling.

16:7 / This verse is a simple statement of Paul's desire to
see the Corinthians for more than a passing visit. He apparently
did not perceive any difficulty in such a visit or stay, and there is
no indication in his writing that at this time he anticipated having to make the painful visit that he refers to later in 2 Corinthians 1–2. That visit apparently came between the writing of
1 Corinthians and the writing of 2 Corinthians, and before Paul
arrived in Corinth immediately prior to going to Jerusalem to deliver the collection.

16:8–9 / Paul refers to his stay in Ephesus, indicating success and opposition; yet, he sees that the end of that sojourn is at hand. In speaking of his work in Ephesus, Paul writes, **a great** [or wide] **door for effective work has opened to me, and there are many who oppose me.** The form of the statement (recognizing the divine opening of a door) shows that Paul understood both opportunities and successes in ministry to be the results of God's own involvement in his life and work.

16:10–11 / Timothy was working on or was about to work on some commission from Paul, as is clear from both this admonition to the Corinthians and the earlier mention (4:17) of Paul's sending Timothy. The cautious character of the present verse is, however, striking, recognizing the possibility that Timothy might find opposition in Corinth which he should fear. This opposition apparently would have been to Paul, as one of those cited as a leader, among competitive cliques (ch. 1), and so Timothy as Paul's agent might have encountered difficulties. Indeed, the labored manner in which Paul addresses Timothy's possible reception—or lack of a reception—in Corinth probably indicates the strength of the opposition that Paul perceived toward himself. Timothy is going as Paul's representative, so Paul attempts to shield his emissary with these words. Finally, exactly what Paul means by saying that he expected Timothy to return to him **along with the brothers** is obscure.

16:12 / From the opening of the verse, **Now about . . . ,** apparently the Corinthians requested that Apollos come to them. Paul states explicitly that he had **strongly urged** Apollos to make a visit. He writes, however, that this development would not take place. He explains that Apollos would not be coming by saying literally "it was not the will" (NIV: **He was quite unwilling**). From Paul's statement, one wonders, Whose will? Apollos's or God's? The sentence is ambiguous. In any case, Paul and Apollos could and did discuss the matter, and while they apparently disagreed with each other, there is no indication in Paul's report that there was friction between himself and Apollos. Paul does suggest that Apollos would come at another, better time— literally, "good opportunity" (Gk. *eukaireō*).

Additional Notes §52

16:1 / On 16:1–2 in general see V. D. Verbrugge, *Paul's Style of Church Leadership Illustrated by His Instruction to the Corinthians on the Collection* (San Francisco: Mellen Research University Press, 1992).

16:2 / Although there is no way to be certain, the mention of **the first day of every week** probably indicates that the Christians in Corinth already had developed the practice of meeting on Sunday, which became the Christian Sabbath, recalling the day on which Jesus was resurrected. Should this be Paul's assumption in making this remark, this is the earliest mention of the practice of Christian Sunday worship.

The suggestion of Orr and Walther (*I Corinthians*, p. 355) that Paul designated this particular day because the Jews were forbidden to handle money on the Sabbath is unpersuasive. In fact, their attempt to defend this notion from the silence of Paul's letter about Sunday worship is an unbelievable argument from double silence.

16:3 / Paul's phraseology in reference to sending the Corinthians representatives to Jerusalem is ambiguous. The NIV renders a portion of this verse with the words, **I will give letters of introduction to the men you approve and send them,** and so agrees with the sense of the statement that is suggested by most contemporary translations of this verse. The Gk. phrases, however, are loosely sequential and may be understood to say, "whomever you approve through letter, these I will send"; some translations understand and render Paul's words in this way. Both translations are possible, sensible, and equally defensible. Orr and Walther (*I Corinthians*, p. 355) offer the more literal and ambiguous translation, "those whom you approve by letter I shall send off," which may be the best solution. Orr and Walther (pp. 355–56) explain their rendering as a result of a disagreement concerning the proper sense of the original statement. Yet, it does seem less likely that Paul anticipated that the Corinthians would report their choice by letter and then later he would send the representatives with the collection, than that he intended to provide a letter for the delegates chosen in Corinth as he sent them on their way. Thus, the NIV and similar translations may have a common-sense claim to accuracy.

16:4 / More literally Paul states that he would go "if it may be *fitting*" (Gk. *ean de axion ē*). The Gk. word *axios* connotes something appropriate as being worthy. Paul does not name the standard by which this particular determination would be made, but he seems open to input or direction and has not simply made up his mind for himself. His openness and flexibility is characteristic of the charismatic disposition to which he has been calling the Corinthians throughout this letter and which would be typical of his own attentiveness to the leadership of the Spirit.

16:6 / This verse contains the final of only three recognitions of a "possibility" (NIV: **perhaps**) by Paul in this epistle. See 14:10 and 15:37, where Paul also uses forms of the Gk. verb *tygchanō*. In fact, this usage of the word is striking because it is the only historically real possibility that Paul observes; the other instances are rhetorical possibilities in rhetorical illustrations. Possibility was not a primary theological category for Paul.

The importance of this visit for Paul may be indicated in the placement of the words **with you** in a striking emphatic position at the beginning of the sentence. He writes, in odd order, lit. "With you possibly I will remain. . . ."

16:8 / Paul writes explicitly of **Pentecost** (Gk. *pentēkostē*), referring by technical title to the Feast of Weeks, which was observed on the fiftieth day after the Passover. This is a religious, traditionally Jewish, designation of time, although since the original Christian empowering on Pentecost, this term may have become a normal designation or celebration in Christianity. If so, this reference is the earliest indication of the Christian recognition of the time or celebration.

16:9 / More literally Paul writes, "for to me opened a great and effective door." Orr and Walther (*I Corinthians*, p. 357) note that this figure is fairly common in the NT (see Acts 14:27; 2 Cor. 2:12; Col. 4:3; Rev. 3:8). Indeed, the notion of God's opening doors and the believers' being responsible to perceive and pass through such doors is a theological cliché in Western Christianity.

16:10 / Paul's imperative, **see to it** (Gk. *blepete*, from *blepō*) is direct and forceful, not merely polite and encouraging. Furthermore, Paul writes in a well-formed purpose clause, "in order that he may become without fear," that indicates possible reservation but confidently implies compliance with the directive.

16:11 / The NIV offers a smoother, more polite statement than Paul makes with the words, **No one, then, should refuse to accept him.** The Gk. verb *exoutheneō* is normally translated "to disdain." Thus, the NASB renders the words, "Let no one therefore despise him." The potential problem is much stronger than the wording of the NIV suggests with the use of the English verb "to accept." Paul is not merely registering a concern that some in Corinth might not be open to Timothy, nor is he merely stating what the Corinthians should and should not do. Paul's statement is concern that some in Corinth might be actively hostile to Timothy, and he effectively demands that the Corinthians not treat Timothy inappropriately.

In good ancient letter form, Paul addresses a set of practical matters in these essentially paranetic verses. He gives a series of admonitions, focusing on the life of the Corinthian congregation as a whole and in relation to particular outstanding figures in the church. In these fairly straightforward statements Paul still registers perceptions and commentary from a theological point of view that gives a deeper significance to the remarks than might at first meet the eye of a reader.

16:13–14 / These two verses are a bit of *stock paranesis,* or plain, direct, and often conventional advice concerning practical issues. Paul's vocabulary in these verses communicates a more nuanced statement than may be communicated in simple translations.The tone is traditional and eschatological. The initial exhortation to "watch" sounds an eschatological note, and the final reference to "love" recognizes the one disposition (and gift of grace) that defines and anticipates all that is truly eternal.

One may understand the phrase "in the faith" in different ways. At one level some interpreters argue that Paul is naming the definite content of belief and practice; other commentators insist that this reference does not intend to focus on the content of belief. Frequently, this phrase which is translated quite literally in the NIV is rendered "in your faith" in other versions. The use of the definite article "the" as if it were a personal pronoun is common or normal in Greek, and that understanding or translation is acceptable in this verse. Exactly what Paul means by this phrase is unclear. Perhaps he does intend to indicate certain basic matters of belief, such as those already registered in 15:3–8, but he may well mean to indicate the dynamic relationship between the Corinthian believers and the Lord that was a matter of trust and not simply a point of doctrine.

16:15–16 / Paul passes out praise for prominent Christian workers in Corinth. **The household of Stephanas** is given special recognition, especially in the demonstration of spiritual gifts employed in **service** to God's will and the well-being of the church. Paul declares that they should be rightfully acknowledged, not because of status, but because of the presence and the power of the Lord at work in their lives. Such persons are presented as models for the congregation, so that in honoring these persons the congregation devotes itself to genuinely charismatic leadership for living out God's will for their lives in the present situation. From their giving themselves in service, Paul recognizes that these persons demonstrate the true characteristics of leadership that will form and direct the life of the whole church.

The discussion of whether or not and how "the household of Stephanas" could have been the first converts in Achaia makes too much of the sense given to Paul's statements in the NIV and other similar translations. Paul says that this group (their exact identity is unclear and impossible to determine) was "the first-fruit of Achaia." Paul's own reference is vague and perhaps not intended to identify or even interested in recognizing exactly who the first converts were in chronological terms.

The term **household** (Gk. *oikia*) is a general reference that could indicate family, or servants, or family and servants. The practice of some English translations in rendering *oikia* with the word "family" is questionable, since it eliminates genuine ambiguities and gives an anachronistic connotation to Paul's words. The issue of the inclusion of children in the reference to an ancient household is truly moot at this point in Paul's writing, although there is some sense to the observation by Orr and Walther (*I Corinthians*, p. 362) that "since the reference here indicates that the *oikia* rendered *diakonia* ['service'], it is highly probable that only adults are in focus."

16:17–18 / Paul also explicitly mentions and praises the three Corinthians who visited him in Ephesus (Stephanas, Fortunatus, and Achaicus). He expresses both joy and gratitude for these three men's having represented the Corinthians, especially for their bringing him encouragement on the mission field. As Paul phrases the matter, **they have supplied what was lacking from you,** he reveals that he regarded the very presence of these men as an offering for the absence of the other Corinthian Christians. Paul declares that the visit of these three **refreshed** [his] **spirit.** In Philemon (v. 7) Paul recognizes the capacity for "refreshing the hearts of the saints" as an endowment character-istic of a gift of grace from the Spirit. Thus, in a sense Paul means more than that the visit of the Corinthian delegates gave him an emotional lift, for he adds that the visit by the Corinthians' repre-sentatives also refreshed the spirit of the Corinthians (**yours also**). Because of the reality of this charismatic exchange, Paul declares that these persons who have served faithfully are due appropriate recognition.

Additional Note §53

16:13–14 / The Corinthians are admonished to "watch" (Gk. *grēgoreō;* NIV: **be on guard**). They are told "to stand courageously in the faith" (Gk. *stēkete en tē pistei;* NIV: **stand firm in the faith**), the founda-tion of their existence; they are exhorted quite literally to "be manly" (Gk. *andrizomai;* NIV: **be men of courage**)—an ancient euphemistic id-iom for displaying courage; and they are urged to **be strong** (Gk. *krataioomai*), an admonition to firmness or steadfastness. Above all, they are to "do everything in love" (Gk. *en agapē . . . ginomai;* NIV: **do . . . in love**)—the chief criterion for all Christian living (see ch. 13).

16:17 / Remarkably the word for **arrived,** or as other transla-tions render the designation, "coming," in Gk. is *parousia,* which is the term often employed in reference to the future coming (or the second coming) of the Lord Jesus Christ. The word does signify a "coming," but it indicates presence as well as arrival. Paul's discussion in the ensuing comments focuses more on the presence of the delegates from Corinth than on their mere coming, so that **arrived** may misstate Paul's thought or emphasis in this verse.

Paul passes closing greetings in verses 19–20. Then, the last lines open with Paul's autograph before issuing a quick series of energetic final declarations. These verses could be viewed as six or more separate but related statements, since Paul does not string the statements together with a series of conjunctions. Such a serial closing is not in strict keeping with the normal conventions of ancient letter writing, although Paul's letters generally demonstrate a penchant for ending with a set of brief final remarks.

16:19 / Paul mentions **the churches in the province of Asia** (lit. "the churches of Asia"), thus clustering the distinct assemblies in a distinct geographical region into a network of congregations. **Aquila and Priscilla** also send greetings through Paul to the Corinthians, so that the reader learns that these former residents of Rome and Corinth, whom Paul met in Corinth, are now present with him in Ephesus as companions and fellow workers. Above all, however, Paul passes greetings to the Corinthians from **the church that meets at** [Aquila's and Priscilla's] **house.** This reference both locates Paul and his co-workers in the context of the church and recognizes that Aquila and Priscilla were house hosts to the Ephesian congregation. The reader of Paul's letters will once again hear of this couple in Paul's letter to Rome (Rom. 16:3), where Paul sends greetings to them, not from them.

16:20 / Paul offers a general greeting (**All the brothers here,** a manner of reference that would have included both the men and women in the Ephesian church), and then he mentions an enigmatic form of greeting, **a holy kiss.** Though many have guessed what this "holy kiss" was, no one really knows. Nevertheless, the suggestion that this greeting was similar to "a passing of the peace" seems reasonable in light of later references to this practice in subsequent Christian writings. Here, however, the "holy kiss" is a congregational activity, apparently meant to be done vicariously among one group in recognition and solidarity with another group of acknowledged believers who were not present at the greeting.

16:21 / This line and the ones that follow are Paul's autograph. A scribe had written for Paul to this point, but now Paul takes pen in hand and gives the letter a truly personal touch.

16:22 / As Paul writes these final lines, he declares a hex (**a curse;** Gk. *anathema*) on **anyone** who **does not love the Lord**, a probable reference to those who opposed the Lord by resisting the work of the early church—the agency through which the Lord was understood by Christians to be at work in the world. Whether Paul intends to pronounce this anathema on someone in or outside the church is impossible to determine. Then, Paul makes an eschatological cry for the Lord to come (**Come, O Lord;** Gk. *marana tha*), a calling out that declares what Paul must have regarded as a proper attitude toward the Lord. The anathema is in good Greek and the eschatological call is Aramaic that has been transliterated into Greek, yet the words form a sound pair that contrast spiritual discord and spiritual concord.

16:23 / The greeting is the typical fashion in which Paul concluded his letters, **The grace of the Lord Jesus be with you.** At times this element of final greeting is expanded with an explicit mention of God and, less frequently, of the Spirit. Throughout this letter Paul's concern has been with the reality and the experience of **grace** in the life of the Corinthian church, and while the letter is thoroughly theological, Paul has given a christological cast to the main lines of his reflection. Thus, this particular ending is highly appropriate for this epistle.

16:24 / The last line of the letter is remarkable, for Paul ends with an unusual assertion of his love for all the Corinthians in Christ Jesus; he sends his love **to all of** the Corinthians. Even this moving declaration of love, however, is qualified as being **in Christ Jesus,** so that Paul ends on the note of emphasis that he has sounded regularly if not constantly throughout the letter. This location and relationship is the most important aspect of Christian life for Paul in regard to all of Christian faith, belief, and practice.

Additional Notes §54

16:19 / The way Paul meets Priscilla and Aquila in the story in Acts 18 suggests that they were Christians at the time that Paul met them in Corinth. The explanation in Acts that the couple came to Corinth after the emperor Claudius expelled "the Jews" from Rome is probably an indirect recognition that the preaching of the gospel had made its way to Rome by the late 40s and that the controversy it produced required Roman intervention to keep the peace—a kind of story often heard in Acts and alluded to by Paul in his letters.

16:20 / References to the **holy kiss** occur in such diverse places in the NT as Rom. 16:16; 2 Cor. 13:12; 1 Thess. 5:26; 1 Pet. 5:14; and in subsequent early Christian literature: Justin Martyr, *First Apology* 65.2; Clement of Alexandria; and Tertullian.

16:21 / Paul mentions his "autograph" in Gal. 6:11; Col. 4:18; 2 Thess. 3:17. It would not have been necessary for Paul to declare that he was writing in this way, since the readers could easily distinguish his untrained hand from the refined writing of the scribe who had been taking down Paul's words in dictation (see Rom. 16:22). That he does so here may indicate that he anticipated the reading of this particular letter to the assembled congregation.

16:22 / Cf. Rev. 22:20, where the same style declaration is made in Gk. The cry is clear in basic intention, but still enigmatic; since the Aramaic could be read as a perfect ("our Lord has come") or an imperative ("Come, our Lord"). The use of this declaration in the closing of this letter, near the end of Rev., and apparently as an eschatological cry in corporate worship, probably indicates the imperative sense of the statement (see further, *Didache* 10.6).

Some interpreters have suggested that both elements of this verse, the curse and the call, were liturgical declarations that Paul incorporated into the conclusion of his letter. This understanding is possible, and if so the Corinthians would probably recognize the materials for what they were, but nothing in the letter indicates that this pair of statements is quoted material in its entirety (see J. A. T. Robinson, "The Earliest Christian Liturgical Sequence?" in *Twelve New Testament Studies* [London: SCM, 1962], pp. 154–57; compare C. F. D. Moule, "A Reconsideration of the Context of *Maranatha*," *NTS* 6 [1960], pp. 307–10).

16:24 / The NIV concludes with an **Amen,** included in many manuscripts, but the omission in a few crucial ancient witnesses (e.g., Codex Vaticanus) probably means that this final word was by a copyist and was a liturgical addition to the original text of the letter.

For Further Reading

Allen, E. L. "The Lost Kerygma." *NTS* 3 (1957), pp. 349–53.

Aune, D. *Prophecy in Early Christianity and the Ancient Mediterranean World.* Grand Rapids, Mich.: Eerdmans, 1983.

Balch, D. L. "1 Cor 7:32–35 and Stoic Debate about Marriage, Anxiety, and Distraction." *JBL* 102 (1983), pp. 429–39.

Balz, H., and G. Schneider, eds. *Exegetical Dictionary of the New Testament.* 3 vols. Grand Rapids, Mich.: Eerdmans, 1990–1993.

Banks, R. "Romans 7.25a: An Eschatological Thanksgiving?" *ABR* 26 (1978), pp. 34–42.

Barré, M. "To Marry or to Burn: *pyrousthai* in 1 Cor 7:9." *CBQ* 36 (1974), pp. 193–202.

Barrett, C. K. *The First Epistle to the Corinthians.* HNTC. New York: Harper & Row, 1968.

Bartchy, S. S. *Mallon Chrēsai: Slavery and the Interpretation of 1 Corinthians 7:21.* SBLDS 11. Cambridge, Mass.: SBL, 1973.

Bassler, J. M. "1 Cor 12:3—Curse and Confession in Context." *JBL* 103 (1982), pp. 415–18.

———. "1 Corinthians." In *The Women's Bible Commentary.* Ed. C. A. Newsom and S. H. Ringe. Louisville, Ky.: Westminster John Knox, 1992.

Berger, A., and B. Nicholas. "Marriage, Law of." *OCD.* Pages 649–50.

———. "Law and Procedure, Roman." *OCD.* Pages 583–90.

Best, E. "1 Corinthians 7:14 and Children in the Church." *IBS* 12 (1990), pp. 158–66.

Bertram, G. "*paideuō/paidagōgos.*" *TDNT.* Vol. 5, pp. 596–625.

Bornkamm, G. "The Missionary Stance of Paul in I Corinthians and in Acts." Pages 194–207 in *Studies in Luke–Acts.* Ed. L. E. Keck and J. L. Martyn. Nashville: Abingdon, 1966.

Boswell, J. *Christianity, Social Tolerance, and Homosexuality: Gay People in Western Europe from the Beginning of the Christian Era to the Fourteenth Century.* Chicago: University of Chicago, 1980.

Brewer, D. I. "1 Corinthians 9.9–11: A Literal Interpretation of 'Do Not Muzzle the Ox.' " *NTS* 38 (1992), pp. 554–65.

Brown, R. E. "The Semitic Background of the New Testament Mysterion (I)." *Bib* 39 (1958), pp. 426–48.

Brox, N. "ANATHEMA IESOUS (1 Kor 12,3)." *BZ* 12 (1968), pp. 103–11.

Bruce, F. F. *1 and 2 Corinthians.* NCB. Grand Rapids, Mich.: Eerdmans, 1987.

Cadbury, H. J. "The Macellum of Corinth." *JBL* 53 (1934), pp. 134–41.

Caird, G. B., and L. D. Hurst. *New Testament Theology.* Oxford: Clarendon, 1994.

Callan, T. "Prophecy and Ecstasy in Greco-Roman Religion and in 1 Corinthians." *NovT* 27 (1985), pp. 125–40.

Campbell, R. A. "Does Paul Acquiesce in Divisions at the Lord's Supper?" *NovT* 33 (1991), pp. 61–70.

Carr, W. *Angels and Principalities: The Background, Meaning, and Development of the Pauline Phrase* hai archai kai hai exousiai. SNTSMS 42. Cambridge: Cambridge University Press, 1981.

———, "The Rulers of This Age—I Corinthians II.6–8." *NTS* (1976), pp. 20–35.

Carson, D. A. "Pauline Inconsistency: Reflections on I Corinthians 9.19–23 and Galatians 2.11–14." *Chm* 100 (1986), pp. 6–45.

Castelli, E. A. *Imitating Paul. A Discourse of Power.* Literary Currents in Biblical Interpretation. Louisville, Ky.: Westminster John Knox, 1991.

Ciocchi, D. M. "Understanding Our Ability to Endure Temptation: A Theological Watershed." *JETS* 35 (1992), pp. 463–79.

Collins, R. F. " 'It was indeed written for our sake' (1 Cor 9,10): Paul's Use of Scripture in the First Letter to the Corinthians." *Studien zum Neuen Testament und seiner Umwelt* 20 (1995), pp. 151–70.

Conzelmann, H. *1 Corinthians.* Hermeneia. Philadelphia: Fortress, 1975.

———. "On the Analysis of the Confessional Formula in I Corinthians 15:3–5." *Int* 20 (1966), pp. 15–25.

Cottle, R. E. " 'All Were Baptized.' " *JETS* 17 (1974), pp. 75–80.

Cullmann, O. "All Who Call on the Name of Our Lord Jesus Christ." *JES* 1 (1964), pp. 1–21.

_____. *Christ and Time: The Primitive Christian Conception of Time and History*. Rev. ed. Philadelphia: Westminster, 1964.

Dahl, N. A. "The Messiahship of Jesus in Paul." Pages 37–47 in *The Crucified Messiah and Other Essays*. Minneapolis: Augsburg, 1974.

DeBoer, M. C. "The Composition of 1 Corinthians." *NTS* 40 (1994), pp. 229–45.

Deissmann, G. A. *Light from the Ancient East: The New Testament Illustrated by Recently Discovered Texts of the Graeco-Roman World*. Trans. L. R. M. Strachan. 1927. Repr., Peabody, Mass.: Hendrickson, 1995.

_____. *Paul: A Study in Social and Religious History*. 2d ed. Trans. W. E. Wilson. London: Hodder & Stoughton, 1926. Repr. New York: Harper, 1957.

DeMaris, R. E. "Corinthian Religion and Baptism for the Dead (1 Corinthians 15:29): Insights from Archeology and Anthropology." *JBL* 114 (1995), pp. 661–82.

Deming, W. "The Unity of 1 Corinthians 5–6." *JBL* 115 (1996), pp. 289–312.

Derrett, J. D. M. "Cursing Jesus (I Cor xii.3): The Jews as Religious 'Persecutors.' " *NTS* 21 (1975), pp. 544–54.

Dittberner, A. " 'Who Is Apollos and Who Is Paul?': I Cor. 3:5." *BiTod* 71 (1974), pp. 1549–52.

Dodd, B. J. "Paul's Paradigmatic 'I' and 1 Corinthians 6:12." *JSNT* 59 (1995), pp. 39–58.

Doughty, D. J. "The Presence and Future of Salvation in Corinth." *ZNW* 66 (1975), pp. 61–90.

Downing, F. G. "Reflecting the First Century: 1 Corinthians 13:12." *ExpT* 95 (1984), pp. 176–77.

Eitrem, S., and J. E. Fontenrose. "Sacrifice," *OCD*. Pages 943–45.

Elliott, J. K. "In Favour of *kauthēsomai* at I Corinthians 13:3." *ZNW* 62 (1971), pp. 297–98.

Ellis, E. E. "A Note on First Corinthians 10:4." *JBL* 76 (1957), pp. 53–56.

Fee, G. D. "1 Corinthians 7:1 in the NIV." *JETS* 23 (1980), pp. 307–14.

_____. "*Eidōlothyta* Once Again: An Interpretation of 1 Corinthians 8–10." *Bib* 61 (1980), pp. 172–97.

_____. *The First Epistle to the Corinthians*. NICNT. Grand Rapids, Mich.: Eerdmans, 1987.

_____. "Toward a Pauline Theology of Glossolalia." *Crux* 31 (1995), pp. 22–23, 26–31.

Feuillet, A. "The enigma of 1 Cor. 2:9." *TD* 14 (1966), pp. 143–48.

Finley, M. I. "Freedmen." *OCD*. Pages 447–48.

_____. "Slavery." *OCD*. Pages 994–96.

Fiore, B. " 'Covert Allusion' in 1 Corinthians 1–4." *CBQ* 47 (1985), pp. 85–102.

Fishbane, M. "Through the Looking Glass: Reflections on Ezek 42:3, Num 12:8 and 1 Cor 13:12." *HAR* 10 (1986), pp. 63–75.

Fishburne, C. W. "I Corinthians III.10–15 and the Testament of Abraham." *NTS* 17 (1970), pp. 109–15.

Fisk, B. N. "Eating Meat Offered to Idols: Corinthian Behavior and Pauline Response in 1 Corinthians 8–10 (A Response to Gordon Fee)." *TJ* 10 (1989), pp. 49–70.

_____. "PORNEUEIN as Body Violation: The Unique Nature of Sexual Sin in 1 Corinthians 6.18." *NTS* 42 (1996), pp. 540–58.

Fitch, W. O. "Paul, Apollos, Cephas, Christ [1 Cor 1:12]." *Theology* 74 (1971), pp. 18–24.

Fitzgerald, J. T. *Cracks in an Earthen Vessel: An Examination of the Catalogues of Hardships in the Corinthian Correspondence.* SBLDS 99. Atlanta: Scholars Press, 1988.

Fitzmyer, J. A. "Another Look at KEPHALE in 1 Corinthians 11.3." *NTS* 35 (1989), pp. 503–11.

_____. "*Kephalē* in I Corinthians 11:3." *Int* 47 (1993), pp. 52–59.

Francis, J. " 'As babes in Christ': Some proposals regarding 1 Corinthians 3.1–3." *JSNT* 7 (1980), pp. 41–60.

Furnish, V. P. " 'Fellow Workers in God's Service.' " *JBL* 80 (1961), pp. 364–70.

Gärtner, B. E. "The Pauline and Johannine Idea of 'to know God' against the Hellenistic Background: The Greek Philosophical Principle 'Like by Like' in Paul and John." *NTS* 14 (1968), pp. 209–31.

Garland, D. E. "The Christian's Posture Toward Marriage and Celibacy: 1 Corinthians 7." *RevExp* 80 (1983), pp. 351–62.

Garrison, R. "Paul's use of the athlete metaphor in 1 Corinthians 9." *SR* 22 (1993), pp. 209–17.

Gibbs, J. A. "An Exegetical Case for Close(d) Communion: 1 Corinthians 10:14–22; 11:17–34." *Concordia Journal* 21 (1995), pp. 148–63.

Gill, D. W. J. "The Importance of Roman Portraiture for Head-Coverings in 1 Corinthians 11:2–16." *TynB* 41 (1990), pp. 245–60.

_____. "The Meat-Market at Corinth (1 Corinthians 10:25)." *TynB* 43 (1992), pp. 389–93.

Goppelt, L. *Typos: The Typological Interpretation of the Old Testament in the New.* German original, 1939. Grand Rapids, Mich.: Eerdmans, 1982.

Goulder, M. D. "Sophia in 1 Corinthians." *NTS* 37 (1991), pp. 516–34.

Grabbe, L. L. *The Roman Period.* Vol. 2 of *Judaism from Cyrus to Hadrian.* Minneapolis: Fortress, 1992.

Grayston, K. "Not With a Rod." *ExpT* 88 (1976), pp. 13–16.

Greig, J. C. G. "Women's Hats: 1 Corinthians xi.1–16." *ExpT* 69 (1958), pp. 156–57.

Grudem, W. "1 Corinthians 14.20–25: Prophecy and Tongues as Signs of God's Attitude." *WTJ* 41 (1979), pp. 381–96.

Gundry-Volf, J. M. "Celibate Pneumatics and Social Power: On the Motivations for Sexual Asceticism in Corinth." *USQR* 48 (1994), pp. 105–26.

Hammond, N. G. L., and H. H. Scullard, eds. *The Oxford Classical Dictionary.* 2d ed. Oxford: Clarendon, 1970.

Hanson, A. "1 Corinthians 4:13b and Lamentations 3:45." *ExpT* 93 (1982), pp. 214–15.

Harris, G. "The Beginnings of Church Discipline: 1 Corinthians 5." *NTS* 37 (1991), pp. 1–21.

Harris, W. " 'Sounding Brass' and Hellenistic Theology." *BAR* 8 (1982), pp. 38–41.

Hartman, L. "Baptism." *ABD.* Vol. 1, pp. 583–94.

_____. "Some remarks on 1 Cor. 2:1–5." *SEÅ* 39 (1974), pp. 109–20.

Hays, R. B. "Ecclesiology and Ethics in 1 Corinthians." *Ex Auditu* 10 (1994), pp. 31–43.

Hengel, M. *Crucifixion.* Philadelphia: Fortress, 1977.

Hill, David. *New Testament Prophecy.* Atlanta: John Knox, 1979.

Hock, R. *The Social Context of Paul's Ministry: Tentmaking and Apostleship.* Philadelphia: Fortress, 1980.

Hollander, H. W. "The Testing by Fire of the Builders' Works: 1 Corinthians 3.10–15." NTS 40 (1994), pp. 89–104.

Hollander, H. W., and G. E. Van der Hout. "The Apostle Paul Calling Himself an Abortion: 1 Cor. 15:8 within the Context of 1 Cor. 15:8–10." *NovT* 38 (1996), pp. 224–36.

Holloway, J. O. *PERIPATEO as a Thematic Marker in Pauline Ethics.* San Francisco: Mellen Research University Press, 1992.

Hooker, M. D. "Hard Sayings. I Corinthians 3:2." *Theology* 69 (1966), pp. 19–22.

Horsley, R. A. " 'How can some of you say that there is no resurrection of the dead?' Spiritual Elitism in Corinth." *NovT* 20 (1978), pp. 203–31.

_____. "Pneumatikos vs. Psychikos: Distinctions of Spiritual Status among the Corinthians." *HTR* 69 (1976), pp. 269–88.

_____. "Wisdom of Word and Words of Wisdom in Corinth." *CBQ* 39 (1977), pp. 224–39.

Isenberg, M. "The Sale of Sacrificial Meat." *CP* 70 (1975), pp. 271–73.

Jervis, L. A. "1 Corinthians 14.34–36: A Reconsideration of Paul's Limitation of the Free Speech of Some Corinthian Women." *JSNT* 58 (1995), pp. 51–74.

Johanson, B. C. "Tongues, a Sign for Unbelievers? A Structural and Exegetical Study of I Corinthians xiv.20–25." *NTS* 25 (1979), pp. 180–203.

Jones, P. R. "1 Corinthians 15:8: Paul the Last Apostle." *TynB* 36 (1985), pp. 3–34.

Judge, E. A. *The Social Pattern of Christian Groups in the First Century.* London: Tyndale, 1960.

Käsemann, E. "Eine paulinische Variation des 'amor fati.' " *ZTK* 56 (1959), pp. 138–54.

Kaiser, Jr., W. C. "The Current Crisis in Exegesis and the Apostolic Use of Deuteronomy 25:4 in 1 Corinthians 9:8–10." *JETS* 21 (1978), pp. 3–18.

Keck, L. E. "God the Other Who Acts Otherwise: An Exegetical Essay on 1 Cor 1:26–31." *Word & World* 16 (1996), pp. 437–43.

Kistemaker, S. J. " 'Deliver This Man to Satan' (1 Cor 5:5): A Case Study in Church Discipline." *MSJ* 3 (1992), pp. 33–46.

Kittel, G., and G. Friedrich, eds. *Theological Dictionary of the New Testament.* Trans. G. Bromiley. 10 vols. Grand Rapids, Mich.: Eerdmans, 1964–1976.

Klauck, H.-J. " 'Christus, Gottes Kraft und Gottes Weisheit' (1 Kor 1,24): Jüdische Weisheitsüberlieferungen im Neuen Testament." *Wissenschaft und Weisheit* 55 (1992), pp. 3–22.

Klein, W. W. "Noisy Gong or Acoustic Vase? A Note on 1 Corinthians 13.1." *NTS* 32 (1986), pp. 286–89.

Kloppenborg, J. "An Analysis of the Pre-Pauline Formula [in] 1 Cor 15:3b–5 in Light of Some Recent Literature." *CBQ* 40 (1978), pp. 351–67.

Kovacs, J. L. "The Archons, the Spirit, and the Death of Christ: Do We Need the Hypothesis of Gnostic Opponents to Explain 1 Corinthians 2:6–16?" Pages 217–36 in *Apocalyptic and the New Testament. Essays in Honor of J. Louis Martyn*. Ed. J. Marcus and M. L. Soards. Sheffield: JSOT Press, 1989.

Kubo, S. "I Corinthians vii.16: Optimistic or Pessimistic?" *NTS* 24 (1978), pp. 539–44.

Kuck, D. W. *Judgment and Community Conflict. Paul's Use of Apocalyptic Judgment Language in 1 Corinthians 3:5–4:5*. NovTSup 66. Leiden: Brill, 1992.

Lambrecht, J. "Line of Thought in 1 Cor 15,1–11." *Greg* 72 (1991), pp. 655–70.

_____. "Paul's Christological Use of Scripture in 1 Cor. 15.20–28." *NTS* 28 (1982), pp. 502–27.

_____. "Universalism in 1 Cor 8:1–11:1." *Greg* 77 (1996), pp. 333–39.

Lampe, P. "The Eucharist. Identifying with Christ on the Cross." *Int* 48 (1994), pp. 36–49.

_____. "Theological Wisdom and the 'Word about the Cross': The Rhetorical Scheme in I Corinthians 1–4." *Int* 44 (1990), pp. 117–31.

Lee, G. M. "Studies in Texts: I Corinthians 9:9–10." *Theology* 71 (1968), pp. 122–23.

Legrand, L. "The Spiritual Value of Virginity according to Paul." *Indian Ecclesiastical Studies* 1 (1962), pp. 175–95.

Lim, T. H. " 'Not in Persuasive Words of Wisdom, but in the Demonstration of the Spirit and Power' (I Cor. 2:4)." *NovT* 29 (1987), pp. 137–49.

Ling, T. "A Note on 1 Corinthians ii.8." *ExpT* 68 (1956), p. 26.

Lowery, D. K. "The Head Covering and the Lord's Supper in 1 Corinthians 11:2–34." *BibSac* 143 (1986), pp. 155–63.

Lucy, L. "Talbott on Paul as a Universalist." *Christian Scholar's Review* 21 (1992), pp. 395–407.

Luke, L. " 'The Night in Which He Was Delivered Up' (1 Cor 11:23)." *Bible Bhashyam* 10 (1984), pp. 261–79.

Maccoby, H. "Paul and the Eucharist." *NTS* 37 (1991), pp. 247–67.

MacMullen, R. *Roman Social Relations*. New Haven/London: Yale University Press, 1974.

Malherbe, A. J. "MEGENOITO in the Diatribe and Paul." *HTR* 73 (1980), pp. 231–40.

_____ . *Social Aspects of Early Christianity*. Baton Rouge/London: Louisiana State University Press, 1977.

Marcus, J. "The Circumcision and the Uncircumcision in Rome."
    NTS 35 (1989), pp. 67–81.

Martyn, J. Louis. "Epistemology at the Turn of the Ages: 2 Corinthians 5:16." Pages 269–87 in *Christian History and Interpretation: Studies Presented to John Knox.* Ed. W. R. Farmer, C. F. D. Moule, and R. R. Niebuhr. Cambridge: University Press, 1967.

McArthur, H. K. "On the Third Day." *NTS* 18 (1971), pp. 81–86.

McGinn, S. E. "*exousian echein epi tēs kephalēs*: 1 Cor 11:10 and the Ecclesial Authority of Woman." *List* 31 (1996), pp. 91–104.

Meeks, W. A. " 'And Rose up to Play': Midrash and Paraenesis in 1 Corinthians 10:1–22." *JSNT* 16 (1982), pp. 64–78.

_____. *The First Urban Christians: The Social World of the Apostle Paul.* New Haven/London: Yale University Press, 1983.

Metzger, B. M. *A Textual Commentary on the Greek New Testament.* Stuttgart: United Bible Societies, 1971.

Michel, O. "*patēr.*" *EDNT.* Vol. 3, pp. 53–57.

Moule, C. F. D. "A Reconsideration of the Context of Maranatha." *NTS* 6 (1960), pp. 307–10.

Murphy-O'Connor, J. " 'Baptized for the Dead' (I Cor XV,29): A Corinthian Slogan?" *RB* 88 (1981), pp. 532–43.

_____. "Co-Authorship in the Corinthian Correspondence." *RB* 100 (1993), pp. 562–79.

_____. "Corinthian Slogans in 1 Cor 6:12–20." *CBQ* 40 (1978), pp. 391–96.

_____. "The Non-Pauline Character of 1 Corinthians 11:2–16." *JBL* 95 (1976), pp. 615–21.

_____. "St. Paul: Promoter of the Ministry of Women." *Priests & People* 6 (1992), pp. 307–11.

_____. *St. Paul's Corinth: Texts and Archaeology.* Good New Studies 6. Collegeville, Minn.: Liturgical Press, 1983.

_____. "Sex and Logic in 1 Corinthians 11:2–16." *CBQ* 42 (1980), pp. 482–500.

Neller, K. V. "1 Corinthians 9:19–23: A Model for Those Who Seek to Win Souls." *RQ* 29 (1987), pp. 129–42.

Nickel, K. "A Parenthetical Apologia: 1 Corinthians 9:1–3." *CurTM* 1 (1974), pp. 68–70.

Nickelsburg, G. W. E. "An *ektrōma,* Though Appointed from the Womb: Paul's Apostolic Self-Description in 1 Corinthians 15 and Galatians 1." *HTR* 79 (1986), pp. 198–205.

Nolland, J. "Women in the Public Life of the Church." *Crux* 19 (1983), pp. 17–23.

Nygren, A. *Agape and Eros*. Rev. ed. London: SPCK, 1953.

O'Brien, J. "Sophocles's Ode on Man and Paul's Hymn on Love: A Comparative Study." *Classical Journal* 71 (1975/76), pp. 138–51.

O'Brien, P. T. *Introductory Thanksgivings in the Letters of Paul*. NovTSup 49. Leiden: Brill, 1977.

_____. "Thanksgiving and the Gospel in Paul." *NTS* 21 (1974), pp. 144–55.

O'Day, G. R. "Jeremiah 9:22–23 and 1 Corinthians 1:26–31: A Study in Intertextuality." *JBL* 109 (1990), pp. 259–67.

Odell-Scott, D. W. "Let the Women Speak in Church: An Egalitarian Interpretation of 1 Cor 14:33b–36." *BTB* 13 (1983), pp. 90–93.

Omanson, R. L. "Acknowledging Paul's Quotations." *BT* 43 (1992), pp. 201–13.

_____. "Some Comments about Style and Meaning: 1 Corinthians 9.15 and 7.10." *BT* 34 (1983), pp. 135–39.

Orr, W. F., and J. A. Walther. *I Corinthians*. AB 32. Garden City, N.Y.: Doubleday, 1976.

Oster, R. E. "Use, Misuse and Neglect of Archaeological Evidence in Some Modern Works on 1 Corinthians (1 Cor 7,1–5; 8,10; 11,2–16; 12,14–26)." *ZNW* 83 (1992), pp. 52–73.

Papadapoulos, K. N. "Sēmeiōma gia to 1 Kor 7,36–38." *Deltion Biblikon Meleton* 19 (1990), pp. 10–12.

Paulsen, H. "Schima and Häresie: Untersuchungen zu 1 Kor 11,18.19." *ZTK* 79 (1982), pp. 180–211.

Pearson, B. A. "Did the Gnostics Curse Jesus?" *JBL* 86 (1967), pp. 301–5.

Petzer, J. H. "Contextual Evidence in Favour of KAUCHESOMI in 1 Corinthians 13.3." *NTS* 35 (1989), pp. 229–53.

Phipps, W. E. "Is Paul's Attitude toward Sexual Relations Contained in 1 Cor 7.1?" *NTS* 28 (1982), pp. 125–31.

Reaume, J. D. "Another Look at 1 Corinthians 15:29, 'Baptized for the Dead.' " *BibSac* 152 (1995), pp. 457–75.

Reese, J. M. "Paul Proclaims the Wisdom of the Cross: Scandal and Foolishness." *BTB* 9 (1979), pp. 147–53.

Rengstorf, K. H. "*didaskō/didaskalos*." *TDNT*. Vol. 2, pp. 135–65.

Richardson, P., and P. W. Gooch. "Accommodation Ethics." *TynB* 29 (1978), pp. 89–142.

Ringe, S. H. "Hospitality, Justice, and Community: Paul's Teaching on the Eucharist in 1 Corinthians 11:17–34." *Prism* 1 (1986), pp. 59–68.

Robertson, A. T. *Word Pictures in the New Testament*. Nashville: Broadman, 1931.

Robinson, J. A. T. "The Earliest Christian Liturgical Sequence?" Pages 154–57 in *Twelve New Testament Studies*. London: SCM, 1962.

Rosner, B. S. " *'ouchi mallon epenthēsate'*: Corporate Responsibility in 1 Corinthians 5." *NTS* 38 (1992), pp. 470–73.

_____. " 'Stronger Than He?' The Strength of 1 Corinthians 10:22b." *TynB* 43 (1992), pp. 171–79.

Schneider, G. *"paidagōgos."* *EDNT*. Vol. 3, pp. 2–3.

Schrenk, G., *"patēr."* *TDNT*. Vol. 5, pp. 945–1022.

Schubert, P. *Form and Function of the Pauline Thanksgivings*. BZNW 20. Berlin: Töpelmann, 1939.

Schweizer, E. "The Service of Worship: An Exposition of I Corinthians 14." *Int* 13 (1959), pp. 400–408.

Scroggs, R. "The Exaltation of the Spirit by Some Early Christians." *JBL* 84 (1965), pp. 359–73.

_____. *The Last Adam: A Study in Pauline Anthropology*. Philadelphia: Fortress, 1966.

Scroggs, Robin. *The New Testament and Homosexuality: Contextual Background for Contemporary Debate*. Philadelphia: Fortress, 1983.

Seaford, R. "1 Corinthians XIII.12." *JTS* 35 (1984), pp. 117–20.

Sebothoma, W. A. *"Koinōnia* in 1 Corinthians 10:16." *Neot* 24 (1990), pp. 63–69.

Sider, R. J. "St. Paul's Understanding of the Nature and Significance of the Resurrection in 1 Corinthians xv 1–19." *NovT* 19 (1977), pp. 124–41.

Sigal, P. "Another Note on 1 Corinthians 10.16." *NTS* 29 (1983), pp. 134–39.

Sigountos, J. G. "The Genre of 1 Corinthians 13." *NTS* 40 (1994), pp. 246–60.

Sirks, G. J. "The Cinderella of Theology: The Doctrine of the Holy Spirit." *HTR* 50 (1957), pp. 77–89.

Smit, J. "The Genre of 1 Corinthians 13 in the Light of Classical Rhetoric." *NovT* 33 (1991), pp. 193–216.

Smit, J. F. M. "Two Puzzles: 1 Corinthians 12.31 and 13.3: A Rhetorical Solution." *NTS* 39 (1993), pp. 246–64.

Smith, B. D. "The More Original Form of the Words of Institution." *ZNW* 83 (1992), pp. 166–86.

Soards, M. L. *The Passion According to Luke: The Special Material of Luke 22*. JSNTSup 14. Sheffield: JSOT Press, 1987.

_____. "Paul." *Mercer Dictionary of the Bible*. W. E. Mills, ed. Macon, Ga.: Mercer University Press, 1990.

South, J. T. "A Critique of the 'Curse/Death' Interpretation of 1 Corinthians 5:1–8." *NTS* 39 (1993), pp. 539–61.

Stambaugh, J. E., and D. L. Balch. *The New Testament in Its Social Environment*. Library of Early Christianity 2. Philadelphia: Westminster, 1986.

Stendahl, K. "The Apostle Paul and the Introspective Conscience of the West." *HTR* 56 (1963), pp. 199–215. Repr. pp. 178–96 in *Paul among Jews and Gentiles*. Philadelphia: Fortress, 1976.

Stuart, E. "Love is . . . Paul." *ExpT* 102 (1991), pp. 264–66.

Talbert, C. H. *Reading Corinthians: A Literary and Theological Commentary on 1 and 2 Corinthians*. New York: Crossroad, 1987.

Tenney, M. C. "The Essence of the Gospel." *Christianity Today* 3 (1959), pp. 9–12.

Theissen, G. *Psychological Aspects of Pauline Theology*. Philadelphia: Fortress, 1987.

_____. *Social Reality and the Early Christians: Theology, Ethics, and the World of the New Testament*. Minneapolis: Fortress, 1992.

_____. *The Social Setting of Pauline Christianity: Essays on Corinth*. Philadelphia: Fortress, 1982.

Thompson, C. L. "Hairstyles, Head-coverings, and St. Paul: Portraits from Roman Corinth." *BA* 51 (1988), pp. 99–115.

Thrall, M. E. "The Pauline Use of *Synedēsis*." *NTS* 14 (1967), pp. 118–25.

Titus, E. L. "Did Paul Write I Corinthians 13?" *JBR* 27 (1959), pp. 299–302.

Vander Broek, L. "Discipline and Community: Another Look at 1 Corinthians 5." *RR* 48 (1994), pp. 5–13.

Vander Stichele, C. "Is Silence Golden? Paul and Women's Speech in Corinth." *LS* 20 (1995), pp. 241–53.

van Roon, A. "The Relation between Christ and the Wisdom of God according to Paul." *NovT* 16 (1974), pp. 207–39.

Verbrugge, V. D. *Paul's Style of Church Leadership Illustrated by His Instruction to the Corinthians on the Collection*. San Francisco: Mellen Research University Press, 1992.

Walker, Jr., W. O. "1 Corinthians 11:2–16 and Paul's Views Regarding Women." *JBL* 94 (1975), pp. 94–110.

Watson, D. F. "1 Corinthians 10:23–11:1 in the Light of Greco-Roman Rhetoric: The Role of Rhetorical Questions." *JBL* 108 (1989), pp. 301–18.

Watson, N. *The First Epistle to the Corinthians*. Epworth Commentaries. London: Epworth, 1992.

Watson, N. M. " 'The Philosopher Should Bathe and Brush His Teeth': Congruence between Word and Deed in Graeco-Roman Philosophy and Paul's Letter to the Corinthians." *ABR* 42 (1994), pp. 1–16.

Wedderburn, A. J. M. *"en tē sophia tou theou*—1 Kor 1:21." *ZNW* 64 (1973), pp. 132–34.

Willis, W. "An Apostolic Apologia? The Form and Function of 1 Corinthians 9." *JSNT* 24 (1985), pp. 33–48.

_____. "The 'Mind of Christ' in 1 Corinthians 2,16." *Bib* 70 (1989), pp. 110–22.

Willis, W. L. *Idol Meat in Corinth: The Pauline Argument in 1 Corinthians 8 and 10*. SBLDS 68. Chico, Calif.: Scholars Press, 1985.

Wimbush, V. L. "The Ascetic Impulse in Ancient Christianity." *ThTo* 50 (1993), pp. 417–28.

Wire, A. C. *The Corinthian Women Prophets: A Reconstruction through Paul's Rhetoric*. Minneapolis: Fortress, 1990.

Witherington, III, B. "Not So Idle Thoughts about *eidolōthutōn*." *TynB* 44 (1993), pp. 237–54.

Wong, E. "1 Corinthians 13:7 and Christian Hope." *LS* 17 (1992), pp. 232–42.

Worden, T. "The Remission of Sins—I." *Scripture* 9 (1957), pp. 65–79.

Zaas, P. S. "Catalogues and Context: 1 Corinthians 5 and 6." *NTS* 34 (1988), pp. 622–29.

Zerwick, Max, and Mary Grosvenor. *A Grammatical Analysis of the Greek New Testament*. Rome: Biblical Institute, 1981.

Subject Index

Scripture Index